BLOOM'S PERIOD STUDIES

The American Renaissance

Edited and with an introduction by

Harold Bloom
Sterling Professor of the Humanities
Yale University

CHELSEA HOUSE
PUBLISHERS
A Haights Cross Communications Company
Philadelphia

©2004 by Chelsea House Publishers, a subsidiary of
Haights Cross Communications.

A Haights Cross Communications ◄┼ Company

Introduction © 2004 by Harold Bloom.

Printed and bound in the United States of America.

10 9 8 7 6 5 4 3 2 1

Library of Congress Cataloging-in-Publication Data
Applied For
  ISBN: 0-7910-7676-8

Chelsea House Publishers
1974 Sproul Road, Suite 400
Broomall, PA 19008-0914

http://www.chelseahouse.com

Contributing Editor: Stuart Watson

Cover designed by Keith Trego

Layout by EJB Publishing Services

Contents

Editor's Note

My Introduction, questing for the American Sublime's difference from England and Continental Europe, follows Emerson and Whitman into the abyss of the American self.

D.H. Lawrence, now an absurdly neglected English poet-novelist-prophet, is represented by his extraordinary critique of *Moby Dick*, "the doom of our white race."

The classic *American Renaissance* by the tragic Francis Otto Matthiessen defines forever the "Method and Scope" of the greatest era, to date, of the literature of the United States.

Charles Olson, poet and Harvard maverick, follows Matthiessen by a pioneer uncovering of Shakespeare's intense influence upon *Moby-Dick*, after which the Argentine fabulist, Jorge Luis Borges, renders tribute to Hawthorne, one of his two prime North American precursors.

Sherman Paul, Thoreau's best expositor, illuminates both *Walden* and the fierce essay, "Civil Disobedience."

The editor, who continues to regard Whitman's "When Lilacs Last in the Dooryard Bloom'd" as the crown of our literature, reveals the significance of the grand metaphor of "tally" in the elegy, and elsewhere in our national poet, true ancestor of Wallace Stevens and the Pindaric Hart Crane.

Emerson's most accomplished essay, "Experience," is explicated by Barbara Packer, while Julie Ellison rhetorically analyzes Emerson's seminal "The Poet," which inspired Whitman.

Richard Brodhead, Yale's Dean, brings together Hawthorne and Melville as prophetic makers of fiction, after which Lawrence Buell learnedly studies the transition from Unitarianism into literary Transcendentalism.

In what I regard as our best essay on Whitman's poetry, John Hollander shows why and how *Leaves of Grass* feigns simplicity, yet is fascinatingly difficult.

This volume ends with the first publication of two essays from books-in-progress, Kathy Kurtzman Lawrence's superb study of Margaret Fuller, and Elizabeth Schmidt's incisively close readings of the poems founded upon Emily Dickinson's refusal of her Calvinist heritage. I have encountered nothing more helpful upon the two most accomplished women creators of the American Renaissance.

Introduction

EMERSON AND WHITMAN: THE AMERICAN SUBLIME

Parable—Those thinkers in whom all stars move in cyclic orbits are not the most profound: whoever looks into himself as into vast space and carries galaxies in himself also knows how irregular all galaxies are; they lead into the chaos and labyrinth of existence.

NIETZSCHE

What is the American Sublime, and how does it differ from its European precursor? When Emerson set out to define *The American Scholar*, in 1837, he began with "the old fable" of One Man, taking this vision of a primordial being from Plutarch's Platonizing essay on "Brotherly Love." Characteristically, Emerson saw the division and fall of man as a reification and as an undoing by the trope of metonymy:

> Man is thus metamorphosed into a thing, into many things. The planter, who is Man sent out into the field to gather food, is seldom cheered by any idea of the true dignity of his ministry. He sees his bushel and his cart, and nothing beyond, and sinks into the farmer, instead of Man on the farm. The tradesman scarcely ever gives an ideal worth to his work, but is ridden by the routine of his craft, and the soul is subject to dollars. The priest becomes a form; the attorney a statute-book; the mechanic a machine; the sailor a rope of the ship.

From *Poetry and Repression: Revisionism from Blake to Stevens*. © 1976 by Yale University.

Parallel to these metonymic reductions is the undoing of the scholar as "the delegated intellect" whereas: "In the right state he is *Man Thinking*." To account for the scholar's fall, Emerson first considers the scholar as a problem in influence. The main influences directed upon the scholar—who for Emerson, as for Stevens, comprises also the poet—are (1) Nature, (2) Books, (3) Action. But Nature is revealed to be only the print of the scholar's seal. As for Books: "One must be an inventor to read well." Finally, Action turns out to be "instinct," the world of will and drive. The three precursors of the scholar thus fade away, leaving "self-trust," freedom or wildness. His ground cleared, Emerson attains to the center of his oration: "It is a mischievous notion that we are come late into nature; that the world was finished a long time ago." The wild or free notion is that: "This time, like all times, is a very good one, if we but know what to do with it." From this follows the prophecy that made possible the drastic grandeur of the American Sublime: "A nation of men will for the first time exist, because each believes himself inspired by the Divine Soul which also inspires all men."

Emerson delivered *The American Scholar: An Oration*, at Harvard on August 31, 1837. A few months before, in the spring of 1837, there was a business crash, banks suspended nearly all payments, and a general economic depression dominated society. It is noteworthy, and has been noted, that Emerson's two great outbursts of prophetic vocation coincide with two national moral crises, the Depression of 1837 and the Mexican War of 1846, which Emerson, as an Abolitionist, bitterly opposed. The origins of the American Sublime are connected inextricably to the business collapse of 1837. I want to illustrate this connection by a close reading of relevant entries in Emerson's journals of 1837, so as to be able to ask and perhaps answer the invariable question that antithetical criticism learns always to ask of each fresh instance of the Sublime. *What is being freshly repressed?* What has been forgotten, on purpose, in the depths, so as to make possible this sudden elevation to the heights? Here is the seer, apparently stimulated to an ascent, by a meditation upon a business depression:

> Behold the boasted world has come to nothing. Prudence itself is at her wits' end. Pride, and Thrift, and Expediency, who jeered and chirped and were so well pleased with themselves, and made merry with the dream, as they termed it, of Philosophy and Love,—behold they are all flat, and here is the Soul erect and unconquered still. What answer is it now to say, It has always been so? I acknowledge that, as far back as I can see the widening procession of humanity, the marchers are lame and blind and

deaf; but to the soul that whole past is but one finite series in its infinite scope. Deteriorating ever and now desperate. Let me begin anew. Let me teach the finite to know its master. Let me ascend above my fate and work down upon my world.

The Yankee virtues, as internalized by Emerson himself, no longer triumph over the Transcendental vision, which indeed now turns transumptive, projecting all the past as a lame, blind, deaf march, and introjecting a Sublime future, mounted over fate, the finite, the cosmos. What Emerson represses is *Ananke*, the Fate he has learned already to call "compensation." His vision of repetition is a metonymic reduction, an undoing of all other selves, and his restituting *daemonization* renders him solipsistic and free. That a poetic repression brings about the Sublime wildness of freedom is almost the most Emersonian of all Emersonian rhetorical paradoxes; and one that he himself carried to its apocalypse eventually in the grand death-march of the essay *Fate*, in *The Conduct of Life*:

> But Fate against Fate is only parrying and defence: there are also the noble creative forces. The revelation of Thought takes man out of servitude into freedom. We rightly say of ourselves, we were born again, and many times. We have successive experiences so important that the new forgets the old, and hence the mythology of the seven or the nine heavens. The day of days, the great day of the feast of life, is that in which the inward eye opens to the Unity in things, to the omnipresence of law:—sees that what is must be and ought to be, or is the best. This beatitude dips from on high down on us and we see. It is not in us so much as we are in it. If the air come to our lungs, we breathe and live; if not, we die. If the light come to our eyes, we see; else not. And if truth come to our mind we suddenly expand to its dimensions, as if we grew to worlds. We are as lawgivers; we speak for Nature; we prophesy and divine.

I want to defer comment on this magnificent instance of the American Sublime by first comparing Emerson, as a moral theorist of interpretation, to Freud and to St. Augustine. Augustine, as Peter Brown says, parallels Freud by speaking of a "Fall" in consciousness:

> Augustine ... produced a singularly comprehensive explanation of why allegory should have been necessary in the first place. The

need for such a language of 'signs' was the result of a specific dislocation of the human consciousness. In this, Augustine takes up a position analogous to that of Freud. In dreams also, a powerful and direct message is said to be deliberately diffracted by some psychic mechanism, into a multiplicity of 'signs' quite as intricate and absurd, yet just as capable of interpretation, as the 'absurd' or 'obscure' passages in the Bible. Both men, therefore, assume that the proliferation of images is due to some precise event, to the development of some geological fault across a hitherto undivided consciousness: for Freud, it is the creation of an unconscious by repression; for Augustine, it is the outcome of the Fall.

Augustine's vision of the Fall, as Brown also shows, had changed from an early, quasi-Plotinian belief, which was that Adam and Eve had "fallen" into physicality: "that the prolific virtues they would have engendered in a purely 'spiritual' existence had declined, with the Fall, into the mere literal flesh and blood of human families." In the mature Augustinian doctrine, the dualizing split in human consciousness is no technical descent to a lower degree of being, but is the most wilful and terrible of catastrophes. How does this compare with catastrophe theory in Freud, and in Emerson? Do all three doctors-of-the-soul, Augustine, Emerson, and Freud agree fundamentally that consciousness, as we know it, cannot inaugurate itself without a catastrophe? The Christian Augustine and the Empedoclean-Schopenhauerian Freud do not surprise us in this regard, but why should the Idealizing quasi-Neoplatonist Emerson insist upon catastrophe as the invariable inaugural act for consciousness?

Here is Emerson's equivalent of the Augustinian or psychoanalytic division into consciousness, from his greatest essay, *Experience*:

> It is very unhappy, but too late to be helped, the discovery we have made that we exist. That discovery is called the Fall of Man. Ever afterwards we suspect our instruments. We have learned that we do not see directly, but mediately, and that we have no means of correcting these colored and distorting lenses which we are, or of computing the amount of their errors. Perhaps these subject-lenses have a creative power; perhaps there are no objects. Once we lived in what we saw; now, the rapaciousness of this new power, which threatens to absorb all things, engages us.

This is surely the authentic vision of the daemonic in Emerson, the apocalyptic frenzy of an American Sublime. The mystery of this passage; as of the other rhapsodies I have quoted from Emerson, is in the paradox of repression, of the power brought into being by an enormous fresh influx of repression. More even than the British Romantic Sublime, Emerson's American Sublime exposes what I am tempted to call the deep structure of rhetoric, by which I mean the defensive nature of rhetoric. I oppose myself here not only to what passes for "Freudian literary criticism" but to the much more formidable "deconstructive" literary criticism in which de Man and Derrida follow Rousseau and Nietzsche. De Man, analyzing Nietzsche, concludes that between rhetoric as a system of tropes and rhetoric as persuasion there is an *aporia*, a limit or doubt that cannot be defined. I venture an analysis now of this *aporia*, for what relates one trope to another in a systematic way, and carries each trope from evasion to persuasion, is that trope's function as defense, its imagistic maskings of those detours to death that make up the highway map of the psyche, the drives from anterior fixations to entropic self-destructions.

Emerson followed Vico in declining to confuse meaning with signification, a confusion still evident even in the most advanced models of, post-Structuralist thought. For Emerson, meaning is concerned with survival, and signification is only an instrumentality of meaning, this being a distinction in which Peirce followed Emerson. What holds together rhetoric as a system of tropes, and rhetoric as persuasion, is the necessity of defense, defense against everything that threatens survival, and a defense whose aptest name is "meaning." Vico named poetic defense as "divination," which in our vocabulary translates best as "over-determination of meaning." But here I must allow myself a digression into theory-of-misprision.

The poetic defense of repression is always a ratio of representation (the Lurianic *tikkun* or restitution) because in poetic repression *you forget something in order to present something else*. Whereas, poetic sublimation is always a ratio of limitation (*zimzum* or contraction) because by it *you remember something (concentrate it) in order to avoid presenting that something, and you choose to present something else in its place*. Substitution or breaking-of-the-vessels between poetic repression and poetic sublimation is a transformation from the unconscious to consciousness just as the movement from poetic sublimation to poetic introjection or projection restores or returns representations to the unconscious. Tropes, defenses, images, ratios of limitation withdraw representations from the unconscious without replenishing the unconscious, while the countermovements of representation restitute the unconscious. When Emerson experiences and describes his influxes of the American Sublime, he is at work creating the great trope of the specifically American Unconscious, or what he himself in *Self-Reliance* calls "Spontaneity or Instinct":

> The magnetism which all original action exerts is explained when we inquire the reason of self-trust. Who is the Trustee? What is the aboriginal Self on which a universal reliance may be grounded? What is the nature and power of that science-baffling star, without parallax, without calculable elements, which shoots a ray of beauty even into trivial and impure actions, if the least mark of independence appear? The inquiry leads us to that source, at once the essence of genius, of virtue, and of life, which we call Spontaneity or Instinct. We denote this primary wisdom as Intuition, whilst all later teachings are tuitions. In that deep force, the last fact behind which analysis cannot go, all things find their common origin.

How does the Freudian Unconscious contrast with this Emersonian American Sublime? Freud's concept of the unconscious was first obtained from his theory of repression, and was intended to explain *discontinuities* in the psychic life of every individual. But these were active discontinuities, so that Freud's notion of the unconscious rapidly became a dynamic conception, and not merely a descriptive one. Ideas had been repressed and then continued to be shut out from consciousness, by an ongoing process of repression. Unconscious ideas that could break back through into consciousness, Freud referred to as "preconscious" and distinguished sharply from repressions that could never return, which constituted the unconscious proper. These latter repressions, according to Freud, are ideas and not affects. If they *seem* affects, then they are "potential beginnings which are preventing *by* developing." Yet even these permanently repressed ideas do not make up the whole of the Freudian unconscious. Mysteriously, there is an original unconscious; indeed Freud finally thought that the mind originally was totally unconscious, and that gradually part of the mind became preconscious and part conscious, with yet another part always remaining unconscious. To this unrepressed unconscious, the augmenting ego added materials through fresh repressions.

Emerson's version of the unconscious is a purer instance of poetic or hyperbolical repression. Whatever one may want to say about the structure of the Freudian unconscious (and I do *not* believe it is structured like a language), I think that Emersonian "Spontaneity or Instinct" *is* structured like a rhetoric, that is, is both a system of tropes and also a mode of persuasion. Like Freud's unconscious, it is originary, and again like Freud's giant trope, it is augmented by fresh and purposeful forgettings, by evasions that are performed in order to present something other than the something that is being evaded. But, in Freud, the something evaded is any drive objectionable to ego-ideals, whereas in Emerson the something must take the name of a single drive, the thrust of anteriority, the mystifying strength of the past, which is profoundly objectionable to Emerson's prime ego-ideal, Self-Reliance. Emerson's pugnacity on this theme is in the Optative Mood; as he says: "When we have new perception, we shall gladly disburden the memory of its hoarded treasures as old rubbish." As for what became Nietzsche's "guilt of indebtedness," which is so profoundly analyzed in *Towards the Genealogy of Morals*, Emerson dismisses it with a Sublime shrug, a shrug directed against Coleridge: "In the hour of vision there is nothing that can be called gratitude, or properly joy."

With so daemonic an unconscious as his support, Emerson cheerfully places the spirit wholly in the category that Kierkegaard called only "the aesthetic." I turn again to "The Rotation Method" in *Either* of *Either/Or*, so as to illuminate Emerson's kind of repression:

> Forgetting is the shears with which you cut away what you cannot use, doing it under the supreme direction of memory. Forgetting and remembering are thus identical arts, and the artistic achievement of this identity is the Archimedean point from which one lifts the whole world. When we say that we *consign* something to oblivion, we suggest simultaneously that it is to be forgotten and yet also remembered.

Kierkegaard is playing upon his own notion of "repetition," which is his revision of the Hegelian "mediation" into a Christian conception "of the anxious freedom." Emerson's Transcendental equivalent is his famous declaration in the journal for April 1842: "I am *Defeated* all the time; yet to Victory I am born." Less than a year later, Kierkegaard wrote: "The difficulty facing an existing individual is how to give his existence the continuity without which everything simply vanishes.... The goal of movement for an existing individual is to arrive at a decision, and to renew it." I think we can remark on this that Kierkegaard does not want us to be able to distinguish between the desire for repetition, and repetition itself, since it is in the blending of the two that the "anxious freedom" of "becoming a Christian" truly consists. But Emerson was post-Christian; for him that "Great Defeat" belonged totally to the past. What Kierkegaard called "repetition" Emerson called by an endless variety of names until he settled on Fate or Necessity, and he insisted always that we had to distinguish between our desire for such reality, and the reality itself. In the grand passage from the essay *Fate* that I quoted earlier, the emphasis is sublimely upon what Emerson calls successive rebirths, while meaning successive re-begettings of ourselves, during this, our one life. Perpetually, Emerson insists, our new experience forgets the old, so that perhaps Nietzsche should have remarked of Emerson, not that he did not know how old he was already or how young he still was going to be, but only that Emerson did know that always he was about to become his own father. This, I now assert, is the distinguishing mark of the specifically American Sublime, that it begins anew not with restoration or rebirth, in the radically displaced Protestant pattern of the Wordsworthian Sublime, but that it is truly past even such displacement, despite the line from Edwards to Emerson that scholarship accurately continues to trace. Not merely rebirth, but the even more hyperbolical trope of self-rebegetting, is the starting point of the last Western Sublime, the great sunset of selfhood in the Evening Land.

But what does this hyperbolical figuration mean, or rather, how are we to transform its signification into meaning? We all of us go home each evening, and at some moment in time, with whatever degree of overt consciousness, we go back over all the signs that the day presented to us. In those signs, we seek only what can aid the continuity of our own discourse, the survival of those ongoing qualities that will give what is vital in us even more life. This seeking is the Vichian and Emersonian making of signification into meaning, by the single test of aiding our survival. By such a test, the American Sublime is a trope *intending* to forget the father in order to present the son or daughter. In this trope, the father is a limitation or what Stevens called a reduction to a First Idea, an idea of an origin, and the son or daughter intends to be a restituting representation in which a First Idea is reimagined, so as to become the idea of an aim. But what is a First Idea, unless it be what Freud termed a primal fixation or an initial repression? And what did that initial repression forget, or at least intend to forget? Here Freud touched his *aporia*, and so I turn beyond him to Kabbalah again, to seek a more ultimate paradigm for the Scene of Instruction than even Kierkegaard affords me, since here too Kierkegaard touched his *aporia*, and accepted the Christian limit of the Incarnation. The Orphic Emerson demands an ultimate paradigm which is beyond the pleasure-principle, yet also beyond these competing reality-principles.

Lacan, in his revision of Freud, tells us that the ego is essentially paranoid, that it is a structure founded upon a contradictory or double-bind relationship between a self and an other, or relationship that is at once an opposition and an identity. I reject this as interpretation of Freud, and reject it also as an observation upon the psyche. But Lacan, as I remarked in another context, joins himself to those greater theorists, including Nietzsche and Freud, who talk about people in ways that are more valid even for poems. I do not think that the psyche is a text, but I find it illuminating to discuss texts as though they were psyches, and in doing so I consciously follow the Kabbalists. For, in poems, I take it that the other is always a person, the precursor, however imagined or composite, whereas for Lacan the other is principle, and not person.

The fourth of the six *behinot* or aspects of each *sefirah*, according to Moses Cordovero, is the aspect of a particular *sefirah* that allows the *sefirah* above it to give that particular *sefirah* the strength enabling it, the later *sefirah*, to emanate out further *sefirot*. Or to state it more simply, yet still by a Kabbalistic trope, *it is from a son that a father takes the power, that in turn will enable the son to become a father*. This hyperbolical figuration is a rather complex theory of repression, because the son or, later poem initially needs to forget the autonomy of its own power in order to express any *continuity* of power. But this is very close also to the peculiar nature of Sublime representation, where there is an implication always that what is being represented is somehow absent, and so must be restituted by an image. But the image, which in Sublime representation tends to be of a fathering force, as it were, remains distinct from what it represents, at least in the Continental and British Sublime. This is where I would locate the *difference* in the Emersonian or American Sublime, which is closer to the Kabbalistic model of Cordovero in its reversal between the roles of the fathering force and the new self of the son, that is, of the later or belated poem. In Emerson and in his progeny from Whitman, Thoreau, Dickinson on through Hart Crane, Stevens, and our contemporaries, the fathering force and the poetic self tend to merge together, but the aim of self-presentation is not defeated, because the fathering force or representative tends to disappear into the poetic self or son, rather than the self into the image of the fathering force.

I turn to *The Divinity School Address* for a proof-text here, and offer an Emerson cento of the American Sublime from it:

> That is always best which gives me to myself. The sublime is excited in me by the great stoical doctrine, Obey thyself. That which shows God in me, fortifies me. That which shows God out of me, makes me a wart and a wen....

Wherever a man comes, there comes revolution. The old is for slaves. When a man comes, all books are legible, all things transparent, all religions are forms....

Let me admonish you, first of all, to go alone; to refuse the good models....

I look for the hour when that supreme Beauty which ravished the souls of those Eastern men, and chiefly of those Hebrews, and through their lips spoke oracles to all time, shall speak in the West also.... I look for the new Teacher that shall follow so far those shining laws that he shall see them come full circle....

There are the two central Emersonian images of the Sublime: "all things transparent" and the Central Man who shall see the transparency and thus see also the laws of reality "come full circle." That transparency, to appear again in Whitman and in Stevens, can be interpreted two ways, transumptively or reductively. The second would relate it to Anna Freud's observation, in *The Ego and the Mechanisms of Defense*, that: "The obscurity of a successful repression is only equalled by the transparency of the repressive process when the movement is reversed." The first would relate it to the Hebrew idea of God as avoiding the Greek notions either of immanence or of transcendence. Thorlief Boman, in his *Hebrew Thought Compared with Greek*, shows that the Hebraic image of transparency, as a trope for God, sees the Divine as being neither *in* the world nor *over* the world, but rather *through* the world, not spatially but discontinuously. Let us allow both meanings, this Hebraic transumption and the Freudian reduction, and combine both with Emerson's bringing-forth a father-god out of himself, even as we examine again the two most famous of all American Sublime passages, the epiphanies in the first and last chapters of Emerson's *Nature*:

I become a transparent eyeball; I am nothing; I see all; the currents of the Universal Being circulate through me; I am part or parcel of God.

The problem of restoring to the world original and eternal beauty is solved by the redemption of the soul. The ruin or the blank that we see when we look at nature, is in our own eye. The axis of vision is not coincident with the axis of things, and so they appear not transparent but opaque.

Reductively, the first passage represents a partial return of the repressed, while the second appears to be what Anna Freud calls "the obscurity of a successful repression." But transumptively, the first passage records a successful repression, and the second the failed perspectivism of sublimation. The Emersonian repressiveness attains to a discontinuity with everything that is anterior, and in doing so it accomplishes or prepares for a reversal in which the self is forgotten ("I am nothing") and yet through seeing introjects the fathering force of anteriority. By seeing the transparency, the poet of the American Sublime *contains* the father-god, and so augments the poetic self even as he remembers to forget that self. Wordsworth celebrated the continuities of hearing, and dreaded the discontinuities of seeing. Emerson, in the defensive discontinuities of seeing, found a path to a more drastic, immediate, and total Sublime than European tradition wished or needed to discover. His greatest disciple, Whitman, an American bard at last, illustrates better than his master, the seer, both the splendor and the disaster of so aboriginal a repression.

My proof-text in Whitman is inevitably *Song of Myself*, but of its fifty-two sections I will concentrate only upon some Sublime centers, though I want to give a mapping-out of the revisionary pattern of the entire poem, for Whitman's romance of the self does follow essentially the model of the British Romantic crisis-poem, though with revealing, Emersonian, further distortions of the model. Employing my own shorthand, this is the pattern of ratios in *Song of Myself*:

Sections:

1–6	*Clinamen*, irony of presence and absence
7–27	*Tessera*, synecdoche of part for whole
28–30	*Kenosis*, metonymy of emptying out
31–38	*Daemonization*, hyperbole of high and low
39–49	*Askesis*, metaphor of inside vs. outside
50–52	*Apophrades*, metalepsis reversing early and late

To adumbrate this pattern fully would take too long, but the principal contours can be sketched. The opening six sections are overtly a celebration, and what they celebrate presumably is a return of the repressed, an ecstatic union of soul and self, of primary and antithetical, or, more simply, they celebrate the American Sublime of influx, of Emersonian self-recognition and consequent self-reliance. What ought to be overwhelmingly present in the first six sections is what Whitman, criticizing Keats, referred to as the great poet's "powerful press of himself." But in these opening sections, the reader confronts instead images of absence rather than of presence; indeed, the reader is led inevitably to the bewildered observation that the poet's absence is so sacred a void that his presence never could hope to fill it. Defensively, Whitman opens with a reaction-formation against his precursor Emerson, which rhetorically becomes not the digressiveness or "permanent parabasis" of German Romantic irony, but the sharper, simpler irony of saying one thing while meaning another. Whitman says "I celebrate" and he cunningly means: "I contract and withdraw while asserting that I expand." Thus in section 2, he evades being intoxicated by an outward fragrance, narcissistically preferring "the smoke of my own breath." This characteristic and beautiful evasiveness intensifies in section 4, where the true self, "the Me myself," takes up a stance in total contradiction to the embracings and urgings that the poet only ostensibly celebrates:

> Apart from the pulling and hauling stands what I am,
> Stands amused, complacent, compassionating, idle, unitary,
> Looks down, is erect, or bends an arm on an impalpable certain
>   rest,
> Looking with side-curved head curious what will come next,
> Both in and out of the game and watching and wondering at it.

If this dialectical evasion is a *clinamen* away from Emerson, then precisely what sort of guilt of indebtedness does it seek to void? Is there a crucial enough difference between the Emersonian and Whitmanian versions of an American Sublime so as to allow Whitman enough breathing-space? I need to digress again, upon antithetical theory and the American Sublime, if I am to answer this question and thus be able to get back to mapping *Song of Myself*. What I want to be able to explain is why Whitman, in section 5, resorts to the image of transparency when he describes the embrace between his self and his soul, and why in section 6 he writes so firmly within the materialist tradition of Epicurus and Lucretius. Epicurus said: "The what is unknowable," and Whitman says he cannot answer the child's question: *What is the grass?* Poetically, he does answer, in a magnificent series of tropes, much admired by the hesitant Hopkins, and progressing from the Homeric: "And now it seems to me the beautiful uncut hair of graves" until we are given the astonishing and very American: "This grass is very dark to be from the white heads of old mothers."

In the 1856, Second Edition of *Leaves of Grass*, Whitman addressed Emerson directly, acknowledging that "it is yours to have been the original true Captain who put to sea, intuitive, positive, rendering the first report, to be told less by any report, and more by the mariners of a thousand bays, in each tack of their arriving and departing, many years after this." But Whitman aspired after strength, and so could not abide in this perfectly accurate tribute. In 1863, in a private notation, full of veneration for the precursor, he subtly described Emerson, perhaps better than even Nietzsche was to describe him:

> America in the future, in her long train of poets and writers, while knowing more vehement and luxurious ones, will, I think, acknowledge nothing nearer [than] this man, the actual beginner of the whole procession-and certainly nothing purer, cleaner, sweeter, more canny, none, after all, more thoroughly her own and native. The most exquisite taste and caution are in him, always saving his feet from passing beyond the limits, for he is transcendental of limits, and you see underneath the rest a secret proclivity, American maybe, to dare and violate and make escapades.

By the time he wrote *Specimen Days* (1882), the consequences of misprision had triumphed in Whitman. Emerson was then condemned as having only a gentleman's admiration of power, and as having been an influence upon Whitman just "for a month or so." Five years later, Whitman lied outright, saying: "It is of no importance whether I had read Emerson before starting *L. of G.* or not. The fact happens to be positively that I had *not*." Rather desperately, Whitman went on to say: "*L. of G.'s word is the body, including all*, including the intellect and soul; E's word is mind (or intellect or soul)." Though I will return to this last remark of Whitman's later, in studying his opening swerve away from Emerson, I wish to end these citations from Whitman-on-Emerson by quoting the truest of them, again from *Specimen Days*:

> The best part of Emersonianism is, it breeds the giant that destroys itself. Who wants to be any man's mere follower? lurks behind every page. No teacher ever taught, that has so provided for his pupil's setting up independently—no truer evolutionist.

Here, Whitman has provided antithetical theory with the inevitable trope for Emersonianism or the American Sublime: "it breeds the giant that destroys itself." We need not be surprised to discover that the trope was, however, Emerson's own invention, crucial in the essay *Self-Reliance* (which Whitman certainly *had* read before he wrote *Song of Myself*):

I affect to be intoxicated with sights and suggestions, but I am
not intoxicated. My giant goes with me wherever I go.

We can contrast another Emersonian-Whitmanian giant, a double one
indeed, that dominates the opening section of the most Emersonian poem in
our literature, *An Ordinary Evening in New Haven*:

I

The eye's plain version is a thing apart,
The vulgate of experience. Of this,
A, few words, an and yet, and yet, and yet—

As part of the never-ending meditation,
Part of the question that is a giant himself:
Of what is this house composed if not of the sun,

These houses, these difficult objects, dilapidate
Appearances of what appearances,
Words, lines, not meanings, not communications,

Dark things without a double, after all,
Unless a second giant kills the first—
A recent imagining of reality,

Much like a new resemblance of the sun,
Down-pouring, up-springing and inevitable,
A larger poem for a larger audience,

As if the crude collops came together as one,
A mythological form, a festival sphere,
A great bosom, beard and being, alive with age.

"The question that is a giant himself" is a late version of the Stevensian
reduction to the First Idea, while the second giant who kills the first is
another reimagining of the otherwise intolerable First Idea or winter vision.
This second giant is the Emersonian giant or daemonic agent of the
American Sublime, a "giant that destroys itself." A transumption of these
giants, difficult as it was to accomplish, is one of the beautiful achievements
of our contemporary master of this tradition, A. R. Ammons, when he
concludes an early venture into the American Sublime by saying:

that is the
  expression of sea level,
the talk of giants,
of ocean, moon, sun, of everything,
spoken in a dampened grain of sand.

Those giants carry me, at last, into my promised theoretical digression, after which I intend to make a return to *Song of Myself* where I left it, in its first six sections. Giantism, as a trope, whether in Milton, or in Emerson and his descendants, is related to sightlessness, or rather to a repressive process that substitutes itself for tropes and defenses of *re-seeing*, which I take as a synonym for *limitation*, in my particular sense of the Lurianic *zimzum* or "contraction." To recapitulate a distinction made at the start of *A Map of Misreading*, "revisionism" as a word and as a notion contains the triad of re-seeing, re-esteeming or re-estimating, and re-aiming, which in Kabbalistic terms becomes the triad of contraction, breaking-of-the-vessels, and restitution, and in poetic terms the triad of limitation, substitution, and representation. In these terms, sublimation is a *re-seeing* but repression is a *re-aiming*, or, rhetorically, a metaphor re-sees, that is, it changes a perspective, but an hyperbole *re-aims*, that is, redirects a response.

Even so, an irony re-sees, but a synecdoche re-aims; a metonymy reduces a seeing, but a metalepsis redirects a purpose or desire. In re-seeing, you have translated desire into an act, but in re-aiming, you have failed to translate, and so what you re-aim is a desire. In poetic terms, *acting is a limitation, but desiring is a representation*. To get back from an act to a desire, or to translate a desire into an act, you must re-estimate and re-esteem either act or desire, and by preferring one to the other, you substitute and so shatter the vessels, break and remake the forms again. Another way of putting this is that a revisionary ratio (trope, defense, image) of limitation is closer to an act than to a desire, but a ratio of representation is closer to a desire or repurposing. To use Kenneth Burke's rhetorical terms, of his four Master Tropes, three (irony, metonymy, metaphor; or dialectic, reduction, perspective) are acts of re-seeing, or simple revisionism, while the fourth (synecdoche or representation) is a desire that redirects purpose, and so is a more complex revisionism. Hyperbole and transumption, as successively more heightened representations, are even more strongly tropes of desire.

Expanding Burke to my purposes, I would say that the prime poetic acts are to make presence more dialectical, to reduce differences, and to change our sense of otherness, of being elsewhere, by perspectivizing it. But the prime poetic desires are to be elsewhere, to be different, and to represent that otherness, that sense of difference and of being elsewhere. I would add, as a surmise, that all of us tend to value poetry more for its desires than for its acts, more for its re-aimings or purposiveness, than for its re-seeings. The Sublime, and particularly the American Sublime, is not a re-seeing but rather is a re-aiming. To achieve the Sublime is to experience a greater desire than you have known before, and such an achievement results from a failure to translate anterior or previous desires into acts. As the Emersonian, American sense of anteriority was greater, ours being. the Evening Land, even so the Sublime heightened, or repression augmented, if only because there was more unfulfilled desire to repress.

Emerson forgets English poetic tradition, in his most Sublime prose passages, because his purpose is to present something else, an American individuality. This forgetting is not primarily a limitation, that is, a calling attention to a lack both in language and in the self. Rather, this forgetting aims to reinforce a potentiality for response in the self, though unfortunately no act of forgetting can do much to reinforce a potentiality in language. Emerson therefore founds his Sublime upon a refusal of history, particularly literary history. But no poetic Sublime can be so founded without a compensating isolation and even a crippling sublimation of the self, as Wordsworth's Sublime already had demonstrated. Emerson's new desire forgets the old desire, only at the expense of increasing the distance between desire and act, which is probably the psychic reason why Emerson's prose style is so discontinuous. More even than Nietzsche, Emerson's unit of thought and expression tends to be the aphoristic, single sentence. Yet Emerson, unlike Nietzsche, was primarily an orator, a proud and knowing continuator of the Oral Tradition. Nietzsche is consistent with his own deepest purposes in so emphasizing the aphoristic energy of *writing*, whereas Emerson gives us the endless paradox of a mode of inspired speech that resorts always to aphorisms, which is what we can accept happily in Oscar Wilde, yet bewilders us in the American moralist.

The Emersonian or American Sublime, I am asserting, differs from the British or the Continental model not by a greater or lesser degree of positivity or negativity, but by a greater acceptance or affirmation of discontinuities in the self. Only Emerson could permit himself, within one page of the same essay (*Circles*), first to say: "There is no outside, no inclosing wall, no circumference to us," but then to cry out: "Alas for this infirm faith, this will not strenuous, this vast ebb of a vast flow! I am God in nature; I am a weed by the wall," and then outrageously to add: "The only sin is limitation." At the end of so discontinuous a Sublime, so strong yet so uncertain a repression, there must be also a heightened sense of the void, of the near-identity between the Sublime as a solitary ecstasy and the terrible raptures of nihilism, Nietzsche's *unheimlich* guest hovering by the door. Emerson's odyssey did not end in madness, and yet Emerson burned out, soon after the Civil War. Nietzsche became insane, Emerson became prematurely senile, Wordsworth merely became very boring, and so alas did Whitman, after *Drum-Taps*. In thirty years punctuated by many influxes of sublimity, Emerson went from saying: "It is a mischievous notion that we are come late into nature; that the world was finished a long time ago" to saying, in 1866: "There may be two or three or four steps, according to the genius of each, but for every seeing soul there are two absorbing facts,—*I and the Abyss*." For "the Abyss," we can read: tradition, history, the other, while for "I" we can read "any American." The final price paid for the extreme discontinuities of Emersonian vision is that we are left with a simple, chilling formula: the American Sublime equals *I and the Abyss*.

I return finally to the opening six sections of *Song of Myself*, with their defensive swerve away from Emerson, even as they appear to celebrate an Emersonian realization of the self. Whitman, not a poet-of-ideas like Emerson, but more traditionally a poet (however odd that sounds), seems to have known implicitly that a poetic representation of a desire tends to be stronger (that is, less limiting) than a poetic representation of an act. *Song of Myself*, in its beginnings, therefore substitutes the desires for union between split parts of the self, and between self and soul, for the acts of union proper, whatever those might be. Whitman wishes to originate his own mode, but he cannot do so without some discontinuity with Emerson, a prophet of discontinuity, and how do you cast off an influence that itself denounces all influence? Emersonianism urges itself to breed a giant that will destroy itself, but this most gigantic of its giants painfully found himself anticipated in nearly every trope, and in every movement of the spirit, a pain that Whitman shared with Thoreau.

It is evident, both from the opening emphases in *Song of Myself*, and from Whitman's comments in *Specimen Days*, on the rival words of precursor and ephebe, that Whitman's intended swerve from Emerson is to deny Emerson's distinction between the Soul and Nature, in which Nature includes all of the NOT ME, "both nature and art, all other men and my own body." Whitman's ME must include his own body, or so he would persuade us. He writes what in 1881 he would title at last *Song of Myself*, and not *Song of the Soul* or even *Song of My Soul*. But the embrace between his soul and his self in section 5, which makes the axis of things appear not opaque but transparent, oddly makes "you my soul" the active partner, and the self, "the other I am," wholly passive in this courtship. If we translate soul as "character" and self as "personality," then we would find it difficult to identify so passive a personality with "Walt Whitman, a kosmos, of Manhattan the son, / Turbulent, fleshy, sensual, eating, drinking and breeding" of section 24. Clearly, there is a division in Whitman between two elements in the self, as well as between self and soul, and it is the first of these divisions that matters, humanly and poetically. Indeed, it was from the first of these divisions that I believe Emerson initially rescued Whitman, thus making it possible for Whitman to become a poet. The "real me" or "me myself" in Whitman could not bear to be touched, ever, except by the maternal trinity of night, death, and the sea, while Walt Whitman, one of the roughs, learned from Emerson to cry: "Contact!" There is a sublime pathos in Whitman making his Epicurean *clinamen* away from Emerson by overproclaiming the body. Emerson had nothing to say about two subjects and two subjects only, sex and death, because he was too healthy-minded to believe that there was much to say about either. Emerson had no sexual problems, and was a Stoic about death.

I return to mapping *Song of Myself*, with its implicit contrast that Whitman, gloriously and plangently, always had much too much to say about sex and death, being in this the ancestor not only of Hart Crane and, perhaps surprisingly, of Wallace Stevens and, these days, of Ammons and Ashbery, but also of such prose obfuscators of sex and death as Hemingway and his egregious ephebe, Norman Mailer. Whitman, surpassing all his descendants, makes of a linked sex–and–death a noble synecdoche for all of existence, which is the figurative design of sections 7–27 of *Song of Myself*. A universalizing flood tide of reversals-into-the-opposite reaches a great climax in section 24, which is an antithetical completion of the self without rival in American poetry, astonishing both for its dignity and its pathos, and transcending any other modern poet's attempt to think and represent by synecdoche. The reader cannot know whether to admire this proclamation more for its power or for its precision:

> Unscrew the locks from the doors!
> Unscrew the doors themselves from their jambs!
>
> Whoever degrades another degrades me,
> And whatever is done or said returns at last to me.
>
> Through me the afflatus surging and surging, through me
>   the current and index.

I speak the pass-word primeval, I give the sign of democracy,
By God! I will accept nothing which all cannot have their
    counterpart of on the same terms.

Through me many long dumb voices,
Voices of the interminable generations of prisoners and slaves,
Voices of the diseas'd and despairing and of thieves and dwarfs,
Voices of the threads that connect the stars, and of wombs and
    of the father-stuff,
And of the rights of them the others are down upon,
Of the deform'd, trivial, flat, foolish, despised,
Fog in the air, beetles rolling balls of dung.

We can say of this astonishing chant that as completing synecdoche it
verges on emptying-out metonymy, reminding us of the instability of all
tropes and, of all psychic defenses. Primarily, Whitman's defense in this
passage is a fantasy reversal, in which his own fear of contact with other
selves is so turned that no outward overthrow of his separateness is possible.
It is as though he were denying denial, negating negation, by absorbing every
outward self, every outcast of society, history, and even of nature. To say that
one will accept nothing which all cannot have their counterpart of on the
same terms is indeed to say that one will accept no overthrow from outside
oneself, no negation or denial. Whitman, with the genius of his enormous
drive towards antithetical completion, can be judged to end the *tessera* phase
of his poem in the remarkable triad of sections 25–27. For in section 25,
nature strikes back against the poet, yet he is strong enough to sustain
himself, but in 26–27 he exhaustedly begins to undergo a kind of passive
slide-down of spirit that precludes the fierce *kenosis* or emptying-out of his
poethood in sections 28–30. At the end of 27, Whitman confesses: "To touch
my person to some one else's is about as much as I can stand." The
Whitmanian *kenosis*, in 28–30, appears to make of masturbation a metonymic
reduction of the self, where touch substitutes for the whole being, and a
pathetic salvation is sought through an exaltation of the earth that the poet
has moistened:

A minute and a drop of me settle my brain,
I believe the soggy clods shall become lovers and lamps,
And a compend of compends is the meat of a man or woman,
And a summit and flower there is the feeling they have for
    each other,

And they are to branch boundlessly out of that lesson until it
    becomes omnific,
And until one and all shall delight us, and we them.

This is the prelude to the most awesome repression in our literature,
the greatest instance yet of the American Sublime, sections 31–38. Rather
than map the glories of this Sublime, I will examine instead the violent
descent into the abyss that culminates it in section 38. Having merged both
the fathering force and the universal brotherhood into himself, with
terrifying eloquence ("I am the man, I suffer'd, I was there"; and "Agonies
are one of my changes of garments"), Whitman pays the fearful price of
Emersonian Compensation. Nothing indeed is gotten for nothing:

Enough! enough! enough!
Somehow I have been stunn'd. Stand back!
Give me a little time beyond my cuff'd head, slumbers, dreams,
    gaping,
I discover myself on the verge of a usual mistake.
That I could forget the mockers and insults!
That I could forget the trickling tears and the blows of the
    bludgeons and hammers!
That I could look with a separate look on my own crucifixion
    and bloody crossing.

I remember now,
I resume the overstaid fraction,
The grave of rock multiplies what has been confided to it, or
    to any graves,
Corpses rise, gashes heal, fastenings roll from me.

Emerson had prophesied a Central Man who would reverse the "great
Defeat" of Christ, insisting that "we demand Victory." Whitman, more
audacious even than his precursor, dares to present himself both as a
repetition of the great Defeat and as the Victory of a Resurrection: "I troop
forth replenish'd with supreme power, one of an average unending
procession." What are we to do with a hyperbolical Sublime this
outrageous? Whitman too is saying: "*I and the Abyss*," despite the self-
deception of that "average unending procession." But Whitman's repression
is greater, as it has to be, since a crucial part of its anteriority is a primal
fixation upon Emerson, a fixation that I want to explore in the conclusion of

this chapter once I have concluded my sketchy mapping of the later ratios in *Song of Myself*.

Sections 39–49 are an attempt at a sublimating consolidation of the self, in which Whitman presents us with his version of the most characteristic of High Romantic metaphors, his self as inside reciprocally addressing the natural world as a supposedly answering outside. The final or reductive form of this perspectivizing is summed up in an appropriately entitled poem of Wallace Stevens, *The American Sublime*:

> But how does one feel?
> One grows used to the weather,
>
> The landscape and that;
> And the sublime comes down
> To the spirit itself,
>
> The spirit and space,
> The empty spirit
> In vacant space.

That is to say: the Sublime comes down to the Abyss in me inhabiting the Abyss of space. Whitman's version of this coming down completes his great *askesis*, in section 49:

> I hear you whispering there O stars of heaven,
> O suns—O grass of graves—O perpetual transfers and
>   promotions,
> If you do not say any thing how can I say any thing?
> . . . .
> Of the turbid pool that lies in the autumn forest,
> Of the moon that descends the steeps of the soughing twilight,
> Toss, sparkles of day and dusk-toss on the black stems that
>   decay in the muck,
> Toss to the moaning gibberish of the dry limbs.
>
> I ascend from the moon, I ascend from the night,
> I perceive that the ghastly glimmer is noonday sunbeams
>   reflected,
> And debouch to the steady and central from the offspring great
>   or small.

The steadiness of the central is reached here only through the rhetorical equivalent of sublimation, which is metaphor, the metaphor of two lights, sun and moon, with the sun necessarily dominating, and taking as its tenor the Emersonian "steady and central." I return to the formula for poetic sublimation ventured earlier in this discourse. The sublimating ratio is a limitation because what it concentrates is being evaded, that is, is remembered only in order *not* to be presented, with something else substituted in the presentation. Whitman does not present what he is remembering, his dream of divination, of being a dazzling sunrise greater than the merely natural sun. Instead of this autonomous splendor, he accepts now a perspectivizing, a balancing of "sparkles of day and dusk." His restitution for this *askesis* comes in his great poem's close, in sections 50–52, which form a miraculous transumption of all that has gone before. Yet the Whitmanian metaleptic reversal differs crucially from the Wordsworthian-Tennysonian model, in that it places the burden upon the reader, rather than upon the poet. It is the reader, and not the poet, who is challenged directly to make his belatedness into an earliness. Whitman was to perfect this challenge in *Crossing Brooklyn Ferry*, appropriately called *Sun-Down Poem* when it first appeared in the second *Leaves of Grass*, in 1856. Here, in *Song of Myself*, the challenge is made explicit at the close of section 51: "Will you speak before I am gone? will you prove already too late?" Nowhere in Emerson (and I concede to no reader in my fanatical love of Emerson) is there so strong a representation of the Central Man who is coming as there is in Whitman's self-presentation in section 52. I would select this as the greatest of Emerson's prophecies of the Central Man, from the journals, April 1846:

> He or That which in despair of naming aright, some have called the *Newness*,—as the Hebrews did not like to pronounce the word,—he lurks, he hides, he who is success, reality, joy, power,—that which constitutes Heaven, which reconciles impossibilities, atones for shortcomings, expiates sins or makes them virtues, buries in oblivion the crowded historical past, sinks religions, philosophies, nations, persons to legends; reverses the scale of opinion, of fame; reduces sciences to opinion, and makes the thought of the moment the key to the universe, and the egg of history to come.
>
> ... 'Tis all alike,—astronomy, metaphysics, sword, spade, pencil, or instruments and arts yet to be invented,—this is the inventor, the worth-giver, the worth. This is He that shall come;

or, if He come not, nothing comes: He that disappears in the moment when we go to celebrate Him. If we go to burn those that blame our celebration, He appears in them. The Divine Newness. Hoe and spade, sword and pen, cities, pictures, gardens, laws, bibles, are prized only because they were means He sometimes used. So with astronomy, music, arithmetic, castes, feudalism,—we kiss with devotion these hems of his garment,—we mistake them for Him; they crumble to ashes on our lips.

The Newness is Influx, or fresh repression, lurking and hiding, imaged in depth, in burying and in sinking. This daemonic force then projects the past and introjects the future, and yet *not now*, but only in the realm of what *shall come*: "He ... disappears in the moment when we go to celebrate Him," and more than his garment would crumble to ashes on our lips. Whitman, as this Newness, is even more splendidly elusive:

> The spotted hawk swoops by and accuses me, he complains of
>   my gab and my loitering.
>
> I too am not a bit tamed, I too am untranslatable;
> I sound my barbaric yawp over the roofs of the world.
>
> The last scud of day holds back for me,
> It flings my likeness after the rest and true as any on the
>   shadow'd wilds,
> It coaxes me to the vapor and the dusk.
>
> I depart as air, I shake my white locks at the runaway sun,
> I effuse my flesh in eddies, and drift it in lacy jags.
>
> I bequeath myself to the dirt to grow from the grass I love,
> If you want me again look for me under your boot-soles.
>
> You will hardly know who I am or what I mean;
> But I shall be good health to you nevertheless,
> And filter and fibre your blood.
>
> Failing to fetch me at first keep encouraged,
> Missing me one place search another,
> I stop somewhere waiting for you.

The hawk accuses Whitman of belatedness, of "loitering," but the poet is one with the hawk, "untranslatable" in that his desire is perpetual, always transcending act. There, in the twilight, Whitman arrests the lateness of the day, dissolving the presentness of the present, and effusing his own presence until it is air and earth. As the atmosphere we are to breathe, the ground we are to walk, the poet introjects our future, and is somewhere up ahead, waiting for us to catch up. So far ahead is he on our mutual quest, that he can afford to stop, though he will not tell us precisely where. His dominant trope remains the grass, but this trope is now transumptive, for it is grass not yet grown but "to grow." Implicit in such a trope is the more-than-Emersonian promise that *this* Central Man will not disappear "in the moment when we go to celebrate him."

I end by returning to Whitman's American Sublime of sections 31–38, with specific reference to the grand march of section 33, where the poet says: "I am afoot with, my vision." Here is a part of this audacious mounting into the Sublime:

> Solitary at midnight in my back yard, my thoughts gone from
>   me a long while,
> Walking the old hills of Judaea with the beautiful, gentle God
>   by my side,
> Speeding through space, speeding through heaven and the stars,
> Speeding amid the seven satellites and the broad ring, and the
>   diameter of eighty thousands miles,
> Speeding with tail'd meteors, throwing fire-balls like the rest,
> Carrying the crescent child that carries its own full mother in
>   its belly,
> Storming, enjoying, planning, loving, cautioning,
> Backing and filling, appearing and disappearing,
> I tread day and night such roads.
>
> I visit the orchards of spheres and look at the product,
> And look at quintillions ripen'd and look at quintillions green.
>
> I fly those flights of a fluid and swallowing soul,
> My course runs below the soundings of plummets.
>
> I help myself to material and immaterial,
> No guard can shut me off, no law prevent me.

As an hyperbolical progression, this sequence is matched only by its misprision or sublime parody, the flight of the Canon Aspirin in *Notes toward a Supreme Fiction*. Whitman's angelic flight breaks down the distinction between material and immaterial, because his soul, as he precisely says, is "fluid and swallowing." Similarly, the Canon's angelic flight breaks down the limits between fact and thought, but the Canon's soul being more limited, the later angelic flight fails exactly where Whitman's cannot fail. The Canon imposes orders upon reality, but Whitman discovers or uncovers orders, because he is discovering himself (even though he does not uncover himself, despite his constant assertions that he is about to do so). I vary an earlier question in order to conclude this discourse. Why is Whitman's American Sublime larger and stronger than either the Sublime of his precursor, Emerson, or the Sublime of his ephebe, Stevens? In the language of misprision, this means: why and how is Whitman's poetic repression greater and more forceful than that of the other major figures in his own tradition?

Whitman's ego, in his most Sublime transformations, wholly absorbs and thus pragmatically forgets the fathering force, and presents instead the force of the son, of his own self or, in Whitman's case, perhaps we should say of his own selves. Where Emerson *urges* forgetfulness of anteriority, Whitman more strenuously *does* forget it, though at a considerable cost. Emerson says: "*I and the Abyss*"; Whitman says: "*The Abyss of My Self*." The second statement is necessarily more Sublime and, alas, even more American.

D.H. LAWRENCE

Herman Melville's "Moby Dick"

Moby Dick, *or the White Whale*.

A hunt. The last great hunt.

For what?

For Moby Dick, the huge white sperm whale: who is old, hoary, monstrous, and swims alone; who is unspeakably terrible in his wrath, having so often been attacked; and snow-white.

Of course he is a symbol.

Of what?

I doubt if even Melville knew exactly. That's the best of it.

He is warm-blooded, he is loveable. He is lonely Leviathan, not a Hobbes sort. Or is he?

But he is warm-blooded and loveable. The South Sea Islanders, and Polynesians, and Malays, who worship shark, or crocodile, or weave endless frigate-bird distortions, why did they never worship the whale? So big!

Because the whale is not wicked. He doesn't bite. And their gods had to bite.

He's not a dragon. He is Leviathan. He never coils like the Chinese dragon of the sun. He's not a serpent of the waters. He is warm-blooded, a mammal. And hunted, hunted down.

It is a great book.

From *Studies in Classic American Literature*. © 1961 by the Estate of the late Mrs. Frieda Lawrence.

At first you are put off by the style. It reads like journalism. It seems spurious. You feel Melville is trying to put something over you. It won't do.

And Melville really is a bit sententious: aware of himself, self-conscious, putting something over even himself. But then it's not easy to get into the swing of a piece of deep mysticism when you just set out with a story.

Nobody can be more clownish, more clumsy and sententiously in bad taste, than Herman Melville, even in a great book like *Moby Dick*. He preaches and holds forth because he's not sure of himself. And he holds forth, often, so amateurishly.

The artist was so *much* greater than the man. The man is rather a tiresome New Englander of the ethical mystical-transcendentalist sort: Emerson, Longfellow, Hawthorne, etc. So unrelieved, the solemn ass even in humour. So hopelessly *au grand sérieux*, you feel like saying: Good God, what does it matter? If life is a tragedy, or a farce, or a disaster, or anything else, what do I care! Let life be what it likes. Give me a drink, that's what I want just now.

For my part, life is so many things I don't care what it is. It's not my affair to sum it up. just now it's a cup of tea. This morning it was wormwood and gall. Hand me the sugar.

One wearies of the *grand sérieux*. There's something false about it. And that's Melville. Oh dear, when the solemn ass brays! brays! brays!

But he was a deep, great artist, even if he was rather a sententious man. He was a real American in that he always felt his audience in front of him. But when he ceases to be American, when he forgets all audience, and gives us his sheer apprehension of the world, then he is wonderful, his book commands a stillness in the soul, an awe.

In his "human" self, Melville is almost dead. That is, he hardly reacts to human contacts any more; or only ideally: or just for a moment. His human-emotional self is almost played out. He is abstract, self-analytical and abstracted. And he is more spellbound by the strange slidings and collidings of Matter than by the things men do. In this he is like Dana. It is the material elements he really has to do with. His drama is with them. He was a futurist long before futurism found paint. The sheer naked slidings of the elements. And the human soul experiencing it all. So often, it is almost over the border: psychiatry. Almost spurious. Yet so great.

It is the same old thing as in all Americans. They keep their old-fashioned ideal frock-coat on, and an old-fashioned silk hat, while they do the most impossible things. There you are: you see Melville hugged in bed by a huge tattooed South Sea Islander, and solemnly offering burnt offering to this savage's little idol, and his ideal frock-coat just hides his shirt-tails and prevents us from seeing his bare posterior as he salaams, while his ethical silk hat sits correctly over his brow the while. That is so typically American: doing the most impossible things without taking off their spiritual get-up. Their ideals are like armour which has rusted in, and will never more come off. And meanwhile in Melville his bodily knowledge moves naked, a living quick among the stark elements. For with sheer physical vibrational sensitiveness, like a marvellous wireless-station, he registers the effects of the outer world. And he records also, almost beyond pain or pleasure, the extreme transitions of the isolated, far-driven soul, the soul which is now alone, without any real human contact.

The first days in New Bedford introduce the only human being who really enters into the book, namely, Ishmael, the "I" of the book. And then the moment's heart's-brother, Queequeg, the tattooed, powerful South Sea harpooner, whom Melville loves as Dana loves "Hope". The advent of Ishmael's bedmate is amusing and unforgettable. But later the two swear "marriage", in the language of the savages. For Queequeg has opened again the flood-gates of love and human connexion in Ishmael.

"As I sat there in that now lonely room, the fire burning low, in that mild stage when, after its first intensity has warmed the air, it then only glows to be looked at; the evening shades and phantoms gathering round the casements, and peering in upon us silent, solitary twain: I began to be sensible of strange feelings. I felt a melting in me. No more my splintered heart and maddened hand were turned against the wolfish world. This soothing savage had redeemed it. There he sat, his very indifference speaking a nature in which there lurked no civilized hypocrisies and bland deceits. Wild he was; a very sight of sights to see; yet I began to feel myself mysteriously drawn towards him."—So they smoked together, and are clasped in each other's arms. The friendship is finally sealed when Ishmael offers sacrifice to Queequeg's little idol, Gogo.

"I was a good Christian, born and bred in the bosom of the infallible Presbyterian Church. How then could I unite with the idolater in worshipping his piece of wood? But what is worship?—to do the will of God—*that* is worship. And what is the will of God?—to do to my fellow man what I would have my fellow man do to me—*that* is the will of God."— Which sounds like Benjamin Franklin, and is hopelessly bad theology. But it is real American logic. "Now Queequeg is my fellow man. And what do I wish that this Queequeg would do to me? Why, unite with me in my particular Presbyterian form of worship. Consequently, I must unite with him; ergo, I must turn idolater. So I kindled the shavings; helped prop up the innocent little idol; offered him burnt biscuit with Queequeg; salaamed before him twice or thrice; kissed his nose; and that done, we undressed and went to bed, at peace with our own consciences and all the world. But we did not go to sleep without some little chat. How it is I know not; but there is no place like bed for confidential disclosures between friends. Man and wife, they say, open the very bottom of their souls to each other; and some old couples often lie and chat over old times till nearly morning. Thus, then, lay I and Queequeg—a cosy, loving pair—"

You would think this relation with Queequeg meant something to Ishmael. But no. Queequeg is forgotten like yesterday's newspaper. Human things are only momentary excitements or amusements to the American Ishmael. Ishmael, the hunted. But much more Ishmael the hunter. What's a Queequeg? What's a wife? The white whale must be hunted down. Queequeg must be just "KNOWN", then dropped into oblivion.

And what in the name of fortune is the white whale? Elsewhere Ishmael says he loved Queequeg's eyes: "large, deep eyes, fiery black and bold." No doubt like Poe, he wanted to get the "clue" to them. That was all.

The two men go over from New Bedford to Nantucket, and there sign on to the Quaker whaling ship, the *Pequod*. It is all strangely fantastic, phantasmagoric. The voyage of the soul. Yet curiously a real whaling voyage, too. We pass on into the midst of the sea with this strange ship and its incredible crew. The Argonauts were mild lambs in comparison. And Ulysses went *defeating* the Circes and overcoming the wicked hussies of the isles. But the *Pequod*'s crew is a collection of maniacs fanatically hunting down a lonely, harmless white whale.

As a soul history, it makes one angry. As a sea yarn, it is marvellous: there is always something a bit over the mark, in sea yarns. Should be. Then again the masking up of actual seaman's experience with sonorous mysticism sometimes gets on one's nerves. And again, as a revelation of destiny the book is too deep even for sorrow. Profound beyond feeling.

You are some time before you are allowed to see the captain, Ahab: the mysterious Quaker. Oh, it is a God-fearing Quaker ship.

Ahab, the captain. The captain of the soul.

"I am the master of my fate,
I am the captain of my soul!"

Ahab!
"Oh, captain, my captain, our fearful trip is done." The gaunt Ahab, Quaker, mysterious person, only shows himself after some days at sea. There's a secret about him! What?

Oh, he's a portentous person. He stumps about on an ivory stump, made from sea-ivory. Moby Dick, the great white whale, tore off Ahab's leg at the knee, when Ahab was attacking him.

Quite right, too. Should have torn off both his legs, and a bit more besides.

But Ahab doesn't think so. Ahab is now a monomaniac. Moby Dick is his monomania. Moby Dick Must DIE, or Ahab can't live any longer. Ahab is atheist by this.

All right.

This *Pequod*, ship of the American soul, has three mates.

1. Starbuck: Quaker, Nantucketer, a good responsible man of reason, forethought, intrepidity, what is called a dependable man. At the bottom, afraid.

2. Stubb: "Fearless as fire, and as mechanical." Insists on being reckless and jolly on every occasion. Must be afraid too, really.

3. Flask: Stubborn, obstinate, without imagination. To him "the wondrous whale was but a species of magnified mouse or water-rat—"

There you have them: a maniac captain and his three mates, three splendid seamen, admirable whalemen, first-class men at their job.

America!

It is rather like Mr. Wilson and his admirable, "efficient" crew, at the Peace Conference. Except that none of the Pequodders took their wives along.

A maniac captain of the soul, and three eminently practical mates. America!

Then such a crew. Renegades, castaways, cannibals Ishmael, Quakers. America!

Three giant harpooners, to spear the great white whale.

1. Queequeg, the South Sea Islander, all tattooed, big and powerful.

2. Tashtego, the Red Indian of the sea-coast, where the Indian meets the sea.

3. Daggoo, the huge black negro.

There you have them, three savage races, under the American flag, the maniac captain, with their great keen harpoons, ready to spear the white whale.

And only after many days at sea does Ahab's own boat-crew appear on deck. Strange, silent, secret, black-garbed Malays, fire-worshipping Parsees. These are to man Ahab's boat, when it leaps in pursuit of that whale.

What do you think of the ship *Pequod*, the ship of the soul of an American?

Many races, many peoples, many nations, under the Stars and Stripes. Beaten with many stripes.

Seeing stars sometimes.

And in a mad ship, under a mad captain, in a mad, fanatic's hunt.

For what?

For Moby Dick, the great white whale.

But splendidly handled. Three splendid mates. The whole thing practical, eminently practical in its working. American industry!

And all this practicality in the service of a mad, mad chase.

Melville manages to keep it a real whaling ship, on a real cruise, in spite of all fantastics. A wonderful, wonderful voyage. And a beauty that is so surpassing only because of the author's awful flounderings in mystical waters. He wanted to get metaphysically deep. And he got deeper than metaphysics. It is a surpassingly beautiful book, with an awful meaning, and bad jolts.

It is interesting to compare Melville with Dana, about the albatross— Melville a bit sententious. "I remember the first albatross I ever saw. It was during a prolonged gale in waters hard upon the Antarctic seas. From my forenoon watch below I ascended to the overcrowded deck, and there, lashed upon the main hatches, I saw a regal feathered thing of unspotted whiteness, and with a hooked Roman bill sublime. At intervals it arched forth its vast, archangel wings—wondrous throbbings and flutterings shook it. Though bodily unharmed, it uttered cries, as some King's ghost in supernatural distress. Through its inexpressible strange eyes methought I peeped to secrets not below the heavens—the white thing was so white, its wings so wide, and in those for ever exiled waters, I had lost the miserable warping memories of traditions and of towns. I assert then, that in the wondrous bodily whiteness of the bird chiefly lurks the secret of the spell—"

Melville's albatross is a prisoner, caught by a bait on a hook.

Well, I have seen an albatross, too: following us in waters hard upon the Antarctic, too, south of Australia. And in the Southern winter. And the ship, a P. and O. boat, nearly empty. And the lascar crew shivering.

The bird with its long, long wings following, then leaving us. No one knows till they have tried, how lost, how lonely those Southern waters are. And glimpses of the Australian coast.

It makes one feel that our day is only a day. That in the dark of the night ahead other days stir fecund, when we have lapsed from existence.

Who knows how utterly we shall lapse.

But Melville keeps up his disquisition about "whiteness". The great abstract fascinated him. The Abstract where we end, and cease to be. White or black. Our white, abstract end!

Then again it is lovely to be at sea on the *Pequod*, with never a grain of earth to us.

"It was a cloudy, sultry afternoon; the seamen were lazily lounging about the decks, or vacantly gazing over into the lead-coloured waters. Queequeg and I were mildly employed weaving what is called a sword-mat, for an additional lashing to our boat. So still and subdued, and yet somehow preluding was all the scene, and such an incantation of reverie lurked in the air that each silent sailor seemed resolved into his own invisible self—"

In the midst of this preluding silence came the first cry: "There she blows! there! there! there! She blows!" And then comes the first chase, a marvellous piece of true sea-writing, the sea, and sheer sea-beings on the chase, sea-creatures chased. There is scarcely a taint of earth—pure sea-motion.

"'Give way, men,' whispered Starbuck, drawing still. further aft the sheet of his sail; 'there is time to kill a fish yet before the squall comes. There's white water again!—Close to!—Spring!' Soon after, two cries in quick succession on each side of us denoted that the other boats had got fast; but hardly were they overheard, when with a lightning-like hurtling whisper Starbuck said: 'Stand up!' and Queequeg, harpoon in hand, sprang to his feet. Though not one of the oarsmen was then facing the life and death peril so close to them ahead, yet, their eyes on the intense countenance of the mate in the stern of the boat, they knew that the imminent instant had come; they heard, too, an enormous wallowing sound, as of fifty elephants stirring in their litter. Meanwhile the boat was still booming through the mist, the waves curbing and hissing around us like the erected crests of enraged serpents.

"'That's his hump. *There*! *There*, give it to. him!' whispered Starbuck.— A short rushing sound leapt out of the boat; it was the darted iron of Queequeg. Then all in one welded motion came a push from astern, while forward the boat seemed striking on a ledge; the sail collapsed and exploded; a gush of scalding vapour shot up near by; something rolled and tumbled like an earthquake beneath us. The whole crew were half-suffocated as they were tossed helter-skelter into the white curling cream of the squall. Squall, whale, and harpoon had all blended together; and the whale, merely grazed by the iron, escaped——"

Melville is a master of violent, chaotic physical motion; he can keep up a whole wild chase without a flaw. He is as perfect at creating stillness. The ship is cruising on the Carrol Ground, south of St. Helena.—"It was while gliding through these latter waters that one serene and moonlight night, when all the waves rolled by like scrolls of silver; and by their soft, suffusing seethings, made what seemed a silvery silence, not a solitude; on such a silent night a silvery jet was seen far in advance of the white bubbles at the bow——"

Then there is the description of brit. "Steering northeastward from the Crozetts we fell in with vast meadows of brit, the minute, yellow substance upon which the Right Whale largely feeds. For leagues and leagues it undulated round us, so that we seemed to be sailing through boundless fields of ripe and golden wheat. On the second day, numbers of Right Whales were seen, who, secure from the attack of a Sperm Whaler like the *Pequod*, with open jaws sluggishly swam through the brit, which, adhering to the fringing fibres of that wondrous Venetian blind in their mouths, was in that manner separated from the water that escaped at the lip. As moving mowers who, side by side, slowly and seethingly advance their scythes through the long wet grass of the marshy meads; even so these monsters swam, making a strange, grassy, cutting sound; and leaving behind them endless swaths of blue on the yellow sea. But it was only the sound they made as they parted the brit which at all reminded one of mowers. Seen from the mastheads, especially when they paused and were stationary, for a while, their vast black forms looked more like lifeless masses of rock than anything else——"

This beautiful passage brings us to the apparition of the squid.

"Slowly wading through the meadows of brit, the *Pequod* still held her way northeastward towards the island of Java; a gentle air impelling her keel, so that in the surrounding serenity her three tall, tapering masts mildly waved to that languid breeze, as three mild palms on a plain. And still, at wide intervals, in the silvery night, that lonely, alluring jet would be seen.

"But one transparent-blue morning, when a stillness almost preternatural spread over the sea, however unattended with any stagnant calm; when the long burnished sunglade on the waters seemed a golden finger laid across them, enjoining secrecy; when all the slippered waves whispered together as they softly ran on; in this profound hush of the visible sphere a strange spectre was seen by Daggoo from the mainmast head.

"In the distance, a great white mass lazily rose, and rising higher and higher, and disentangling itself from the azure, at last gleamed before our prow like a snow-slide, new slid from the hills. Thus glistening for a moment, as slowly it subsided, and sank. Then once more arose, and silently gleamed. It seemed not a whale; and yet, is this Moby Dick? thought Daggoo——"

The boats were lowered and pulled to the scene.

"In the same spot where it sank, once more it slowly rose. Almost forgetting for the moment all thoughts of Moby Dick, we now gazed at the most wondrous phenomenon which the secret seas have hitherto revealed to mankind. A vast pulpy mass, furlongs in length and breadth, of a glancing cream-colour, lay floating on the water, innumerable long arms radiating from its centre, and curling and twisting like a nest of anacondas, as if blindly to clutch at any hapless object within reach. No perceptible face or front did it have; no conceivable token of either sensation or instinct; but undulated there on the billows, an unearthly, formless, chance-like apparition of life. And with a low sucking it slowly disappeared again."

The following chapters, with their account of whale hunts, the killing, the stripping, the cutting up, are magnificent records of actual happening. Then comes the queer tale of the meeting of the *Jeroboam*, a whaler met at sea, all of whose men were under the domination of a religious maniac, one of the ship's hands. There are detailed descriptions of the actual taking of the sperm oil from a whale's head. Dilating on the smallness of the brain of a sperm whale, Melville significantly remarks—"for I believe that much of a man's character will be found betokened in his backbone. I would rather feel your spine than your skull, whoever you are——" And of the whale, he adds

"For, viewed in this light, the wonderful comparative smallness of his brain proper is more than compensated by the wonderful comparative magnitude of his spinal cord."

In among the rush of terrible, awful hunts, come touches of pure beauty.

"As the three boats lay there on that gently rolling sea, gazing down into its eternal blue noon; and as not a single groan or cry of any sort, nay not so much as a ripple or a thought, came up from its depths; what landsman would have thought that beneath all that silence and placidity the utmost monster of the seas was writhing and wrenching in agony!"

Perhaps the most stupendous chapter is the one called *The Grand Armada*, at the beginning of Volume III. The *Pequod* was drawing through the Sunda Straits towards Java when she came upon a vast host of sperm whales. "Broad on both bows, at a distance of two or three miles, and forming a great semicircle embracing one-half of the level horizon, a continuous chain of whale-jets were up-playing and sparkling in the noonday air." Chasing this great herd, past the Straits of Sunda, themselves chased by Javan pirates, the whalers race on. Then the boats are lowered. At last that curious state of inert irresolution came over the whales, when they were, as the seamen say, gallied. Instead of forging ahead in huge martial array they swam violently hither and thither, a surging sea of whales, no longer moving on. Starbuck's boat, made fast to a whale, is towed in amongst this howling Leviathan chaos. In mad career it cockles through the boiling surge of monsters, till it is brought into a clear lagoon in the very centre of the vast,

mad, terrified herd. There a sleek, pure calm reigns. There the females swam
in peace, and the young whales came snuffing tamely at the boat, like dogs.
And there the astonished seamen watched the love-making of these amazing
monsters, mammals, now in rut far down in the sea—"But far beneath this
wondrous world upon the surface, another and still stranger world met our
eyes, as we gazed over the side. For, suspended in these watery vaults, floated
the forms of the nursing mothers of the whales, and those that by their
enormous girth seemed shortly to become mothers. The lake, as I have
hinted, was to a considerable depth exceedingly transparent; and as human
infants while sucking will calmly and fixedly gaze away from the breast, as if
leading two different lives at a time; and while yet drawing moral
nourishment, be still spiritually feasting upon some unearthly reminiscence,
even so did the young of these whales seem looking up towards us, but not
at us, as if we were but a bit of gulf-weed in their newborn sight. Floating on
their sides, the mothers also seemed quietly eyeing us.—Some of the subtlest
secrets of the seas seemed divulged to us in this enchanted pond. We saw
young Leviathan amours in the deep. And thus, though surrounded by circle
upon circle of consternation and affrights, did these inscrutable creatures at
the centre freely and fearlessly indulge in all peaceful concernments; yea,
serenely revelled in dalliance and delight——"

There is something really overwhelming in these whale-hunts, almost
superhuman or inhuman, bigger than life, more terrific than human activity.
The same with the chapter on ambergris: it is so curious, so real, yet so
unearthly. And again in the chapter called *The Cassock*—surely the oldest
piece of phallicism in all the world's literature.

After this comes the amazing account of the Try-works, when the ship
is turned into the sooty, oily factory in mid-ocean, and the oil is extracted
from the blubber. In the night of the red furnace burning on deck, at sea,
Melville has his startling experience of reversion. He is at the helm, but has
turned to watch the fire: when suddenly he feels the ship rushing backward
from him, in mystic reversion—"Uppermost was the impression, that
whatever swift, rushing thing I stood on was not so much bound to any haven
ahead, as rushing from all havens astern. A stark bewildering feeling, as of
death, came over me. Convulsively my hands grasped the tiller, but with the
crazy conceit that the tiller was, somehow, in some enchanted way, inverted.
My God! What is the matter with me, I thought!"

This dream-experience is a real soul-experience. He ends with an
injunction to all men, not to gaze on the red fire when its redness makes all
things look ghastly. It seems to him that his gazing on fire has evoked this
horror of reversion, undoing.

Perhaps it had. He was water-born.

After some unhealthy work on the ship, Queequeg caught a fever and was like to die. "How he wasted and wasted in those few, long-lingering days, till there seemed but little left of him but his frame and tattooing. But as all else in him thinned, and his cheek-bones grew sharper, his eyes, nevertheless, seemed growing fuller and fuller; they took on a strangeness of lustre; and mildly but deeply looked out at you there from his sickness, a wondrous testimony to that immortal health in him which could not die, or be weakened. And like circles on the water, which as they grow fainter, expand; so his eyes seemed rounding and rounding, like the circles of Eternity. An awe that cannot be named would steal over you as you sat by the side of this waning savage——"

But Queequeg did not die—and the *Pequod* emerges from the Eastern Straits, into the full Pacific. "To any meditative Magian rover, this serene Pacific once beheld, must ever after be the sea of his adoption. It rolls the midmost waters of the world——"

In this Pacific the fights go on: "It was far down the afternoon, and when all the spearings of the crimson fight were done, and floating in the lovely sunset sea and sky, sun and whale both stilly died together; then such a sweetness and such a plaintiveness, such inwreathing orisons curled up in that rosy air, that it almost seemed as if far over from the deep green convent valleys of the Manila isles, the Spanish land-breeze had gone to sea, freighted with these vesper hymns. Soothed again, but only soothed to deeper gloom, Ahab, who had sterned off from the whale, sat intently watching his final wanings from the now tranquil boat. For that strange spectacle, observable in all sperm whales dying—the turning of the head sunwards, and so expiring—that strange spectacle, beheld of such a placid evening, somehow to Ahab conveyed wondrousness unknown before. 'He turns and turns him to it; how slowly, but how steadfastly, his homage-rendering and invoking brow, with his last dying motions. He too worships fire ...'"

So Ahab soliloquizes: and so the warm-blooded whale turns for the last time to the sun, which begot him in the waters.

But as we see in the next chapter, it is the Thunder-fire which Ahab really worships: that living sundering fire of which he bears the brand, from head to foot; it is storm, the electric storm of the *Pequod*, when the corposants burn in high, tapering flames of supernatural pallor upon the masthead, and when the compass is reversed. After this all is fatality. Life itself seems mystically reversed. In these hunters of Moby Dick there is nothing but madness and possession. The captain, Ahab, moves hand in hand with the poor imbecile negro boy, pip, who has been so cruelly demented, left swimming alone in the vast sea. It is the imbecile child of the sun hand in hand with the northern monomaniac, captain and master.

The voyage surges on. They meet one ship, then another. It is all ordinary day-routine, and yet all is a tension of pure madness and horror, the approaching horror of the last fight. "Hither and thither, on high, glided the snow-white wings of small unspecked birds; these were the gentle thoughts of the feminine air; but to and fro in the deeps, far down in the bottomless blue, rushed mighty leviathans, sword-fish and sharks; and these were the strong, troubled, murderous thinkings of the masculine sea——" On this day Ahab confesses his weariness, the weariness of his burden. "But do I look very old, so very, very old, Starbuck? I feel deadly faint, and bowed, and humped, as though I were Adam staggering beneath the piled centuries since Paradise—" It is the Gethsemane of Ahab, before the last fight: the Gethsemane of the human soul seeking the last self-conquest, the last attainment of extended consciousness—infinite, consciousness.

At last they sight the whale. Ahab sees him from his hoisted perch at the masthead—"From this height the whale was now seen some mile or so ahead, at every roll of the sea revealing his high, sparkling hump, and regularly jetting his silent spout into the air."

The boats are lowered, to draw near the white whale. "At length the breathless hunter came so nigh his seemingly unsuspectful prey that his entire dazzling hump was distinctly visible, sliding along the sea as if an isolated thing, and continually set in a revolving ring of finest, fleecy, greenish foam. He saw the vast involved wrinkles of the slightly projecting head, beyond. Before it, far out on the soft, Turkish rugged waters, went the glistening white shadow from his broad, milky forehead, a musical rippling playfully accompanying the shade; and behind, the blue waters interchangeably flowed over the moving valley of his steady wake; and on either side bright bubbles arose and danced by his side. But these were broken again by the light toes of hundreds of gay fowl softly feathering the sea, alternate with their fitful flight; and like to some flagstaff rising from the pointed hull of an argosy, the tall but shattered pole of a recent lance projected from the white whale's back; and at intervals one of the clouds of soft-toed fowls hovering, and to and fro shimmering like a canopy over the fish, silently perched and rocked on this pole, the long tail-feathers streaming like pennons.

"A gentle joyousness—a mighty mildness of repose in swiftness, invested the gliding whale——"

The fight with the whale is too wonderful, and too awful, to be quoted apart from the book. It lasted three days. The fearful sight, on the third day, of the torn body of the Parsee harpooner, lost on the previous day, now seen lashed on to the flanks of the white whale by the tangle of harpoon lines, has a mystic dream-horror. The awful and infuriated whale turns upon the ship, symbol of this civilized world of ours. He smites her with a fearful shock. And a few minutes later, from the last of the fighting whale-boats comes the cry: "'The ship! Great God, where is the ship?' Soon they, through dim, bewildering mediums, saw her sidelong fading phantom, as in the gaseous Fata Morgana; only the uppermost masts out of the water; while fixed by infatuation, or fidelity, or fate, to their once lofty perches, the pagan harpooners still maintained their sinking lookouts on the sea. And now concentric circles seized the lone boat itself, and all its crew, and each floating oar, and every lance-pole, and spinning, animate and inanimate, all round and round in one vortex, carried the smallest chip of the *Pequod* out of sight——"

The bird of heaven, the eagle, St. John's bird, the Red Indian bird, the American, goes down with the ship, nailed by Tashtego's hammer, the hammer of the American Indian. The eagle of the spirit. Sunk!

"Now small fowls flew screaming over the yet yawning gulf; a sullen white surf beat against its steep sides; then all collapsed; and the great shroud of the sea rolled on as it rolled five thousand years ago."

So ends one of the strangest and most wonderful books in the world, closing up its mystery and its tortured symbolism. It is an epic of the sea such as no man has equalled; and it is a book of esoteric symbolism of profound significance, and of considerable tiresomeness.

But it is a great book, a very great book, the greatest book of the sea ever written. It moves awe in the soul. The terrible fatality.

Fatality.

Doom.

Doom! Doom! Doom! Something seems to whisper it in the very dark trees of America. Doom!

Doom of what?

Doom of our white day. We are doomed, doomed. And the doom is in America. The doom of our white day. Ah, well, if my day is doomed, and I am doomed with my day, it is something greater than I which dooms me, so I accept my doom as a sign of the greatness which is more than I am.

Melville knew. He knew his race was doomed. His white soul, doomed. His great white epoch, doomed. Himself, doomed. The idealist, doomed. The spirit, doomed.

The reversion. "Not so much bound to any haven ahead, as rushing from all havens astern."

That great horror of ours! It is our civilization rushing from all havens astern.

The last ghastly hunt. The White Whale.

What then is Moby Dick? He is the deepest blood-being of the white race; he is our deepest blood-nature.

And he is hunted, hunted; hunted by the maniacal fanaticism of our white mental consciousness. We want to hunt him down. To subject him to our will. And in this maniacal conscious hunt of ourselves we get dark races and pale to help us, red, yellow, and black, east and west, Quaker and fire-worshipper, we get them all to help us in this ghastly maniacal hunt which is our doom and our suicide.

The last phallic being of the white man. Hunted into the death of upper consciousness and the ideal will. Our blood-self subjected to our will. Our blood-consciousness sapped by a parasitic mental or ideal consciousness.

Hot-blooded sea-born Moby Dick. Hunted by monomaniacs of the idea.

Oh God, oh God, what next, when the *Pequod* has sunk?

She sank in the war, and we are all flotsam.

Now what next?

Who knows? *Quien sabe? Quien sabe, señor?*

Neither Spanish nor Saxon America has any answer. The *Pequod* went down. And the *Pequod* was the ship of the white American soul. She sank, taking with her negro and Indian and Polynesian, Asiatic and Quaker and good, businesslike Yankees and Ishmael: she sank all the lot of them.

Boom! as Vachel Lindsay would say.

To use the words of Jesus, IT IS FINISHED.

Consummatum est!

But *Moby Dick* was first published in 1851. If the Great White Whale sank the ship of the Great White Soul in 1851, what's been happening ever since?

Post-mortem effects, presumably.

Because, in the first centuries, Jesus was Cetus, the Whale. And the Christians were the little fishes. Jesus, the Redeemer, was Cetus, Leviathan. And all the Christians all his little fishes.

F.O. MATTHIESSEN

Method and Scope

The starting point for this book was my realization of how great a number of our past masterpieces were produced in one extraordinarily concentrated moment of expression. It may not seem precisely accurate to refer to our mid-nineteenth century as a *re-birth*; but that was how the writers themselves judged it. Not as a re-birth of values that had existed previously in America, but as America's way of producing a renaissance, by coming to its first maturity and affirming its rightful heritage in the whole expanse of art and culture.

The half-decade of 1850–55 saw the appearance of *Representative Men* (1850), *The Scarlet Letter* (1850), *The House of the Seven Gables* (1851), *Moby-Dick* (1851), *Pierre* (1852), *Walden* (1854), and *Leaves of Grass* (1855). You might search all the rest of American literature without being able to collect a group of books equal to these in imaginative vitality. That interesting fact could make the subject for several different kinds of investigation. You might be concerned with how this flowering came, with the descriptive narrative of literary history. Or you might dig into its sources in our life, and examine the economic, social, and religious causes why this flowering came in just these years. Or you might be primarily concerned with *what* these books were as works of art, with evaluating their fusions of form and content.

By choosing the last of these alternatives my main subject has become the conceptions held by five of our major writers concerning the function

From *American Renaissance: Art and Expression in the Age of Emerson and Whitman*. © 1941 by Oxford University Press, Inc.

and nature of literature, and the degree to which their practice bore out their theories. That may make their process sound too deliberate, but Emerson, Thoreau, and Whitman all commented very explicitly on language as well as expression, and the creative intentions of Hawthorne and Melville can be readily discerned through scrutiny of their chief works. It has seemed to me that the literary accomplishment of those years could be judged most adequately if approached both in the light of its authors' purposes and in that of our own developing conceptions of literature. The double aim, therefore, has been to place these works both in their age and in ours.

In avowing that aim, I am aware of the important books I have not written. One way of understanding the concentrated abundance of our mid-nineteenth century would be through its intellectual history, particularly through a study of the breakdown of Puritan orthodoxy into Unitarianism, and of the quickening of the cool Unitarian strain into the spiritual and emotional fervor of transcendentalism. The first of those two developments has been best sketched by Joseph Haroutunian, *Piety versus Moralism: The Passing of New England Theology* (1932). The whole movement will be genetically traced in Perry Miller's monumental study of *The New England Mind*, the first volume of which (1939), dealing with the seventeenth century, has already extended the horizons of our cultural past. Another notable book could concentrate on how discerning an interpretation our great authors gave of the economic and social forces of the time. The orientation of such a book would not be with the religious and philosophical ramifications of the transcendental movement so much as with its voicing of fresh aspirations for the rise of the common man. Its method could be the one that Granville Hicks has inherited from Taine, and has already applied in *The Great Tradition* (1933) to our literature since the Civil War. An example of that method for the earlier period is Newton Arvin's detailed examination (1938) of Whitman's emergent socialism.

The two books envisaged in the last paragraph might well be called *The Age of Swedenborg* and *The Age of Fourier*. Emerson said in 1854, 'The age is Swedenborg's,' by which he meant that it had embraced the subjective philosophy that 'the soul makes its own world.' That extreme development of idealism was what Emerson had found adumbrated in Channing's 'one sublime idea': the potential divinity of mail. That religious assumption could also be social when it claimed the inalienable worth of the individual and his right to participate in whatever the community might produce. Thus the transition from transcendentalism to Fourierism was made by many at the time, as by Henry James, Sr., and George Ripley and his loyal followers at Brook Farm. *The Age of Fourier* could by license be extended to take up a wider subject than Utopian socialism; it could treat all the radical movements of the period; it would stress the fact that 1852 witnessed not only the appearance of *Pierre* but of *Uncle Tom's Cabin*; it would stress also what had been largely ignored until recently, the anticipation by Orestes Brownson of some of the Marxist analysis of the class controls of action.[1]

But the age was also that of Emerson and Melville. The one common denominator of my five writers, uniting even Hawthorne and Whitman, was their devotion to the possibilities of democracy. In dealing with their work I hope that I have not ignored the implications of such facts as that the farmer rather than the businessman was still the average American, and that the terminus to the agricultural era in our history falls somewhere between 1850 and 1865, since the railroad, the iron ship, the factory, and the national labor union all began to be dominant forces within those years, and forecast a new epoch. The forties probably gave rise to more movements of reform than any other decade in our history; they marked the last struggle of the liberal spirit of the eighteenth century in conflict with the rising forces of exploitation. The triumph of the new age was foreshadowed in the gold rush, in the full emergence of the acquisitive spirit.[2]

The older liberalism was the background from which my writers emerged. But I have concentrated entirely on the foreground, on the writing itself. I have not written formal literary history—a fact that should be of some relief to the reader, since if it required a volume of this length for five years of that record, the consequences of any extension of such a method Would be appalling. Parrington stated in his *Main Currents of American Thought* (1927): 'With aesthetic judgments I have not been greatly concerned. I have not wished to evaluate reputations or weigh literary merits, but rather to understand what our fathers thought ...' My concern has been opposite. Although I greatly admire Parrington's elucidation of our liberal tradition, I think the understanding of our literature has been retarded by the tendency of some of his followers to regard all criticism as 'belletristic trifling.' I am even more suspicious of the results of such historians as have declared that they were not discussing art, but 'simply using art, in a purpose of research.' Both our historical writing and our criticism have been greatly enriched during the past twenty years by the breaking down of arbitrary divisions between them, by the critic's realization of the necessity to master what he could of historical discipline, by the historian's desire to extend his domain from politics to general culture. But you cannot 'use' a work of art unless you have comprehended its meaning. And it is well to remember that although literature reflects an age, it also illuminates it. Whatever the case may be for the historian, the quality of that illumination is the main concern for the common reader. He does not live by trends alone; he reads books, whether of the present or past, because they have an immediate life of their own.

What constitutes the secret of that life is the subject of this volume. It may be held that my choice of authors is arbitrary. These years were also those of Whittier's *Songs of Labor* (1850), of Longfellow's *Hiawatha* (1855), of work by Lowell and Holmes and Simms, of Baldwin's *Flush Times in Alabama and Mississippi*, of T. S. Arthur's *Ten Nights in a Barroom*. Nor were any of my authors best sellers. The five hundred copies of Emerson's first book, *Nature* (1836), had been disposed of so slowly that a second edition was not called for until 1849; and though his lecturing had made him well known by then, the sales of none of his books ran far into the thousands. Thoreau recorded in his journal that four years after the appearance of his *Week on the Concord and Merrimack* (1849) only 219 copies had been sold; so he had the publisher ship the remainder back to him and said: 'I have now a library of nearly nine hundred volumes, over seven hundred of which I wrote myself. Is it not well that the author should behold the fruits of his labor?' After that *Walden* was considered a great risk, but it managed to go through an edition of two thousand. Whitman set up and printed *Leaves of Grass* for himself, and probably gave away more copies than were bought, whereas Longfellow could soon report (1857) that the total sales of his books had run to over three hundred thousand, and *Fern Leaves from Fanny's Portfolio* (1853), by the sister of N. P. Willis, sold a hundred thousand in its first year. Although *Typee* (1846) was more popular than Melville's subsequent work, it never came within miles of such figures. Hawthorne reported that six or seven hundred copies of *Twice-Told Tales (1837)* had been disposed of before the panic of that year descended. To reach a wider audience he had to wait until *The Scarlet Letter*, and reflecting on the triumphant vogue of Susan Warner's *The Wide, Wide World* (1850), Maria Cummins' *The Lamplighter* (1854), the ceaseless flux of Mrs. E.D.E.N. Southworth's sixty novels, he wrote to Ticknor in 1855: 'America is now wholly given over to a damned mob of scribbling women, and I should have no chance of success while the public taste is occupied with their trash—and should be ashamed of myself if I did succeed. What is the mystery of these innumerable editions of *The Lamplighter*, and other books neither better nor worse?—worse they could not be, and better they need not be, when they sell by the hundred thousand.'

Such material still offers a fertile field for the sociologist and for the historian of our taste. But I agree with Thoreau: 'Read the best books first, or you may not have a chance to read them at all.' And during the century that has ensued, the successive generations of common readers, who make the decisions, would seem finally to have agreed that the authors of the pre–Civil War era who bulk largest in stature are the five who are my subject. That being the case, a book about their value might seem particularly unnecessary. But 'the history of an art,' as Ezra Pound has affirmed, 'is the history of masterwork, not of failures or mediocrity.' And owing to our fondness for free generalization, even the masterworks of these authors have been largely taken for granted. The critic knows that any understanding of the subtle principle of life inherent in a work of art can be gained only by direct experience of it, again and again. The interpretation of what he has found demands close analysis, and plentiful instances from the works themselves. With a few notable exceptions, most of the criticism of our past masters has been perfunctorily tacked onto biographies. I have not yet seen in print an adequately detailed scrutiny even of 'When lilacs last in the dooryard bloom'd,' or of *Moby-Dick*. And such good criticism as has been written has ordinarily dealt with single writers; it has not examined many of the interrelations among the various works of the group.

My aim has been to follow these books through their implications, to observe them as the culmination of their authors' talents, to assess them in relation to one another and to the drift of our literature since, and, so far as possible, to evaluate them in accordance with the enduring requirements for great art. That last aim will seem to many only a pious phrase, but it describes the critic's chief responsibility. His obligation is to examine an author's resources of language and of genres, in a word, to be preoccupied with form. This means nothing rarefied, as Croce's description of De Sanctis' great *History of Italian Literature* can testify: form for De Sanctis 'was not the "form" pathologically felt by aesthetes and decadents: it was nothing else than the entire resolution of the intellectual, sentimental, and emotional material into the concrete reality of the poetic image and word, which alone has aesthetic value.'

The phases of my somewhat complex method of elucidating that concrete reality can be briefly described. The great attraction of my subject was its compactness:[3] for though I made no attempt to confine my study of these authors to the strait jacket of a five-year segment of their careers, the fact remained that Emerson's theory of expression was that on which Thoreau built, to which Whitman gave extension, and to which Hawthorne and Melville were indebted by being forced to react against its philosophical assumptions. The nature of Emerson's achievement has caused me to range more widely in my treatment of him than in that of the others. *Representative Men* has no more right to be called his masterpiece than *Nature* (1836) or *The Conduct of Life* (1860). He wrote no masterpiece, but his service to the development of our literature was enormous in that he made the first full examination of its potentialities. To apply to him his own words about Goethe: he was the cow from which the rest drew their milk. My discussion of his theory has always in view his practice of it, and its creative use by the others. My prime intention is not Sainte-Beuve's: to be 'a naturalist of minds,' to relate the authors' works to their lives. I have not drawn upon the circumstances of biography unless they seemed essential to place a given piece of writing;[4] and whenever necessary, especially in the case of Melville, I have tried to expose the modern fallacy that has come from the vulgarization of Sainte-Beuve's subtle method—the direct reading of an author's personal life into his works.

The types of interrelation that have seemed most productive to understanding the literature itself were first of all the obvious debts, of Thoreau to Emerson, or Melville to Hawthorne. In the next place there were certain patterns of taste and aspiration: the intimate kinship to the seventeenth-century metaphysical strain that was felt by Emerson, Thoreau, and Melville; the desire for a functional style wherein Thoreau and Whitman especially were forerunners of our modern interest. That last fact again suggests one of my chief convictions: that works of art can be best perceived if we do not approach them only through the influences that shaped them, but if we also make use of what we inevitably bring from our own lives. That is an unorthodox postulate for literary history. But if we can see *Moby-Dick* and *Pierre* much more accurately by uncovering Melville's extraordinary debt to Shakespeare, and come closer to Hawthorne's intentions by observing that his psychological assumptions were still fundamentally the same as Milton's, it seems equally clear that Henry James and Eliot call cast light back on Hawthorne, and that one way of judging *Leaves of Grass* is by juxtaposing it with the deliberate counterstatement made by Whitman's polar opposite, Hopkins. I have, therefore, utilized whatever interrelations of tills type have seemed to grow organically from my subject. I do not expect the reader to be willing at this point to grant any relevance to the juxtaposition of Whitman with the painters Millet and Eakins, or to that of Thoreau with the theories of the forgotten sculptor Horatio Greenough. It will be my responsibility to demonstrate those relevances.

The phase of my subject in which I am most interested is its challenge to pass beyond such interrelations to basic formulations about the nature of literature. In the chapter, 'Allegory and Symbolism,' Hawthorne and Melville have been its center, but I have attempted, so far as I was able, to write also an account of these two fundamental anodes of apprehending reality. In the concluding chapter, 'Man in the Open Air,' the concern was to bring all five writers together through their subject matter, through their varied responses to the myth of the common man. But these serious responses can be better defined if set into contrast with the comic myth of the frontier, especially in its richest expression by George Washington Harris' *Sut Lovingood*. And the function of myth in literature can be clarified by the rediscovery of its necessity by the age of Joyce and Mann. As a final descriptive instance of my method, I have conceived of the two central books on Hawthorne and Melville as composing a single unit in which the chief value would be the aspects of tragedy that could be discerned through its representative practice by these two writers. I have made no pretence of abstracting a general theory of tragedy, but have crystallized out certain indispensable attributes that are common also to the practice of both Shakespeare and Milton.

After this description of my method, it is obvious that the division into four books is merely to indicate the central emphasis of each. This division, with the index, should make it easy for a reader particularly concerned with a single writer to concentrate on his work alone. Since volumes of criticism are now conventionally supposed to be short, I might have concealed the length of mine by printing it as four separate books, spaced, say, a year apart. But that would have defeated one of my main purposes: to make each writer cast as much light as possible on all the others. Moreover, our chief critical need would seem to be that of full-length estimates. I saw no use in adding further partial portraits to those of Parrington and Van Wyck Brooks, but wanted to deal in both analysis and synthesis. That required extensive quotation, since a critic, to be of any use, must back up his definitions with some of the evidence through which he has reached them. Only thus can the reader share in the process of testing the critic's judgments, and thereby reach his own. I trust that the further division into sixty-odd short essays will help the reader to skip wherever he wants. However, when dealing with the work of one writer, I have made as many transitions as practicable to that of the others.

It may be of some help to the reader to know from the start that the structure of the volume is based on recurrent themes. In addition to the types of interrelation I have mentioned, the most dominant of these themes are: the adequacy of the different writers' conceptions of the relation of the individual to society, and of the nature of good and evil—these two themes rising to their fullest development in the treatment of tragedy; the stimulus that lay in the transcendental conviction that the word must become one with the thing; the effect produced by the fact that when these writers began their careers, the one branch of literature in which America had a developed tradition was oratory; the effect of the nineteenth century's stress on seeing, of its identification of the poet with the prophet or seer; the connection, real if somewhat intangible, between this emphasis on vision and that put on light by the advancing arts of photography and open-air painting; the inevitability of the symbol as a means of expression for an age that was determined to make a fusion between appearance and what lay behind it; the major desire on the part of all five writers that there should be no split between art and the other functions of the community, that there should be an organic union between labor and culture.

The avenue of approach to all these themes is the same, through attention to the writers' use of their own tools, their diction and rhetoric, and to what they could make with them. An artist's use of language is the most sensitive index to cultural history, since a man can articulate only what he is, and what he has been made by the society of which he is a willing or an unwilling part. Emerson, Hawthorne, Thoreau, Whitman, and Melville all wrote literature for democracy in a double sense. They felt that it was incumbent upon their generation to give fulfillment to the potentialities freed by the Revolution, to provide a culture commensurate with America's political opportunity. Their tones were sometimes optimistic, sometimes blatantly, even dangerously expansive, sometimes disillusioned, even despairing, but what emerges from the total pattern of their achievement—if we will make the effort to repossess it[5]—is literature for our democracy. In reading the lyric, heroic, anti tragic expression of our first great age, we can feel the challenge of our still undiminished resources. In my own writing about that age, I have kept in mind the demands made on the scholar by Louis Sullivan, who found a great stimulus for his architecture in the functionalism of Whitman. 'If, as I hold,' Sullivan wrote, 'true scholarship is of the highest usefulness because it implies the possession and application of the highest type of thought, imagination, and sympathy, his works trust so reflect his scholarship as to prove that it has drawn him toward his people, not away from them; that his scholarship has been used as a means toward attaining their end, hence his. That his scholarship has been applied for the good and the enlightenment of all the people, not for the pampering of a class. His works must prove, in short (and the burden of proof is on him), that he is a citizen, not a lackey, a true exponent of democracy, not a tool of the most insidious form of anarchy ... In a democracy there can be but one fundamental test of citizenship, namely: Are you using such gifts as you possess for or against the people?' These standards are the inevitable and right extension of Emerson's demands in *The American Scholar*. The ensuing volume has value only to the extent that it comes anywhere near measuring up to them.

Notes

1. See A. M. Schlesinger, Jr., *Orestes A. Brownson* (1939), and Helen S. Mims, 'Early American Democratic Theory and Orestes Brownson' (*Science and Society*, Spring 1939).

2. See Norman Ware, *The Industrial Worker, 1840–1860* (1924), and E. C. Kirkland, *A History of American Economic Life* (1936).

3. I have avoided, therefore, the temptation to include a full length treatment of Poe. The reason is more fundamental than that his work fell mainly in the decade of 1835–45: for it relates at very few points to the main assumptions about literature that were held by any of my group. Poe was bitterly hostile to democracy, and in that respect could serve as a revelatory contrast. But the chief interest in treating his work would be to examine the effect of his narrow but intense theories of poetry and the short story, and the account of the first of these alone could be the subject for another book: the development from Poe to Baudelaire, through the French symbolists, to modern American and English poetry. My reluctance at not dealing with Poe here is tempered by the fact that his value, even more than Emerson's, is now seen to consist in his influence rather than in the body of his own work. No group of his poems seems as enduring as *Drum-Taps*; and his stories, less harrowing upon the nerves than they were, seem relatively factitious when contrasted with the moral depth of Hawthorne or Melville.

4. I have provided a Chronology of the principal events in the five authors' lives on pages 657–61.

5. Santayana has said that the American mind does not oppose tradition, it forgets it. The kind of repossession that is essential has been described by André Malraux in an essay on 'The Cultural Heritage' (1936): 'Every civilization is like the Renaissance, and creates / its own heritage out of everything in the past that helps it to surpass itself. *A heritage it not transmitted; it must be conquered*; and moreover it is conquered slowly and unpredictably. We do not demand a civilization made to order any more than we demand masterpieces made to order. But let us demand of ourselves a full consciousness that the choice made by each of us out of the past—out of the boundless hopes of the men who came before us—is measured by our thirst for greatness and by our wills.'

CHARLES OLSON

Shakespeare and Melville

Which is the best of Shakespeare's plays? I mean in what mood and with what accompaniment do you like the sea best?"
KEATS, *Letter to Jane Reynolds*
Sept. 14, 1817

SHAKESPEARE, OR THE DISCOVERY OF MOBY-DICK

Moby-Dick was two books written between February, 1850 and August, 1851.
The first book did not contain Ahab.
It may not, except incidentally, have contained Moby-Dick.
On the 7th of August, 1850, the editor Evert Duyckinck reported to his brother:

Melville has a new book mostly done, a romantic, fanciful & most literal & most enjoyable presentment of the Whale Fishery— something quite new.

It is not surprising that Melville turned to whaling in February, 1850, on his return from a trip to England to sell his previous book, *White-Jacket*. It was the last of the materials his sea experience offered him.

From *Call Me Ishmael*. © 1947 by Charles Olson.

51

He had used his adventures among the South Sea islands in *Typee* (1846) and *Omoo* (1847). He had gone further in the vast archipelago of *Mardi*, written in 1847 and 1848, to map the outlines of his vision of life. The books of 1849, *Redburn* and *White-Jacket*, he had based on his experiences aboard a merchant ship and a man-of-war. The whaling voyage in the *Acushnet* was left.

There is no evidence that Melville had decided on the subject before he started to write in February. On the contrary. Melville's reading is a gauge of him, at all points of his life. He was a skald, and knew how to appropriate the work of others. He read to write. Highborn stealth, Edward Dahlberg calls originality, the act of a cutpurse Autolycus who makes his thefts as invisible as possible. Melville's books batten on other men's books. Yet he bought no books on whaling among the many volumes purchased in England on his trip and soon after his return Putnam's the publishers were picking up in London for him such things as Thomas Beale's *The Natural History of the Sperm Whale*.

He went at it as he had his last two books, "two jobs," as he called *Redburn* and *White-Jacket* in a letter to his father-in-law, "which I have done for money-being forced to it, as other men are to sawing wood." He had a family to support.

By May it was half done. So he told Richard Henry Dana in a letter on the 1st, the only other information of the first Moby-Dick which has survived. The book was giving Melville trouble. Referring to it as "the 'whaling voyage,'" he writes:

> It will be a strange sort of a book, I fear; blubber is blubber you know; tho you may get oil out of it, the poetry runs as hard as sap from a frozen maple tree;—& to cook the thing up, one must needs throw in a little fancy, which from the nature of the thing, must be ungainly as the gambols of the whales themselves. Yet I mean to give the truth of the thing, spite of this.

That's the record of Moby-Dick No. 1, as it stands. There is nothing on why, in the summer of 1850, Melville changed his conception of the work and, on something "mostly done" on August 7th, spent another full year until, in August, 1851, he had created what we know as *Moby-Dick or, The Whale*.

"Dollars damn me." Melville had the bitter thing of men of originality, the struggle between money and me. It was on him, hard, in the spring of 1850.

He says as much in the Dana letter: "I write these books of mine almost entirely for 'lucre'—by the job, as a wood-sawyer saws wood," repeating on Moby-Dick what he had said about *Redburn* and *White-Jacket*.

He knew the cost if he let his imagination loose. He had taken his head once, with *Mardi*. In this new work on whaling he felt obliged, as he had, after *Mardi*, with *Redburn* and *White-Jacket*, "to retain from writing the kind of book I would wish to."

He would give the truth of the thing, spite of this, yes. His head was lifted to Dana as it was to his father-in-law seven months earlier. He did his work clean. *Exs*: *Redburn* and *White-Jacket*. "In writing these two books I have not repressed myself much—so far as *they* are concerned; but have spoken pretty much as I feel."

There was only one thing in the spring of 1850 which he did not feel he could afford to do: "So far as I am individually concerned, & independent of my pocket, it is my earnest desire to write those sort of books which are said to 'fail.'"

In the end, in *Moby-Dick*, he did. Within three months he took his head again. Why?

Through May he continued to try to do a quick book for the market: "all my books are botches." Into June he fought his materials: "blubber is blubber." Then something happened. What, Melville tells:

> I somehow cling to the strange fancy, that, in all men hiddenly reside certain wondrous, occult properties—as in some plants and minerals—which by some happy but very rare accident (as bronze was discovered by the melting of the iron and brass at the burning of Corinth) may chance to be called forth here on earth.

When? Melville is his own tell-tale: he wrote these words in July, 1850. They occur in an article he did for Duyckinck's magazine. He gave it the title HAWTHORNE AND HIS MOSSES, WRITTEN BY A VIRGINIAN SPENDING A JULY IN VERMONT.

The subject is Hawthorne, Shakespeare and Herman Melville. It is a document of Melville's rights and perceptions, his declaration of the freedom of a man to fail. Within a matter of days after it was written (July 18 ff.), Melville had abandoned the account of the Whale Fishery and gambled it and himself with Ahab and the White Whale.

The *Mosses* piece is a deep and lovely thing. The spirit is asweep, as in the book to come. The confusion of May is gone. Melville is charged again. *Moby-Dick* is already shadowed in the excitement over genius, and America as a subject for genius. You can feel Ahab in the making, Ahab of "the globular brain and ponderous heart," so much does Melville concern himself with the distinction between the head and the heart in Hawthorne and Shakespeare. You can see the prose stepping off.

The germinous seeds Hawthorne has dropped in Melville's July soil begin to grow: Bulkington, the secret member of the crew in *Moby-Dick*, is here, hidden, in what Melville quotes as Hawthorne's self-portrait—the "seeker," rough-hewn and brawny, of large, warm heart and powerful intellect.

Above all, in the ferment, Shakespeare, the cause. The passages on him—the manner in which, he is introduced, the detail with which he is used, the intensity—tell the story of what had happened. Melville had read him again. His copy of THE PLAYS survives. He had bought it in Boston in February, 1849. He described it then to Duyckinck:

> It is an edition in glorious great type, every letter whereof is a soldier, & the top of every 't' like a musket barrel.
>
> I am mad to think how minute a cause has prevented me hitherto from reading Shakespeare. But until now any copy that was come-atable to me happened to be a vile small print unendurable to my eyes which are tender as young sperms.
>
> But chancing to fall in with this glorious edition, I now exult over it, page after page.

The set exists, seven volumes, with passages marked, and comments in Melville's hand. The significant thing is the rough notes, for the composition of *Moby-Dick* on the fly-leaf of the last volume. These notes involve Ahab, Pip, Bulkington, Ishmael, and are the key to Melville's intention with these characters. They thus relate not to what we know of the Moby-Dick that Melville had been working on up to July but to *Moby-Dick* as he came to conceive it at this time.

Joined to the passages on Shakespeare in the *Mosses* piece, the notes in the Shakespeare set verify what *Moby-Dick* proves: Melville and Shakespeare had made a Corinth and out of the burning came *Moby-Dick*, bronze.

A NOTE OF THANKS

The Melville people are rare people, and this is the right place to tell:

> of Eleanor Melville Metcalf and Henry K. Metcalf, with whom the Shakespeare was only a beginning, for they have made all Melville's things mine, indeed have made me a member of their family;

> of Raymond Weaver and Henry A. Murray, Jr., the other true biographer, who have been my generous friends;

> and of those early criers of Melville, Carl Van Doren and Van Wyck Brooks, who have spoken up for me.

> For the original use of the Shakespeare set and Melville's notes in it I wish also to thank another granddaughter, Mrs. Frances Osborne.

AMERICAN SHILOH

Shakespeare emerged from the first rush of Melville's reading a Messiah: as he put it in the *Mosses* piece in 1850, a "Shiloh"; as he put it to Duyckinck in 1849, "full of sermons-on-the-mount, and gentle, aye, almost as Jesus." Melville had a way of ascribing divinity to truth-tellers, Solomon, Shakespeare, Hawthorne, or Jesus.

He next limited Shakespeare. He advanced a criticism in his second letter to Duyckinck in 1849 which is central to all his later published passages on the poet. It keeps him this side idolatry. It arises from what Melville takes to be an "American" advantage:

> I would to God Shakespeare had lived later, & promenaded in Broadway. Not that I might have had the pleasure of leaving my card for him at the Astor, or made merry with him over a bowl of the fine Duyckinck punch; but that the muzzle which all men wore on their souls in the Elizabethan day, might not have intercepted Shakespeare's free articulations, for I hold it a verity, that even Shakespeare was not a frank man to the uttermost. And, indeed, who in this intolerant universe is, or can be? But the Declaration of Independence makes a difference.

In the *Mosses* piece, a year and a half later, he gives it tone:

> In Shakespeare's tomb lies infinitely more than Shakespeare ever
> wrote. And if I magnify Shakespeare, it is not so much for what
> he did do as for what he did not do, or refrained from doing.
>
> For in this world of lies, Truth is forced to fly like a scared
> white doe in the woodlands; and only by cunning glimpses will
> she reveal herself, as in Shakespeare and other masters of the
> great Art of Telling the Truth,—even though it be covertly and
> by snatches.

In his copy of the PLAYS, when Shakespeare muzzles truth-speakers,
Melville is quick to mark the line or incident. In Antony and Cleopatra he
puts a check beside Enobarbus' blunt answer to Antony's correction of his
speech: "That truth should be silent I had almost forgot."

In Lear he underscores the Fool's answer to Lear's angry threat of the
whip: "Truth's a dog must to kennel; he must be whipp'd out, when Lady the
brach may stand by th' fire and stink." The very language of Melville in the
Mosses thing is heard from the Fool's mouth.

As an artist Melville chafed at representation. His work up to *Moby-Dick* was
a progress toward the concrete and after *Moby-Dick* a breaking away. He had
to fight himself to give truth dramatic location. Shakespeare's dramatic
significance was not lost upon him, but he would have been, as he says, "more
content with the still, rich utterance of a great intellect in repose." Melville's
demand uncovers a flaw in himself.

Fortunately—for *Moby-Dick*—the big truth was not sermons-on-the-
mount. Melville found these in *Measure for Measure*. It is, rather

> those deep far-away things in him; those occasional flashings-
> forth of the intuitive Truth in him; those short, quick probings at
> the very axis of reality;—these are the things that make
> Shakespeare, Shakespeare.

Such reality is in the mouths of the "dark" characters, Hamlet, Timon, Lear
and Iago, where the drama Melville could learn from, lay. For blackness fixed
and fascinated; Melville. Through such dark men Shakespeare

> craftily says, or sometimes insinuates the things which we feel to

be so terrifically true, that it were all but madness for any good
man, in his own proper character, to utter or even hint of them!

It is this side of Shakespeare that Melville fastens on. Madness, villainy
and evil are called up out of the plays as though Melville's pencil were a wand
of black. magic. To use Swinburne's comment on *Lear*, it is not the light of
revelation but the darkness of it that Melville finds most profound in
Shakespeare. He was to write in *Moby-Dick*:

> Though in many of its aspects the visible world seems formed in
> love, the invisible spheres were formed in fright.

MAN, TO MAN

Shakespeare reflects Melville's disillusion in the treacherous world. In *The
Tempest*, when Miranda cries out "O brave new world!", Melville encircles
Prospero's answer "'Tis new to thee," and writes this note at the bottom of
the page:

> Consider the character of the persons concerning whom Miranda
> says this—then Prospero's quiet words in comment—how
> terrible! In *Timon* itself there is nothing like it.

Shakespeare frequently expresses disillusion through friendship and its
falling off. The theme has many variations. Melville misses none of them.
Caesar and Antony on the fickleness of the people to their rulers, in *Antony
and Cleopatra*. Achilles and Ulysses on the people's faithlessness to their
heroes, in *Troilus and Cressida*. Henry V and Richard II on treachery within
the councils of the state. Melville pulls it out of the tragedies: in *Lear*, when
the Fool sings how fathers who bear bags draw forth love and those who wear
rags lose love; and in *Hamlet*, the lines of the Player King:

> For who not needs, shall never lack a friend
> And who in want a hollow friend doth try,
> Directly seasons him his enemy.

To betray a friend was to make—for Melville as for Richard—a second
fall of cursed man. Shakespeare gives the theme its great counterpoint in
Timon. In that play the whole issue of idealism is objectified through

friendship. When his friends fail him Timon's love turns to hate. His world—and with it the play—wrenches into halves as the earth with one lunge tore off from a sun.

Melville took a more personal possession of the tragedy of Timon than of any of the other dark men. In *Lear* he found ingratitude, but what gave *Timon* its special intensity was that Timon was undone by friends, not daughters.

Melville makes little out of the love of man and woman. It is the friendship of men which is love. That is why Hawthorne was so important to him, to whom he wrote his best letters and to whom he dedicated *Moby-Dick*. That is why he never forgot Jack Chase, the handsome sailor he worked under in the Pacific, to whom he dedicated his last book, *Billy Budd*.

Melville had the Greek sense of men's love. Or the Roman's, as Shakespeare gives it in *Coriolanus*. In that play the only place Melville heavily marks is the long passage in which Coriolanus and Aufidius meet and embrace. They are captains, with the soldier's sense of comrade. Melville's is the seaman's, of a shipmate. Aufidius speaks the same passionate images of friendship Melville uses to convey the depth of feeling between Ishmael and Queequeg in *Moby-Dick*. Ishmael and Queequeg are as "married" as Aufidius feels toward Coriolanus:

> that I see thee here
> Thou noble thing, more dances my rapt heart
> Than when I first my wedded mistress saw
> Bestride my threshold.

Like Timon Melville found only disappointment. He lost Jack Chase, and Hawthorne, shyest grape, hid from him. In a poem of his later years Melville wrote:

> To *have* known him, to have loved him
>   After loneness long
> And then to be estranged in life
>   And neither in the wrong
> Ease me, a little ease, my song!

Timon is mocked with glory, as his faithful Steward says, lives, as Melville notes, but in a dream of friendship. Melville uses the blasted hero as a symbol throughout his books, sometimes in Plutarch's convention as a misanthrope, often as another Ishmael of solitude, most significantly—in

Pierre—as disillusion itself, man undone by goodness. It is the subject of *Pierre* and the lesson of *The Confidence Man*.

Melville's feeling for the play is summarized by a line he underscores in it, the Stranger's observation on the hypocrisy of Timon's friends:

Why, this is the world's soul.

LEAR AND MOBY-DICK

Note: Under this title an earlier version of this material appeared in the magazine Twice-A-Year.

It was *Lear* that had the deep creative impact. In *Moby-Dick* the use is pervasive. That its use is also the most implicit of any play serves merely to enforce a law of the imagination, for what has stirred Melville's own most is heaved out, like Cordelia's heart, with most tardiness.

In the Hawthorne-Mosses article it is to Lear's speeches that Melville points to prove Shakespeare's insinuations of "the things we feel to be so terrifically true":

Tormented into desperation, Lear, the frantic king, tears off the mask, and speaks the same madness of vital truth.

His copy of the play is marked more heavily than any of the others but *Antony and Cleopatra*. Of the characters the Fool and Edmund receive the attention. I have said Melville found his own words in the Fool's mouth when the Fool cries, "Truth's a dog must to kennel." He found them in such other speeches of that boy, as

Nay, an thou canst not smile as the wind sits, thou'lt catch cold shortly.

For Melville sees the Fool as the Shakespeare he would have liked more of, not one who refrained from hinting what he knew.

Melville is terrified by Edmund who took his fierce quality in the lusty stealth of nature and who, in his evil, leagued with that world whose thick rotundity Lear would strike flat. The sources of this man's evil, and his qualities, attract the writer who is likewise drawn to Goneril, to Iago—and who himself creates a Jackson in *Redburn* and a Claggart in *Billy Budd*.

It is the positive qualities in the depraved: Edmund's courage, and his power of attracting love. When Edmund outfaces Albany's challenge, denies he is a traitor, and insists he will firmly prove his truth and honor, Melville writes this footnote:

The infernal nature has a valor often denied to innocence.

When Edmund is dying he fails to revoke his order for the death of Lear and Cordelia, only looks upon the bodies of Goneril and Regan and consoles himself: "Yet Edmund was belov'd!" This Melville heavily checks. It is a twisting ambiguity like one of his own—Evil beloved.

Melville is dumb with horror at the close, blood-stop double meaning of Shakespeare's language in the scene of the blinding of Gloucester. His comment is an exclamation: "Terrific!" When Regan calls Gloucester "Ingrateful fox!" Melville writes:

Here's a touch Shakespearean—Regan talks of *ingratitude*!

First causes were Melville's peculiar preoccupation. He concentrates on an Edmund, a Regan—and the world of *Lear*, which is almost generated by such creatures, lies directly behind the creation of an Ahab, a Fedallah and the White, lovely, monstrous Whale.

Melville found answers in the darkness of *Lear*. Not in the weak goodness of an Albany who thinks to exclude evil from good by a remark as neat and corrective as Eliphaz in the Book of Job:

Wisdom and goodness to the vile seem vile;
Filths savor but themselves.

The ambiguities do not resolve themselves by such "right-mindedness." Albany is a Starbuck.

Melville turned rather to men who suffered as Job suffered—to Lear and Edgar and Gloucester. Judged by his markings upon the scene in which Edgar discovers, with a hot burst in his heart, his father's blindness. Melville perceived what suggests itself as a symbol so inherent to the play as to leave one amazed it has not been more often observed—that to lose the eye and capacity to see, to lose the physical organ, "vile jelly," is to gain spiritual sight.

The crucifixion in *Lear* is not of the limbs on a crossbeam, but of the eyes put out, the eyes of pride too sharp for feeling. Lear himself in the storm scene senses it, but Gloucester blind speaks it: "I stumbled when I saw."

Lear's words:

> Poor naked wretches, wheresoe'er you are,
> That bide the pelting of this pitiless storm,
> How shall your houseless heads and unfed sides,
> Your loop'd and window'd raggedness, defend you
> From seasons such as these? O, I have ta'en
> Too little care of this! Take physic, pomp;
> Expose thyself to feel what wretches feel,
> That thou mayst shake the superflux to them
> And show the heavens more just.

Gloucester's words come later, Act IV, Sc. 1. It is the purgatorial dispensation of the whole play. Gloucester, who aches to have his son Edgar back—

> Might I but live to *see thee in my touch*,
> I'ld say I had eyes again!

—has his wish and does not know it. He does not know, because he cannot see, that Edgar is already there beside him in the disguise of Tom o' Bedlam. Gloucester takes him for the poor, mad beggar he says he is. He seconds Lear thus:

> Here, take this purse, thou whom the heavens' plagues
> Have humbled to all strokes. That I am wretched
> Makes thee the happier. Heavens, deal so still!
> Let the superfluous and lust-dieted man,
> That slaves your ordinance, <u>that will not see</u>
> <u>Because he does not feel</u>, feel your pow'r quickly;
> So distribution should undo excess,
> And each man have enough.

The underscore is Melville's.

What moves Melville is the stricken goodness of a Lear, a Gloucester, an Edgar, who in suffering feel and thus probe more closely to the truth. Melville is to put Ahab through this humbling.

Shakespeare drew Lear out of what Melville called "the infinite obscure of his background." It was most kin to Melville. He uses it as an immediate obscure around his own world of *Moby-Dick*. And he leaves Ishmael at the end to tell the tale of Ahab's tragedy as Kent remained to speak these last words of Lear:

> Vex not his ghost. O, let him pass! He hates him
> That would upon the rack of this tough world
> Stretch him out longer.

A MOBY-DICK MANUSCRIPT

It is beautifully right to find what I take to be rough notes for *Moby-Dick* in the Shakespeare set itself. They are written in Melville's hand, in pencil, upon the last fly-leaf of the last volume, the one containing *Lear*, *Othello* and *Hamlet*. I transcribe them as they stand:

> Ego non baptizo te in nomine Patris et
> Filii et Spiritus Sancti—sed in nomine
> Diaboli.—madness is undefinable—
> It & right reason extremes of one,
> —not the (black art) Goetic but Theurgic magic—
> seeks converse with the Intelligence, Power, the Angel.

The Latin is a longer form of what Melville told Hawthorne to be the secret motto of *Moby-Dick*. In the novel Ahab howls it as an inverted benediction upon the harpoon he has tempered in savage blood:

> Ego non baptizo te in nomine patris, sed in nomine diaboli.
> I do not baptize thee in the name of the father, but in the name
> of the devil.

The change in the wording from the notes to the novel is of extreme significance. It is not for economy of phrase. The removal of Christ and the Holy Ghost—Filii et Spiritus Sancti—is a mechanical act mirroring the imaginative. Of necessity, from Ahab's world, both Christ and the Holy Ghost are absent. Ahab moves and has his being in a world to which They and what They import are inimical: remember, Ahab fought a deadly scrimmage with a Spaniard before the altar at Santa, and spat into the silver calabash. The conflict in Ahab's world is abrupt, more that between Satan and Jehovah, of the old dispensation than the new. It is the outward symbol of the inner truth that the name of Christ is uttered but once in the book and then it is torn from Starbuck, the only possible man to use it, at a moment of anguish, the night before the fatal third day of the chase.

Ahab is Conjur Man. He invokes his own evil world. He himself uses black magic to achieve his vengeful ends. With the very words "in nomine diaboli" he believes he utters a Spell and performs a Rite of such magic.

The Ahab-world is closer to *Macbeth* than to *Lear*. In it the supernatural is accepted. Fedallah appears as freely as the Weird Sisters. Before Ahab's first entrance he has reached that identification with evil to which Macbeth out of fear evolves within the play itself. The agents of evil give both Ahab and Macbeth a false security through the same device, the unfulfillable prophecy. Ahab's tense and nervous speech is like Macbeth's, rather than Lear's. Both Macbeth and Ahab share a common hell of wicked, sleep-bursting dreams. They both endure the torture of isolation from humanity. The correspondence of these two evil worlds is precise. In either the divine has little place. Melville intended certain exclusions, and Christ and the Holy Ghost were two of them. Ahab, alas, could not even baptize in the name of the Father. He could only do it in the name of the Devil.

That is the Ahab-world, and it is wicked. Melville meant exactly what he wrote to Hawthorne when the book was consummated:

I have written a wicked book, and feel as spotless as the lamb.

Melville's "wicked book" is the drama of Ahab, his hot hate for the White Whale, and his vengeful pursuit of it from the moment the ship plunges like fate into the Atlantic. It is that action, not the complete novel *Moby-Dick*. The *Moby-Dick* universe contains more, something different. Perhaps the difference is the reason why Melville felt "spotless as the lamb." The rough notes in the Shakespeare embrace it.

"Madness is undefinable." Two plays from which the thought could have sprung are in the volume in which it is written down: *Lear* and *Hamlet*. Of the modes of madness in Lear—the King's, the Fool's—which is definable? But we need not rest on supposition as to what Melville drew of madness from *Hamlet*, or from *Lear*: *Moby-Dick* includes both Ahab and Pip. Melville forces his analysis of Ahab's mania to incredible distances, only himself to admit that "Ahab's larger, darker, deeper part remains unhinted." Pip's is a more fathomable idiocy: "his shipmates called him mad." Melville challenges the description, refuses to leave Pip's madness dark and unhinted, declares: "So man's insanity is heaven's sense."

The emphasis in this declaration is the key to resolve apparent difficulties in the last sentence of the notes in the Shakespeare volume:

> It & right reason extremes of one,—not the (black art) Goetic but Theurgic magic—seeks converse with the Intelligence, Power, the Angel.

I take "it" to refer to the "madness" of the previous sentence. "Right reason," less familiar to the 20th century, meant more to the last, for in the Kant–Coleridge terminology "right reason" described the highest range of the intelligence and stood in contrast to "understanding." Melville had used the phrase in *Mardi*. What he did with it there discloses what meaning it had for him when he used it in these cryptic notes for the composition of *Moby-Dick*. *Mardi*:

> Right reason, and Alma (Christ), are the same; else Alma, not reason, would we reject. The Master's great command is Love; and here do all things wise, and all things good, unite. Love is all in all. The more we love, the more we know; and so reversed.

Now, returning to the notes, if the phrase "not the (black art) Goetic but Theurgic magic" is recognized as parenthetical, the sentence has some clarity: "madness" and its apparent opposite "right reason" are the two extremes of one way or attempt or urge to reach "the Intelligence, Power, the Angel" or, quite simply, God.

The adjectives of the parenthesis bear this reading out. "Goetic" might seem to derive from Goethe and thus Faust, but its source is the Greek "goetos," meaning variously trickster, juggler and, as here, magician. (Plato called literature "Goeteia.") Wherever Melville picked up the word he means it, as he says, for the "black art." "Theurgic," in sharp contrast, is an accurate term for a kind of occult art of the Neoplatonists in which, through self-purification and sacred rites, the aid of the divine was evoked. In thus opposing "Goetic" and "Theurgic" Melville is using a distinction as old as Chaldea between black and white magic, the one of demons, the other of saints and angels, one evil, the other benevolent. For white or "Theurgic" magic, like "madness" and "right reason," seeks God, while the "black art Goetic" invokes only the devil.

Now go to *Moby-Dick*. In the Ahab-world there is no place for "converse with the Intelligence, Power, the Angel." Ahab cannot seek it, for understood between him and Fedallah is a compact as binding as Faust's with

Mephistopheles. Melville's assumption is that though both Ahab and Faust may be seekers after truth, a league with evil closes the door to truth. Ahab's art, so long as his hate survives, is black. He does not seek true converse.

"Madness," on the contrary, does, and Pip is mad, possessed of an insanity which is "heaven's sense." When the little Negro almost drowned, his soul went down to wondrous depths and there he "saw God's foot upon the treadle of the loom, and spoke it." Through that accident Pip, of all the crew, becomes "preclusive of the eternal time" and thus achieves the converse Ahab has denied himself by his blasphemy. The chapter on THE DOUBLOON dramatizes the attempts on the part of the chief active characters to reach truth. In that place Starbuck, in his "mere unaided virtue," is revealed to have no abiding faith: he retreats before "Truth," fearing to lose his "righteousness." ... Stubb's jollity and Flask's clod-like stupidity blunt the spiritual.... The Manxman has mere superstition, Queequeg mere curiosity.... Fedallah worships the doubloon evilly.... Ahab sees the gold coin solipsistically: "three peaks as proud as Lucifer" and all name "Ahab!" Pip alone, of all, has true prescience: he names the doubloon the "navel" of the ship—"Truth" its life.

"Right reason" is the other way to God. It is the way of man's sanity, the pure forging of his intelligence in the smithy of life. To understand what use Melville made of it in *Moby-Dick* two characters, both inactive to the plot, have to be brought forth.

Bulkington is the man who corresponds to "right reason." Melville describes him once early in the book when he enters the Spouter Inn. "Six feet in height, with noble shoulders, and a chest like a coffer-dam." In the deep shadows of his eyes "floated some reminiscences that did not seem to give him much joy." In the LEE SHORE chapter Bulkington is explicitly excluded from the action of the book, but not before Melville has, in ambiguities, divulged his significance as symbol. Bulkington is Man who, by "deep, earnest thinking" puts out to sea, scorning the land, convinced that "in landlessness alone resides the highest truth, shoreless, indefinite as God."

The rest of the *Pequod*'s voyage Bulkington remains a "sleeping-partner" to the action. He is the secret member of the crew, below deck always, like the music under the earth in *Antony and Cleopatra*, strange. He is the crew's heart, the sign of their paternity, the human thing. And by that human thing alone can they reach their apotheosis.

There remains Ishmael. Melville framed Ahab's action, and the parts Pip, Bulkington and the rest of the crew played in the action, within a narrative told by Ishmael. Too long in criticism of the novel Ishmael has been confused with Herman Melville himself. Ishmael is fictive, imagined, as are Ahab, Pip and Bulkington, not so completely perhaps, for the very reason that he is so like his creator. But he is not his creator only: he is a chorus through whom Ahab's tragedy is seen, by whom what is black and what is white magic is made clear. Like the Catskill eagle Ishmael is able to dive down into the blackest gorges and soar out to the light again.

He is passive and detached, the observer, and thus his separate and dramatic existence is not so easily felt. But unless his choric function is recognized some of the vision of the book is lost. When he alone survived the wreck of the *Pequod*, he remained, after the shroud of the sea rolled on, to tell more than Ahab's wicked story. Ahab's self-created world, in essence privative, a thing of blasphemies and black magic, has its offset. Ahab has to dominate over a world where the humanities may also flower and man (the crew) by Pip's or Bulkington's way reach God. By this use of Ishmael Melville achieved a struggle and a catharsis which he intended, to feel "spotless as the lamb."

Ishmael has that cleansing ubiquity of the chorus in all drama, back to the Greeks. It is interesting that, in the same place where the notes for *Moby-Dick* are written in his Shakespeare, Melville jots down: "Eschylus Tragedies." Ishmael alone hears Father Mapple's sermon out. He alone saw Bulkington, and understood him. It was Ishmael who learned the secrets of Ahab's blasphemies from the prophet of the fog, Elijah. He recognized Pip's God-sight, and moaned for him. He cries forth the glory of the crew's humanity. Ishmael tells *their* story and *their* tragedy as well as Ahab's, and thus creates the *Moby-Dick* universe in which the Ahab-world is, by the necessity of life—or the Declaration of Independence—*included*.

AHAB AND HIS FOOL

Life has its way, even with Ahab. Melville had drawn upon another myth besides Shakespeare's to create his dark Ahab, that of both Marlowe and Goethe: the Faust legend. But he alters it. After the revolutions of the 18th–19th century the archetype Faust has never been the same. In Melville's alteration the workings of Lear and the Fool can also be discerned.

The change comes in the relation of Ahab to Pip. Ahab does not die in the tempestuous agony of Faustus pointing to Christ's blood and crying for His mercy. He dies with an acceptance of his damnation. Before his final battle with the White Whale Ahab has resigned himself to his fate.

His solipsism is most violent and his hate most engendered the night of THE CANDLES when he raises the burning harpoon over his crew. It is a night of storm. The setting is *Lear*-like. Ahab, unlike Lear, does not in this night of storm discover his love for his fellow wretches. On the contrary, this night Ahab uncovers his whole hate. He commits the greater blasphemy than defiance of sun and lightning. He turns the harpoon, forged and baptized for the inhuman Whale alone, upon his own human companions, the crew, and brandishes his hate over them. The morning after the storm Ahab is most subtly dedicated to his malignant purpose when he gives the lightning-twisted binnacle a new needle. Melville marks this pitch of his ego:

> In his fiery eyes of scorn and triumph, you then saw Ahab in all his fatal pride.

In a very few hours the change in Ahab sets in and Pip—the shadow of Pip—is the agent of the change. Like a reminder of Ahab's soul he calls to Ahab and Ahab, advancing to help, cries to the sailor who has seized Pip: "Hands off that holiness!" It is a crucial act: for the first time Ahab has offered to help another human being. And at that very moment Ahab speaks Lear's phrases:

> Thou touchest my inmost centre, boy; thou art tied to me by cords woven of my heart-strings. Come, let's down.

Though Ahab continues to curse the gods for their "inhumanities," his tone, from this moment, is richer, quieter, less angry and strident. He even questions his former blasphemies, for a bottomed sadness grows in him as Pip lives in the cabin with him. There occurs a return of something Peleg had insisted that Ahab possessed on the day Ishmael signed for the fatal voyage. Peleg then refuted Ishmael's fears of his captain's wicked name—that dogs had licked his blood. He revealed that Ahab had a wife and child, and concluded:

> hold ye then there can be any utter, hopeless harm in Ahab? No, no, my lad; stricken, blasted, if he be, Ahab has his humanities!

These humanities had been set aside in Ahab's hate for the White Whale. One incident: Ahab never thought, as he paced the deck at night in fever of anger, how his whalebone stump rapping the boards waked his crew and officers. The aroused Stubb confronts Ahab. Ahab orders him like a dog to kennel. For Stubb cannot, like Pip, affect Ahab. When it is over Stubb's only impulse is to go down on his knees and pray for the hot old man who he feels has so horribly amputated himself from human feelings.

Pip continues to be, mysteriously, the agent of this bloom once it has started. Says Ahab: "I do suck most wondrous philosophies from thee!" He even goes so far as to ask God to bless Pip and save him. BUT before he asks that, he threatens to murder Pip, Pip so weakens his revengeful purpose.

Though Pip recedes in the last chapters, the suppleness he has brought out of old Ahab continues to grow. Pip is left in the hold as though Ahab would down his soul once more, but above decks Ahab is no longer the proud Lucifer. He asks God to bless the captain of the *Rachel*, the last ship they meet before closing with Moby-Dick, the vessel which later picks Ishmael up after the tragedy. The difference in his speech is commented on: "a voice that prolongingly moulded every word." And it is noticed that when, toward the last days, Ahab prepares a basket lookout for himself to be hoisted up the mast to sight Moby-Dick, he trusts his "life-line" to Starbuck's hands. This running sap of his humanities gives out its last shoots in THE SYMPHONY chapter: observe that Ahab asks God to destroy what has been from the first his boast "God! God! God! stave my brain!" He has turned to Starbuck and talked about his wife and child! And though this apple, his last, and cindered, drops to the soil, his revenge is now less pursued than resigned to. His thoughts are beyond the whale, upon easeful death.

In the three days' chase he is a tense, mastered, almost grim man. He sets himself outside humanity still, but he is no longer arrogant, only lonely: "Cold, cold ..." After the close of the second day, when Fedallah cannot be found, he withers. His last vindictive shout is to rally his angers which have been hurled and lost like Fedallah and the harpoon of lightning and blood. He turns to Fate, the handspike in his windlass: "The whole act's immutably decreed." That night he does not face the whale as was his custom. He turns his "heliotrope glance" back to the east, waiting the sun of the fatal third day like death. It is Macbeth in his soliloquy of tomorrow, before Macduff will meet and match him. On the third day the unbodied winds engage his attention for the first time in the voyage. Even after the White Whale is sighted Ahab lingers, looks over the sea, considers his ship, says goodbye to his masthead. He admits to Starbuck he foreknows his death: the prophecies are fulfilled. In his last speech he moans only that his ship perishes without him:

Oh, lonely death on lonely life! Oh, now I feel my topmost greatness lies in my topmost grief.

He rushes to the White Whale with his old curse dead on his lips.

The last words spoken to him from the ship had been Pip's: "O master, my master, come back!"

What Pip wrought in Ahab throws over the end of *Moby-Dick* a veil of grief, relaxes the tensions of its hate, and permits a sympathy for the stricken man that Ahab's insistent diabolism up to the storm would not have evoked. The end of this fire-forked tragedy is enriched by a pity in the very jaws of terror.

The lovely association of Ahab and Pip is like the relations of Lear to both the Fool and Edgar. What the King learns of their suffering through companionship with them in storm helps him to shed his pride. His hedging and self-deluding authority gone, Lear sees wisdom in their profound unreason. He becomes capable of learning from his Fool just as Captain Ahab does from his cabin-boy.

In *Lear* Shakespeare has taken the conventional "crazy-witty" and brought him to an integral place in much more than the plot. He is at center to the poetic and dramatic conception of the play. Melville grasped the development.

Someone may object that Pip is mad, not foolish. In Shakespeare the gradations subtly work into one another. In *Moby-Dick* Pip is both the jester and the idiot. Before he is frightened out of his wits he and his tambourine are cap and bells to the crew. His soliloquy upon their midnight revelry has the sharp, bitter wisdom of the Elizabethan fool. And his talk after his "drowning" is parallel not only to the Fool and Edgar but to Lear himself.

A remark in *Moby-Dick* throws a sharp light over what has just been said and over what remains to be said. Melville comments on Pip:

> all thy strange mummeries not unmeaningly blended with the black tragedy of the melancholy ship, and mocked it.

For Pip by his madness had seen God.

SHAKESPEARE, CONCLUDED

Melville was no naïve democrat. He recognized the persistence of the "great man" and faced, in 1850, what we have faced in the 20th century. At the time of the rise of the common man Melville wrote a tragedy out of the rise, and the fall, of uncommon Ahab.

In the old days of the Mediterranean and Europe it was the flaw of a king which brought tragedy to men. A calamity was that which "unwar strook the regnes that been proude." When fate was feudal, and a great man fell, his human property, the people, paid.

A whaleship reminded Melville of two things: (1) democracy had not rid itself of overlords; (2) the common man, however free, leans on a leader, the leader, however dedicated, leans on a straw. He pitched his tragedy right there.

America, 1850 was his GIVEN:

"a poor old whale-hunter" the great man;

fate, the chase of the Sperm whale, plot (economics
    is the administration of scarce resources);
the crew the commons, the Captain over them;

EQUALS:

tragedy.

For a consideration of dominance in man, read by all means the chapter in *Moby-Dick* called THE SPECKSYNDER, concerning emperors and kings, the forms and usages of the sea:

through these forms that certain sultanism of Ahab's brain became incarnate in an irresistible dictatorship.

For be a man's intellectual superiority what it will, it can never assume the practical, available supremacy over other men, without the aid of some sort of external arts and entrenchments, always, in themselves, more or less paltry and base.

Nor will the tragic dramatist who would depict mortal indomitableness in its fullest sweep and direct swing, ever forget a hint, incidentally so important in his art, as the one now alluded to.

More, much more.

Melville saw his creative problem clearly:

He had a prose world, a NEW.
But it was "tragedie," old.

Shakespeare gave him a bag of tricks.
The Q.E.D.: *Moby Dick*.

The shape of *Moby-Dick*, like the meaning of its action, has roots deep in THE PLAYS. Melville studied Shakespeare's craft. For example, *characterization*. In at least three places Melville analyzes *Hamlet*. There are two in *Pierre*. One enlarges upon the only note he writes in his copy of the play: "the great Montaignism of Hamlet." The third and most interesting passage is in *The Confidence Man*. There Melville makes a distinction between the making of "odd" and the creation of "original" characters in literature. Of the latter he allows only three: Milton's Satan, Quixote, and Hamlet. The original character is

> like a revolving Drummond light, raying away from itself all round it—everything is lit by it, everything starts up to it (mark how it is with Hamlet).

Melville likens the effect to "that which in Genesis attends upon the beginning of things." In the creation of Ahab Melville made the best use of that lesson he knew how.

Structure, likewise. *Moby-Dick* has a rise and fall like the movement of an Elizabethan tragedy. The first twenty-two chapters, in which Ishmael as chorus narrates the preparations for the voyage, are precedent to the action and prepare for it. Chapter XXIII is an interlude, THE LEE SHORE; Bulkington, because he is "right reason," is excluded from the tragedy. With the next chapter the book's drama begins. The first act ends in the QUARTER-DECK chapter, the first precipitation of action, which brings together for the first time Ahab, the crew, and the purpose of the voyage—the chase of the White Whale. All the descriptions of the characters, all the forebodings, all the hints are brought to their first manifestation.

Another interlude follows: Ishmael expands upon MOBY-DICK and THE WHITENESS OF THE WHALE.

Merely to summarize what follows, the book then moves up to the meeting with the *Jeroboam* and her mad prophet Gabriel (chp. LXXI) and, after that, in a third swell, into the visit of Ahab to the *Samuel Enderby* to see her captain who had lost his arm as Ahab his leg to Moby-Dick (chp. C). The pitch of the action is the storm scene, THE CANDLES. From that point on Ahab comes to repose, fifth act, in his fate.

In this final movement Moby-Dick appears, for the first time. It is a mistake to think of the Whale as antagonist in the usual dramatic sense. (In democracy the antagonisms are wide.) The demonisms are dispersed, and Moby-Dick but the more assailable mass of them. In fact the actual physical whale finally present in *Moby-Dick* is more comparable to death's function in Elizabethan tragedy: when the white thing is encountered first, he is in no flurry, but quietly gliding through the sea, "a mighty mildness of repose in swiftness."

Obviously *Moby-Dick* is a novel and not a play. It contains creations impossible to any stage—a ship the *Pequod*, whales, Leviathan, the vast sea. In the making of most of his books Melville used similar things. In *Moby-Dick* he integrated them as he never had before nor was to again.

The whaling matter is stowed away as he did not manage the ethnology of *Typee* nor was to, the parables of *The Confidence Man*. While the book is getting under way—that is, in the first forty-eight chapters—Melville allows only four "scientific" chapters on whaling to appear. Likewise as the book sweeps to its tragic close in the last thirty chapters, Melville rules out all such exposition. The body of the book supports the bulk of the matter on the Sperm whale—"scientific or poetic." Melville carefully controls these chapters, skillfully breaking them up: the eight different vessels the *Pequod* meets as she moves across the oceans slip in and cut between the considerations of cetology. Actually and deliberately the whaling chanters brake the advance of the plot. Van Wyck Brooks called them "ballast."

Stage directions appear throughout. *Soliloquies*, too. There is a significant use of the special Elizabethan soliloquy to the skull in Ahab's mutterings to the Sperm whale's head in THE SPHINX (clip. LXX). One of the subtlest *supernatural effects*, the "low laugh from the hold" in the QUARTER-DECK scene, echoes Shakespeare's use of the Ghost below ground in *Hamlet*.

Properties are used for precise theater effect. Ahab smashes his quadrant as Richard his mirror. Of them the Doubloon is the most important. Once Ahab has nailed the coin to the mast it becomes FOCUS. The imagery, the thought, the characters, the events precedent and to come, are centered on it. It is there, midstage, Volpone, gold.

Of the soliloquies Ahab's show the presence of *Elizabethan speech* most. The cadences and acclivities of Melville's prose change. Melville characterized Ahab's language as "nervous, lofty." In the soliloquies it is jagged like that of a Shakespeare hero whose speech like his heart often cracks in the agony of fourth and fifth act.

The long ease and sea swell of Ishmael's narrative prose contrasts this short, rent language of Ahab. The opposition of cadence is part of the counterpoint of the book. It adumbrates the part the two characters play, Ishmael the passive, Ahab the active. More than that, it arises from and returns, contrapunto, to the whole concept of the book revealed by the notes in Melville's copy of Shakespeare—the choric Ishmael can, like the Catskill eagle, find the light, but Ahab, whose only magic is Goetic, remains dark. The contrast in prose, repeats the theme of calm and tempest which runs through the novel. Without exception action rises out of calm, whether it is the first chase of a whale, the appearance of the Spirit Spout, the storm, or the final chase of Moby-Dick precipitously following upon THE SYMPHONY.

As the strongest literary force Shakespeare caused Melville to approach tragedy in terms of the drama. As the strongest social force America caused him to approach tragedy in terms of democracy.

It was not difficult for Melville to reconcile the two. Because of his perception of America: Ahab.

It has to do with size, and how you value it. You can approach BIG America and spread yourself like a pancake, sing her stretch as Whitman did, be puffed up as we are over PRODUCTION. It's easy. THE AMERICAN WAY. Soft. Turns out paper cups, lies flat on the brush. N.G.

Or recognize that our power is simply QUANTITY. Without considering purpose, Easy too. That is, so long as we continue to be INGENIOUS about machines, and have the resources.

Or you can take an attitude, the creative vantage. See. her as OBJECT in MOTION, something to be shaped, for use. It involves a first act of physics. You can observe POTENTIAL and VELOCITY separately, have to, to measure THE THING. You get approximate results. They are usable enough if you include the Uncertainty Principle, Heisenberg's law that you learn the speed at the cost of exact knowledge of the energy and the energy at the loss of exact knowledge of the speed.

Melville did his job. He calculated, and cast Ahab, BIG, first of all. ENERGY, next. PURPOSE: lordship over nature. SPEED: of the brain. DIRECTION: vengeance. COST: the people, the Crew.

Ahab is the FACT, the Crew the IDEA. The Crew is where what America stands for got into *Moby-Dick*. They're what we imagine democracy to be. They're Melville's addition to tragedy as he took it from Shakespeare. He had to do more with the people than offstage shouts in a Julius Caesar. This was the difference a Declaration of Independence made. In his copy of the play Melville writes the note

TAMMANY HALL

in heavy strokes beside Casca's description of the Roman rabble before
Caesar:

> If the tag-rag people did not clap him and hiss him, according as
> he pleas'd and displeas'd them, as they use to do the players in the
> theatre, I am no true man.

Melville thought he had more searoom to tell the truth. He was writing in a
country where an Andrew Jackson could, as he put it, be "hurled higher than
a throne." A political system called "democracy" had led men to think they
were "free" of aristocracy. The fact of the matter is Melville couldn't help but
give the "people" a larger part because in the life around him they played a
larger part. He put it this way:

> this august dignity I treat of, is not the dignity of kings and robes,
> but that abounding dignity which has no robed investiture.
>
> Thou shalt see it shining in the arm that wields a pick and
> drives a spike; that democratic dignity which, on all hands,
> radiates without end from God; Himself! The great God
> absolute! The center and circumference of all democracy! His
> omnipresence, our divine equality!
>
> If, then, to meanest mariners, and renegades and castaways, I
> shall hereafter ascribe high qualities, though dark; weave round
> them tragic graces; if even the most mournful, perchance the
> most abased, among them all, shall at times lift himself to the
> exalted mounts; if I shall touch that workman's arm with some
> ethereal light; if I shall spread a rainbow over his disastrous set of
> sun; then against all mortal critics bear me out in it, thou just
> Spirit of Equality, which hast spread one royal mantle of
> humanity over all my kind!

Remember Bulkington.

To MAGNIFY is the mark of *Moby-Dick*. As with workers, castaways,
so with the scope and space of the sea, the prose, the Whale, the Ship and,
OVER ALL, the Captain. It is the technical act compelled by the American
fact. Cubits of tragic stature. Put it this way. Three forces operated to bring
about the dimensions of *Moby-Dick*: Melville, a man of MYTH, antemosaic:
an experience of SPACE. its power and price, America; and ancient
magnitudes of TRAGEDY, Shakespeare.

It is necessary now to consider *Antony and Cleopatra*, the play Melville pencilled most heavily. Rome was the World, and Shakespeare gives his people and the action imperial size. His hero and heroine love as Venus and Mars, as planets might.

> His legs bestrid the ocean; his rear'd arm
> Crested the world.

So Cleopatra dreamed of Antony. Melville marked her words. He marked Antony's joyful greeting to Cleopatra after he has beaten Caesar back to his camp:

> O thou day o' th' world!

And Cleopatra's cry of grief when Antony dies:

> The crown o' th' earth doth melt.

Antony and Cleopatra is an East. It is built as Pyramids were built. There is space here, and objects big enough to contest space. These are men and women who live life large. The problems are the same but they work themselves out on a stage as wide as ocean.

When Enobarbus comments on Antony's flight from Actium in pursuit of Cleopatra, we are precisely within the problems of *Moby-Dick*:

> To be furious
> Is to be frighted out of fear, and in that mood
> The dove will peck the estridge. I see still
> A diminution in our captain's brain
> Restores his heart. When valour preys on reason
> It eats the sword it fights with.

In exactly what way Ahab, furious and without fear, retained the instrument of his reason as a lance to fight the White Whale is a central concern of Melville's in *Moby-Dick*. In his Captain there was a diminution in his heart.

From whaling, which America had made distinctly a part of her industrial empire, he took this "poor old whale-hunter," as he called him, this man of "Nantucket grimness and shagginess." Out of such stuff he had to make his tragic hero, his original. He faced his difficulties. He knew he was denied "the outward majestical trappings and housings" that Shakespeare had for his Antony, his Lear and his Macbeth. Melville wrote:

Oh, Ahab! what shall be grand in thee, must needs be plucked at from the skies, and dived for in the deep, and featured in the unbodied air!

He made him "a khan of the plank, and a king of the sea, and a great lord of leviathans." For the American has the Roman feeling about the world. It is his, to dispose of. He strides it, with possession of it. His property. Has he not conquered it with his machines? He bends its resources to his will. The pax of legions? the Americanization of the world. Who else is lord?

Melville isolates Ahab in "a Grand-Lama-like exclusiveness." He is captain of the *Pequod* because of "that certain sultanism of his brain." He is proud and morbid, willful, vengeful. He wears a "hollow crown," not Richard's. It is the Iron Crown of Lombardy which Napoleon wore. Its jagged edge, formed from a nail of the Crucifixion, galls him. He worships fire and swears to strike the sun.

OVER ALL, hate—huge and fixed upon the imperceptible. Not man but all the hidden forces that terrorize man is assailed by the American Timon. That HATE, extra-human, involves his Crew, and Moby-Dick drags them to their death as well as Ahab to his, a collapse of a hero through solipsism which brings down a world.

At the end of the book, in the heart of the White Whale's destruction, the Crew and Pip and Bulkington and Ahab lie down together.

All scatt'red in the bottom of the sea.

Nathaniel Hawthorne[1]

I shall begin the history of American literature with the history of a metaphor; or rather, with some examples of that metaphor. I don't know who invented it; perhaps it is a mistake to suppose that metaphors can be invented. The real ones, those that formulate intimate connections between one image and another, have always existed; those we can still invent are the false ones, which are not worth inventing. The metaphor I am speaking of is the one that compares dreams to a theatrical performance. Quevedo used it in the seventeenth century at the beginning of the *Sueño de la muerte*; Luis de Góngora made it a part of the sonnet "Varia imaginación," where we read:

> A dream is a playwright
> Clothed in beautiful shadows
> In a theatre fashioned on the wind.

In the eighteenth century Addison will say it more precisely. When the soul dreams (he writes) it is the theatre, the actors, and the audience. Long before, the Persian Omar Khayyam had written that the history of the world is a play that God—the multiform God of the pantheists—contrives, enacts, and beholds to entertain his eternity; long afterward, Jung the Swiss in charming and doubtless accurate volumes compares literary inventions to oneiric inventions, literature to dreams.

From *Other Inquisition: 1937–1952s*. © 1964 by the University of Texas Press.

If literature is a dream (a controlled and deliberate dream, but fundamentally a dream) then Góngora's verses would be an appropriate epigraph to this story about American literature, and a look at Hawthorne, the dreamer, would be a good beginning. There are other American writers before him—Fenimore Cooper, a sort of Eduardo Gutiérrez infinitely inferior to Eduardo Gutiérrez; Washington Irving, a contriver of pleasant Spanish fantasies—but we can skip over them without any consequence.

Hawthorne was born in 1804 in the port of Salem, which suffered, even then, from two traits that were anomalous in America: it was a very old, but poor, city; it was a city in decadence. Hawthorne lived in that old and decaying city with the honest biblical name until 1836; he loved it with the sad love inspired by persons who do not love us, or by failures, illness, and manias; essentially it is not untrue to say that he never left his birthplace. Fifty years later, in London or Rome, he continued to live in his Puritan town of Salem; for example, when he denounced sculptors (remember that this was in the nineteenth century) for making nude statues.

His father, Captain Nathaniel Hawthorne, died in Surinam in 1808 of yellow fever; one of his ancestors, John Hawthorne, had been a judge in the witchcraft trials of 1692, in which nineteen women, among them the slave girl Tituba, were condemned to be executed by hanging. In those curious trials (fanaticism has assumed other forms in our time) Justice Hawthorne acted with severity and probably with sincerity. Nathaniel, our Nathaniel, wrote that his ancestor made himself so conspicuous in the martyrdom of the witches that possibly the blood of those unfortunate women had left a stain on him, a stain so deep as to be present still on his old bones in the Charter Street Cemetery if they had not yet turned to dust. After that picturesque note Hawthorne added that, not knowing whether his elders had repented and begged for divine mercy, he wished to do so in their name, begging that any curse that had fallen on their descendants would be pardoned from that day forward.

When Captain Hawthorne died, his widow, Nathaniel's mother, became a recluse in her bedroom on the second floor. The rooms of his sisters, Louise and Elizabeth, were on the same floor; Nathaniel's was on the top floor. The family did not eat together and they scarcely spoke to one another; their meals were left on trays in the hall. Nathaniel spent his days writing fantastic stories; at dusk he would go out for a walk. His furtive way of life lasted for twelve years. In 1837 he wrote to Longfellow: "... I have secluded myself from society; and yet I never meant any such thing, nor dreamed what sort of life I was going to lead. I have made a captive of myself, and put me into a dungeon, and now I cannot find the key to let myself out."

Hawthorne was tall, handsome, lean, dark. He walked with the rocking gait of a seaman. At that time children's literature did not exist (fortunately for boys and girls!). Hawthorne had read *Pilgrim's Progress* at the age of six; the first book he bought with his own money was *The Faërie Queene*; two allegories. Also, although his biographers may not say so, he read the Bible; perhaps the same Bible that the first Hawthorne, William Hathorne, brought from England with a sword in 1630. I have used the word "allegories"; the word is important, perhaps imprudent or indiscreet, to use when speaking of the work of Hawthorne. It is common knowledge that Edgar Allan Poe accused Hawthorne of allegorizing and that Poe deemed both the activity and the genre indefensible. Two tasks confront us: first, to ascertain whether the allegorical genre is, in fact, illicit; second, to ascertain whether Nathaniel Hawthorne's works belong to that category.

The best refutation of allegories I know is Croce's; the best vindication, Chesterton's. Croce says that the allegory is a tiresome pleonasm, a collection of useless repetitions which shows us (for example) Dante led by Virgil and Beatrice and then explains to us, or gives us to understand, that Dante is the soul, Virgil is philosophy or reason or natural intelligence, and Beatrice is theology or grace. According to Croce's argument (the example is not his), Dante's first step was to think: "Reason and faith bring about the salvation of souls" or "Philosophy and theology lead us to heaven" and then, for *reason* or *philosophy* he substituted *Virgil* and for *faith* or *theology* he put *Beatrice*, all of which became a kind of masquerade. By that derogatory definition an allegory would be a puzzle, more extensive, boring, and unpleasant than other puzzles. It would be a barbaric or puerile genre, an aesthetic sport. Croce wrote that refutation in 1907; Chesterton had already refuted him in 1904 without Croce's knowing it. How vast and uncommunicative is the world of literature!

The page from Chesterton to which I refer is part of a monograph on the artist Watts, who was famous in England at the end of the nineteenth century and was accused, like Hawthorne, of allegorism. Chesterton admits that Watts has produced allegories, but he denies that the genre is censurable. He reasons that reality is interminably rich and that the language of men does not exhaust that vertiginous treasure. He writes:

Man knows that there are in the soul tints more bewildering, more numberless, and more nameless than the colours of an autumn forest; ... Yet he seriously believes that these things can every one of them, in all their tones and semi-tones, in all their blends and unions, be accurately represented by an arbitrary system of grunts and squeals. He believes that an ordinary civilized stockbroker can really produce out of his own inside noises which denote all the mysteries of memory and all the agonies of desire.

Later Chesterton infers that various languages can somehow correspond to the ungraspable reality, and among them are allegories and fables.

In other words, Beatrice is not an emblem of faith, a belabored and arbitrary synonym of the word *faith*. The truth is that something—a peculiar sentiment, an intimate process, a series of analogous states—exists in the world that can be indicated by two symbols: one, quite insignificant, the sound of the word *faith*; the other, Beatrice, the glorious Beatrice who descended from Heaven and left her footprints in Hell to save Dante. I don't know whether Chesterton's thesis is valid; I do know that the less an allegory can be reduced to a plan, to a cold set of abstractions, the better it is. One writer thinks in images (Shakespeare or Donne or Victor Hugo, say), and another writer thinks in abstractions (Benda or Bertrand Russell); a priori, the former are just as estimable as the latter. However, when an abstract man, a reasoner, also wants to be imaginative, or to pass as such, then the allegory denounced by Croce occurs. We observe that a logical process has been embellished and disguised by the author to dishonor the reader's understanding, as Wordsworth said. A famous example of that ailment is the case of José Ortega y Gasset, whose good thought is obstructed by difficult and adventitious metaphors; many times this is true of Hawthorne. Outside of that, the two writers are antagonistic. Ortega can reason, well or badly, but he cannot imagine; Hawthorne was a man of continual and curious imagination; but he was refractory, so to speak, to reason. I am not saying he was stupid; I say that he thought in images, in intuitions, as women usually think, not with a dialectical mechanism.

One aesthetic error debased him: the Puritan desire to make a fable out of each imagining induced him to add morals and sometimes to falsify and to deform them. The notebooks in which he jotted down ideas for plots have been preserved; in one of them, dated 1836, he wrote: "A snake taken into a man's stomach and nourished there from fifteen years to thirty-five, tormenting him most horribly." That is enough, but Hawthorne considers himself obliged to add: "A type of envy or some other evil passion." Another example, this time from 1838: "A series of strange, mysterious, dreadful events to occur, wholly destructive of a person's happiness. He to impute them to various persons and causes, but ultimately finds that he is himself the sole agent. Moral, that our welfare depends on ourselves." Another, from the same year: "A person, while awake and in the business of life, to think highly of another, and place perfect confidence in him, but to be troubled with dreams in which this seeming friend appears to act the part of a most deadly enemy. Finally it is discovered that the dream-character is the true one. The explanation would be—the soul's instinctive perception." Better are those pure fantasies that do not look for a justification or moral and that seem to have no other substance than an obscure terror. Again, from 1838: "The situation of a man in the midst of a crowd, yet as completely in the power of another, life and all, as if they two were in the deepest solitude." The following, which Hawthorne noted five years later, is a variation of the above: "Some man of powerful character to command a person, morally subjected to him, to perform some act. The commanding person to suddenly die; and, for all the rest of his life, the subjected one continues to perform that act." (I don't know how Hawthorne would have written that story. I don't know if he would have decided that the act performed should be trivial or slightly horrible or fantastic or perhaps humiliating.) This one also has slavery—subjection to another—as its theme: "A rich man left by will his mansion and estate to a poor couple. They remove into it, and find there a darksome servant, whom they are forbidden by will to turn away. He becomes a torment to them; and, in the finale, he turns out to be the former master of the estate." I shall mention two more sketches, rather curious ones; their theme, not unknown to Pirandello or André Gide, is the coincidence or the confusion of the aesthetic plane and the common plane, of art and reality. The first one: "Two persons to be expecting some occurrence, and watching for the two principal actors in it, and to find that the occurrence is even then passing, and that they themselves are the two actors." The other is more complex: "A person to be writing a tale, and to find that it shapes itself against his intentions; that the characters act otherwise than he thought; that unforeseen events occur; and a catastrophe comes which he strives in vain to avert. It might shadow forth his own fate—he having made himself one of the personages." These games, these momentary confluences of the imaginative world and the real world—the world we pretend is real when we read—are, or seem to us, modern. Their origin, their ancient origin, is perhaps to be found in that part of the *Iliad* in which Helen of Troy weaves into her tapestry the battles and the disasters of the Trojan War even then in progress. Virgil must have been impressed by that passage, for the *Aeneid* relates that Aeneas, hero of the Trojan War, arrived at the port of Carthage and saw scenes from the war sculptured on the marble of a temple and, among the many images of warriors, he saw his own likeness. Hawthorne liked those contacts of the imaginary and the real, those reflections and duplications of art; and in the sketches I have mentioned we observe that he leaned toward the pantheistic notion that one man is the others, that one man is all men.

Something more serious than duplications and pantheism is seen in the sketches, something more serious for a man who aspires to be a novelist, I mean. It is that, in general, situations were Hawthorne's stimulus, Hawthorne's point of departure—situations, not characters. Hawthorne first imagined, perhaps unwittingly, a situation and then sought the characters to embody it. I am not a novelist, but I suspect that few novelists have proceeded in that fashion. "I believe that Schomberg is real," wrote Joseph Conrad about one of the most memorable characters in his novel *Victory*, and almost any novelist could honestly say that about any of his characters. The adventures of the *Quixote* are not so well planned, the slow and antithetical dialogues—reasonings, I believe the author calls them—offend us by their improbability, but there is no doubt that Cervantes knew Don Quixote well and could believe in him. Our belief in the novelist's belief makes up for any negligence or defect in the work. What does it matter if the episodes are unbelievable or awkward when we realize that the author planned them, not to challenge our credibility, but to define his characters? What do we care about the puerile scandals and the confused crimes of the hypothetical Court of Denmark if we believe in Prince Hamlet? But Hawthorne first conceived a situation, or a series of situations, and then elaborated the people his plan required. That method can produce, or tolerate, admirable stories because their brevity makes the plot more visible than the actors, but not admirable novels, where the general form (if there is one) is visible only at the end and a single badly invented character can contaminate the others with unreality. From the foregoing statement it will be inferred that Hawthorne's stories are better than Hawthorne's novels. I believe that is true. The twenty-four chapters of *The Scarlet Letter* abound in memorable passages, written in good and sensitive prose, but none of them has moved me like the singular story of "Wakefield" in the *Twice-Told Tales*.

Hawthorne had read in a newspaper, or pretended for literary reasons that he had read in a newspaper, the case of an Englishman who left his wife without cause, took lodgings in the next street and there, without anyone's suspecting it, remained hidden for twenty years. During that long period he spent all his days across from his house or watched it from the corner, and many times he caught a glimpse of his wife. When they had given him up for dead, when his wife had been resigned to widowhood for a long time, the man opened the door of his house one day and walked in—simply, as if he had been away only a few hours. (To the day of his death he was an exemplary husband.) Hawthorne read about the curious case, uneasily and tried to understand it, to imagine it. He pondered on the subject; "Wakefield" is the conjectural story of that exile. The interpretations of the riddle can be infinite; let us look at Hawthorne's.

He imagines Wakefield to be a calm man, timidly vain, selfish, given to childish mysteries and the keeping of insignificant secrets; a dispassionate man of great imaginative and mental poverty, but capable of long, leisurely, inconclusive, and vague meditations; a constant husband, by virtue of his laziness. One October evening Wakefield bids farewell to his wife. He tells her—we must not forget we are at the beginning of the nineteenth century—that he is going to take the stagecoach and will return, at the latest, within a few days. His wife, who knows he is addicted to inoffensive mysteries, does not ask the reason for the trip. Wakefield is wearing boots, a rain hat, and an overcoat; he carries an umbrella and a valise. Wakefield—and this surprises me—does not yet know what will happen. He goes out, more or less firm in his decision to disturb or to surprise his wife by being away from home for a whole week. He goes out, closes the front door, then half opens it, and, for a moment, smiles. Years later his wife will remember that last smile. She will imagine him in a coffin with the smile frozen on his face, or in paradise, in glory, smiling with cunning and tranquility. Everyone will believe he has died but she will remember that smile and think that perhaps she is not a widow.

Going by a roundabout way, Wakefield reaches the lodging place where he has made arrangements to stay. He makes himself comfortable by the fireplace and smiles; he is one street away from his house and has arrived at the end of his journey. He doubts; he congratulates himself; he finds it incredible to be there already; he fears that he may have been observed and that someone may inform on him. Almost repentant, he goes to bed, stretches out his arms in the vast emptiness and says aloud: "I will not sleep alone another night." The next morning he awakens earlier than usual and asks himself, in amazement, what he is going to do. He knows that he has some purpose, but he has difficulty defining it. Finally he realizes that his purpose is to discover the effect that one week of widowhood will have on the virtuous Mrs. Wakefield. His curiosity forces him into the street. He murmurs, "I shall spy on my home from a distance." He walks, unaware of his direction; suddenly he realizes that force of habit has brought him, like a traitor, to his own door and that he is about to enter it. Terrified, he turns away. Have they seen him? Will they pursue him? At the corner he turns back and looks at his house; it seems different to him now, because he is already another man—a single night has caused a transformation in him, although he does not know it. The moral change that will condemn him to twenty years of exile has occurred in his soul. Here, then, is the beginning of the long adventure. Wakefield acquires a reddish wig. He changes his habits; soon he has established a new routine. He is troubled by the suspicion that his absence has not disturbed Mrs. Wakefield enough. He decides he will not return until he has given her a good scare. One day the druggist enters the house, another day the doctor. Wakefield is sad, but he fears that his sudden reappearance may aggravate the illness. Obsessed, he lets time pass; before he had thought, "I shall return in a few days," but now he thinks, "in a few weeks." And so ten years pass. For a long time he has not known that his conduct is strange. With all the lukewarm affection of which his heart is capable, Wakefield continues to love his wife, while she is forgetting him. One Sunday morning the two meet in the street amid the crowds of London. Wakefield has become thin; he walks obliquely, as though hiding or escaping; his low forehead is deeply wrinkled; his face, which was common before, is extraordinary, because of his extraordinary conduct. His small eyes wander or look inward. His wife has grown stout; she is carrying a prayer. book and her whole person seems to symbolize a placid and resigned widowhood. She is accustomed to sadness and would not exchange it, perhaps, for joy. Face to face, the two look into each other's eyes. The crowd separates them, and soon they are lost within it. Wakefield hurries to his lodgings, bolts the door, and throws himself on the bed where he is seized by a fit of sobbing. For an instant he sees the miserable oddity of his life. "Wakefield, Wakefield! You are mad!" he says to himself.

Perhaps he is. In the center of London he has severed his ties with the world. Without having died, he has renounced his place and his privileges among living men. Mentally he continues to live with his wife in his home. He does not know, or almost never knows, that he is a different person. He keeps saying, "I shall soon go back," and he does not realize that he has been repeating these words for twenty years. In his memory the twenty years of solitude seem to be an interlude, a mere parenthesis. One afternoon, an afternoon like other afternoons, like the thousands of previous afternoons, Wakefield looks at his house. He sees that they have lighted the fire in the second-floor bedroom; grotesquely, the flames project Mrs. Wakefield's shadow on the ceiling. Rain begins to fall, and Wakefield feels a gust of cold air. Why should he get wet when his house, his home, is there. He walks heavily up the steps and opens the door. The crafty smile we already know is hovering, ghostlike, on his face. At last Wakefield has returned. Hawthorne does not tell us of his subsequent fate, but lets us guess that he was already dead, in a sense. I quote the final words: "Amid the seeming confusion of our mysterious world, individuals are so nicely adjusted to a system, and systems to one another, and to a whole, that by stepping aside for a moment a man exposes himself to a fearful risk of losing his place for ever. Like Wakefield, he may become, as it were, the Outcast of the Universe."

In that brief and ominous parable, which dates from 1835, we have already entered the world of Herman Melville, of Kafka—a world of enigmatic punishments and indecipherable sins. You may say that there is nothing strange about that, since Kafka's world is Judaism, and Hawthorne's, the wrath and punishments of the Old Testament. That is a just observation, but it applies only to ethics, and the horrible story of Wakefield and many stories by Kafka are united not only by a common ethic but also by a common rhetoric. For example, the protagonist's profound triviality, which contrasts with the magnitude of his perdition and delivers him, even more helpless, to the Furies. There is the murky background against which the nightmare is etched. Hawthorne invokes a romantic past in other stories, but the scene of this tale is middle-class London, whose crowds serve, moreover, to conceal the hero.

Here, without any discredit to Hawthorne, I should like to insert an observation. The circumstance, the strange circumstance, of perceiving in a story written by Hawthorne at the beginning of the nineteenth century the same quality that distinguishes the stories Kafka wrote at the beginning of the twentieth must not cause us to forget that Hawthorne's particular quality has been created, or determined, by Kafka. "Wakefield" prefigures Franz Kafka, but Kafka modifies and refines the reading of "Wakefield." The debt is mutual; a great writer creates his precursors. He creates and somehow justifies them. What, for example, would Marlowe be without Shakespeare?

The translator and critic Malcolm Cowley sees in "Wakefield" an allegory of Nathaniel Hawthorne's curious life of reclusion. Schopenhauer has written the famous words to the effect that no act, no thought, no illness is involuntary; if there is any truth in that opinion, it would be valid to conjecture that Nathaniel Hawthorne left the society of other human beings for many years so that the singular story of Wakefield would exist in the universe, whose purpose may be variety. If Kafka had written that story, Wakefield would never have returned to his home; Hawthorne lets him return; but his return is no less lamentable or less atrocious than is his long absence.

One of Hawthorne's parables which was almost masterly, but not quite, because a preoccupation with ethics mars it, is "Earth's Holocaust." In that allegorical story Hawthorne foresees a moment when men, satiated by useless accumulations, resolve to destroy the past. They congregate at evening on one of the vast western plains of America to accomplish the feat.

Men come from all over the world. They make a gigantic bonfire kindled
with all the genealogies, all the diplomas, all the medals, all the orders, all the
judgments, all the coats of arms, all the crowns, all the sceptres, all the tiaras,
all the purple robes of royalty, all the canopies, all the thrones, all the
spirituous liquors, all the bags of coffee, all the boxes of tea, all the cigars, all
the love letters, all the artillery, all the swords, all the flags, all the martial
drums, all the instruments of torture, all the guillotines, all the gallows trees,
all the precious metals, all the money, all the titles of property, all the
constitutions and codes of law, all the books, all the miters, all the vestments,
all the sacred writings that populate and fatigue the Earth. Hawthorne views
the conflagration with astonishment and even shock. A man of serious mien
tells him that he should be neither glad nor sad, because the vast pyramid of
fire has consumed only what was consumable. Another spectator—the
Devil—observes that the organizers of the holocaust have forgotten to throw
away the essential element—the human heart—where the root of all sin
resides, and that they have destroyed only a few forms. Hawthorne concludes
as follows:

> The heart, the heart—there was the little yet boundless sphere
> wherein existed the original wrong of which the crime and misery
> of this outward world were merely types. Purify that inward
> sphere, and the many shapes of evil that haunt the outward, and
> which now seem almost our only realities, will turn to shadowy
> phantoms and vanish of their own accord; but if we go no deeper
> than the intellect, and strive, with merely that feeble instrument,
> to discern and rectify what is wrong, our whole accomplishment
> will be a dream, so unsubstantial that it matters little whether the
> bonfire, which I have so faithfully described, were what we
> choose to call a real event and a flame that would scorch the
> finger, or only a phosphoric radiance and a parable of my own
> brain.

Here Hawthorne has allowed himself to be influenced by the Christian, and
specifically the Calvinist, doctrine of the inborn depravation of mankind and
does not appear to have noticed that his parable of an illusory destruction of
all things can have a philosophical as well as a moral interpretation. For if the
world is the dream of Someone, if there is Someone who is dreaming us now
and who dreams the history of the universe (that is the doctrine of the
idealists), then the annihilation of religions and the arts, the general burning
of libraries, does not matter much more than does the destruction of the

trappings of a dream. The Mind that dreamed them once will dream them again; as long as the Mind continues to dream, nothing will be lost. The belief in this truth, which seems fantastic, caused Schopenhauer, in his book *Parerga and Paralipomena*, to compare history to a kaleidoscope, in which the figures, not the pieces of glass, change; and to an eternal and confused tragicomedy in which the roles and masks, but not the actors, change. The presentiment that the universe is a projection of our soul and that universal history lies within each man induced Emerson to write the poem entitled "History."

As for the fantasy of abolishing the past, perhaps it is worth remembering that this was attempted in China, with adverse fortune, three centuries before Christ. Herbert Allen Giles wrote that the prime minister Li Su proposed that history should begin with the new monarch, who took the title of First Emperor. To sever the vain pretensions of antiquity, all books (except those that taught agriculture, medicine, or astrology) were decreed confiscated and burned. Persons who concealed their books were branded with a hot iron and forced to work on the construction of the Great Wall. Many valuable works were destroyed; posterity owes the preservation of the Confucius canon to the abnegation and valor of obscure and unknown men of letters. It is said that so many intellectuals were executed for defying the imperial edict that melons grew in winter on the burial ground.

Around the middle of the seventeenth century that same plan appeared in England, this time among the Puritans, Hawthorne's ancestors. Samuel Johnson relates that in one of the popular parliaments convoked by Cromwell it was seriously proposed that the archives of the Tower of London be burned, that every memory of the past be erased, and that a whole new way of life should be started. In other words, the plan to abolish the past had already occurred to men and—paradoxically—is therefore one of the proofs that the past cannot be abolished. The past is indestructible; sooner or later all things will return, including the plan to abolish the past.

Like Stevenson, also the son of Puritans, Hawthorne never ceased to feel that the task of the writer was frivolous or, what is worse, even sinful. In the preface to *The Scarlet Letter* he imagines that the shadows of his forefathers are watching him write his novel. It is a curious passage. "What is he?" says one ancient shadow to the other. "A writer of story-books! What kind of a business in life—what mode of glorifying God, or being serviceable to mankind in his day and generation—may that be? Why, the degenerate fellow might as well have been a fiddler!" The passage is curious, because it is in the nature of a confidence and reveals intimate scruples. It harks back to the ancient dispute between ethics and aesthetics or, if you prefer, theology and aesthetics. One early example of this dispute was in the Holy Scriptures and forbade men to adore idols. Another example, by Plato, was in the *Republic*, Book X: "God creates the Archetype (the original idea) of the table; the carpenter makes an imitation of the Archetype; the painter, an imitation of the imitation." Another is by Mohammed, who declared that every representation of a living thing will appear before the Lord on the day of the Last Judgment. The angels will order the artisan to animate what he has made; he will fail to do so and they will cast him into Hell for a certain length of time. Some Moslem teachers maintain that only images that can project a shadow (sculptured images) are forbidden. Plotinus was said to be ashamed to dwell in a body, and he did not permit sculptors to perpetuate his features. Once, when a friend urged him to have his portrait painted, he replied, "It is enough to be obliged to drag around this image in which nature has imprisoned me. But why shall I consent to the perpetuation of the image of this image?"

Nathaniel Hawthorne solved that *difficulty* (which is not a mere illusion). His solution was to compose moralities and fables; he made or tried to make art a function of the conscience. So, to use only one example, the novel *The House of the Seven Gables* attempts to show that the evil committed by one generation endures and persists in its descendants, like a sort of inherited punishment. Andrew Lang has compared it to Émile Zola's novels, or to Émile Zola's theory of novels; to me the only advantage to be gained by the juxtaposition of those heterogeneous names is the momentary surprise it causes us to experience. The fact that Hawthorne pursued, or tolerated, a moral purpose does not invalidate, cannot invalidate his work. In the course of a lifetime dedicated less to living than to reading, I have been able to verify repeatedly that aims and literary theories are nothing but stimuli; the finished work frequently ignores and even contradicts them. If the writer has something of value within him, no aim, however trite or erroneous it may be, will succeed in affecting his work irreparably. An author may suffer from absurd prejudices, but it will be impossible for his work to be absurd if it is genuine, if it responds to a genuine vision. Around 1916 the novelists of England and France believed (or thought they believed) that all Germans were devils; but they presented them as human beings in their novels. In Hawthorne the germinal vision was always true; what is false, what is ultimately false, are the moralities he added in the last paragraph or the characters he conceived, or assembled, in order to represent that vision. The characters in *The Scarlet Letter*—especially Hester Prynne, the heroine—are more independent, more autonomous, than those in his other stories; they are more like the inhabitants of most novels and not mere projections of

Hawthorne, thinly disguised. This objectivity, this relative and partial objectivity, is perhaps the reason why two such acute (and dissimilar) writers as Henry James and Ludwig Lewisohn called *The Scarlet Letter* Hawthorne's masterpiece, his definitive testimony. But I would venture to differ with those two authorities. If a person longs for objectivity, if he hungers and thirsts for objectivity, let him look for it in Joseph Conrad or Tolstoi; if a person looks for the peculiar flavor of Nathaniel Hawthorne, he will be less apt to find it in the laborious novels than on some random page or in the trifling and pathetic stories. I don't know exactly how to justify my difference of opinion; in the three American novels and *The Marble Faun* I see only a series of situations, planned with professional skill to affect the reader, not a spontaneous and lively activity of the imagination. The imagination (I repeat) has planned the general plot and the digressions, not the weaving together of the episodes and the psychology—we have to call it by some name of the actors.

Johnson observes that no writer likes to owe something to his contemporaries; Hawthorne was as unaware of them as possible. Perhaps he did the right thing; perhaps our contemporaries—always—seem too much like us, and if we are looking for new things we shall find them more easily in the ancients. According to his biographers, Hawthorne did not read De Quincey, did not read Keats, did not read Victor Hugo—who did not read each other, either. Groussac would not admit that an American could be original; he denounced "the notable influence of Hoffmann" on Hawthorne, an opinion that appears to be based on an impartial ignorance of both writers. Hawthorne's imagination is romantic; in spite of certain excesses, his style belongs to the eighteenth century, to the feeble end of the admirable eighteenth century.

I have quoted several fragments from the journal Hawthorne kept to entertain his long hours of solitude; I have given brief resumes of two stories; now I shall quote a page from *The Marble Faun* so that you may read Hawthorne's own words. The subject is that abyss or well that opened up, according to Latin historians, in the center of the Forum; a Roman, armed and on horseback, threw himself into its blind depths to propitiate the gods. Hawthorne's text reads as follows:

> "Let us settle it," said Kenyon, "that this is precisely the spot where the chasm opened, into which Curtius precipitated his good steed and himself. Imagine the great, dusky gap, impenetrably deep, and with half-shaped monsters and hideous faces looming upward out of it, to the vast affright of the good

citizens who peeped over the brim! Within it, beyond a question, there were prophetic visions,—intimations of all the future calamities of Rome,—shades of Goths, and Gauls, and even of the French soldiers of today. It was a pity to close it up so soon!, I would give much for a peep into such a chasm."

"I fancy," remarked Miriam, "that every person takes a peep into it in moments of gloom and despondency; that is to say, in his moments of deepest insight.

"The chasm was merely one of the orifices of that pit of blackness that lies beneath us, everywhere. The firmest substance of human happiness is but a thin crust spread over it, with just reality enough to bear up the illusive stage-scenery amid which we tread. It needs no earthquake to open the chasm. A footstep, a little heavier than ordinary, will serve; and we must step very daintily, not to break through the crust at any moment. By and by, we inevitably sink! It was a foolish piece of heroism in Curtius to precipitate himself there, in advance; for all Rome, you see, has been swallowed up in that gulf, in spite of him. The Palace of the Caesars has gone down thither, with a hollow, rumbling sound of its fragments! All the temples have tumbled into it; and thousands of statues have been thrown after! All the armies and the triumphs have marched into the great chasm, with their martial music playing, as they stepped over the brink..."

From the standpoint of reason, of mere reason—which should not interfere with art—the fervent passage I have quoted is indefensible. The fissure that opened in the middle of the Forum is too many things. In the course of a single paragraph it is the crevice mentioned by Latin historians and it is also the mouth of Hell "with half-shaped monsters and hideous faces"; it is the essential horror of human life; it is Time, which devours statues and armies, and Eternity, which embraces all time. It is a multiple symbol, a symbol that is capable of many, perhaps incompatible, values. Such values can be offensive to reason, to logical understanding, but not to dreams, which have their singular and secret algebra, and in whose ambiguous realm one thing may be many. Hawthorne's world is the world of dreams. Once he planned to write a dream, "which shall resemble the real course of a dream, with all its inconsistency, its eccentricities and aimlessness," and he was amazed that no one had ever done such a thing before. The same journal in which he wrote about that strange plan—which our "modern" literature tries vainly to achieve and which, perhaps, has only been achieved by Lewis Carroll—contains his notes on thousands of trivial impressions, small concrete details (the movement of a hen, the shadow of a branch on the wall); they fill six volumes and their inexplicable abundance is the consternation of all his biographers. "They read like a series of very pleasant, though rather dullish and decidedly formal, letters, addressed to himself by a man who, having suspicions that they might be opened in the post, should have determined to insert nothing compromising." Henry James wrote that, with obvious perplexity. I believe that Nathaniel Hawthorne recorded those trivialities over the years to show himself that he was real, to free himself, somehow, from the impression of unreality, of ghostliness, that usually visited him.

One day in 1840 he wrote:

Here I sit in my old accustomed chamber, where I used to sit in days gone by ... Here I have written many tales—many that have been burned to ashes, many that have doubtless deserved the same fate. This' claims to be called a haunted chamber, for thousands upon thousands of visions have appeared to me in it; and some few of them have become visible to the world ... And sometimes it seems to me as if I were already in the grave, with only life enough to be chilled and benumbed. But oftener I was happy ... And now I begin to understand why I was imprisoned so many years in this lonely chamber, and why I could never break through the viewless bolts and bars; for if I had sooner made my escape into the world, I should have grown hard and rough, and been covered with earthly dust, and my heart might have become callous ... Indeed, we are but shadows ..."

In the lines I have just quoted, Hawthorne mentions "thousands upon thousands of visions." Perhaps this is not an exaggeration; the twelve volumes of Hawthorne's complete works include more than a hundred stories, and those are only a few of the very many he outlined in his journal. (Among the stories he finished, one—"Mr. Higginbotham's Catastrophe"—prefigures the detective story that Poe was to invent.)

Miss Margaret Fuller, who knew him in the utopian community of Brook Farm, wrote later, "Of that ocean we have had only a few drops," and Emerson, who was also a friend of his, thought Hawthorne had never given his full measure. Hawthorne married in 1842, when he was thirty-eight; until that time his life had been almost purely imaginative, mental. He worked in the Boston customhouse; he served as United States consul at Liverpool; he lived in Florence, Rome, and London. But his reality was always the filmy twilight, or lunar world, of the fantastic imagination.

At the beginning of this essay I mentioned the doctrine of the psychologist Jung, who compared literary inventions to oneiric inventions, or literature to dreams. That doctrine does not seem to be applicable to the literatures written in the Spanish language, which deal in dictionaries and rhetoric, not fantasy. On the other hand, it does pertain to the literature of North America, which (like the literatures of England or Germany) tends more toward invention than transcription, more toward creation than observation. Perhaps that is the reason for the curious veneration North Americans render to realistic works, which induces them to postulate, for example, that Maupassant is more important than Hugo. It is within the power of a North American writer to be Hugo, but not, without violence, Maupassant. In comparison with the literature of the United States, which has produced several men of genius and has had its influence felt in England and France, our Argentine literature may possibly seem somewhat provincial. Nevertheless, in the nineteenth century we produced some admirable works of realism—by Echeverria, Ascasubi, Hernández, and the forgotten Eduardo Gutiérrez—the North Americans have not surpassed (perhaps have not equaled) them to this day. Someone will object that Faulkner is no less brutal than our Gaucho writers. True, but his brutality is of the hallucinatory sort—the infernal, not the terrestrial sort of brutality. It is the kind that issues from dreams, the kind inaugurated by Hawthorne.

Hawthorne died on May 18, 1864, in the mountains of New Hampshire. His death was tranquil and it was mysterious, because it occurred in his sleep. Nothing keeps us from imagining that he died while dreaming and we can even invent the story that he dreamed—the last of an infinite series—and the manner in which death completed or erased it. Perhaps I shall write it some day; I shall try to redeem this deficient and too digressive essay with an acceptable story.

Van Wyck Brooks in *The Flowering of New England*, D. H. Lawrence in *Studies in Classic American Literature*, and Ludwig Lewisohn in *Story of American Literature* analyze and evaluate the work of Hawthorne. There are many biographies. I have used the one Henry James wrote in 1879 for the English Men of Letters Series.

When Hawthorne died, the other writers inherited his task of dreaming. At some future time we shall study, if your indulgence permits, the glory and the torment of Poe, in whom the dream was exalted to a nightmare.

NOTE

1. This is the text of a lecture given at the Colegio Libre de Estudios Superiores in March, 1949.

SHERMAN PAUL

Introduction to *Walden* and *Civil Disobedience*

I

Life—the "irrepressible satisfaction with the gift of life"—is the single theme of Thoreau's writing, all of which is biographical, the record of an aspiring soul's exploration of reality. "I ... require of every writer," Thoreau said in explaining the "I," the subjective center of *Walden*, "a simple and sincere account of his own life...." From first to last, all his work was devoted to telling not only how he had lived but how alive he had been, how much life he had got. But founded as it was on actual first-hand experience, it was never the immediate report of his experiment on life. Instead, it was the fruit of a slow growth, ripened by recollection, deeply colored by the hues of his mind, and "folded many times thick" by the seasons through which it matured. Place the day-to-day entries in his *Journals* against their final appropriation in his finished work, and the imaginative alchemy—the symbolization of his materials—becomes apparent. For he discovered early that "what is actually present and transpiring is commonly perceived by the common sense and understanding only, is bare and bald, without halo or the blue enamel of intervening air," but that "let it be past ... and it is at once idealized." Then, he said, "it is a deed ripe and with the bloom on it. It is not simply the understanding now, but the imagination that takes cognizance of it."

Now, this is true of *Walden*, which, for all of its riches of common sense

From *Walden* and *Civil Disobedience*. © 1960 by Sherman Paul.

and actual things, was the "flower and fruit of a man," a deed ripe with the bloom on it, full of fragrance. According to Thoreau's intention, *Walden* was not to lead men to strict economies, not even to a life in the woods. In a letter to his "disciple" Harrison Blake, telling of his first encounter with Daniel Ricketson (a spiritual seeker who having read *Walden* turned to Thoreau for guidance), he reported that Ricketson wanted him, "having common sense," to "write in plain English always" in order to "*teach* men in detail how to live a simpler life...." But, Thoreau told Blake, "I have no scheme about it,—no designs on men at all; and, if I had, my mode would be to tempt them with the fruit, and not with the manure." Give man, he added, changing the metaphor, "the bread of life compared with which *that* is bran," let him "only taste these loaves, and he becomes a skillful economist at once. He'll not waste much time in earning those." Unfortunately, like Ricketson, the reviewers and readers misunderstood Thoreau's intention: the symbolism— or *extra-vagant* expression, as he called it (page 221)—they thought only extravagance ("namby-pamby," "stuff," "mystical," Ricketson claimed); they did not see that "the words which express our faith and piety are not definite" but "significant and fragrant like frankincense"; and even Thoreau's warning that words have several meanings, a "volatile truth," went unheeded. He did not intend, of course, to "level downward to our dullest perception always, and praise that as common sense"; and he had adopted symbolism because he had seen his universe symbolically and because it was the only way to truly communicate his valuable experiences, to speak "like a man in a waking moment, to men in their waking moments...." If the "commonest sense is the sense of men asleep, which they express by snoring," nothing less would awaken them or cure their "brain-rot." Indeed, to get men to see their universe symbolically, to read beyond its lessons of matter-of-fact, was one of the most liberating things Thoreau had to offer.

Having misunderstood his method, however, these literalists of common sense also misunderstood what he had to say. They read *Walden* only as an account of Thoreau's life in the woods; they took the "residual statement," the factual record of his life at the pond, for the whole story, once more forgetting Thoreau's instructions-that the heavier element, the narrative fact, was required to float the lighter or spiritual fact. Seizing upon the dramatic act of his withdrawal from society, they thought him uncivil and, like Emerson who provided his Walden acres but did not approve of the experiment, branded him a hermit. As Holmes later remarked, giving the judgment of his generation, Thoreau was "the nullifier of civilization, who insisted on nibbling his asparagus at the wrong end...." And perhaps to heal the sting of his remarks on economy, they saw in this simple means of dodging the pressures of society an end they considered worthless. Did this crank (and there were cranks aplenty in New England preaching the salvation of fresh air and water, of graham flour, of going without money) expect them, so happily satisfied with the luxurious benefits of civilization, to listen to his exultation over a needless belt-tightening? At best, as American society compounded the evils Thoreau had avoided, *Walden* was read as a social gospel—and *Walden* today is most often associated with his doctrine of simplicity, with escape from the burdens of complicated urban existence. That escape, however, is usually associated with the woods, with a return to a long-lost pastoralism; and even in Thoreau's time the identification of his experiment with the woods, as if only the woods promised fulfillment, forced him to clarify his intention by dropping the subtitle, *Life in the Woods*. If *Walden* needed any subtitle, it should have been *Life*; and to this end he offered, and continues to offer, not an escape, but the greatest discovery and gift: an open universe, forever novel, alive, and full of life, forever awaiting and sustaining the untried enterprises of man.

This was the discovery he had made when he went to Walden in the spring of 1845, a discovery that had certified the transcendental faith he had learned from Emerson and that, in the years of "decay" following Walden, he cherished and maintained by writing his book. Only after the fact, when he was powerless to perform the deed again, did he relive it in words; and then he more poignantly and fully realized its significance. With the trials and losses of these years, those glorious years of achievement climaxing the endeavors of his youth were subtly transformed into a testament of prospective hope, and *Walden* affirmed his faith in "the unquestionable ability of man to elevate his life by a conscious endeavor." The ecstasy *of* his former life in the Elysian fields—as he called Walden then—was magnificently reported because it was now colored by his resolution; and the season of joy was given its natural place among the other seasons he had known in such a way that joy was not only the gift of youth but the reward of a mature remaking of one's life.

That one does not readily separate these chronological strands, however, was due in part to Thoreau himself. He knew the artistic value of his narrative facts, that his "fable" had to have a firm foundation, and he minimized all that time had wrought by speaking of Walden as the record of his residence at the pond in 1845–47, claiming that only a few details had been added. And because he believed that the hero hides his struggles and that one should not communicate his dyspepsia but his joy, he did not "propose to write an ode to dejection, but to brag as lustily as chanticleer in the morning...." His spiritual history, nevertheless, was woven into the texture of *Walden*. The resolute tone, if nothing else, proclaims it; and the chapter on "Higher Laws," full of his later determination for discipline and purity, and indeed the very structure of the book, with its culmination in rebirth, disclose it. To read *Walden*, then, as the account of only the Walden years—and it has been read in this way because it has long been assumed that he wrote the book at the pond—is to miss the tremendous struggle that makes *Walden* so glorious. It is to overlook the obstacles and evils that transcendentalists, like all human kind, have known, to make the faith that Thoreau enacted easy, when he himself knew the abyss beneath unity and the horrors of spiritual emptiness, and confessed during the years he was writing *Walden* that "a ticket to Heaven must include tickets to Limbo, Purgatory and Hell." And it is to disregard the fact that the years at Walden yielded two books, that there he wrote *A Week on the Concord and Merrimack Rivers* and infused it with the new found joys of his adventure. For *Walden* was his second book and his second attempt to find a form that would express his life; it was primarily the spiritual history of the years from 1845 to 1854, just as the *Week* was the spiritual history of the years from 1839 to 1849. Companion volumes, they cover the course of his quest for an organic life in Nature, the easy, available communion of his youth and the hard-won, intellectual communion of his manhood; taken together, they are the American equivalent of Wordsworth's *Prelude*; they are the richest account we have of American transcendental experience.

II

One would have to know more of Thoreau's life than he provides in *Walden* in order to explain the "private business" he referred to when he said that "my purpose in going to Walden Pond was not to live cheaply nor to live dearly there, but to transact some private business with the fewest obstacles...." For his private business was a concern of long standing, a matter long delayed that he preferred to speak of in whimsy and allegory. When he told of how he had desired to spend his life in years past, he said that he had been anxious "to stand on the meeting of two eternities, the past and the future, which is precisely the present moment," that he had been eager "to anticipate, not the sunrise and the dawn merely, but, if possible, Nature herself," and that he wanted "to hear what was in the wind, to hear and carry it express!" He told how in trying to achieve these ends—to live in the moment or eternal now, to know the laws of Nature so well that in her every phenomenon his mood would find its correspondence, and to participate in spirit and express it for all mankind—he had kept a journal "of no very wide circulation," had been the "self-appointed inspector" and warden of Nature and the wild, and had "woven a kind of basket of a delicate texture [the *Week*]" which no one would buy. His townsmen, he said, would not "make my place a sinecure with a moderate allowance," and his accounts—he punned—had never been "audited." And so he turned "more exclusively than ever to the woods"—for these reasons, and for other losses darkly hinted at in the hound, bay horse, and turtle-dove that he said he had lost long ago. Not one to postpone his life, he went to the pond, built a hut (his "small counting house"), and, entering the business without any capital but his own self-reliance, began his trade with the "Celestial Empire."

It was an unusual trade, and "a labor to task the faculties of a man"— certainly one that he had not been trained for at Harvard College, although there he had first been stirred by a nascent transcendentalism to follow it. Already dedicated to Truth and Principle, and hungry for the superiority and public influence he believed were the warrants of a devotion to Reason (as his college essays clearly show), he was one of those young men who illustrated, according to Henry James, the "queer search" of the New England character for "something to expend itself upon." He was one of the "young men of the fairest promise," whom Emerson addressed in "The American Scholar" on the occasion of the commencement of Thoreau's class: young men "who begin life upon our shores, inflated by the mountain winds, shined upon by all the stars of God" but who "find the earth below not in unison with these" and "are hindered from action by the disgust which the principles on which business is managed inspire...." "The American Scholar" and the Emerson who represented him were, of course, a challenging alternative to the professions of expediency; especially since Emerson had wrapped about the scholar the mantle of greatness and had made his work "the study and the communication of principles" and "the conversion of the world" at the same time that he united this public end with individual fulfillment—with the "peculiar fruit ... each man was created to bear...." The scholar, he said at Dartmouth College in the following year, "is the favorite of Heaven and earth, the excellency of his country, the happiest of men.... His successes are occasions of the purest joy to all men."

The way to that vocation, however, was difficult because it required self-reliance—the repudiation of the traditional, social institutions of culture—because one's vocation was unique, ultimately one's own character, and even the calling Emerson had created for himself would not afford, as both Alcott and Thoreau were to learn, a sufficient model for others. Like many ideas Emerson announced in his early years with the expectation of immediate enactment, that of the scholar was slow in being fulfilled. Do what he would to instruct the youth who answered his summons, he found—and most painfully in the case of his "brave Henry," in whom he saw the promise of an executive genius and the active powers to engineer for all America that would complement his own passivity—that if the young men "do not wish to go into trade" and "reject all the ways of living of other men," as he told Carlyle in 1842, still they "have none to offer in their stead."

The problem of vocation troubled Thoreau all his life—not that he was without one, but that his was not covered by any respectable label. It was not proper for a youth educated at Harvard, and at great sacrifice on the part of his family, to walk idly, in the woods; and while all his classmates were "choosing their profession, or eager to begin some lucrative employment ... it required rare decision," Emerson admitted in his funeral tribute, "to refuse all the accustomed paths and keep his solitary freedom at the cost of disappointing the natural expectations of his family and friends...." Disappoint them he did, even Emerson who in "Self-Reliance" had approved of Thoreau's determination to follow his genius: "He walks abreast with his days and feels no shame in not 'studying a profession,' for he does not postpone his life, but lives already."

It was easier, perhaps, to walk abreast of the day in the years immediately following his graduation, when schoolteaching put off the expectations of his friends and he was free to begin his apprenticeship as a writer—for that was the vocation he had chosen. He could even delay long enough to get the graduate training Emerson provided him during his stay at the Emersons in 1841–43. Apprenticeships, however, have their term and even Emerson's benign help had its obligations: when Thoreau's lectures before the Concord Lyceum and his poems and essays in *The Dial* (which he edited with Emerson) showed that he was ready, Emerson shipped him off to Staten Island, to his brother William, as a tutor, with the understanding that this scholar and poet "as full of buds of promise as a young apple tree" should have the time and place to continue his work, "pending the time when he shall procure for himself literary labor from some quarter in New York." Unfortunately, Thoreau did not carry his siege against the literary capital; he could not write "companionable" articles, and what he could and did write the Knickerbockers would not pay for. He returned home, having paid his debt to Emerson with failure, and having, meanwhile, acquired other debts, which he paid off in the following year in his father's pencil factory. Once more an Apollo enslaved to Admetus, as he frequently lamented his condition, he simply wrote in his biographical record of the year before he went to Walden Pond, "Made pencils in 1844."

Thoreau had chosen writing because to be socially useful the transcendental life had to be expressed and because writing permitted him to live the transcendental life that was "agreeable to his imagination." Success in the literary marketplace would have made this possible: then the very life he had chosen to live would have paid its way with its own fruit. But having failed to sell his "baskets," his vocation set him another problem, that of getting his living without losing his life, that of mingling in the world where "trade curses everything" without impoverishing those inspirations and perceptions for which he lived. "If we live truly," Emerson had posed the problem in "Self-Reliance," "we shall see truly." To be self-reliant was to live an organic life, to cut the bonds of artificial social life and remake one's relations according to the primary laws of Nature; it was self-culture, nothing less than making one's life one's vocation, tending it as one would a plant or as a poet shapes a poem. Thoreau never fully achieved this goal, though at the end of his life, as he recounted it in "Wild Apples," he was proud of his hardy, long-matured, and spicy fruit, sure that his determination to grow wild had been a good thing even though it had left him dwarfed and stunted and encrusted with thorns. That was the price he had paid to go his own way: the wild apple tree that "emulates man's independence and enterprise" had been browsed on by fate, by the coercions and importunities of society and friends, by the pencil-making and surveying which were, for the rest of his life, in spite of his continued efforts to succeed as a lecturer and writer, the servitudes by which he earned his freedom.

Even by the time he went to Walden, and especially afterwards, his problem was not so much finding a vocation as finding the conditions that would make the one he had never postponed possible; and then the success he sought became the moments of ecstatic communion with Nature, the perceptions and the insights that were *life* and that, by radiating him, vindicated his endeavor to live truly. Everything he wrote from the "Natural History of Massachusetts" to "Walking" was an attempt to define this vocation, from the sympathetic way of beholding "facts" by the "finer organization" of his senses, by an "Indian wisdom," to the sauntering that enabled him by long association with his environment to make the fact "flower in a truth." The bravery this life demanded, and which was one of its attractions for Thoreau, had been proclaimed as early as his lecture on "Society," in his youthful testament, *The Service: Qualities of the Recruit*, where the military imagery that figures in his work was first made explicit, and in "A Winter Walk"; and the leisure it required, and the richer experience it offered, which the pace and tone as well as the actual narrative of his writing always conveyed, were already in his earliest excursions, "A Winter Walk" and "A Walk to Wachusett."

In this early work, however, he defined his vocation only to announce it; from the *Week* on, with growing insistence, he defined it to defend it. For his vocation was defined or focused by the life he lived, by his deepening awareness of the struggle to wrest meaning from Nature and so make his life significant, and by a widening awareness of the uses of Nature. Indeed, the definition which took the final form of the saunterer—though walking had always been the mode of his life—was that of the student of environment. The loss of the private ecstasy of his youth, when his own delight in Nature had been sufficient, had transformed him into a student of human culture. Though life remained the heart of his vision, his vision had become public, scanning wide reaches of human history, even turning to close scientific scrutiny, that he might learn the essential lessons of man's interaction with the organic world. This was a greater "fruit" than the wild apple, simply because it opened to all men the possibility of self-culture that Thoreau's own life dramatized. And perhaps it was the greatest fruit of transcendentalism as well: for though the function of the organic environment in human culture no longer rests on the transcendental philosophy of Nature—as one sees in Benton MacKaye's *The New Exploration*, a landmark in regional planning directly inspired by Thoreau, "the philosopher of environment"—the transcendental view had led Thoreau to the first American exploration of that relationship. Here, in fact, Thoreau had gone beyond Emerson's *Nature*, which had been the manual of his vocation and his introduction to the uses of Nature, and, unrecognized by his teacher, had engineered for all America.

Although Emerson's treatise, which Thoreau had read during his college years, had awakened him to the new vistas of a life in Nature, he did not at first associate this life with the woods. When he left college, Nature for him was a rather indefinite concept, a "prospect" of untried fields for heroism, a new way of seeing the possibilities of life. It answered his desire, as he wrote in his commencement part on "The Commercial Spirit," for a manly and independent life. Repudiating the "blind and unmanly love of wealth," he would be a "Lord of Creation" rather than a "slave of matter"; he would live in "this curious world which ... is more wonderful than it is convenient; more beautiful than it is useful; ... more to be admired and enjoyed than used." To do this, moreover, he would reverse the order of things—a promise he carried out in the *Week* and *Walden*, where vocation became vacation; for "the seventh should be man's day of toil," he said, "and the other six his Sabbath of the affections and the soul,—in which to range this widespread garden, and drink in the soft influences and sublime revelations of Nature."

Such was the life that was agreeable to his imagination, one that he felt was guaranteed by the stimulating assurances of Emerson's *Nature*. There he had learned not only that Nature was beneficent, that it supplied the needs of spirit as well as commodity, but that by means of the wonderful correspondence of man and Nature he could "enjoy an original relation to the universe"—share the currents of Being and thereby become a "creator in the finite." Armed with the idealistic philosophy Emerson had reclaimed for his generation, a philosophy in which ideas were sovereign, he felt that he could "walk even with the Builder of the Universe" and put the foundations under the castles he had built in the air. For Nature, Emerson had shown, was not mechanical but organic, the continuing handiwork of God; the life in Nature was the ever-present spirit of God, and her phenomena "the present expositor of the divine mind." Man, therefore, had "access to the entire mind of the Creator" because the ideas he had in his communion with Nature were Ideas, the constitutive Reality of the universe as well as the reality of his mind.

In this organically-spiritualized idealism, every fact of Nature answered to a fact of consciousness in the human mind, and because of this correspondence the life of consciousness could best be pursued in Nature. Everything in Nature, the entire external world, could be taken possession of by the mind: the brute fact transformed in this experience into value, fused with the inner and subjective and given its human-spiritual significance. Seized in this way the fact flowered in a truth; or rather projected in this way—since Emerson in going beyond "Idealism" to "Spirit" had internalized the whole process and had made Nature, the facts themselves, the issue of spirit—every mood of the mind found its objective expression. As Thoreau described his youthful confidence in this subjective idealism in "The Inward Morning,"

> Packed in my mind lie all the clothes
>   Which outward nature wears,
> And in its fashion's hourly change
>   It all things else repairs.
>
> In vain I look for change abroad,
>   And can no difference find,
> Till some new ray of peace uncalled
>   Illumes my inmost mind.

The inward morning, the wakefulness he sought later on, was, of course, the influx of inspiration without which Nature, as he found, was barren. Then his universe was indeed broken in two, the galvanic ecstasy gone. But rather than disown the faith in which he had invested his life, he accepted the implication of Emerson's statement that to see truly one must live truly: "The ruin or the blank that we see when we look at nature, is in our own eye." He found the fault, not in the Emersonian theory, but in his own unworthiness: he acknowledged the guilt of impurity. And where once, in his youth, he had all unconsciously had a perfect communion, he now determined, with a heroism he never dreamed he would be called on to show, to rebuild his universe and his faith. He tried to bring the poles of the Emersonian universe together by purifying the channels of perception, by living a disciplined and ascetic life, and by studying Nature more objectively. By the one he hoped to renew his worthiness, by the other to know Nature so intimately that he could anticipate her moods—together, he hoped, he would once more complete the circuit of inspiration. But if this conscious endeavor had its rewards in the richer symbolic readings of Nature of his mature writing, it did not bring with it the fullness of ecstasy, the flow of inspiration through him. "The unconsciousness of man," he said in the *Week*, where he criticized Goethe for being too consciously the artist, "is the consciousness of God." By conscious means he could not retrieve the unconsciousness of his youth, that glorious passivity he recalled in *Walden*, when he spent his life lavishly "dreaming awake," "floating over its [the pond's] surface as the zephyr willed...." This was the personal tragedy that humanized the youth who had had eternity in his eye; this rooted him and socialized his vision; but it was also the struggle that the hero tried to hide.

When he first read *Nature* he was hardly aware that the mountain by which he symbolized his transcendent aspirations would be so steep. He had been dazzled by the American scholar who had personally set him to work journalizing and who later sheltered him—the Emerson in whose world "every man would be a poet, Love would reign, Beauty would take place, Man and Nature harmonize." He had been stirred more deeply than anyone else in his generation by the power of Emersonian perception for the conduct of life, by the possibility of making life an art. For *Nature* affirmed that man was no longer the slave of matter but the shaper of the external circumstances of his life. These he could build around him with the same organic fitness with which the bark fits the tree, as a function of the idea that controlled his life, in the very way the Creator—the Supreme Artist—"put forth" the organic world as the expression of His Ideas. Man's life would grow out of him in the way a tree springs from the seed, puts forth leaves; flowers, and fruit, assimilating and transforming all that Nature provides for its nurture into a resplendent ripeness. Man would be the poem of his own creation, or the statue, as Thoreau said, that he would carve out of the elements about him. And even more grandly, he would make his own world, the landscape would radiate from him; he would have as Thoreau had at Walden, "my own sun and moon and stars, and a little world all to myself." This was the exhilarating prospect Emerson had opened: "'Nature is not fixed but fluid,'" he said. "'Spirit alters, moulds, makes it. The immobility or bruteness of nature is the absence of spirit; to pure spirit it is fluid, it is volatile, it is obedient. Every spirit builds itself a house, and beyond its house a world, and beyond its world a heaven. Know then that the world exists for you. For you is the phenomenon perfect. What we are, that only can we see.... Build therefore your own world. As fast as you conform your life to the pure idea in your mind, that will unfold its great proportions.'"

To conform one's life to the idea in one's mind, to live, as Thoreau wrote while he was composing *Walden*, "that you may the more completely realize and live, in the idea which contains the reason of your life, that you may build yourself up to the height of your conceptions"—this was to live greatly, to use one's life wisely. "The whole duty of life," Thoreau said in 1841, recognizing the problem of vocation, "is contained in the question how to respire and aspire both at once." Already discontented with the tame life he was living as a schoolteacher, and with the fact that he was not marching to his own music, he proposed that he help himself by "withdrawing ... [by] determining to meet myself face to face sooner or later." The solitary position in which he had pictured himself in his lecture on "Society" now became the "most positive life that history notices"—"a constant retiring out of life, a wiping one's hands of it seeing how mean it is, and having nothing to do with it." And farming, which he always felt was a noble vocation, first suggested itself as a solution. But before he could act on it, he went to the Emersons as handy-man, expecting in the adventure of friendship that "a great person ... will constantly give you great opportunities to serve him...."

Friendship was the supreme transcendental relationship, for without it, Thoreau learned, Nature ceased to be morally significant. He had gone to Emerson with high hopes that in their relationship the world would learn "what men can build each other up to be, when both master and pupil work in love." Their relationship, however, had its undercurrent of antagonism, if only because of Thoreau's ideal expectancies and Emerson's benevolent but patronizing attitude toward his superserviceable Henry. "We do [not] wish friends to feed and clothe our bodies—neighbors are kind enough for that," Thoreau complained, "but to do the like offices to ourselves. We wish to spread and publish ourselves, as the sun spreads its rays...." Before long he found that "life in gardens and parlors" was unpalatable to him, that he was growing "savager and savager every day," that his wish, still unfulfilled, was to be "nature looking into nature," that from this recess he might "put forth sublime thoughts daily, as the plant puts forth leaves." "When any scorn your love," he wrote at this time, "let them see plainly that you serve not them but another. If these bars are up, go your way to other of God's pastures.... When your host shuts his door on you he incloses you in the dwelling of nature.... My foes restore me to my friends." Even at Emerson's, Nature became the refuge for his discontent, and before a year had passed, he wrote: "I want to go soon and live away by the pond, where I shall hear only the wind whispering among the reeds. It will be success if I shall have left myself behind. But my friends ask what I will do when I get there. Will it not be employment enough to watch the progress of the seasons?" And the next day he added: "I don't want to feel as if my life were a sojourn any longer. That philosophy cannot be true which so paints it. It is time now that I begin to live."

But he lingered because, with Emerson so much away lecturing, his services were indispensable, and because the deaths of his brother John and Emerson's son Waldo had united them in grief. Still the feeling of delay did not abate, but intensified in plaintiveness: "What ... can I do to hasten that other time ... [when] there will be no discords in my life? ... My life, my life! why will you linger? ... How often has long delay quenched my aspiration! Can God afford that I should forget him? Is he so indifferent to my career? Can heaven be postponed with no more ado?" And when he went to Staten Island it was with reluctance, the stigmata of which were an "unaccountable" bronchitis and a "skirmishing with drowsiness" that interfered with his literary projects. The city, moreover, unmanned him, for though he was always the most perceptive of travelers, he did not have a traveler's temperament; the strange surroundings and the multiplicity of sensations disturbed the tranquillity and stability, the pastoral routine, that he needed. The herds of people—"the pigs in the street" that he wrote of to Emerson— a great tide entering the Narrows and flowing West, all bent on progress, taught him, as he said in "Paradise (To Be) Regained," that "we must first succeed alone, that we may enjoy our success together."

But the most valuable thing his first—and longest—stay in the city taught him was his need for roots; it crystallized his longing and discontent into a hut beside a pond in Concord. When he wrote "The Landlord" for the *Democratic Review* he not only described a hut in a retired place but made it a symbol of his own sincerity and sociality—here was the open and hospitable hut, that one lofty room in which all the secrets of housekeeping were exposed, that he imagined in "House-Warming" in *Walden*; and in "A Winter Walk," which he also wrote at this time, he first canvassed the scenery of his life: Walden Pond, Fair Haven Cliffs and Bay, and the Concord River. Here, too, was a deserted woodman's hut that suggested the rude shelter he later built. And as he sat within it, he enjoyed "the friendship of the seasons" that he described in "Sounds" and "Solitude" in *Walden*, and felt the appeal of the life it would permit him to live. The pond, furthermore, first began to acquire the personal associations that he would explicitly develop in *Walden*, but the lesson it symbolized now was the Oriental wisdom in which the Staten Island interlude had schooled him: "'sitting still at home is the heavenly way; the going out is the way of the world.'"

Staten Island, then, drove him back to Concord and to Nature. "Where nature ceases to be supernatural to a man what will he do then?" he had asked despairingly in this first crisis. "Of what worth is human life if its actions are no longer to have this sublime and un explored scenery? Who will build a cottage and dwell in it with enthusiasm if not in the Elysian fields?" His determination on Walden, however, even after the delay of a year in the pencil factory, was not made easy. His friends, understanding his proposal in theory—as one sees in Charles Lane's "Life in the Woods" in *The Dial*—did not approve of the "simple, fibrous life" in practice; and when one considers that Thoreau's experiment was one of the most daring and dramatic of transcendental acts, their sullen silence during his years at the pond, as if he had gone out of the world, showed the strength of their disapproval. In fact, it was partly to get away from the ceaseless transcendental debates in Concord parlors that Thoreau wanted to go to the pond. To live in the woods was not only an economic expedient that would permit him the leisure to write; it would permit him to make his relationships on his own terms, free from the expectations of his friends.

Once there, at last face to face with "the great facts of his existence," Thoreau was overwhelmed by a joy that was everything he had anticipated. This, he later realized, was the great occasion of his life—an adventure that mounts in excitement from day to day as one follows in the journal his own sudden sense of release from bondage. At last, he said, he walked the fields "with unexpected expansion and long-missed content, as if there were a field worthy of me." The usual boundaries of his life were dispersed, and he learned, as he later dramatized his belief in the uncommitted life in his conversation with John Field (pages 140 ff.), that "your fetters are knocked off; you are really free." "Yes," he told himself, "roam far, grasp life and conquer it, learn much and live.... Dismiss prudence, fear, conformity. Remember only what is promised." Free "to adventure on life now, his vacation from humbler toil having commenced" and blest by his "hard and emphatic life" in the Elysian fields, his joy at the pond helped him transform his 1839 excursion on the Concord and Merrimack into the spiritual holiday of the *Week*. This book, in fact, with its confidence in Nature and its daily adventures in ecstasy, was a rhapsody to wakefulness, the record of his "morning work," a form for thought itself. And compared with *Walden*, which was the form for the growth of consciousness and the record of his wakening, it was more faithful in spirit to the life he had had at the pond.

There was nothing in this life, moreover, that justified the fears of his friends that he would lose himself in the solitudes of his own ecstasy. For as it had for Whitman, self-realization in Nature suffused him with love. Neither life nor love could be shared, he learned, until he had found his own center, the pride that rested on the security of his own self-reliance. Then, indeed, he could brag for mankind. And then he saw the representative value of his private reform; he even saw himself as a stock personality, better able to speak for common working men than Emerson because he had known and sur mounted the conditions of their lives. His life in the woods had put in perspective the life of village and city, and counting his gains, he hoped that his example would begin the social redemption of New England. For unlike the many social experiments of his day (Alcott had gone to Fruitlands in 1843, and Brook Farm was in its Fourieristic phase when Thoreau lived at Walden)—unlike the ideal lives that Alcott had said "none of us were prepared to actualize practically," Thoreau's experiment had been successful. He had "reduced a fact of the imagination to be a fact to his understanding," as he said in *Walden*, in the hope "that all men will at length establish their lives on that basis."

He had not planned to live permanently at the pond, however, and the Walden experiment came to an end when Thoreau, at the bidding of Mrs. Emerson, returned to manage the household during Emerson's absence in England in 1847–48. In many respects, Thoreau took up his life where he had left it before going to Staten Island, with the advantages, however, of now being the master of the house and of having the manuscript of a publishable book in his possession. Walden had healed his defeat and restored his confidence, and he felt ready now for a life of successful authorship. He immediately set to work preparing lectures, and the reception of some of them seemed to promise success. But again he was thwarted by delay, this time by the refusal of publishers to print the *Week*, his bid for fame. Advised by Emerson to issue the book at his own expense, he finally published the *Week* in 1849, but the sale was so poor that Thoreau did not hazard another book until he had paid his debts. That delay, however, providing the background of new and more difficult obstacles, was the making of *Walden*.

For faced once more with the problem of economy in the years following Emerson's return, Thoreau had turned again, this time permanently, to the pencil factory—and had added to his chains those of the surveyor. This life, of course, was hardly satisfactory; it robbed him of the time to work for and with his nobler faculties; it was "trivial"; and surveying, which forced him "to live grossly or inattentive to [his] diet," he felt, had made his life "prosaic, hard, and coarse." In "Life Without Principle," where the bitterness of these years was distilled, leaving his gladness for *Walden*, he said that "a man had better starve at once than lose his innocence in the process of getting his bread." Indeed, the despair of his later years, those autumnal years of "decay" in which he was literally the "'god in ruins'" Emerson spoke of in *Nature*—the god who was once "'permeated and dissolved by spirit,'" who "'filled nature with his overflowing currents,'" and the laws of whose mind had "'externized themselves into day and night, into the year and the seasons'"—was over his lost innocence. This loss, this impurity, was measured by the loss of communion with Nature, and his world, as Emerson said of the fallen man, now lacked unity, and lay "broken and in heaps...." There were, of course, other contributory "stains": that bustling nineteenth century that destroyed his repose, binding him to society with the ligature of his own desire for social justice—Negro slavery and Irish "slavery," the Mexican War, the Anthony Burns' affair, and his own night in jail, all teaching him that "life itself being worthless, all things with it, that feed it, are worthless"; and more personally, the irreparable alienation from his friends, and his strenuous efforts to overcome the first advances of illness by an outdoor life, which, intensified by the strain of the scientific attention he had given to Nature in his attempt to find communion, became a permanent disability. Moreover, from his arduous study of Nature—he had now embarked on the staggering labor of finding in the seasons of Nature the corresponding seasons of man—he learned that his pristine youth or springtime was passed, that the "second spring" of autumn was not a time of germination but of ripening, and that to achieve this seasoned virtue, the sloth and sensuality and impurity of the hot summer of growth had to be overcome. Summer was no longer the extended spring it had been in his youth, but the season of his present manhood, when "Pegasus," he confessed, "has lost his wings; he has turned a reptile and gone on his belly." The reptilian imagery of *Walden* (as well as the imagery of carrion, stagnation, and slumber) were the result of these years when, living "this slimy, beastly kind of life," Thoreau felt that he had become "the very sewers, the cloacae of nature."

In his desire for purity, Thoreau transferred the values of spring to autumn, for autumn was a rejuvenescence, with its cooler days and purer atmosphere, its returning birds and late flowerings and running crystal streams. At the same time, however, he returned in memory to his youth. He longed again for "those youthful days!" He wished again to be a child. Nothing; he felt, was "comparable with the experiences of my boyhood...." If the seasons of Nature taught him the inevitability of the seasons of man, and even assured him that harvest was superior to seedtime, still the "knowledge of ourselves" that came with manhood spoiled his satisfaction. In spite of (and because of) his discipline and asceticism, he could not win back the time when "nature developed as I developed, and grew up with me" and "my life was ecstasy." He could only remember that before his "losses" he had been "all alive, and inhabited my body with irrepressible satisfaction...." As he wrote *Walden* in these years, he knew that his life had been one of obstacles; that once, at the pond, he had overcome them. The spring he now desired was the rebirth he hoped to earn by the purity of his manhood, a rebirth that he believed was possible because of his former victory, and guaranteed by a law of Nature as certain as that of the seasons—the law of renewal. With this double truth, he found that he could be true to the course of his life: to the seasons of life and to his faith in an eternal spring that would transcend the seasons themselves. In *Walden*, the fruit of his ripening year, he hoped to keep this faith alive by memorializing the period that had crowned his life. Still undaunted, he believed, as he once told Harrison Blake, that "what can be expressed in words can be expressed in life."

III

The knowledge of the seasons was the most important addition to Thoreau's thought after 1850. It made possible the metaphors of ripening and completion that give his last work a tone of acceptance and quiet satisfaction; and it also made possible the fable of the renewal of life in *Walden*. When "for convenience" Thoreau put the experience of his two years at the pond into one, when he saw that the narrative action might be related to the seasons, he had the "fable with a moral" with which to express the meaning he now gave to that period of his life. Unlike that of the *Week*, which made the day the unit of time and of inspiration, the fable of the seasons enabled Thoreau to be true to the trials, changes, and growth he had known—to actualize by means of his former life his present aspirations. "Some men's lives are but an aspiration, a yearning toward a higher state," he wrote in

1851, "and they are wholly misapprehended, until they are referred to, or traced through, all their metamorphoses." In the seasons of *Walden* he could trace his metamorphoses: the passage from servitude to liberation, and the self-transcendence of his transformation from impurity to purity—the rebirth of new life out of the old.

The day, of course, had its seasons; it was the epitome of the year: "The night is winter, the morning and evening are the spring and fall, and the noon is summer." The spiritual change from sleep to wakefulness—the prospect of the dawn that closes *Walden*—was proper to it; and the chapters nearest in fact to his ecstatic years employed it—"Where I Lived, and What I Lived For," with its morning philosophy, and "Sounds," with its account of his summer reverie, of a full day in Nature. He had used the day in the *Week* as the very possession of ecstasy, but now that he was earning it, he needed a longer cycle of time in order to participate in the organic processes of rebuilding and renewing his world. There had to be time to clear his land, build his hut, plant his seeds, and harvest his crop: time for that "something even in the lapse of time by which time recovers itself." Change, gradual transformation, now preoccupied him, and sleeping and waking, admirably fitted to the sudden advent of inspiration, were neither as adequate nor as rich in the details of change as the metaphors he now chose: ice–thaw–flux, seed–flower–fruit, grub–chrysalis–butterfly. These natural facts became the metaphors in terms of which he told of his desire to pass from a lower to a higher form of life, from fixity to fluidity (he would share again the "circulations" of Being), from the innocence of youth to the wisdom of maturity, from larval sensuality to aerial purity.

These transformations, moreover, were examples of change in obedience to the organic principle, by means of an inner expansion. In terms of Thoreau's personal life, their possibility was dramatized by his withdrawal from society to Nature, that is to say, from a condition fixed beyond growth (society for Thoreau was always a machine) to a condition permitting him to build his life from the inside out in obedience to his idea. "Our moulting season, like that of the fowls, must be the crisis of our lives," he explained. "The loon retires to solitary ponds to spend it. Thus also the snake casts its slough, and the caterpillar its wormy coat, by an internal industry and expansion..." In society, however, he remained his old "scurvy self," and society, as he now used it in *Walden* to enclose his experiment in renewal, was the sum of all the anxieties and constraints and failures he wished to leave behind. Not only because he was preaching self-reform, but because he wanted to show what he had surmounted, he began *Walden* with the long social analysis of "Economy," setting up the emphatic polarities and perspectives that would awaken his readers to see their—and his—condition absolutely, from a vantage outside of society. As Emerson had done in *Nature*, he began with commodity before turning to spirit. But more fully than Emerson, whose treatise had its point-by-point parallels in *Walden*, he employed history, anthropology, books (even Scripture), paradox, humor, irony, ridicule, scorn, philological puns, parables, dramatization, utopian prospects, and every variety of symbolic statement to establish the contrasting values of surface and depth (appearance and reality), transient and permanent, complex and simple, disease and health, tradition and the uncommitted life, desperation and joy, spiritual emptiness and spiritual fullness. From externality and circumstance, he turned to the inner dominion of self-reliance, from collective "humanitarian" reform to self-discovery, from a world broken and in heaps to the cosmos he had made. Indeed, in dramatizing these changes from society and commodity to spirit and self, *Walden* worked inward from the circumferential to the central life, from the external to the real self, from extrinsic to intrinsic success.

Thoreau also began with "Economy" because it was the aspect of his experiment that had aroused the most curiosity. The life of quiet desperation that he so brilliantly anatomized, however, had been (or was) his own, and the economic anxieties merely pointed to deeper anxieties—those of a life gone stale, without savor or animating purpose. The economy he proposed, therefore, was to the end of getting and spending one's life, an economy of spirit his readers little expected, one that denied the Puritan necessity of working with the sweat of the brow, one that made work itself a joy and a pastime rather than a duty. The irony of his economy, given to the fraction of a cent, was that on so little, he had got so much, that he did not carry a house on his back or possess a corner of the world, but had all the landscape for his own, and time (which Franklin said was money) to read, to sit idle all day, to boat and fish, and to saunter at his ease and enjoy those bounties of Nature that were reserved for a "Lord of Creation." He had a self that he could hug, one that was not at society's beck and call or twisted and thwarted by relations, which, he had found by experiment, were customary rather than essential. And if the simplicity of his economy seemed Franklinian, he was not burning incense to the patron saint of State Street: the end of his economy was enrichment, not denial, and he spent lavishly. "Give me the poverty," he exclaimed when cursing Flint (pages 135 ff.), "that enjoys true wealth." If anything, he was undermining the Franklinian virtues, replacing the *Autobiography* with a model for another kind of success—utilizing the very terminology of business to raise the uncomfortable question of whether possessions actually helped one possess life. This was the purpose of his reductiveness in treating the goods of the world, for the only good he wished to appropriate (and here he added his voice to the swelling clamor of American literature) was experience, the quality or bloom of life. The burden of "Economy," in fact, was that the way to wealth was not the way to health, but to lives of quiet desperation. When he wrote Blake, who was trying to use *Walden* as his guide, he said: "It is surprising how contented one can be with nothing definite,—only a sense of existence.... O how I laugh when I think of my vague, indefinite riches. No run on my bank can drain it, for my wealth is not possession but enjoyment."

Standing in the way of this enjoyment, however, was the confusion concerning the means and ends of life which Thoreau had tried to clarify by reducing his life to its simplest terms; and, accordingly, the central issue to those who either rejected or accepted his life was his doctrine of simplicity. He had reduced the means of life, of course, not because he wanted to prove that he could go without them, or to disclaim their value in enriching life, but because they were usually factitious—they robbed one of life itself. And though, like *Walden*, the "shallow meaning" of this economy was "but too clear," the meaning it had for him was not. His economy, like his withdrawal to Nature, was not an ultimate abdication from social life; it was only the means of the self-emancipation, which many, accepting social bondage as the inevitable condition of life, did not find necessary. Economy freed him from society, and Nature provided him the opportunity to share the recreative processes of life; but this life in Nature was also a means, the goal being another, a "higher" and an organic society, shaped by the same principles whose efficacy Thoreau had demonstrated. To this end, rather than to the renunciation of society, *Walden* was a social gospel.

He himself had adopted simplicity for many reasons. He believed, for example, that it would bring him nearer to those common influences in which Emerson had taught the poet to delight. And as a social critic, he believed that the only honest or absolute view required the detached prospect of "voluntary poverty." Considering his personal experiment, however, the most important reason was his need to clear away the obstacles that stood between him and the "grand fact" of life. For in order to front the fact and recover reality, he had to reduce the problem of perception to its simplest terms—self and Nature. Simplicity, then, was a discipline and an ascetic, as necessary to his purification as the labor in the beanfield or the dietary practices of "Higher Laws," and he often hallowed it with religious associations by calling it "poverty." "By poverty, *i.e.* simplicity of life and fewness of incidents," he wrote in 1857, bringing to the surface the sunken imagery of *Walden*, "I am solidified and crystallized, as a vapor or liquid by cold. It is a singular concentration of strength and energy and flavor. Chastity is perpetual acquaintance with the All [In "Higher Laws" he said that "Chastity is the flowering of man.... Man flows at once to God when the channel of purity is open."].... You think that I am impoverishing myself by withdrawing from men, but in my solitude I have woven for myself a silken web or chrysalis, and nymph-like, shall ere long burst forth a more perfect creature, fitted for a higher society. By simplicity ... my life is concentrated and so becomes organized, or a Κόσμος [cosmos], which before was inorganic and lumpish."

When simplicity, finally, was associated with his life in the woods and his hunger for the wild, it raised another issue—that of primitivism vs. civilization. In espousing Nature, the transcendentalists, of course, had also glorified the primitive life. But having experienced the wilderness on his trips to the Maine woods in 1846 and 1853, Thoreau knew that his life at the pond and in Concord pastures was far from wild; and though he always maintained that the health of civilization needed the tonic of the wild, his experience had taught him that the pastoral landscape was the best setting for human life. On one level, in fact, he intended *Walden* for a modern epic of farming, and he had purposely begun his life from scratch in order to relive all history and test this mode of life against the achievements of civilization.

Had his problem been merely that of doing without society, it would have been easily solved; but his problem—the one that Lane had posed in *The Dial*—was what to do with it: how to join the values of urban and sylvan life. The paradox of civilization that Thoreau exploited (though it was hardly a paradox to one who recognized the enslavement to means) was that it did not civilize but barbarized most men, reducing them to a level of want below that of the savage. His own simple life, however, had been remarkably civil, and much of his satisfaction in it was due to the fact that it had provided the uncluttered and leisurely conditions of truly civilizing himself: savages, after all, did not read Homer or write books in the woods. His stance as a philosopher, moreover, made it clear that his demands on life were not simple or primitive, that only the self-sufficiency and adjustment of the Indians to the natural environment appealed to him—the style of their life rather than the "barren simplicity" of their elementary demands on it. "There are two kinds of simplicity," he had observed in the journal, "one that is akin to foolishness, the other to wisdom. The philosopher's style of living is only outwardly simple, but inwardly complex. The savage's style is both outwardly and inwardly simple." The complex and refined life of society, however, did not necessarily yield a complex inner life. And when he proposed that the civilized man become a more experienced and wiser savage, he hoped that he would retain the physical simplicity of the one in order to achieve the complex goals of the other, that he would "spend as little time as possible in planting, weaving, building, etc." and devote his freedom to cultivating "the highest faculties." This could be done, he believed, as he had done it, not only by simplicity, but by making the organic communion of the sylvan the foundation of a higher life.

In showing the "positive hindrances" of civilization—that its means did not fit the ends of man—Thoreau used examples that also enabled him to develop the theory of organic functionalism so essential to his faith in the renewal of life. Everything—education, reform, clothing, shelter, and furniture—was tested by its fitness to living needs, by whether it answered to the inner necessities of man. Clothing, he found, for example, seldom fit the character of the wearer, in many cases did not even serve its basic function of preserving the "vital heat"; instead it was an outer covering worn in conformity to society. Houses, too, were "*exo*strious" [a pun on *indu*strious], a building from without, a more cumbersome clothing, indeed a "tomb" built by the "coffin-maker," as he called the carpenter, for the next generation. Fine houses, like fashionable clothes, he said, were not the expression or function of the indweller; they had not been built up from the "foundation" of "beautiful housekeeping and beautiful living." And furniture was *exuviae*, the cast skins of others, that cluttered the house, the spider's web of tradition that trapped the "gay butterfly." Accordingly, having by his withdrawal and simplicity divested himself of these impediments, he built his life from the inside out; and he proposed that others build in the same "Orphean fashion," that they "grow" their houses: "Let our houses first be lined with beauty," he said, "where they come in contact with our lives, like the tenement of the shellfish, and not overlaid with it." If he acknowledged that in building his hut he had built too heedlessly to build well, still he recommended that others consider "what foundation a door, a window, a cellar, a garret, have in the nature of man...." For he knew that the circumstances that man creates also shape him, that "this frame," as he said of his hut, "was a sort of crystallization around me, and reacted on the builder."

These principles, as well as the prospectus of his hopes and the initial stages of his experiment, were placed in the intervals of the social analysis of "Economy." The contrast they provided, however, was immediately realized in "Where I Lived, and What I Lived For," for in his determination to adventure on life Thoreau was already reborn. When he went to the pond in March, 1845, he had already felt the influence of "the spring of springs"; he had overcome his "torpidity"; in the woods, as Emerson said in *Nature*, he had "cast off his skin, as a snake his slough," and had again become "a child."

Though Thoreau buried this spring in "Economy," and deliberately began his account with summer, with his going to the pond to live on Independence Day, the imagery of the melting pond, the returning birds, and the stray goose were the same as in his second "Spring." This additional season, of course, made it possible for Thoreau to recapitulate the entire history of his life from youth to maturity: the first spring, the dewy, pure, auroral season of the Olympian life, was true to his youth, and the subsequent seasons and the second spring were the record of the growth of consciousness and of his conscious endeavor to earn the new world of his springtime again.

Thoreau most patently dramatized this process of organic growth and renewal by building his hut, the container of his vital heat and the symbol of the self, to meet the developing seasons of man and consciousness. The seasons of man, of course, corresponded to the seasons of Nature: summer representing the outdoor life, when man was alive in all his senses and Nature supplied his vital heat; autumn, the gathering of consciousness; and winter, the withdrawal inward to self-reflection. This development, moreover, had its counterpart in the seasons of history, for, as Emerson had noted, "The Greek was the age of observation; the Middle Age, that of fact and thought; ours, that of reflection and ideas." Thus, when Thoreau went to Walden, he found that "both place and time were changed and I dwelt nearer to those parts of the universe and to those eras in history which had most attracted me." Spring was the Golden Age, that morning time of heroic endeavor that he always. associated with Greece; and this explained why his first spring was so full of allusions to Greece, why Homer was the proper scripture for his morning discipline, and why the second spring recalled his reading in Ovid's *Metamorphoses* and brought back the Golden Age. His year was the cycle of human history, and by renewing it he was trying to prove his proposition that the joys of life were not exhausted, that the counsel of despair of his elders, who believed that the whole ground of human life had already been gone over, was untrue.

The frame and foundation of Thoreau's hut came from Nature, the boards or outer covering from a shanty Thoreau purchased from James Collins, an Irish laborer whose life, like his "dank, clammy, and aquish" dwelling, was the very sum of quiet desperation. Dismantling this hut, Thoreau bleached and warped the boards in the sun; he purified the materials of his life, as he did again the second-hand bricks he used for his chimney; and with the stuff of the old, for he knew that men must borrow from civilization, he built the new after an Orphean fashion. When he first occupied his house in the summer, it was "merely a defence against the rain, without plastering or chimney," with "wide chinks" between the boards, open, as he had been in the summer, to the influence of Nature. "I did not need to go out doors to take the air," he observed, "for the atmosphere within had lost none of its freshness." This was the time of his rich communion with Nature, when there were no barriers to the rapture he celebrated in "Sounds," when his solitude (which he defined in terms of his nearness to God) was a satisfaction his friends never suspected. As long as possible, therefore, he preferred to remain outdoors, warmed by these genial influences; but, anticipating the bleaker seasons, toward the end of summer he began to build his chimney and fireplace—"the most vital part of the house." The foundation had already been laid in the spring, and now in the cooler days of autumn, he carefully and slowly built his chimney a layer of bricks at a time. The chimney, of course, was his very self or "soul"—an "independent structure, standing on the ground and rising through the house to the heavens," and he built it deliberately because it "was calculated to endure for a long time." Finally, when the north wind came and the pond began to cool and he needed a fire to warm him, he first "inhabited" his house; he plastered and shingled, completely closing himself off from the elements—he internalized his life. "I withdrew yet farther into my shell," he wrote, and endeavored to keep a bright fire both within my house and within my breast." In this season, as he told of it in "House-Warming," his chief employment was gathering wood for his fire: he was trying to keep alive, to maintain "a kind of summer in the midst of winter...." For he found, during this "barren" season when he had only his heart to gnaw, that he began to grow torpid, that what he had gained in maturity by his self-confinement— by the change from outer to inner, from unconsciousness to consciousness— had brought with it an estrangement from Nature, the sense of "otherness" that bespoke his greatest loss.

If this development was true to Thoreau's life, so were the occupations or disciplines by which he hoped to burst the shell of his cocoon. His summer and morning work, for example, was cultivating beans, a discipline that was hardly consonant with the "fertile idleness" he had appropriately described in "Sounds" and "Solitude." During the Walden period he had, of course, hoed beans, but solely for the purpose of paying his way; from the vantage of his later years, however, this labor became the discipline by means of which he participated in the natural process and renewed his intimacy with Nature. "They attached me to the earth," he said of his beans, "and so I got strength like Antaeus." The value of farming, or of any unspecialized vocation in Nature, he also found, was that it helped one catch Nature unaware, that it restored unconsciousness and permitted one to see out of the side of the eye. He advised the American scholar to live by this manual labor, moreover, not only because it was honest and because it rooted one in the native soil, but because it taught one how to reason from the hands to the head: here was the very creative process that would instruct him in the symbolic use of things, that would make the concrete object yield its truth, and that, accordingly, would remove the "palaver" from his style. In his own case, he had been "a plastic artist in the dewy and crumbling sand" in order that his work might bear the "instant and immeasurable crop" of "tropes and expression." And the expression it yielded was the parable of the chapter itself: how to plant the seeds of "sincerity, truth, simplicity, faith, innocence, and the like," how by constant vigilance to make the "germ of virtue" bear, how by redeeming the "lean and effete" soil of Massachusetts—the "dust of my ancestors" —the seed of one man might bear the harvest of "a new generation of men." Here was a parable of both individual and social reform, of the kind of moral reform that went to the root of things and that could not fail because, as Thoreau pointed out in the case of the word "seed," its root was "spica," "spe," and "gerendo"—hope-bearing.

The most important result of this discipline was that it helped him "clothe that fabulous landscape of my infant dreams...." At the beginning of "The Bean-Field" he told how he had first been brought to the pond in his childhood, and in "The Ponds" he told how the woodchoppers had since laid waste its shores. These alterations in the shore, he now realized, were the evidence of his own coarsened, actual self. For the pond itself, he discovered, was "the same water which my youthful eyes fell on," that "all the change," as he confessed, "is in me." The pond then was his own pristine, eternal self, and by cultivating beans, by discipline, he was changing the aspect of its shore, making it more agreeable to his imagination. If in his "decay" he lamented that the poet could not sing because his groves were cut down, he was heartened now because, he said, "one of the results of my presence and influence is seen in these bean leaves, corn blades, and potato vines."

That the pond was his real or essential self and the shore his actual self was made clear in "The Ponds." "It is no dream of mine," he said of Walden. "I cannot come nearer to God and Heaven / Than I live to Walden even. / I am its stony shore...." In a variant of this verse, he wrote: "It is a part of me which I have not profaned / I live by the shore of me detained." And he even punned on its name—"*Walled-in* Pond." In "The Ponds," however, he did not linger over his shores, but lovingly related all the details of the "crystal well" that he had once been made. There he described the remarkable purity, depth, and transparency of the pond, its coolness and constancy, the cerulean color that made it a "Sky water," the "earth's eye," the very window of the soul. It was the "distiller of celestial dews" whose seasonal tides and daily evaporations kept it pure; it was alive with the motion imparted by the "spirit" of the air, and its surface was "a perfect forest mirror," reflecting all phenomena perfectly as an untarnished mind should. Even its bottom was "pure sand," with only the sediment of fallen leaves (Thoreau's autumnal decay); "a bright green weed," the token of life, could be found growing there in winter; and its fish—its "ascetic fish"—were "cleaner, handsomer, and firmer." Having in his *Journal* thanked God for making "this pond deep and pure for a symbol," Thoreau accounted for its creation with a "myth" of the "old settler," the same old settler he had used to explain why he was not lonely in "Solitude" and was to refer to again in "Former Inhabitants; and Winter Visitors" to explain his notion of society. "That ancient settler [God] ... came here with his divining-rod [pun]," he wrote, "saw a thin vapor rising from the sward, and the hazel pointed steadily downward, and he concluded to dig a well here." Walden was "'God's Drop.'" He also gave it Edenic associations, describing its immemorial breaking up in the imagery of his first and second springs, making the rebirth this signified Adamic. Finally, having told of the ecstasy of his youth upon its waters, he likened it to himself; for it was "the work of a brave man," it lived "reserved and austere, like a hermit in the woods," and like his life, which he had "deepened and clarified," it was "too pure to have a market value." And yet he "bequeathed it to Concord," hoping that it would serve society as an example of "greater steadfastness," that "this vision of serenity and purity" would "wash out State-street and the engine's soot."

"The Ponds" was a summer chapter, the record of the time when he floated on the bosom of Nature and even in the darkest night communicated with her by fishing her mysterious depths. Now, fishing, he explained in "Higher Laws," was the proper vocation of the Golden Age; with hunting, it was "the young man's introduction to the forest, and the most original part of himself." Following the inevitable cycle of the seasons, however, this youthful pursuit was soon over: "He goes thither at first as a hunter and fisher, until at last, if he has the seeds of a better life in him, he distinguishes his proper objects, as a poet or naturalist it may be...." When unconscious communion was gone, showing him what his proper object was, the fisher angled instead (in "The Pond in Winter") for the pond itself, seeking the bottom or foundation "that will hold an anchor, that it may not drag."

But before this conscious exploration became necessary, Thoreau went afishing in the summer days. In "Baker Farm," he extolled the easy self-sufficiency of this uncommitted life in the wild and contrasted it with John Field's grubbing. Coming home with his string of fish, however, he turned to "Higher Laws," as if suddenly aware of the fact that in respect to diet at least he was as much in the larval condition as Field. Aware now that only discipline would help him continue his culture after manhood, that the instinct for the wild had been challenged by an instinct toward a higher or spiritual life, he repudiated his former mode of life and adopted the Oriental rituals of purification—bathing and diet and the conscious discipline of earnest labor. This resolution on purity, like the invocation to Hebe in "Solitude" and the martial vigilance of "The Bean-Field," betrayed an autumnal mood which Thoreau tried to dispel by the humorous dialogue that began "Brute Neighbors." There his going fishing was a breach of discipline that destroyed his "budding ecstasy"; but, having covered his loss by his self-protective humor, he nevertheless seriously explained the higher uses of Nature for which he was purifying himself. Nature, as Emerson said and as Thoreau first introduced this theme in "Sounds," was language. Thoreau's proper objects now were the correspondences of Nature; his brute neighbors were "beasts of burden ... made to carry some portion of our thoughts." The partridge, for example, suggested "not merely the purity of infancy, but a wisdom clarified by experience." And the loon, whose return marked the advent of autumn, carried the heavy burden of his personal lapse. Enacting the play of inspiration by chasing this deep-diving bird, Thoreau told the story of his decay: consciously trying to pursue it—"While he was thinking one thing in his brain, I was endeavoring to divine his thought in mine"—he was balked; and even his passivity would no longer help him. Always the loon, he said, raised its "demoniac" laugh "in derision of my efforts...." Finally, he wrote, the east wind came and "filled the whole air with misty rain, and I was impressed as if it were the prayer of the loon answered, and his god was angry with me...." Like the "tumultuous surface" of the pond, here were the signs that the serene communion of summer was over.

The chapters that followed—"House-Warming," "Former Inhabitants; and Winter Visitors," "Winter Animals," "The Pond in Winter"— recapitulated the themes of the summer chapters, taking up solitude, the resources of the natural scene, sounds, and the pond. With the change to the season of inwardness, however, the good had changed: now was the time of Thoreau's greatest solitude, a sleepy time when life was reduced to routine and staying alive was a problem, a time when he retreated to memory and held communion with the former inhabitants whose lives suggested the possibility of failure. Every image, from the pond whooping as it turned in its sleep to the fox "seeking expression" and "struggling for light," conveyed a sense of impoverishment and spiritual restlessness, and the need for bravery under duress. Now he longed for the "Visitor" who never came, and turned to the spiritual necessity of friendship, recalling those days when the faithful

Alcott had come and their discourse had summoned the "old settler" and "expanded and racked my little house...." But if "moral reform," as he said, "was the effort to throw off sleep," and "to be awake is to be alive," he found that, like the pond, he could not escape his dormant season. "Every winter," he observed, "the liquid and trembling surface of the pond, which was so sensitive to every breath, and reflected every light and shadow, becomes solid to the depth of a foot or a foot and a half.... it closes its eyelids and becomes dormant for three months or more.... After a cold and snowy night it needed a divining rod to find it."

In the midst of his winter of discontent, however, Thoreau began his intellectual search for faith. In "The Pond in Winter," he told of the question that he had tried to answer in his sleep, the question of "what-how-when-where?" which only dawning Nature, by her living presence, had answered for him. This awakening to life was the preparation for his rebirth, the beginning of the long process of conscious penetration to the law of the "spring of springs." This finally brought the rewards of "Spring," warranted his injunctions on self-exploration, and provided the testimony of his "Conclusion"—"Only that day dawns to which we are awake." Now his morning work was the "scientific" exploration of the bottom of the pond; for he "was desirous," he said, "to recover the long-lost bottom of Walden Pond," that "infinite" which its reputed bottomlessness suggested. In this survey he found that the fabulous pickerel (fish and fishing, as early as the *Week*, were symbols of thought and contemplation) still lived beneath the surface of the ice and that the "bright sanded floor" of the pond was "the same as in summer." And what was even more important for the foundation of his faith, he discovered and verified by accurate measurement the spiritual law of correspondences. The general regularity of the bottom—of the unseen—conformed to the shores: the correspondence was so perfect that "a distant promontory betrayed itself in the soundings quite across the pond, and its direction could be determined by observing the opposite shore." This universal law, which he applied to his own character, was also supported by the fact that "the line of greatest length intersected the line of greatest breadth exactly at the point of greatest depth...." By these soundings he renewed his faith in the transcendental method; and reading his own life correspondentially, he found that the disciplines of his outer life indicated the purity of his inner life. Though winter was the barren season, it brought the compensation of "concentration"; in the purity of the Walden ice he could see the symbol of his steadfastness. He could meet the priest of Brahma at his well—and the pure Walden water could mingle with the sacred water of the Ganges—because he had observed the purificatory disciplines, had bathed his "intellect in the stupendous and cosmogonal philosophy of the Bhagvat Geeta...."

At the bottom of the pond he also found the "bright green weed" that symbolized the everlasting life of organic Nature, the law of life to which even the frozen pond undulated in its sleep, to which it thundered "obedience ... as surely as the buds expand in the spring." Its booming, accordingly, was the sign of its awakening, a morning phenomenon, when, responding to the sun, it "stretched itself and yawned like a waking man...." It sounded the signal of spring, prefigured that irresistible thaw when "all things give way to the impulse of expression." Indeed, with the warmer weather, the snow and ice began to melt, the "circulations" began, and the blood of winter was purged. Once more Nature supplied her "vital heat" and, in the thawing clay of the railroad cut, gave way to the impulse of expression—to the impulse of life.

The most brilliant passage in "Spring," Thoreau's description of the thaw was a myth of creation as expression. This elaborate metaphor of the organic process that proceeds from the inside out, that creates and shapes by means of the Idea—the process of Nature, art, moral reform, and social reform—was also for Thoreau the metaphor of his purification and rebirth. Not only did the "bursting out" of the "insides of the earth" and the unfolding of "the piled-up history" of geology prove that there was nothing inorganic and that life provided fresh materials for the fictile arts of man, it showed that "Nature has some bowels, and ... is mother of humanity...." The frost coming out of the ground was Spring, a newly delivered child; and the flowing clay was an analogy of the development of the human body. The shapes and forms it took in its passage reminded him of "brains or lungs or bowels, and excrements of all kinds," but, as he explained this process in terms of "sand-foliage," the leaf-like character not only appeared in liver and lungs, but in feathers and wings. This evolution from excrementitious to aerial forms was a process of purification: "You pass from the lumpish grub in the earth," he wrote, "to the airy and fluttering butterfly. The very globe continually transcends and translates itself, and becomes winged in its orbit."

If the thawing made him feel that he was "nearer to the vitals of the globe," its leaf-like forms also reminded him that he was in the presence of "the Artist who made the world...." The Creator was still in his laboratory, "still at work, sporting on this bank, and with excess of energy strewing his fresh designs about." In this analogy to the creative process, the earth was laboring with "the idea inwardly" and expressing itself "outwardly in leaves...." For, as he had learned from Goethe, the leaf was the unit-form of all creation, the simplest form of which the most complex, even the world, was composed. "This one hill side illustrated the principle of all the operations of Nature," he explained. "The Maker of this earth but patented a leaf." This process, of course, not only applied to art, but to all reforming and shaping. It illustrated Emerson's belief that "Nature is not fixed but fluid. Spirit alters, moulds, makes it"—that not only poems and individual lives, but institutions were "plastic like clay in the hands of the potter." Hoeing beans, Thoreau had himself been a plastic artist making the earth—that granary of seeds—express itself in leaves; and of all the former inhabitants he had identified himself with Wyman the potter, whose fictile art pleased him. Moreover, unknown to his neighbors, he had practiced that fictile art himself—for himself and society. He was not the reformer, however, who broke things, but one whose method, like that of the thaw with its "gentle persuasion," melted things. By recasting his life he hoped that Nature again would try, with him "for a first settler." For he was a "Champollion," deciphering the hieroglyphics of Nature, that "we may turn over a new leaf at last."

As a symbol of ecstasy, however, the thaw, even with its remarkable suddenness, was spoiled by the intellectual purposes Thoreau made it serve. Whatever ecstasy the passage conveyed was intellectual rather than spontaneous or unconscious; it followed from his long observation of Nature, and it showed that he had with his intellect riven into the "secret of things." The faith he had earned by this conscious endeavor, however, was rewarded, at least in the pages of *Walden,* by his long-awaited ecstasy. This "memorable crisis"—"seemingly instantaneous at last"—came with the melting of the pond, when he saw its "bare face ... full of glee and youth, as if it spoke the joy of the fishes within it, and of the sands on its shore...." For in the sparkling water, he realized the contrast between winter and spring: "Walden was dead," he said, "and is alive again." The change he had awaited—"the change from storm and winter to serene and mild weather, from dark and sluggish hours to bright and elastic ones"—was at hand. "Suddenly," he wrote, "an influx of light filled my house, though the evening was at hand, and the clouds of winter still overhung it, and the eaves were dripping with sleety rain. I looked out of my window, and lo! where yesterday was cold gray ice there lay the transparent pond already calm and full of hope as in a summer evening, reflecting a summer sky in its bosom, though none was visible overhead, as if it had intelligence with some remote horizon. I heard a robin in the distance, the first I had heard for many a thousand years ... the same sweet and powerful song as of yore.... The pitch-pines and shrub-oaks about my house, which had so long drooped, suddenly resumed their several characters, looked brighter, greener, and more erect and alive, as if effectually cleansed and restored by the rain.... As it grew darker, I was startled by the *honking* of geese.... Standing at my door, I could hear the rush of their wings.... they suddenly spied my light, and with hushed clamor wheeled and settled in the pond. So I came in, and shut the door, and passed my first spring night in the woods."

With the coming of spring, with renewal and rebirth, had come "the creation of Cosmos out of Chaos and the realization of the Golden Age." Like Ovid, Thoreau was ready to tell of bodies changed by the gods into new forms, even glad, in the presence of this alchemy, to accept the life in Nature—served though it was by death—as the grand fact. Once again he lived in the eternal present, reborn to innocence, with an overwhelming sense of freedom, release, hope, and pardon. But even though he had regained the Golden Age before the fall of man, his metamorphosis took the form of the hawk rather than that of the butterfly; for having won his renewal by lonely heroism, he saw his transcendence in the soaring, solitary hawk, the bird he associated with nobleness and knightly courage. The hawk, he wrote in his *Journal*, soared so loftily and circled so steadily and without effort because it had "earned this power by faithfully creeping on the ground as a reptile in a former state of existence." It symbolized his ultimate liberation, the emancipation from the senses. At last, as he copied from *The Harivansa*, he was "free in this world, as birds in the air, disengaged from every kind of chain."

As the logic of his metaphors demanded, however, Thoreau closed his book with the fable of the beautiful bug that had come out of the dry leaf of an old apple-wood table. This fable, of course, recapitulated his themes: "Who knows what beautiful and winged life, whose egg has been buried for ages under many concentric layers of woodenness in the dead dry life of society, deposited at first in the alburnum of the green and living tree, which has been gradually converted into the semblance of its well-seasoned tomb ... may unexpectedly come forth from amidst society's most trivial and handselled furniture, to enjoy its perfect summer life at last!" This was the fable of organic renewal. But the fable of the creative enterprise that made it possible—the transparent parable of his own life and vocation—was that of the artist of the city of Kouroo. This artist, Thoreau wrote, "was disposed to strive after perfection." Determined to make a staff, he went to the woods to select the proper materials, rejecting stick after stick, until "his friends gradually deserted him...." In his striving, however, he lived in the eternal now of inspiration which made the passing of dynasties, even eras, an illusion. Finally, in fashioning his staff, merely by minding his destiny and his art, he discovered that he had "made a new system ... a world with full and fair proportions...." And because "the material was pure, and his art was pure," the result, Thoreau knew, could not be "other than wonderful." *Walden* was that staff, that fuller and fairer and supremely organic world, because it was, by Thoreau's own test of sincerity, the form and expression of the life he had lived in the desire to live. But it was also—for in it he had enacted the process of creating scripture—the kind of heroic book that was worthy of morning discipline, a book so true "to our condition" that reading it might date a new era in our lives.

HAROLD BLOOM

Whitman's Image of Voice:
To the Tally of My Soul

Where does the individual accent of an American poetry begin? How, then and now, do we recognize the distinctive voice that we associate with an American Muse? Bryant, addressing some admonitory lines, in 1830, *To Cole, the Painter, Departing for Europe*, has no doubts as to what marks the American difference:

> Fair scenes shall greet thee where thou goest—fair,
>> But different—everywhere the trace of men,
> To where life shrinks from the fierce Alpine air.
>> Gaze on them, till the tears shall dim thy sight,
>> But keep that earlier, wilder image bright.

Only the Sublime, from which life shrinks, constitutes a European escape from the trace of men. Cole will be moved by that Sublime, yet he is to keep vivid the image of priority, an American image of freedom, for which Emerson and Thoreau, like Bryant before them, will prefer the trope of "wildness." The wildness triumphs throughout Bryant, a superb poet, always and still undervalued, and one of Hart Crane's and Wallace Stevens's legitimate ancestors. The voice of an American poetry goes back before Bryant, and can be heard in Bradstreet and Freneau (not so much, I think, in Edward Taylor, who was a good English poet who happened to be living in

From *Agon: Towards a Theory of Revisionism.* © 1982 by Oxford University Press, Inc.

America). Perhaps, as with all origins, the American poetic voice cannot be traced, and so I move from my first to my second opening question: how to recognize the Muse of America. Here is Bryant, in the strong opening of his poem *The Prairies*, in 1833:

> These are the gardens of the Desert, these
> The unshorn fields, boundless and beautiful,
> For which the speech of England has no name—
> The Prairies. I behold them for the first
> And my heart swells, while the dilated sight
> Takes in the encircling vastness....

Bryant's ecstatic beholding has little to do with what he sees. His speech swells most fully as he intones "The Prairies," following on the prideful reflection that no English poet could name these grasslands. The reflection itself is a touch awkward, since the word after all is French, and not Amerindian, as Bryant knew. No matter; the beholding is still there, and truly the name is little more important than the sight. What is vital is the dilation of the sight, an encircling vastness more comprehensive even than the immensity being taken in, for it is only a New England hop, skip and a jump from this dilation to the most American passage that will ever be written, more American even than Huck Finn telling Aunt Polly that he lies just to keep in practice, or Ahab proclaiming that he would strike the sun if it insulted him. Reverently I march back to where I and the rest of us have been before and always must be again, crossing a bare common, in snow puddles, at twilight, under a clouded sky, in the company of our benign father, the Sage of Concord, teacher of that perfect exhilaration in which, with him, we are glad to the brink of fear:

> ... Standing on the bare ground,—my head bathed by the blithe
> air and uplifted into infinite space,—all mean egotism vanishes. I
> become a transparent eyeball; I am nothing; I see all; the currents
> of the Universal Being circulate through me; I am part or parcel
> of God....

Why is this ecstasy followed directly by the assertion: "The name of the nearest friend sounds then foreign and accidental ..."? Why does the dilation of vision to the outrageous point of becoming a transparent eyeball provoke a denaturing of even the nearest name? I hasten to enforce the obvious, which nevertheless is crucial: the name is not forgotten, but loses the sound of immediacy; it becomes foreign or out-of-doors, rather than domestic; and accidental, rather than essential. A step beyond this into the American Sublime, and you do not even forget the name; you never hear it at all:

> And now at last the highest truth on this subject remains unsaid; probably cannot be said; for all that we say is the far-off remembering of the intuition. That thought by what I can now nearest approach to say it, is this. When good is near you, when you have life in yourself, it is not by any known or accustomed way; you shall not discern the footprints of any other; you shall not see the face of man; you shall not hear any name;—the way, the thought, the good, shall be wholly strange and new....

"This subject" is self-reliance, and the highest truth on it would appear to be voiceless, except that Emerson's voice does speak out to tell us of the influx of the Newness, in which no footprints or faces are to be seen, and no name is to be heard. Unnaming always has been a major mode in poetry, far more than naming; perhaps there cannot be a poetic naming that is not founded upon an unnaming. I want to leap from these prose unnamings in Emerson, so problematic in their possibilities, to the poem in which, more than any other, I would seek to hear Emerson's proper voice for once in verse, a voice present triumphantly in so many hundreds of passages throughout his prose:

> Pour, Bacchus! the remembering wine;
> Retrieve the loss of me and mine!
> Vine for vine be antidote,
> And the grape requite the lote!
> Haste to cure the old despair,—
> Reason in Nature's lotus drenched,
> The memory of ages quenched;
> Give them again to shine;
> Let wine repair what this undid;
> And where the infection slid,
> A dazzling memory revive;
> Refresh the faded tints,
> Recut the aged prints,
> And write my old adventures with the pen
> Which on the first day drew,
> Upon the tablets blue,
> The dancing Pleiads and eternal men.

But why is Bacchus named here, if you shall not hear any name? My question would be wholly hilarious if we were to literalize Emerson's splendid chant. Visualize the Sage of Concord, gaunt and spare, uncorking a bottle in Dionysiac abandon, before emulating the Pleiads by breaking into a Nietzschean dance. No, the Bacchus of Ralph Waldo is rather clearly another unnaming. As for voice, it is palpably absent from this grand passage, its place taken up not even by writing, but by rewriting, by that revisionary pen which has priority, and which drew before the tablets darkened and grew small.

I am going to suggest shortly that rewriting is an invariable trope for voicing, within a poem, and that voicing and reseeing are much the same poetic process, a process reliant upon unnaming, which rhetorically means the undoing of a prior metonymy. But first I am going to leap ahead again, from Emerson to Stevens, which is to pass over the great impasse of Whitman, with whom I have identified always Hart Crane's great trope: "Oval encyclicals in canyons heaping / The impasse high with choir." Soon enough this discourse will center upon Whitman, since quite simply he is the American Sublime, he is voice in our poetry, he is our answer to the Continent now, precisely as he was a century ago. Yet I am sneaking up on him, always the best way for any critic to skulk near the Sublime Walt. His revisionism, of self as of others, is very subtle; his unnamings and his voices come out of the Great Deep. Stevens's are more transparent:

Throw away the lights, the definitions,
And say of what you see in the dark
That it is this or that it is that,
But do not use the rotted names.

*   *   *

Phoebus is dead, ephebe. But Phoebus was
A name for something that never could be named.
There was a project for the sun and is.

There is a project for the sun. The sun
Must bear no name, gold flourisher, but be
In the difficulty of what it is to be.

*   *   *

This is nothing until in a single man contained,
Nothing until this named thing nameless is
And is destroyed. He opens the door of his house

On flames. The scholar of one candle sees
An Arctic effulgence flaring on the frame
Of everything he is. And he feels afraid.

What have these three unnaming passages most in common? Well,
what are we doing when we give pet names to those we love, or give no
names to anyone at all, as when we go apart in order to go deep into
ourselves? Stevens's peculiar horror of the commonplace in names emerges
in his litany of bizarre, fabulistic persons and places, but though that
inventiveness works to break casual continuities, it has little in common with
the true break with continuity in poets like Lewis Carroll and Edward Lear.
Stevens, *pace* Hugh Kenner, is hardly the culmination of the poetics of Lear.
He may not be the culmination of Whitman's poetics either, since that begins
to seem the peculiar distinction of John Ashbery. But like Whitman, Stevens
does have a link to the Lucretian Sublime, as Pater the Epicurean did, and
such a Sublime demands a deeper break with commonplace continuities than
is required by the evasions of nonsense and fantasy. The most authentic of
literary Sublimes has the Epicurean purpose of rendering us discontented
with easier pleasures in order to prepare us for the ordeal of more difficult
pleasures. When Stevens unnames he follows, however unknowingly, the
trinity of negative wisdom represented by Emerson, Pater and Nietzsche.
Stevens himself acknowledged only Nietzsche, but the unfashionable
Emerson and Pater were even stronger in him, with Emerson (and
Whitman) repressedly the strongest of strains. Why not, after all, use the
rotted names? If the things were things that never could be named, is not one
name as bad anyway as another? Stevens's masterpiece is not named *The
Somethings of Autumn*, and not only because the heroic desperation of the
Emersonian scholar of one candle is not enough. Whether you call the
auroras flames or an Arctic effulgence or call them by the trope now stuck
into dictionaries, auroras, you are giving your momentary consent to one
arbitrary substitution or another. Hence Emerson's more drastic and Bacchic
ambition; write your *old* adventures, not just your new, with the Gnostic pen
of our forefather and foremother, the Abyss. I circle again the problematic
American desire to merge voicing and revisionism into a single entity, and
turn to Whitman for a central text, which will be the supposed elegy for
Lincoln, *When Lilacs Last in the Dooryard Bloom'd*. So drastic is the amalgam

of voicing, unnaming and revisionism here that I take as prelude first Whitman's little motto poem, *As Adam Early in the Morning*, so as to set some of the ways for approaching what is most problematic in the great elegy, its images of voice and of voicing.

What can we mean when we speak of the *voice* of the poet, or the voice of the critic? Is there a pragmatic sense of voice, in discussing poetry and criticism, that does not depend upon the illusions of metaphysics? When poetry and criticism speak of "images of voice," what is being imaged? I think I can answer these questions usefully in the context of my critical enterprise from *The Anxiety of Influence* on, but my answers rely upon a post-philosophical pragmatism which grounds itself upon what has worked to make up an American tradition. Voice in American poetry always necessarily must include Whitman's oratory, and here I quote from it where it is most economical and persuasive, a five-line poem that centers the canon of our American verse:

As Adam early in the morning,
Walking forth from the bower refresh'd with sleep,
Behold me where I pass, hear my voice, approach,
Touch me, touch the palm of your hand to my body as I pass,
Be not afraid of my body.

What shall we call this striding stance of the perpetually passing Walt, prophetic of Stevens's singing girl at Key West, and of Stevens's own Whitman walking along a ruddy shore, singing of death and day? Rhetorically the stance is wholly transumptive, introjecting earliness, but this is very unlike the Miltonic transuming of tradition. Walt is indeed Emerson's new Adam, American and Nietzschean, who can live as if it were morning, but though he is *as* the Biblical and Miltonic Adam, that "as" is one of Stevens's "intricate evasions of as." The Old Adam was not a savior, except in certain Gnostic traditions of Primal Man; the new, Whitmanian Adam indeed is Whitman himself, more like Christ than like Adam, and more like the Whitmanian Christ of Lawrence's *The Man Who Died* than like the Jesus of the Gospels.

Reading Whitman's little poem is necessarily an exercise both in a kind of repression and in a kind of introjection. To read the poem strongly, to voice its stance, is to transgress the supposed boundary between reading or criticism, and writing or poetry. "As" governs the three words of origins— "Adam," "early" and "morning"—and also the outgoing movement of Whitman, walking forth refreshed from a bower (that may be also a tomb), emerging from a sleep that may have been a kind of good death. Whitman placed this poem at the close of the *Children of Adam* division of *Leaves of Grass*, thus positioning it between the defeated American pathos of *Facing West from California's Shores* and the poignant *In Paths Untrodden* that begins the homoerotic *Calamus* section. There is a hint, in this contextualization, that the astonished reader needs to cross a threshold also. Behold Whitman as Adam; do not merely regard him when he is striding past. The injunctions build from that "behold" through "hear" and "approach" to "touch," a touch then particularized to the palm, as the resurrected Walt passes, no phantom, but a risen body. "Hear my voice" is the center. As Biblical trope, it invokes Jehovah walking in Eden in the cool of the day, but in Whitman's American context it acquires a local meaning also. Hear my voice, and not just my words; *hear me as voice*. Hear me, as in my elegy for President Lincoln, I hear the hermit thrush.

Though the great elegy finds its overt emblems in the lilac-bush and the evening star, its more crucial tropes substitute for those emblems. These figures are the sprig of lilac that Whitman places on the hearse and the song of the thrush that floods the western night. Ultimately these are one trope, one image of voice, which we can follow Whitman by calling the "tally," playing also on a secondary meaning of "tally," as double or agreement. "Tally" may be Whitman's most crucial trope or ultimate image of voice. As a word, it goes back to the Latin *talea* for twig or cutting, which appears in this poem as the sprig of lilac. The word meant originally a cutting or stick upon which notches are made so as to keep count or score, but first in the English and then in the American vernacular it inevitably took on the meaning of a sexual score. The slang words "tallywoman," meaning a lady in an illicit relationship, and "tallywhack" or "tallywags," for the male genitalia, are still in circulation. "Tally" had a peculiar, composite meaning for Whitman in his poetry, which has not been noted by his critics. In the odd, rather luridly impressive death-poem *Chanting the Square Deific*, an amazing blend of Emerson and an Americanized Hegel, Whitman identifies himself with Christ, Hermes and Hercules and then writes: "All sorrow, labor, suffering, I, tallying it, absorb it in myself." My comment would be: "Precisely *how* does he tally it?" and the answer to that question, grotesque as initially it must seem, would be: "Why, first by masturbating, and then by writing poems." I am being merely accurate, rather than outrageous, and so I turn to *Song of Myself*, section 25, as first proof-text:

Dazzling and tremendous how quick the sunrise would kill me,
If I could not now and always send sunrise out of me.

We also ascend dazzling and tremendous as the sun,
We found our own O my soul in the calm and cool of the
    daybreak.
My voice goes after what my eyes cannot reach,
With the twirl of my tongue I encompass worlds and volumes
    of worlds.

Speech is the twin of my vision, it is unequal to measure itself,
It provokes me forever, it says sarcastically,
Walt you contain enough, why don't you let it out then?

Come now I will not be tantalized, you conceive too
    much of articulation,
Do you not know O speech how the buds beneath you are folded?
Waiting in gloom, protected by frost,
The dirt receding before my prophetical screams,
I underlying causes to balance them at last,
My knowledge my live parts, it keeping tally with the
    meaning of all things,
Happiness, (which whoever hears me let him or her set out in
    search of this day.)

My final merit I refuse you, I refuse putting from me what I
    really am,
Encompass worlds, but never try to encompass me,
I crowd your sleekest and best by simply looking toward you.

Writing and talk do not prove me,
I carry the plenum of proof and every thing else in my face,
With the hush of my lips I wholly confound the skeptic.

At this, almost the mid-point of his greatest poem, Whitman is sliding knowingly near crisis, which will come upon him in the crossing between sections 27 and 28. But here he is too strong, really too strong, and soon will pay the price of that over-strength, according to the Emersonian iron Law of Compensation, that nothing is got for nothing. Against the sun's mocking taunt: "See then whether you shall be master!" Whitman sends forth his own sunrise, which is a better, a more Emersonian answer than what Melville's Ahab threatens when he cries out, with surpassing Promethean eloquence: "I'd strike the sun if it insulted me!" As an alternative dawn, Whitman crucially identifies himself as a voice, a voice overflowing with presence, a presence that is a sexual self-knowledge: "My knowledge my live parts, it keeping tally with the meaning of all things." His knowledge and sexuality are one, and we need to ask: how does that sexual self-knowing keep tally with the meaning of all things? The answer comes in the crisis sequence of sections 26–30, where Whitman starts with listening and then regresses to touch, until he achieves both orgasm and poetic release through a Sublime yet quite literal masturbation. The sequence begins conventionally enough with bird song and human voice, passes to music, and suddenly becomes very extraordinary, in a passage critics have admired greatly but have been unable to expound:

> The orchestra whirls me wider than Uranus flies,
> It wrenches such ardors from me I did not know I possess'd them,
> It sails me, I dab with bare feet, they are lick'd by the indolent
>   waves,
> I am cut by bitter and angry hail, I lose my breath,
> Steep'd amid honey'd morphine, my windpipe throttled in fakes
>   of death,
> At length let up again to feel the puzzle of puzzles,
> And that we call Being.

This Sublime antithetical flight (or repression) not only takes Whitman out of nature, but makes him a new kind of god, ever-dying and ever-living, a god whose touchstone is of course voice. The ardors wrenched from him are operatic, and the cosmos becomes stage machinery, a context in which the whirling bard first loses his breath to the envious hail, then sleeps a drugged illusory death in uncharacteristic silence, and at last is let up again to sustain the enigma of Being. For this hero of voice, we expect now a triumphant ordeal by voice, but surprisingly we get an equivocal ordeal by sexual self-touching. Yet the substitution is only rhetorical, and establishes the model for the tally in the Lincoln elegy, since the sprig of lilac will represent Whitman's live parts, and the voice of the bird will represent those ardors so intense, so wrenched from Whitman, that he did not know he possessed them.

After praising his own sensitivity of touch, Whitman concludes section 27 with the highly equivocal line: "To touch my person to some one else's is about as much as I can stand." The crisis section proper, 28, centers upon demonstrating that to touch his own person is also about as much as Whitman can stand. By the time he cries out: "I went myself first to the headland, my own hands carried me there," we can understand how the whole 1855 *Song of Myself* may have grown out of an early notebook jotting on the image of the headland, a threshold stage between self-excitation and orgasm. Section 28 ends with frankly portrayed release:

> You villain touch! what are you doing? my breath is tight in its
>   throat,
> Unclench your floodgates, you are too much for me.

The return of the image of breath and throat, of voice, is no surprise, nor will the attentive reader be startled when the lines starting section 29 take a rather more affectionate view of touch, now that the quondam villain has performed his labor:

> Blind loving wrestling touch, sheath'd hooded sharp-tooth'd
>   touch!
> Did it make you ache so, leaving me?

Since Whitman's "rich showering rain" fructifies into a golden, masculine landscape, we can call this sequence of *Song of Myself* the most productive masturbation since the ancient Egyptian myth of a god who masturbates the world into being. I suggest now (and no Whitman scholar will welcome it) that a failed masturbation is the concealed reference in section 2 of the Lilacs elegy:

> O powerful western fallen star!
> O shades of night—O moody, tearful night!
> O great star disappear'd—O the black murk that hides the star!
> O cruel hands that hold me powerless—O helpless soul of me!
> O harsh surrounding cloud that will not free my soul.

The cruel hands are Whitman's own, as he vainly seeks relief from his repressed guilt, since the death of Father Abraham has rekindled the death, a decade before, of the drunken Quaker carpenter-father, Walter Whitman, Senior. Freud remarks, in *Mourning and Melancholia*, that

> ... there is more in the content of melancholia than in that of normal grief. In melancholia the relation to the object is no simple one; it is complicated by the conflict of ambivalence. This

latter is either constitutional, i.e. it is an element of every love-relation formed by this particular ego, or else it proceeds from precisely those experiences that involved a threat of losing the object.... Constitutional ambivalence belongs by nature to what is repressed, while traumatic experiences with the object may have stirred to activity something else that has been repressed. Thus everything to do with these conflicts of ambivalence remains excluded from consciousness, until the outcome characteristic of melancholia sets in. This, as we know, consists in the libidinal cathexis that is being menaced at last abandoning the object, only, however, to resume its occupation of that place in the ego whence it came. So by taking flight into the ego love escapes annihilation....

Both conflicts of ambivalence are Whitman's in the Lilacs elegy, and we will see love fleeing into Whitman's image of voice, the bird's tallying chant, which is the last stance of his ego. Freud's ultimate vision of primal ambivalence emphasized its origin as being the dialectical fusion/defusion of the two drives, love and death. Whitman seems to me profounder even than Freud as a student of the interlocking of these antithetical drives that darkly combine into one Eros and its shadow of ruin, to appropriate a phrase from Shelley. Whitman mourns Lincoln, yes, but pragmatically he mourns even more intensely for the tally, the image of voice he cannot as yet rekindle into being, concealed as it is by a "harsh surrounding cloud" of impotence. The miraculous juxtaposition of the two images of the tally, sprig of lilac and song of the hermit thrush, in sections 3 and 4 following, points the possible path out of Whitman's death-in-life:

> 3
> In the dooryard fronting an old farm-house near the white-
>   wash'd palings,
> Stands the lilac-bush tall-growing with heart-shaped leaves
>   of rich green,
> With many a pointed blossom rising delicate, with the perfume
>   strong I love,
> With every leaf a miracle—and from this bush in the dooryard,
> With delicate-color'd blossoms and heart-shaped leaves of rich
>   green,
> A sprig with its flower I break.

4

In the swamp in secluded recesses,
A shy and hidden bird is warbling a song.

Solitary the thrush,
The hermit withdrawn to himself, avoiding the settlements,
Sings by himself a song.

Song of the bleeding throat,
Death's outlet song of life, (for well dear brother I know,
If thou wast not granted to sing thou would'st surely die.)

Whitman breaks the *talea*, in a context that initially suggests a ritual of castration, but the image offers more than a voluntary surrender of manhood. The broken lilac sprig is exactly analogous to the "song of the bleeding throat," and indeed the analogy explains the otherwise baffling "bleeding." For what has torn the thrush's throat? The solitary song itself, image of wounded voice, is the other *talea*, and has been broken so that the soul can take count of itself. Yet why must these images of voice be broken? Whitman's answer, a little further on in the poem, evades the "why" much as he evades the child's "What is the grass?" in *Song of Myself* 6, for the *why* like the *what* is unknowable in the context of the Epicurean-Lucretian metaphysics that Whitman accepted. Whitman's answer comes in the hyperbolic, daemonic, repressive force of his copious over-breaking of the tallies:

Here, coffin that slowly passes,
I give you my sprig of lilac.

7

(Nor for you, for one alone,
Blossoms and branches green to coffins all I bring,
For fresh as the morning, thus would I chant a song for you
        O sane and sacred death.

All over bouquets of roses,
O death, I cover you over with roses and early lilies,
But mostly and now the lilac that blooms the first,
Copious I break, I break the sprigs from the bushes,
With loaded arms I come, pouring for you,

For you and the coffins all of you O death.)

Why should we be moved that Whitman intones: "O sane and sacred death," rather than: "O insane and obscene death," which might seem to be more humanly accurate? "Death" here is a trope for the sane and sacred Father Abraham, rather than for the actual father. Whitman's profuse breaking of the tallies attempts to extend this trope, so as to make of death itself an ultimate image of voice or tally of the soul. It is the tally and not literal death, our death, that is sane and sacred. But that returns us to the figuration of the tally, which first appears in the poem as a verb, just before the carol of death:

And the charm of the carol rapt me,
As I held as if by their hands my comrades in the night,
And the voice of my spirit tallied the song of the bird.

"My knowledge my live parts, it keeping tally with the meaning of all things" now transfers its knowledge from the vital order to the death-drive. I am reminded that I first became aware of Whitman's crucial trope by pondering its remarkable use by Hart Crane, when he invokes Whitman directly in the "Cape Hatteras" section of *The Bridge*:

O Walt!—Ascensions of thee hover in me now
As thou at junctions elegiac, there, of speed,
With vast eternity, dost wield the rebound seed!
The competent loam, the probable grass,—travail
Of tides awash the pedestal of Everest, fail
Not less than thou in pure impulse inbred
To answer deepest soundings! O, upward from the dead
Thou bringest tally, and a pact, new bound
Of living brotherhood!

Crane's allusion is certainly to the *Lilacs* elegy, but his interpretation of what it means to bring tally "upward from the dead" may idealize rather too generously. That Walt's characteristic movement is ascension cannot be doubted, but the operative word in this elegy is "passing." The coffin of the martyred leader passes first, but in the sixteenth and final section it is the bard who passes, still tallying both the song of the bird and his own soul. That the tally is crucial, Crane was more than justified in emphasizing, but then Crane was a great reader as well as a great writer of poetry. Flanking the famous carol of death are two lines of the tally: "And the voice of my spirit tallied the song of the bird" preceding, and "To the tally of my soul" following. To tally the hermit thrush's carol of death is to tally the soul, for what is measured is the degree of sublimity, the agonistic answer to the triple question: more? less? equal? And the Sublime answer in death's carol is surely "more"

> Come lovely and soothing death,
> Undulate round the world, serenely arriving, arriving,
> In the day, in the night, to all, to each,
> Sooner or later delicate death.
>
> Prais'd be the fathomless universe,
> For life and joy, and for objects and knowledge curious,
> And for love, sweet love—but praise! praise! praise!
> For the sure-enwinding arms of cool-enfolding death.
>
> Dark mother always gliding near with soft feet,
> Have none chanted for thee a chant of fullest welcome?
> Then I chant it for thee, I glorify thee above all,
> I bring thee a song that when thou must indeed come, come unfalteringly.
>
> Approach strong deliveress,
> When it is so, when thou hast taken them I joyously sing the dead,
> Lost in the loving floating ocean of thee,
> Laved in the flood of thy bliss O death.

If this grand carol, as magnificent as the Song of Songs which is Solomon's, constitutes the tally or image of voice of the soul, then we ought now to be able to describe that image. To tally, in Whitman's sense, is at once to measure the soul's actual and potential sublimity, to overcome object-loss and grief, to gratify one's self sexually by one's self, to compose the thousand songs at random of *Leaves of Grass*, but above all, as Crane said, to bring a new covenant of brotherhood, and, here that pact is new bound with the voice of the hermit thrush: The bird's carol, which invokes the oceanic mother of Whitman's *Sea Drift* cosmos, is clearly not its tally but Whitman's own, the transgressive verbal climax of his own family romance. When, in the elegy's final section, Whitman chants himself as "Passing the song of the hermit bird and the tallying song of my soul," he prepares himself and us for his abandonment of the image of the lilac. And, in doing so, he prepares us also for his overwhelming refusal or inability to yield up similarly the darker image of the tally:

> Yet each to keep and all, retrievements out of the night,
> The song, the wondrous chant of the gray-brown bird,
> And the tallying chant, the echo arous'd in my soul....

The tally is an echo, as an image of voice must be, yet truly it does not echo the carol of the hermit thrush. Rather, it echoes the earlier Whitman, of *Out of the Cradle Endlessly Rocking*, and his literary father, the Emerson of the great *Essays*. But here I require an *excursus* into poetic theory in order to explain image of voice and its relation to echo and allusion, and rather than rely upon as recondite a theorist as myself, I turn instead to a great explainer, John Hollander, who seems to me our outstanding authority upon all matters of lyrical form. Here is Hollander upon images of voice and their relation to the figurative interplay I have called "transumption," since that is what I take "tally" to be: Whitman's greatest transumption or introjection or Crossing of Identification, his magnificent overcoming both of his own earlier images of poetic origins and of Emerson's story of how poetry comes into being, particularly American poetry. First Hollander, from his forthcoming book, *The Figure of Echo*:

> ... we deal with diachronic trope all the time, and yet we have no name for it as a class.... the echoing itself makes a figure, and the interpretive or revisionary power which raises the echo even louder than the original voice is that of a trope of diachrony....
>
> I propose that we apply the name of the classical rhetoricians' trope of *transumption* (or *metalepsis* in its Greek form) to these diachronic, allusive figures....
>
> Proper reading of a metaphor demands a simultaneous appreciation of the beauty of a vehicle and the importance of its freight.... But the interpretation of a metalepsis entails the recovery of the transumed material. A transumptive style is to be distinguished radically from the kind of conceited one which we usually associate with baroque poetic, and with English seventeenth-century verse in particular. It involves an ellipsis, rather than a relentless pursuit, of further figuration....

Hollander then names transumption as the proper figure for

interpretive allusion, to which I would add only the description that I gave before in *A Map of Misreading*: this is the trope-undoing trope, which seeks to reverse imagistic priorities. Milton crowds all his poetic precursors together into the space that intervenes between *himself and the truth*. Whitman also crowds poetic anteriority—Emerson and the Whitman of 1855–1860—into a little space between the carol of death and the echo aroused in the soul of the elegist of *Lilacs*. Emerson had excluded the questions of sex and death from his own images-of-voice, whether in a verse chant like *Bacchus* or a prose rhapsody like *The Poet*. The earlier Whitman had made of the deathly ocean at night his maternal image of voice, and we have heard the hermit thrush in its culmination of that erotic cry. Whitman's tally transumes the ocean's image of voice, by means of what Hollander calls an ellipsis of further figuration. The tally notches a restored Narcissism and the return to the mode of erotic self-sufficiency. The cost is high as it always is in transumption. What vanishes here in Whitman is the presence of others and of otherness, as object-libido is converted into ego-libido again. Father Abraham, the ocean as dark mother, the love of comrades, and even the daemonic *alter ego* of the hermit thrush all fade away together. But what is left is the authentic American image of voice, as the bard brings tally, alone there in the night among the fragrant pines except for his remaining comrades, the knowledge of death and the thought of death.

In 1934 Wallace Stevens, celebrating his emergence from a decade's poetic silence, boldly attempted a very different transumption of the Whitmanian images of voice:

> It was her voice that made
> The sky acutest at its vanishing.
> She measured to the hour its solitude.
> She was the single artificer of the world
> In which she sang....

The tally, in *The Idea of Order at Key West*, becomes the "ghostlier demarcations, keener sounds" ending the poem. A year later, Stevens granted himself a vision of Whitman as sunset in our evening land:

> In the far South the sun of autumn is passing
> Like Walt Whitman walking along a ruddy shore.
> He is singing and chanting the things that are part of him,
> The worlds that were and will be, death and day.
> Nothing is final, he chants. No man shall see the end.
> His beard is of fire and his staff is a leaping flame.

It is certainly the passing bard of the end of *Lilacs*, but did he chant that nothing is final? Still, this is Walt as Moses and as Aaron, leading the poetic children of Emerson through the American wilderness, and surely Whitman was always proudly provisional. Yet, the tally of his soul had to present itself as a finality, as an image of voice that had achieved a fresh priority and a perpetually ongoing strength. Was that an American Sublime, or only another American irony? Later in 1935, Stevens wrote a grim little poem called *The American Sublime* that seems to qualify severely his intense images of voice, of the singing girl and of Whitman:

> But how does one feel?
> One grows used to the weather,
> The landscape and that;
> And the sublime comes down To the spirit itself,
>
> The spirit and space,
> The empty spirit
> In vacant space.
> What wine does one drink?
> What bread does one eat?

The questions return us full circle to Emerson's *Bacchus*, nearly a century before:

> We buy ashes for bread;
> We buy diluted wine....

This is not transumptive allusion, but a repetition of figurations, the American baroque defeat. But that is a secondary strain in Stevens, as it was in Emerson and in Whitman. I leap ahead, past Frost and Pound, Eliot and Williams, past even Hart Crane, to conclude with a contemporary image-of-voice that is another strong tally, however ruefully the strength regards itself. Here is John Ashbery's *The Other Tradition*, the second poem in his 1977 volume, *Houseboat Days*:

> They all came, some wore sentiments
> Emblazoned on T-shirts, proclaiming the lateness
> Of the hour, and indeed the sun slanted its rays
> Through branches of Norfolk Island pine as though
> Politely clearing its throat, and all ideas settled

In a fuzz of dust under trees when it's drizzling:
The endless games of Scrabble, the boosters,
The celebrated omelette au Cantal, and through it
The roar of time plunging unchecked through the sluices
Of the days, dragging every sexual moment of it
Past the lenses: the end of something.
Only then did you glance up from your book,
Unable to comprehend what had been taking place, or
Say what you had been reading. More chairs
Were brought, and lamps were lit, but it tells
Nothing of how all this proceeded to materialize
Before you and the people waiting outside and in the next
Street, repeating its name over and over, until silence
Moved halfway up the darkened trunks,
And the meeting was called to order.

                         I still remember
How they found you, after a dream, in your thimble hat,
Studious as a butterfly in a parking lot.
The road home was nicer then. Dispersing, each of the
Troubadours had something to say about how charity
Had run its race and won, leaving you the ex-president
Of the event, and how, though many of these present
Had wished something to come of it, if only a distant
Wisp of smoke, yet none was so deceived as to hanker
After that cool non-being of just a few minutes before,
Now that the idea of a forest had clamped itself
Over the minutiae of the scene. You found this
Charming, but turned your face fully toward night,
Speaking into it like a megaphone, not hearing
Or caring, although these still live and are generous
And all ways contained, allowed to come and go
Indefinitely in and out of the stockade
They have so much trouble remembering, when your forgetting
Rescues them at last, as a star absorbs the night.

I am aware that this charming poem urbanely confronts, absorbs and in some sense seeks to overthrow a critical theory, almost a critical climate, that has accorded it a canonical status. Stevens's Whitman proclaims that nothing is final and that no man shall see the end. Ashbery, a Whitman somehow more studiously casual even than Whitman, regards the prophets of belatedness and cheerfully insists that his forgetting or repression will rescue us at last, even as the Whitmanian or Stevensian evening star absorbs the night. But the price paid for this metaleptic reversal of American belatedness into a fresh earliness is the yielding up of Ashbery's tally or image of voice to a deliberate grotesquerie. Sexuality is made totally subservient to time, which is indeed "the end of something," and poetic tradition becomes an ill-organized social meeting of troubadours, leaving the canonical Ashbery as "ex-president / Of the event." As for the image of voice proper, the Whitmanian confrontation of the night now declines into: "You found this / Charming, but turned your face fully toward night, / Speaking into it like a megaphone, not hearing / Or caring." Such a megaphone is an apt image for Paul de Man's deconstructionist view of poetic tradition, which undoes tradition by suggesting that every poem is as much a random and gratuitous event as any human death is.

Ashbery's implicit interpretation of what he wants to call *The Other Tradition* mediates between this vision of poems as being totally cut off from one another and the antithetical darkness in which poems carry over-determined relationships and progress towards a final entropy. Voice in our poetry now tallies what Ashbery in his *Syringa*, a major Orphic elegy in *Houseboat Days*, calls "a record of pebbles along the way." Let us grant that the American Sublime is always also an American irony, and then turn back to Emerson and hear the voice that is great within us somehow breaking through again. This is Emerson in his journal for August 1859, on the eve of being burned out, with all his true achievement well behind him; but he gives us the true tally of his soul

> *Beatitudes of Intellect.*—Am I not, one of these days, to write consecutively of the beatitude of intellect? It is too great for feeble souls, and they are over-excited. The wineglass shakes, and the wine is spilled. What then? The joy which will not let me sit in my chair, which brings me bolt upright to my feet, and sends me striding around my room, like a tiger in his cage, and I cannot have composure and concentration enough even to set down in English words the thought which thrills me—is not that joy a certificate of the elevation? What if I never write a book or a line? for a moment, the eyes of my eyes were opened, the affirmative experience remains, and consoles through all suffering.

BARBARA PACKER

The Curse of Kehama

How shall we face the edge of time? We walk
In the park. We regret we have no nightingale.
We must have the throstle on the gramophone.
Where shall we find more than derisive words?
When shall lush chorals spiral through our fire
And daunt that old assassin, heart's desire?
                    —Wallace Stevens, "A Duck for Dinner"

"EXPERIENCE"

Emerson's final version of the Fall story is his shortest and most epigrammatic. It is remarkable not so much for its content as for its tone, and the startling nature of the "facts" it is invented to explain. The voice we hear in "Experience" has neither the rhapsodic intensity of the Orphic chants, nor the chill impersonality of the axis-of-vision formula, nor the militancy of "The Protest" or "Circles." It is instead the voice of a man of the world: urbane, rueful, a little weary. "It is very unhappy, but too late to be helped, the discovery we have made that we exist. That discovery is called the Fall of Man."

Equating self-consciousness with the Fall is of course one of the commonest Romantic ways of allegorizing the story of Genesis. And the myth of ossification, with its insistence that the conscious intellect was the

From *Emerson's Fall:* 148–179. © 1982 by B. L. Packer.

enemy of that central power accessible only by surprise or abandonment, may be regarded as containing or at least implying this final myth (which we may call the myth of *reflection*).

But this new version differs from its predecessors in two significant respects. It is considerably more pessimistic in its implications (there is no suggestion that the catastrophe of self-consciousness is either potentially or temporarily reversible), and the evidence adduced to support it is more shocking, in its quiet way, than anything Emerson had ever written. In *Nature* he had based his argument for the original divinity of the Self on its surviving capacity for ecstasy; in "Circles," on its refusal to accept limitation. In "Experience" what is taken as proof of the "ill-concealed Deity" of the Self is neither its joy nor its zeal but simply its ruthlessness:

> There are moods in which we court suffering, in the hope that here at least we shall find reality, sharp peaks and edges of truth. But it turns out to be scene-painting and counterfeit. The only thing grief has taught me, is to know how shallow it is. That, like all the rest, plays about the surface, and never introduces me into the reality, for contact with which we would even pay the costly price of sons and lovers.

> We believe in ourselves as we do not believe in others. We permit all things to ourselves, and that which we call sin in others is experiment for us. It is an instance of our faith in ourself that men never speak of crime as lightly as they think; or that every man thinks a latitude safe for himself which is nowise to be indulged to another.... No man at last believes that he can be lost, or that the crime in him is as black as in the felon.

Emerson had once wanted to write a book like the Proverbs of Solomon; "Experience" sounds more like the *Maxims* of La Rochefoucauld.

The necessary ruthlessness of the Self had been a corollary of the doctrine of self-reliance from the beginning, of course; it is implicit in Emerson's exhortation to "shun father and mother and wife and brother" when genius calls, even if it causes them pain. And it is avowed even more frankly in "Circles," where Emerson argues that "men cease to interest us when we find their limitations. The only sin is limitation. As soon as you once come up with a man's limitations, it is all over with him." As individuals, we are always in the position of the disappointed child in "Experience" who asks his mother why the story he enjoyed yesterday fails to please him as much the second time around. And the only answer Emerson can give us is the one he offers the child: "will it answer thy question to say, Because thou wert born to a whole and this story is a particular?" This information is hardly an unmixed blessing. If our hunger for "sphericity" is on the one hand the only defense we have against the soul's tendency to ossification, it is on the other hand the restlessness that "ruins the kingdom of mortal friendship and of love."

Emerson's deliberate emphasis in essays like "Circles" and "Experience" on the ruthlessness and secret cruelty of the Self shocks us, and is meant to. It is not merely (as Firkins guesses) "that a parade of hardness may have seemed to him a wholesome counterpoise to the fashionable parade of sensibility,"[1] though that was doubtless an added attraction. Emerson says these unpleasant things chiefly because he thinks they are true. Of course it would be easier for us and for society as a whole if they were not true, if there were some way of living without the ruinous ferocity of desire, which never ceases to torment us in thought, even if our outward behavior is decorous. Our mortal condition would be easier to endure if the divine Providence had *not* "shown the heaven and earth to every child and filled him with a desire for the whole; a desire raging, infinite; a hunger, as of space to be filled with planets; a cry of famine, as of devils for souls"—as Emerson puts it in a memorable passage in "Montaigne." That desire sends us off on a perpetual quest through the world of experience, and at the same time foredooms the quest to failure, since each particular satisfaction can only frustrate a being whose desire is for the whole. As questers, we are partly like Tennyson's Ulysses—

> .... all experience is an arch wherethrough
> Gleams that untravelled world whose margin fades
> For ever and for ever when I move ... [2]

but even more like Tennyson's Percivale—

> "Lo, if I find the Holy Grail itself
> And touch it, it will crumble into dust."[3]

Romance—the glamour or beauty that could transmute life's baser metals into gold—is always somewhere else, somewhere just beyond our grasp. "Every ship is a romantic object, except that we sail in. Embark, and the romance quits our vessel and hangs on every other sail in the horizon." Or, as he had put it in the. earlier essay "Love": "each man sees his own life defaced and disfigured, as the life of man is not, to his imagination."

Sensible people, hearing these confessions of frustration and despair, counsel renunciation of the Self's imperial ambitions. But Emerson denies that any permanent renunciation is possible. For one thing, that glimpse of the whole we were granted as children survives in adult life as more than a memory. Just when we have, as we think, managed to adjust our desires to reality, the old vision reappears to tantalize us:

> How easily, if fate would suffer it, we might keep forever these beautiful limits, and adjust ourselves, once for all, to the perfect calculation of known cause and effect.... But ah! presently comes a day, or is it only a half-hour, with its angel-whispering,—which discomfits the conclusions of notions and years!

And this reminder, while it distresses us, calls to our attention something we cannot safely ignore. The desire that torments us is also the only "capital stock" we have to invest in the actions and relationships of life. The man who tried to conduct his business on the principles of common sense alone "would quickly be bankrupt. Power keeps quite another road than the turnpikes of choice and will; namely the subterranean and invisible tunnels and channels of life."

These meditations on power and ruthlessness are an important part of the essay "Experience." They constitute a sort of ground bass heard at intervals beneath the constantly varying melodies of the essay, and contribute not a little to the impression of toughness it makes on the reader's mind. Yet toughness is hardly the essay's most significant characteristic. What is strikingly new about "Experience" is the voice that is heard in its opening paragraph, a voice neither powerful nor ruthless, but instead full of bewilderment, exhaustion, and despair:

> Where do we find ourselves? In a series of which we do not know the extremes, and believe that it has none. We wake and find ourselves on a stair; there are stairs below us, which we seem to have ascended; there are stairs above us, many a one, which go upward and out of sight. But the Genius which according to the old belief stands at the door by which we enter, and gives us the lethe to drink, that we may tell no tales, mixed the cup too strongly, and we cannot shake off the lethargy now at noonday. Sleep lingers all our lifetime about our eyes, as night hovers all

day in the boughs of the fir-tree. All things swim and glitter. Our life is not so much threatened as our perception. Ghostlike we glide through nature, and should not know our place again.

When Dr. Beard, in his *American Nervousness*, wanted a phrase that would convey to a popular audience an accurate sense of the new disease he had identified and named *neurasthenia*, he instinctively chose a metaphor Emerson would have admired: "nervous bankruptcy."[4] In the peculiar lassitude of the prose here—so different from the militant assertiveness of "Circles" or "Self-Reliance"—Emerson has managed to create a stylistic correlative to the "Feeling of Profound Exhaustion" Dr. Beard found characteristic of the nervously bankrupt.[5] Insufficiency of vital force is in fact Emerson's chief complaint in this opening passage.

> Did our birth fall in some fit of indigence and frugality in nature, that she was so sparing of her fire and so liberal of her earth that it appears to us that we lack the affirmative principle, and though we have health and reason, yet we have no superfluity of spirit for new creation? We have enough to live and bring the year about, but not an ounce to impart or invest. Ah that our Genius were a little more of a genius! We are like the millers on the lower levels of a stream, when the factories above them have exhausted the water. We too fancy that the upper people have raised their dams.

No reader of Emerson's journals can be unfamiliar with the mood described here. Recurrent laments over want of stamina and of animal spirits, over feelings of exhaustion and despair, punctuate the earliest notebooks. "I have often found cause to complain that my thoughts have an ebb & flow," he noted in one of them. "The worst is, that the ebb is certain, long, & frequent, while the flow comes transiently & seldom." A few pages earlier, a pious composition intended as a meditation "Upon Men's Apathy to their Eternal interests" turns into a meditation upon apathy of a more personal sort—a meditation whose systematic hopelessness, coming from a youth of nineteen, almost raises a smile:

> In the pageant of life, Time & Necessity are the stern masters of ceremonies who admit no distinctions among the vast train of aspirants.... And though the appetite of youth for marvels & beauty is fain to draw deep & strong lines of contrast between one & another character we early learn to distrust them & to

acquiesce in the unflattering & hopeless picture which Experience exhibits.

This grim lesson Emerson hastens to apply to his own disappointing life:

> We dreamed of great results from peculiar features of Character. We thought that the overflowing benevolence of our youth was pregnant with kind consequences to the world; that the agreeable qualities in the boy of courage, activity, intelligence, & good temper would prove in the man Virtues of extensive & remarkable practical effect.

The passage is revealing; it provides a glimpse of what Emerson's boyhood ambition had really been—not to become a reclusive scholar and occasional lecturer, but to be a public figure, an eloquent mover of men, like his hero Daniel Webster. The disinterest of his elders in his visionary schemes of regeneration had not dampened his personal ambitions; if anything, it had increased them. "The momentary ardour of childhood found that manhood & age were too cold to sympathise with it, & too hastily inferred that its own merit was solitary & unrivalled & would by and by blaze up, & make an era in Society." But this childhood ardor, like Wordsworth's "visionary gleam," eventually died away of its own accord:

> Alas. As it grew older it also grew colder & when it reached the period of manhood & of age it found that the waters of time, as they rolled had extinguished the fire that once glowed & there was no partial exemption for itself. The course of years rolls an unwelcome wisdom with them which forcibly teaches the vanity of human expectations.

And he concludes: "The dreams of my childhood are all fading away & giving place to some very sober & very disgusting views of a quiet mediocrity of talents & condition."

The intellectual revolution of the early 1830s—the discovery of the God within—liberated Emerson from the hopelessness that had oppressed his young manhood, but it could not do much for his stamina. He circumvented the limitations of his constitution by carefully husbanding his time and strength, and he learned to make the best of his alarming "*periods of mentality*" ("one day I am a doctor, & the next I am a dunce") by means of the unique method of composition he had already perfected by the mid-thirties. He spent his mornings barricaded in his study, writing isolated paragraphs in his journal when the spirit was upon him. When a longer composition was needed—a sermon or a lecture—he quarried in these journals for material and, as Chapman says, "threw together what seemed to have a bearing on some subject, and gave it a title." Chapman adds, correctly, I think, that what keeps this method from resulting in an "incomprehensible chaos" is Emerson's single-mindedness:

> There was only one thought which could set him aflame, and that was the unfathomed might of man. This thought was his religion, his politics, his ethics, his philosophy. One moment of inspiration was in him own brother to the next moment of inspiration, although they might be separated by six weeks.[6]

What keeps this procedure from resulting in monotony for the reader, is first, the sheer power and felicity of Emerson's prose; next, the perpetual surprise of his observations (who else would have thought of comparing readers at the Boston Athenaeum to flies, aphids, and sucking infants?); and finally, his unflinching honesty, which will not let him rest until he has subjected his claim for the unfathomed might of man to every shred of negative evidence that can reasonably be urged against it. The combination of his single-mindedness and his insistence upon recognizing all the "opposite negations between which, as walls, his being is swung" is responsible for the curious fact about his work noticed long ago by Firkins. "Emerson's wish to get his whole philosophy into each essay tended toward sameness and promiscuity at once; it made the *essays similar* and the *paragraphs diverse*."[7] (It is also responsible for the fact that while his paragraphs are extraordinarily easy to remember word for word, they can be almost impossible to locate. Anything can be anyplace. The most time-consuming feature of being a student of Emerson is the necessity it places one under of repeatedly rereading half the collected *Works* and *Journals* in the maddening pursuit of some paragraph one can remember but not find.)

But his habits of composition, though they enabled him to produce a body of written work that would be remarkable enough for even a vigorous man, probably contributed to his sense of the unbridgeable gap between the life of the soul and the life of the senses, between the Reason and the Understanding. His ecstasies were carefully reserved for his study; the price he paid for them was an abnormally lowered vitality for the acts and perceptions of everyday life. He repeatedly complains of the "Lethean stream" that washes through him, of the "film or haze of unreality" that separates him from the world his senses perceive. How to transfer "nerve capital" (as a follower of Dr. Beard termed it[8]) from the column of the Reason to the column of the Understanding seemed to him life's chief insoluble problem. In "Montaigne" he writes:

> The astonishment of life is the absence of any appearance of reconciliation between the theory and practice of life. Reason, the prized reality, the Law, is apprehended, now and then, for a serene and profound moment amidst the hubbub of cares and works which have no direct bearing on it; is then lost for months and years, and again found for an interval, to be lost again. If we compute it in time, we may, in fifty years, have half a dozen reasonable hours. But what are these cares and works the better? A method in the world we do not see, but this parallelism of great and little, which never discover the smallest tendency to converge.

Or, as he had once laconically observed: "Very little life in a lifetime."

Yet despite this discouraging arithmetic Emerson had always refused to abandon his insistence that the visionary moments constituted our *real* life, the one in which we felt most truly ourselves. This insistence is not quite as suicidal as it sounds, for the visionary moments, however brief they may be when measured by the clock; have a way of expanding while they are occurring into an eternal present that makes a mockery of duration. In a paragraph of "Circles" that looks forward to Thoreau's parable of the artist of Kouroo, Emerson had written:

> It is the highest power of divine moments that they abolish our contritions also. I accuse myself of sloth and unprofitableness, day by day; but when these waves of God flow into me, I no longer reckon lost time. I no longer poorly compute my possible achievements by what remains to me of the month or the year; for these moments confer a sort of omnipresence and omnipotence, which asks nothing of duration, but sees that the energy of the mind is commensurate with the work to be done, without time.

With this proviso in mind it is easier to understand why Emerson could speculate in his journal that "in the memory of the disembodied soul the days or hours of pure Reason will shine with a steady light as the life of life & all the other days & weeks will appear but as hyphens which served to join these."

In "Experience" Emerson tries for the first time in his career to describe life as it looks from the standpoint of the hyphens rather than the heights, from the "waste sad time" (as Eliot calls it) separating the moments of vision rather than from the moments themselves. It is his attempt to confront the only form of suffering he recognized as genuinely tragic, because it was the only one for which his imagination could discover no answering compensation—the haze of unreality that sometimes suggested to him that we were "on the way back to Annihilation."

Emerson had originally planned to call the essay "Life." At first glance the difference between the two titles does not seem very great. Everything that happens in life can be described as an experience: a visionary moment as much as a bump on the head. Emerson himself uses the word this way in "The Transcendentalist" when he says that a transcendentalist's faith is based on a "certain brief experience" that surprises him in the midst of his everyday worries and pursuits.

Yet the word "experience" also had a technical meaning in empirical philosophy, where it refers to that portion of the world accessible to the senses, the world of time and space. This is the meaning it has in the works of Hume, whose skepticism had provoked the young Emerson into his first spiritual crisis during the decade of the 1820s. "Experience" is the weapon Hume uses to demolish belief in miracles and the argument for God's existence based on inferences from the evidence of design in the universe. If one accepted Hume's thesis—that "we have no knowledge but from Experience"—it was difficult to avoid his conclusion—that "we have no Experience of a Creator & therefore know of none." Hume could also use arguments from experience to shake belief in more fundamental assumptions: in the existence of matter, in the relationship of cause and effect, in the stability of personal identity. Emerson puzzled over these problems. In a high-spirited letter to his Aunt Mary written in 1823 he confessed that the doubts raised by this "Scotch Goliath" were as distressing to him as worries about the origin of evil or the freedom of the will. "Where," he asked rhetorically, "is the accomplished stripling who can cut off his most metaphysical head? Who is he that can stand up before him & prove the existence of the Universe, & of its Founder?" All the candidates in the "long & dull procession of Reasoners that have followed since" only proved, by their repeated attempts to confute Hume, that Hume had not been confuted.

Here, it is evident, Emerson is still accepting his teachers' argument that an attack on the existence of the material universe led inevitably to an attack on the existence of God. Whicher points out that "though Berkeley had denied the existence of matter independent of perception to confute sceptical materialism," to the Scottish Realists whose philosophical works dominated the Harvard scene in Emerson's youth, "the end product of the Ideal Theory was the scepticism of Hume."[9]

Emerson's discovery of "the God within" released him from the necessity of clinging to proofs of the existence of matter, since once the confirmation of the truths of religion had been made a purely intuitive affair, no longer dependent for its ratification on miracles perceivable by the senses, the "Ideal Theory" no longer seemed dangerous. The endless, fussy debates about whether we could trust the testimony of the Apostles who claimed to have witnessed the miracles of Jesus, about how the immutable laws of nature could have been temporarily suspended (e.g., whether Jesus made the water he walked on temporarily solid or himself temporarily weightless), about whether the gospels in which these events were recorded were genuine or spurious, neutral historical records or (as the German Higher Critics alleged) legendary or mythological narratives, could all be dispensed with in one liberating gesture. "Internal evidence outweighs all other to the inner man," Emerson wrote in 1830. "If the whole history of the New Testament had perished & its teachings remained—the spirituality of Paul, the grave, considerate, unerring advice of James would take the same rank with me that now they do." It is the truth of the doctrine that confirms the truth of the miracle, not the other way round. If it were not so, Emerson frankly confesses, he would probably "yield to Hume or any one that this, like all other miracle accounts, was probably false."

Hume's argument against the possibility of miracles had rested on the observation that our opinions about the reliability of testimony and about the probability of matters of fact are both drawn from experience. We usually believe the testimony of honorable witnesses, because we have found from experience that such men usually tell the truth. But we also form our opinions about the probability of matters of fact from our experience: whether it is likely to snow in July, whether a man can walk on water or rise from the dead. "The reason, why we place any credit in witnesses and historians, is not derived from any *connexion*, which we perceive *a priori*, between testimony and reality, but because we are accustomed to find a conformity between them. But when the fact attested is such a one as has seldom fallen under our observation, here is a contest of two opposite experiences; of which the one destroys the other, as far as its force goes, and the superior can only separate on the mind by the force, which remains."[10]

Emerson's mature position can best be characterized by saying that he accepts Hume's argument but reverses his conclusions. When the testimony involved is not the testimony of witnesses but the testimony of consciousness, the "superior force" clearly belongs to consciousness. Experience and consciousness are indeed in perpetual conflict: "life is made up of the intermixture and reaction of these two amicable powers, whose marriage appears beforehand monstrous, as each denies and tends to abolish the other." When an irreconcilable conflict occurs, it is consciousness, not experience, whose testimony we believe. Hence Emerson's delight in the "scientific" equivalent to this assertion: the law he attributed to the Swiss mathematician Euler and quoted in the "Idealism" chapter of *Nature*. "The sublime remark of Euler on his law of arches, 'This will be found contrary to all experience, yet it is true;' had already transferred nature into the mind, and left matter like an outcast corpse."

Idealism had always held a secret attraction for Emerson, which had survived unchanged even during the years when his teachers were telling him to regard it as dangerous. In a letter to Margaret Fuller in 1841 he writes: "I know but one solution to my nature & relations, which I find in the remembering the joy with which in my boyhood I caught the first hint of the Berkleian philosophy, and which I certainly never lost sight of afterwards." What Emerson means by the "Berkleian philosophy," as Whicher notes, is not Berkeley's particular system but

> simply the "noble doubt … whether nature outwardly exists." The seductive reversal of his relations to the world, with which the imagination of every child is sometimes caught, transferring his recurrent sense of a dreaminess in his mode of life to outward nature, and releasing him in his imagination into a solitude peopled with illusions, was scepticism of a special kind—

but a kind that increasingly seemed not the murderer of faith but rather its midwife.[11] The man who believes that the mind alone is real, matter only a phenomenon, is easier to convince of spiritual realities than the empiricist who continually demands sensible proofs. "Idealism seems a preparation for a strictly moral life & so skepticism seems necessary for a universal holiness," Emerson noted in an early journal. Indeed, if what he asserts in "Montaigne" is correct—that "belief consists in accepting the affirmations of the soul; unbelief, in denying them"—it is the empiricist, not the idealist, who deserves the title of skeptic. With this in mind, the history of philosophy begins to look very different. The classical skeptics no longer look frightening—Emerson quotes with approval de Gerando's opinion that Sextus Empiricus' skepticism had been directed only at the external world, not at metaphysical truths. Even the Scotch Goliath begins to look less formidable. "Religion does that for the uncultivated which philosophy does for ~~Hume~~ Berkeley & Viasa; makes the mountains dance & smoke & disappear before the steadfast gaze of Reason." Emerson crossed out Hume's name (enlisting Hume as an ally of religion was presumably too radical an idea for Emerson at this point in his career, though the Emerson of "Circles" would have found it plausible), but that he thought of Hume in context at all is significant enough.

But Idealism as a doctrine was more than philosophically important to Emerson; it was emotionally important as well. *Nature* as originally planned was to have ended with the chapter "Idealism"; and in that chapter he suggests some of the chief attractions the doctrine possessed. When "piety or passion" lifts us into the realm of Ideas, "we become physically nimble and lightsome; we tread on air; life is no longer irksome, and we think it will never be so. No man fears age or misfortune or death in their serene company, for he is transported out of the region of change." "The best, the happiest moments of life are these delicious awakenings of the higher powers, and the reverential withdrawing of nature before its God."

No wonder Emerson seized eagerly upon every philosopher whose system tended toward idealism of one kind or another: Plato, Plotinus, Berkeley, Kant, Fichte, Schelling. Religious doctrines, too, he tends to judge by their approximations to idealism. In an early journal he notes with approval that idealism seems to be a primeval theory, and quotes from the Mahabharata (one of the sacred books of India) a sentence that neatly inverts the Peripatetic formula (*nihil in intellectu quod non ante fuerit in sensu*) upon which Locke had based his philosophy. "The senses are nothing but the soul's instrument of action, *no knowledge can come to the soul by their channel*" (emphasis added).

I have made this digression into Emerson's philosophical interests for a reason: the essay "Experience" cannot, I think, be fully understood without some grasp of the metaphorical ways in which he employs the technical vocabulary of epistemology to talk about things like grief, guilt, ruthlessness, and isolation. Stanley Cavell sees in Emerson the only thinker who can be said to have anticipated the Heidegger of *Being and Time* in an attempt "to formulate a kind of epistemology of moods":

> The idea is roughly that moods must be taken as having at least as sound a role in advising us of reality as sense-experience has; that, for example, coloring the world, attributing to it the

qualities "mean" or "magnanimous," may be no less objective or subjective than coloring an apple, attributing to it the colors red and green. Or perhaps we should say: sense-experience is to objects what moods are to the world.[12]

What makes this difficult subject more complicated still is Emerson's own recognition that the various epistemological theories proposed by every philosopher from Plato to Kant might themselves be little more than metaphorical equivalents of moods or habitual ways of taking the world. "I fear the progress of Metaphysical philosophy may be found to consist in nothing else than the progressive introduction of apposite metaphors," Emerson had dryly remarked in an early journal. "Thus the Platonists congratulated themselves for ages upon their knowing that Mind was a dark chamber whereon ideas like shadows were painted. Men derided this as infantile when they afterwards learned that the Mind was a sheet of white paper whereon any & all characters might be written." The real difficulty in arriving at an epistemology of moods is that moods are likely to dictate beforehand the shape of one's epistemology. A soul in a state of exaltation will instinctively incline to the mystical idealism of the Mahabharata; a soul in a state of depression, to the skepticism of Hume. A healthy but nonreflective man might find the epistemology of the Scottish Realists sufficiently convincing; a more introspective man might not rest content until he had seen the relation between subject and object given transcendental ground in the philosophy of Kant.

Words like "experience" and "idealism" have different meanings in each of these systems, and different from any are the meanings they have acquired in popular use, where "idealism" is taken to mean any rosy or elevated estimate of human possibilities, and "experience" the process by which that estimate is lost. In "Experience" Emerson does not so much attempt to introduce order into this confusion as to exploit its ironies. If the essay, like life itself, is a "train of moods" or succession of "many-colored lenses which paint the world their own hue," each showing only what lies in its focus, then one of the chief ways of arriving at an epistemology of moods is by studying the shadings these words take on as the paragraphs pass by. From some moods within the essay, "experience" looks like a neutrally descriptive word; from others, a term of bitterness or contempt; from others still, the most savage of ironies. And the same thing holds true for "idealism," as one can see from the sentence (which may be the bitterest Emerson ever wrote) taken from the paragraphs of the essay that deal with the death of his son: "Grief too will make us idealists."

From the beginning of the essay the concept of experience is already involved in ironies. The opening image, which compares life to the climbing of an endless staircase, has reminded more than one critic of a Piranesi engraving, and Porte has pointed out that Emerson's references to "lethe" and "opium" recall a passage in DeQuincey's *Confessions of an English Opium-Eater*, where Piranesi's *Carceri d'Invenzione* is explicitly mentioned.[13] But DeQuincey was describing dreams induced by an actual drug; Emerson is describing the ordinary waking consciousness, life as it presents itself to. the senses.

Hume, who thought that all knowledge came through experience, divided the contents of the mind into "IMPRESSIONS and IDEAS," the former derived from sensation (whether from external nature or the passions themselves), the latter the "faint images" of the former.[14] Since the two are different not in kind but only in degree, he pauses at the beginning of the *Treatise of Human Nature* to consider whether the two can ever be confused. He admits that in madness or fever or dreams ideas may become almost as lively as impressions, and that conversely there are some states in which "it sometimes happens, that our impressions are so faint and low, that we cannot distinguish them from our ideas."[15] What Emerson suggests in the opening paragraph of "Experience" is that the state Hume admitted as exceptional is in fact closer to being the norm: our impressions are most of the time as faint as our ideas, and a system of philosophy that separated one from the other according to the "degrees of force and liveliness, with which they strike upon the mind"[16] would very shortly lose the power to tell reality from phantasmagoria. The first irony we can record about experience is that it chiefly menaces the very philosophical system supposed to revere it. The exhaustion that attends it numbs the mind so that all the things we perceive "swim and glitter" like apparitions—a condition that, as Emerson accurately says, threatens not so much our life as our perception.

The second paragraph of the essay lodges a different complaint: the fact that experience and whatever wisdom can be derived from it are never coincident. Our life becomes meaningful only retroactively. "If any of us knew what we were doing, or where we are going, then when we think we best know! We do not know today whether we are busy or idle. In times when we have thought ourselves indolent, we have afterwards discovered that much was accomplished and much was begun in us." The most valuable experiences Wordsworth discovered in his childhood as he looked back on it were not the incidents a biographer would be likely to record but rather certain uncanny moments of heightened perception that occurred unexpectedly in the midst of ordinary childish sports—ice skating, robbing birds' nests, going for a night ride in a stolen boat—just as the most significant experience during the European tour he made as a young man turned out to be not the visions of sublime Alpine scenery but the vague feeling of depression that had succeeded the peasant's revelation that he and his companion had passed the highest point on their Alpine journey without recognizing it. Life and the meaning of life can never be apprehended simultaneously; like Pandarus in *Troilus and Criseyde* we can all justly complain "I hoppe alwey byhynde."[17]

Nor can any illumination ever prove final. "What a benefit if a rule could be given whereby the mind could at any moment *east* itself, & find the sun," Emerson had written in his journal. "But long after we have thought we were recovered & sane, light breaks in upon us & we find we have yet had no sane moment. Another morn rises on mid-noon." That final Miltonic allusion (along with its demonic counterpart, "under every deep a lower deep opens") may be regarded as a slightly more cheerful version of the staircase image that opens "Experience": it combines the suggestion of interminability with the suggestion that with each new layer of experience there is at least a widening of circumference or gain in wisdom. As Emerson says later on in the essay, "the years teach much that the days never know." Unfortunately, this wisdom clarifies only the past; each new situation finds us blundering like novices. "The individual is always mistaken." This melancholy but resigned conclusion resembles the opinion Yeats expresses in *Per Amica Silentia Lunae*, that since no disaster in life is exactly like another, there must always be "new bitterness, new disappointment";[18] it is perhaps even closer to the remark made by a contemporary Zen master, Shunryu Suzuki, to the effect that the life of a Zen master in pursuit of enlightenment "could be said to be so many years of *shoshaku jushaku*—'to succeed wrong with wrong,' or one continuous mistake."[19]

It is important to realize that at this point in the essay Emerson is *not* contrasting the wisdom that comes from experience with the higher wisdom that comes from consciousness. He is exploring a curious paradox that exists within experience itself. "All our days are so unprofitable while they pass, that 'tis wonderful where or when we ever got anything of this which we call wisdom, poetry, virtue. We never got it on any dated calendar day." The contrast between the pettiness of our daily lives and the accumulated wisdom that somehow results from them is so vast that even a resolute empiricist will be driven to mythology or fiction to account for it. "Some heavenly days must have been intercalated somewhere, like those that Hermes won with the dice of the Moon, that Osiris might be born."

Yet the cruelest feature of experience is the power it possesses of alienating *us* not only from our perceptions and our interpretations but even from our own sorrows:

> What opium is instilled into all disaster! It shows formidable as we approach it, but there is at last no rough rasping friction, but the most slippery sliding surfaces; we fall soft on a thought; *Ate Dea* is gentle,—
>
> > *"Over men's heads walking aloft,*
> > *With tenderfeet treading so soft."*
>
> People grieve and bemoan themselves, but it is not half so bad with them as they say. There are moods in which we court suffering, in the hope that here we shall find reality, sharp peaks and edges of truth. But it turns out to be only scene-painting and counterfeit. The only thing grief has taught me, is to know how shallow it is. That, like all the rest, plays about the surface, and never introduces me into the reality, for contact with which we would even pay the costly price of sons and lovers. Was it Boscovich who found out that bodies never come in contact? Well, souls never touch their objects. An innavigable sea washes with silent waves between us and the things we aim at and converse with. Grief too will make us idealists. In the death of my son, now more than two years ago, I seem to have lost a beautiful estate,—no more. I cannot get it nearer to me. If tomorrow I should be informed of the bankruptcy of my principle debtors, the loss of my property would be a great inconvenience to me, perhaps, for many years; but it would leave me as it found me,— neither better nor worse. So it is with this calamity; it does not touch me; something which I fancied was a part of me, which could not be torn away without tearing me nor enlarged without enriching me, falls off and leaves no scar. It was caducous. I grieve that grief can teach me nothing, nor carry me one step into real nature. The Indian who was laid under a curse that the wind should not blow to him, nor fire burn him, is a type of us all. The dearest events are summer-rain and we the Para coats that shed every drop. Nothing is left us now but death. We look to that with a grim satisfaction, saying, There at least is a reality that will not dodge us.

I have quoted the whole of this magnificent passage because it is chiefly in its cumulative force that it achieves its great and disturbing power over us. I have never yet read a commentary on it that I thought did justice to the peculiar kind of shock it administers to the reader who is encountering the essay for the first time. The casual brutality of the sentence in which Emerson introduces the death of his son *as an illustration* is unmatched by anything I know of in literature, unless it is the parenthetical remark in which Virginia Woolf reports the death of Mrs. Ramsay in the "Time Passes" section of *To the Lighthouse*.

Not that the unreality or numbness Emerson reports is itself shocking. Many writers before and after Emerson have said as much. A similar experience forms the subject of Dickinson's chilling lyric, "After great pain, a formal feeling comes"; it is also analyzed in a passage of Sir Thomas Browne's *Hydrotaphia* from which Emerson had copied sentences into one of his early journals. "There is no antidote against the Opium of time," Browne reminds us, and then goes on to say:

> Darknesse and light divide the course of time, and oblivion shares with memory a great part even of our living beings; we slightly remember our felicities, and the smartest stroaks of affliction leave but short smart upon us. Sense endureth no extremities, and sorrows destroy us or themselves. To weep into stones are fables. Afflictions induce callosities, miseries are slippery, or fall like snow upon us, which notwithstanding is no unhappy stupidity. To be ignorant of evils to come, and forgetfull of evils past, is a mercifull provision in nature, whereby we digest the mixture of our few and evil dayes, and our delivered senses not relapsing into cutting remembrances, our sorrows are not kept raw by the edge of repetitions.[20]

The whole passage, even down to the details of its tactile imagery, is a striking anticipation of "Experience." Yet the differences are as noteworthy as the similarities. The slipperiness of misery, which Browne calls a "mercifull provision in nature," is for Emerson "the most unhandsome part of our condition." And this is so because Emerson, unlike Browne, sees in the unreality of grief only an intensification of our normal state of alienation or dislocation from the world our senses perceive. This distance—the "innavigable sea" that washes between us and the world—is the real torture. If grief could relieve it, if suffering could introduce us to the reality behind the glittering and evanescent phenomena, we would welcome it. For contact with that reality we would be *willing* to pay (as Emerson says in what is surely the most chilling of all his hyperboles) "even the costly price of sons and lovers."

But grief proves to be as shallow as everything else. In a letter written a week after the death of his son Emerson laments: "Alas! I chiefly grieve that I cannot grieve; that this fact takes no more deep hold than other facts, is as dreamlike as they; a lambent flame that will not burn playing on the surface of my river. Must every experience—those that promised to be dearest & most penetrative,—only kiss my cheek like the wind & pass away? I think of Ixion & Tantalus & Kehama." "Kehama" is an allusion to Robert Southey's long narrative poem *The Curse of Kehama*, in which a virtuous character named Ladurlad is laid under a curse by the wicked ruler Kehama, who, though himself a mere mortal, has learned to wrest such power from the gods that he is able to send a burning fire into Ladurlad's heart and brain, and at the same time order the elements to flee from him. As Ladurlad laments:

> The Winds of Heaven must never breathe on me;
> The Rains and Dews must never fall on me;
> Water must mock my thirst and shrink from me;
> The common earth must yield no fruit to me;
> Sleep, blessed Sleep! must never light on me;
> And Death, who comes to all, must fly from me,
> And never, never set Ladurlad free.[21]

Ladurlad is the "Indian" mentioned in "Experience": in making him a "type of us all" Emerson gives us his grimmest assessment of the human condition: an endless, goalless pilgrimage, driven by an inner but unquenchable fire through a world that recedes perpetually before the pilgrim. The bitter lesson we learn from experience is the soul's imperviousness to experiences. The traumas are not traumatic. "The dearest events are summer-rain, and we the Para coats that shed every drop." If we look forward with a "grim satisfaction" to death, it is because it is the one event in life that we can be sure will not slip through our fingers. "There at least is a reality that will not dodge us."

Yet the central portion of the passage is the most explicitly self-lacerating. In observing that grief, like poetry or religion, convinces us of the insubstantiality of the phenomenal world, in offering as evidence for this assertion his own imperviousness to the death of his son, whose loss he likens, with deliberate vulgarity, to the loss of an estate, Emerson is indulging in a candor so "dreadful" (as Bishop puts it) that it has driven more than one critic to suppose that he either did not mean what he said or else was unaware of his meaning.[22]

Part of the problem comes from the difficulty of determining Emerson's tone in the passage. Bishop has pointed out Emerson's fondness for what he calls "tonal puns." He instances a sentence from *The Conduct of Life*: "Such as you are, the gods themselves could not help you." Bishop says: "One can hear a voice that says this insultingly and another voice, intimate and quiet, that says it encouragingly."[23] But he confesses that sentences like "*Ate Dea* is gentle" and "Grief too will make us idealists" and "I cannot get it nearer to me" leave him puzzled. Are they straightforward or ironical, desperate or resigned?[24] The answer, I think, is that we *can* imagine a voice that says all of these things with bitter irony, but that we can also imagine them being said in a voice as toneless and detached as that of a witness giving evidence in a war crimes trial, or that of the wasted and suffering discharged soldier whom Wordsworth questions about his experiences in Book IV of *The Prelude*:

> ... in all he said
> There was a strange half-absence, as of one
> Knowing too well the importance of his theme
> But feeling it no longer.[25]

Emerson is driven to offer his testimony by an inner necessity. I admire Maurice Gonnaud's fine remark about this compulsion: "The greatness of an essay like 'Experience' lies, I suggest, in our sense of the author's being engaged in a pursuit of truth which has all the characters of faith except its faculty of radiating happiness."[26]

What sharpens the sting of the revelations is Emerson's tacit acknowledgment, through his phrasing and imagery, that fate itself has retroactively conferred upon some brave assertions of the past the one kind of irony it was beyond his power to intend. Thus "grief too will make us idealists" both echoes and answers a journal entry of 1836 in which Emerson was working out the concepts that later became part of the sixth chapter of *Nature*: "Religion makes us idealists. Any strong passion does. The best, the happiest moments of life are these delicious awakenings of the higher powers & the reverential withdrawing of nature before its god." His remark that his relationship to his son proved to be "caducous" recalls a happy declaration, made after the departure of some friends in August of 1837, that he had faith in the soul's powers of infinite regeneration: "these caducous relations are in the soul like leaves ... & how often soever they are lopped off, yet still it renews them ever." Even more chilling is the prophetic remark he made to Jones Very during the latter's visit in 1838: "I told Jones Very that I had never suffered, & that I could scarce bring myself to feel a concern for the safety & life of my nearest friends that would satisfy them: that I saw clearly that if my wife, my child, my mother, should be taken from me, I should still remain whole with the same capacity of cheap enjoyment from all things." There is a kind of self-contempt in this passage; Emerson had already survived so many losses that he felt confident in predicting his response to more. But this passage was written when little Waldo was barely two. In the intervening years—years in which Emerson had delightedly recorded his small son's doings and sayings in his otherwise austerely intellectual journal—he had evidently come to hope that this relationship was somehow different, that it was something that "could not be torn away without tearing me nor enlarged without enriching me."

Alas. Though Elizabeth Hoar's brother Rockwood "was never more impressed with a human expression of agony than by that of Emerson leading the way into the room where little Waldo lay dead,"[27] Rusk tells us, Emerson discovered to his sorrow that the prophecy he had made in 1838 was true. In his young manhood he had been greatly stirred by the remark of a Methodist farmer he worked with one summer that men were always praying and that their prayers were always answered. "Experience" records Emerson's grim awareness that the price you pay for invulnerability is invulnerability.

The passages here recanted were all confined to Emerson's private journals—a fact that helps explain why the opening pages of "Experience," almost alone among Emerson's works, give the impression of being not heard but overheard. But these privately recorded passages are not the only ones to be so retracted. Nearly every critic of the essay has pointed out the connection between some detail of its imagery or argument and those of an earlier work that it systematically recants or retracts. Thus the opening question—"Where do we find ourselves?"—when compared to the boldness of *Nature*'s opening—"Let us inquire, to what end is nature?"—suggests the bewilderment that has overtaken this latter-day Oedipus as he turns from riddle solving to self-examination. The opening image of an endless staircase recalls the "mysterious ladder" of "Circles," but where the latter saw a new prospect of power from every rung, "Experience" sees only repetition and exhaustion. Idiosyncrasy or subjectivity, which in "Self-Reliance" was felt to be the source of one's chief value, now becomes part of the limitation of temperament, which shut us out from every truth our "colored and distorting lenses" cannot transmit. The horizon that in "Circles" was a promise of perpetual expansion has now become merely a metaphor for frustration: "Men seem to have learned of the horizon the art of perpetual retreating and reference." In *Nature* Emerson was a Transparent Eye-ball; in "Experience" he is shut in "a prison of glass which [he] cannot see." The "noble doubt" whether nature outwardly exists, the exhilarating suggestion that perhaps the whole of the outward universe is only a projection from the apocalypse of the mind, has become in "Experience" the Fall of Man.[28]

But if "Experience" is in one way a palinode, it is in another way a continuation, under grimmer conditions, of the faith Emerson had never relinquished. That faith first enters the essay only as a kind of recoil against the reductiveness of the argument in the section devoted to temperament. Life is a string of moods, each showing only what lies in its focus; temperament is the iron wire on which these beads are strung. "Men resist the conclusion in the morning, but adopt it as the evening wears on, that temper prevails over everything of time, place, and condition, and is inconsumable in the flames of religion."

Yet in the midst of this determinism Emerson suddenly pauses to note the "capital exception" every man makes to general or deterministic laws— that is, himself. Although every man believes every other to be "a fatal partialist," he never sees himself as anything other than a "universalist." (In a similar passage later on in the essay Emerson will observe that we make the same exception to moral laws, which is why no man can believe that "the crime in him is as black as in the felon.") In "Circles" Emerson had noted that "every man supposes himself not to be fully understood; and if there is any truth in him, if he rests at last on the divine soul, I see not how it can be otherwise. The last chamber, the last closet, he must feel was never opened; there is always a residuum unknown, unanalyzable. That is, every man believes he has a greater possibility." However much we may appear to one another as creatures limited by a given temperament, bound by the "links of the chain of physical necessity," the very fact that our consciousness rebels utterly at such a description of *ourselves* is the best evidence we have of the falsity of the doctrine. On its own level—the level of nature, of experience— temperament may be final, relativism inescapable.

> But it is impossible that the creative power should exclude itself. Into every intelligence there is a door which is never closed, through which the creator passes. The intellect, seeker of absolute truth, or the heart, lover of absolute good, intervenes for our succor, and at one whisper of these high powers we awake from our ineffectual struggles with this nightmare. We

hurl it into its own hell, and cannot again contract ourselves to
so base a state.

Yet this recovery, though it suggests the direction the essay will take, is by no
means a final triumph over the lords of life. After Temperament there is
Succession, by which Emerson means both the succession of "moods"—
which he has already discussed—and the succession of "objects." The
succession of moods is something we suffer; the succession of objects is
something we choose. "We need change of objects." Our hunger for the
whole keeps us restlessly searching through the world of experience in
pursuit of a final consummation forever denied us. But if there are no final
satisfactions, there are at least partial ones. In *The American Scholar* Emerson
had compared inspiration to the "one central fire which flaming now out of
the lips of Etna, lightens the capes of Sicily; and now out of the throat of
Vesuvius, illuminates the towers and vineyards of Naples." The image he
uses in "Experience" is considerably less apocalyptic, but the faith it
expresses is the same: "Like a bird which alights nowhere, but hops
perpetually from bough to bough, is the Power which abides in no man and
no woman, but for a moment speaks from this one, and for another from that
one."

The essay by this point seems to have established a pattern—a dip into
despair, followed by a recoil of hope. But suddenly and unexpectedly
Emerson turns on himself and his method: "what help from these fineries or
pedantries? What help from thought? Life is not dialectics." This yawing
back and forth between despair and hope is not, after all, how we spend most
of our time. "Life is not intellectual or critical, but sturdy." Some way must
be found to redeem the time, to treat it as something other than an emptiness
separating moments of vision. "To fill the hour,—that is happiness; to fill the
hour and leave no crevice for a repentance or an approval. We live amid
surfaces, and the true art of life is to skate well on them." In these sentences
we hear a different voice emerging, a voice that will become stronger in
"Montaigne" and dominant in a book like *English Traits*. It is the voice of
strong common sense, giving a view of the world Emerson had indeed
expressed earlier, in things like the "Commodity" chapter of *Nature* and in
essays like "Prudence" and "Compensation," but had never before offered as
a serious *alternative* to the world of Reason. Now, for the first time, he
proposes the "mid-world" as something other than a step on the way to
vision.

Yet the mid-world offers no permanent anchorage either; moments of
illumination will return whether we want them to or not, upsetting all our

resolutions to keep "due metes and bounds." "Underneath the inharmonious and trivial particulars, is a musical perfection, the Ideal journeying always with us, the heaven without rent or seam." This region is something we do not make, but find, and when we find it all the old exhilaration returns. We respond with joy and amazement to the opening of "this august magnificence, old with the love and homage of innumerable ages, young with the life of life, the sunbright Mecca of the desert. And what a future it opens! I feel a new heart beating with the love of the new beauty. I am ready to die out of nature and be born again into this new yet unapproachable America I have found in the West."

For a vision of life that assessed man only from the platform of "experience" would leave out half his nature. "If I have described life as a flux of moods, I must now add that there is that in us which changes not and which ranks all sensations and states of mind." This something is the "central life" mentioned at the end of "Circles," the center that contains all possible circumferences. "The consciousness in each man is a sliding scale, which identifies him now with the First Cause, and now with the flesh of his body; life above life, in infinite degrees." Different religions have given this First Cause different names—Muse, Holy Ghost, *nous*, love—but Emerson confesses that he likes best the one ventured by the Chinese sage Mencius: "vast-flowing vigor." Asked what he means by this, Mencius describes it as the power that can "fill up the vacancy between heaven and earth" and that "leaves no hunger." With this definition we have come as far as possible from the terminal exhaustion and depletion of the essay's opening paragraphs: "we have arrived as far as we can go. Suffice it for the joy of the universe that we have arrived not at a wall, but at interminable oceans. Our life seems not so much present as prospective; not for the affairs on which it is wasted, but as a hint of this vast-flowing vigor."

But if this is the end of the dialectic, it is not the end of the essay, which—like life itself—will not let us remain in any state of illumination for long. We are brought back to the mid-world in a paragraph that summarizes all that has come before:

> It is very unhappy, but too late to be helped, the discovery we have made that we exist. That discovery is called the Fall of Man. Ever afterwards we suspect our instruments. We have learned that we do not see directly but mediately, and that we have no means of correcting these colored and distorting lenses which we

are, or of computing the amount of their errors. Perhaps these subject-lenses have a creative power; perhaps there are no objects. Once we lived in what we saw; now, the rapaciousness of this new power, which threatens to absorb all things, engages us. Nature, art, persons, letters, religions, objects, successively tumble in, and God is but one of its ideas.

As Michael Cowan notes, this investigation of Subjectiveness in some ways "represents a spiralling back to the lord of Illusion, but now seen from the viewpoint of the saved rather than the damned imagination."[29] What has made the difference is the discovery that there is an irreducible something in the soul that rebels fiercely at any attempt to reduce it to a mere "bundle of perceptions," and that is hence the best proof that any such definition is false. Knowing that the soul retains even in its grimmest moments "a door which is never closed, through which the creator passes" is the saving revelation that transforms the hell of Illusion into the purgatory of Subjectiveness. We are still unable to transcend the limitations of our vision, but now we seem not so much cut off from the real as the unconscious progenitors of it. Our "subject-lenses," unlike the object-lenses of a telescope or microscope, do not merely magnify reality, they determine its characteristics: "the chagrins which the bad heart gives off as bubbles, at once take form as ladies and gentlemen in the street, shopmen or barkeepers in hotels, and threaten or insult whatever is threatenable or insultable in us." This is a trivial example of a principle, anything but trivial, whose gradual triumph one can witness in the history of the race. Realism is the philosophical system of every primitive tribe, but as civilization advances, men come gradually to suspect that as it is the eye that makes the horizon, so it is the beholder who creates the things he perceives.

It is not to be denied that there is something melancholy about such self-awareness. In a lecture entitled "The Present Age," delivered in 1837, Emerson expresses the traditional Romantic envy of those luckier ages that lived in what they saw:

Ours is distinguished from the Greek and Roman and Gothic ages, and all the periods of childhood and youth by being the age of the second thought. The golden age is gone and the silver is gone—the blessed eras of unconscious life, of intuition, of genius.... The ancients were self-united. We have found out the difference of outer and inner. They described. We reason. They acted. We philosophise.

The act of reflection severs us as with an "innavigable sea" from the "things we aim at and converse with," and at the same time plants in our minds the suspicion that these things, which *feel* so distant, may not be "out there" at all. On this point modern empiricism and idealism coincide. Hume wrote: "Let us fix our attention out of ourselves as much as possible: Let us chace our imagination to the heavens, or to the utmost limits of the universe; we can never really advance a step beyond ourselves, nor can conceive of any kind of existence, but those perceptions, which have appear'd in that narrow compass."[30] As Emerson remarked of a similar passage from the materialist Condillac, "what more could an idealist say?"

This imprisonment has some lamentable consequences, as Emerson is the first to acknowledge, for the kingdoms of mortal friendship and of love. "Marriage (in which is called the spiritual world) is impossible, because of the inequality between every subject and every object.... There will be the same gulf between every me and every thee as between the original and the picture." For the soul, though it incarnates itself in time as an ordinary mortal with ordinary limitations, is in fact "of a fatal and universal power, *admitting no co-life*" (emphasis added). To say this is to push one's philosophy considerably beyond antinomianism; it ought logically to lead to a state in which everything—theft, arson, murder—is permitted. Emerson does not attempt to refute this objection. Instead (in what is surely one of the more audacious gestures in American literature) he coolly embraces it. That crime occurs at all is the best evidence we have of our unshakable belief in the divinity of the self. "It is an instance of our faith in ourselves that men never speak of crime as lightly as they think.... Murder in the murderer is no such ruinous thought as poets and romancers will have it; it does not unsettle him or fright him from his ordinary notice of trifles; it is an act quite easy to be contemplated." Our reasons for abstaining from murder are (by a nice irony) purely empirical, derived from experience: "in its sequel [murder] turns out to be a horrible confounding of all relations." Emerson's own version of the categorical imperative derives from the same ontology. Just as the highest praise we can offer any artist is to think that he actually possessed the thought with which he has inspired us, so the highest tribute we can pay to a fellow human being is to assume that his exterior—which must remain to us merely a part of the phenomenal—conceals a Deity as central to itself as our own. "Let us treat the men and women well; treat them as if they were real; perhaps they are."

We have here reached the shadowy ground where philosophy and psychology merge. In the letter to Margaret Fuller quoted earlier Emerson had claimed that the Berkleian philosophy was the clue to his nature *and relations*. Idealism as a philosophical doctrine appealed to him partly because it offered a credible way of accounting for the loneliness and isolation to which he felt temperamentally condemned. In 1851, after a rambling talk with Thoreau in which both of them had "stated over again, to sadness, almost, the Eternal loneliness," Emerson exclaimed, "how insular & pathetically solitary, are all the people we know!" We are inclined to try to find excuses for our separation from others, but in more honest moments we admit the grimmer truth: "the Sea, vocation, poverty, are seeming fences, but Man is insular and cannot be touched. Every man is an infinitely repellent orb, and holds his individual being on that condition." Existence for each of us is a drama played out in a private theater that admits only one spectator:

> Men generally attempt early in life to make their brothers first, afterwards their wives, acquainted with what is going forward in their private theater, but they soon desist from the attempt on finding that they also have some farce or perhaps some ear- & heart-rending tragedy forward on their secret boards on which they are intent, and all parties acquiesce at last in a private box with the whole play performed before him Bolus.

The same haunting notion prompts the question that closes this section of "Experience": "How long before our masquerade will end its noise of tambourines, laughter and shouting, and we will find it was a solitary performance?"

It is true, as Emerson says, that the muses of love and religion hate these developments. But our inescapable subjectivity has its own compensations. The "sharp peaks and edges of truth" we had hoped to find in reality we discover at last in the soul. God himself is "the native of these bleak rocks," an insight that "makes in morals the capital virtue of self-trust. We must hold hard to this poverty, however scandalous, and by more vigorous self-recoveries, after the sallies of action, possess our axis more firmly. The life of truth is cold and so far mournful; but it is not the slave of tears, contritions, and perturbations. It does not attempt another's work, nor adopt another's facts." As James Cox notes, "if 'Self-Reliance' was a ringing exhortation to trust the self, 'Experience' turns out to disclose that, after the last disillusion, there is nothing to rely on *but* the self.[31]

And the sunbright Mecca of the West? The New Jerusalem, the kingdom of man over nature? What has become of it? In a journal Emerson had once noted sadly that "it takes a great deal of elevation of thought to produce a very little elevation of life.... Gradually in long years we bend our living to our idea. But we serve seven years & twice seven for Rachel." In "Experience" Emerson admits that he has served his time—"I am not the novice I was fourteen, nor yet seven years ago"—and still must be content only with Leah. "Let who will ask, Where is the fruit? I find a private fruit sufficient." This private fruit is, as Yoder says, "consciousness without correspondent results"[32]—but I think it is not quite true to say that it is the only paradise offered us after the circuitous journey of "Experience." The view from Pisgah is as clear as it ever was.

In a letter to Margaret Fuller written to mark the second anniversary of his son's death Emerson declared himself no closer to reconciling himself to the calamity than when it was new, and compared himself to a poor Irishman who, when a court case went against him, said to the judge, "I am not satisfied." The senses have a right to perfection as well as the soul, and the soul will never rest content until these "ugly breaks" can be prevented. The attitude of defiance and the feeling of impotence recall a famous journal entry written a few months after his son's death. Speaking of Christ's sacrifice, he says:

> He did well. This great Defeat is hitherto the highest fact we have. But he that shall come shall do better. The mind requires a far higher exhibition of character, one which shall make itself good to the senses as well as the soul. This was a great Defeat. We demand Victory.

If it is not clear how long we will have to wait for this victory, how wide is the distance between ourselves and the Promised Land, Emerson refuses to give up hope. "Patience and patience, we shall win at the last." Experience may counsel only despair, "but in the solitude to which every man is always returning" there is a "sanity" that gives a very different kind of advice. "Never mind the ridicule, never mind the defeat; up again, old heart!—it seems to say." The "romance" that fled from our ship at the beginning of "Experience" returns at the end to become the goal of our weary but still hopeful pilgrimage. The "true romance which the world exists to realize"— the point at which desire and fact, the pleasure principle and the reality principle, will coincide "will be the transformation of genius into practical power."

Yet the ending of "Experience," if it restates the old hope—or at least restates the impossibility of giving it up—hardly leaves us cheered. As Firkins says, "the victory is gained in the end, idealism is reestablished, but the world in which its authority is renewed looks to the common eye like a dismantled, almost a dispeopled, universe."[33] After such knowledge, what consolation?

Emerson develops two main answers to his question in the decade of the 1840s, one of them given in "The Poet," the other in "Montaigne." Both are attempts to find some sort of "paradise within" to compensate the individual for his loss of Eden and for his failure to reach the New Jerusalem. One is designed to satisfy the Reason, the other the Understanding. (The very fact that this distinction still remains is a sign that the consolations offered are clearly thought of as *second bests*.[34]) And both essays, in their imagery and structure, show that by now Emerson's four fables— contraction, dislocation, ossification, and reflection—have become a system of significances as useful to him as the Biblical stories had been to his ancestors: a series of types or analogies by which the chaotic impressions of experience could be ordered and understood.

NOTES

1. Firkins, *Ralph Waldo Emerson*, p. 112.

2. Alfred Lord Tennyson, "Ulysses," lines 18–21, in *The Poems of Tennyson*, ed. Christopher Ricks (New York: W. W. Norton & Co., 1972), p. 563.

3. "The Holy Grail," lines 438–439, from *Idylls of the King*, in *Poems of Tennyson*, p. 1674.

4. Beard, *American Nervousness*, p. 9.

5. George M. Beard, *A Practical Treatise on Nervous Exhaustion (Neurasthenia) Its Symptoms, Nature, Sequences, Treatment* (New York: William Wood & Co., 1880), p. 66.

6. Chapman, *Selected Writings*, p. 163.

7. Firkins, *Ralph Waldo Emerson*, p. 239.

8. Albert Abrams, *The Blues (Splanchnic Neurasthenia): Causes and Cures*, 2nd. ed., enlarged (New York: E. B. Treat & Co., 1905) p. 16.

9. Whicher, *Freedom and Fate*, p. 15.

10. David Hume, "Of Miracles," in *An Enquiry Concerning Human Understanding*, in: *Essays, Moral, Political, and Literary*, ed. T. H. Green and T. H. Grose, 2 vols. (London: Longmans, Green, & Co., 1875), I, 91–92.

11. Whicher, *Freedom and Fate*, p. 16.

12. Cavell, *The Senses of Walden*, p. 125.

13. Porte, *Representative Man*, p. 181, n. 10.

14. David Hume, *A Treatise of Human Nature, Being an Attempt to Introduce the Experimental Method of Reasoning into Moral Subjects*, ed. T. H. Green and T. H. Grose, 2 vols. (London: Longmans, Green, & Co., 1898), I, 311.

15. Ibid., I, 311–312.

16. Ibid., I, 311.

17. Chaucer, *Troilus and Criseyde*, Bk. 2, line 1107.

18. W.B. Yeats, *Per Amica Silentia Lunae* (London: Macmillan & Co., 1918), p. 41.

19. Shunryu Suzuki, *Zen Mind, Beginner's Mind*, ed. Trudy Dixon, with an introduction by Richard Baker (New York: John Weatherhill, 1970), p. 35.

20. *Hydrotaphia: Urne-Burial, or, A Brief Discourse of the Sepulchral Urnes Lately Found in Norfolk* (1658), in *Sir Thomas Browne: Selected Writings*, ed. Sir Geoffrey Keynes (Chicago: University of Chicago Press, 1968), pp. 150, 152. Among the sentences Emerson copied were "There is no antidote against the *Opium* of time," and "miseries are slippery, or fall like snow upon us, which notwithstanding is no unhappy stupidity." See *JMN*, III, 219–220.

21. *The Poetical Works of Robert Southey*, 10 vols. (London: Longman, Orme, Brown, Green, & Longmans, 1840), VIII, 21.

22. Bishop, *Emerson on the Soul*, p. 198.

23. Ibid., p. 139.

24. Ibid., pp. 196–197.

25. Wordsworth, *The Prelude*, 1850 version, Bk. 4, lines 442–445.

26. Gonnaud, *Emerson: Prophecy*, pp. 121–122.

27. Rusk, *Life*, p. 294.

28. See Bishop, *Emerson on the Soul*, pp. 193–194; Porte, *Representative Man*, p. 182; Whicher, *Freedom and Fate*, p. 121. For additional examples, see Yoder, *Orphic Poet*, pp. 45, 48.

29. Michael Cowan, *City of the West: Emerson, America, and Urban Metaphor* (New Haven, Conn.: Yale University Press, 1967), p. 120. Cowan's reading of "Experience" is excellent.

30. Hume, *Treatise of Human Nature*, p. 371.

31. Cox, *Emerson: Prophecy*, p. 80.

32. Yoder, *Orphic Poet*, p. 46.

33. Firkins, *Ralph Waldo Emerson*, p. 194.

34. Whicher points out that Emerson's later thought is "characteristically an affirmation of a *second best*." *Freedom and Fate*, p. 126.

JULIE ELLISON

"The Poet"

I turn now to "The Poet" (1844) in, order to trace in greater detail the motions that have become apparent in *Nature*, "The American Scholar," and the Divinity School "Address." "The Poet" has the advantage of being typical; it is not generically one of a kind, like *Nature*, nor can its aggressiveness be attributed to the tensions of a particular occasion, like that of "The American Scholar" and the "Address." The significance of its structural similarity to those works emerges all the more clearly because of the difference in its ostensible subject. In fact, almost any essay would do for a rather exhaustive (I hope not exhausting) investigation of the cycle of antithetical personae that generates an Emersonian essay, in which I will ask more insistently what motivates the shifts from one attitude to another. The kinds of transitions that become problematic in "The Poet" are the sudden plunges from sublimity to irony, the abrupt substitutions of nature and instinct for self-conscious human authors, and the manifestations of the usual figures—the needy reader, the creative reader, the anxious young poet, the poet in his apotheosis as liberating god. Although sorting out these roles becomes more difficult the more closely one looks at the essays, an intensive reading of "The Poet" confirms, as well as complicates, the patterns we have traced in earlier works. It enables us to analyze with greater precision the defensive and aggressive functions of Emerson's irony, his repetitions, and his contradictions.

From *Emerson's Romantic Style*. © 1984 by Princeton University Press.

Emerson defines his initial stance in "The Poet" by two oppositions: first, us versus them, that is, the speaker and his audience versus the "selfish and sensual" "umpires of taste" and second, us as distinct from him, the Poet. Emerson stands over conventional critics, his selfish inferiors, but, as a reader himself, looks up to the heroic poet. Three similes in the first paragraph instigate this hierarchical self-definition. The worthless cultivation of "amateurs" is merely local, "as if you should rub a log of dry wood in one spot to produce fire, all the rest remaining cold." Next "We"— Emerson and ourselves—possess sparks of the spirit only "as fire is put into a pan to be carried about." But, finally, as "children of the fire" we may aspire to join the "highest minds of the world" which attain "accurate adjustment" (*W*.III.3–4).

In the opening movement of the essay, then, we know Emerson first by what he is against—what Bishop calls "enemy values"—and second by what he lacks and desires.[1] False critics, referred to abstractly as "Criticism ... infested with a cant of materialism," are his antagonists. Their knowledge consists only of "some study of rules and particulars, or some limited judgment of color or form ... exercised for amusement or for show." Emerson, as the true critic, occupies the middle ground between "them" and "Him." He damns the unnamed contemporary poet (who the journals show to be Tennyson [*JMN*.VII.471]) with the faint praise of resembling "the landscape-garden of a modern house." Yet he remains, like us, a listener and reader. We "need an interpreter," he confesses, including himself among the needy: "Too feeble fall the impressions of nature on us to make us artists." We who "miswrite the poem" admit the superiority of "men of more delicate ear"; unlike contemporary wits, we "know that the secret of the world is profound, but who or what shall be our interpreter, *we* know not" (*W*.III.3–9, 11, emphasis added). As Bishop finely intuits, there is in this prose—as perhaps in all prose—"a latent connection among aggression, writing, and identity." Affirmation of Emerson's "new self," Bishop observes, necessitates opponents: "One's identity is found by distinguishing a self from those who are not oneself."[2] Emerson, like the general he pictured in the Divinity School "Address," is "not himself until the battle [begins] to go against him"; he is one of those men "who rise refreshed on hearing a threat" (*CW*.I.91–92).

The speaker's position in the hierarchy between "theologians" and "the highest minds" is revealed stylistically as Emerson's rhetoric moves from diminution to dilation:

Theologians think it a pretty air-castle to talk of the spiritual meaning of a ship or a cloud, of a city or a contract, but they prefer to come again to the solid ground of historical evidence.... But the highest minds of the world have never ceased to explore the double meaning, or shall I say the quadruple or the centuple or much more manifold meaning, of every sensuous fact. (*W*.III.4)

The scornful miniaturization of "a pretty air-castle" yields to the explosive multiplication of meanings available to the poet. Similarly, the "recent writer of lyrics" has a head that resembles "a music-box of delicate tones," whereas the "eternal man" of superhuman dimensions stands "out of our low limitations" like a mountain peak (*W*.III.9).

Emerson's position as the man in the middle accounts for many such tonal variations. As critic, he argues and insists; as aspiring poet, he yearns. He belittles heroes and sages as "secondaries and servants, as sitters or models in the studio of a painter, or as assistants who bring building-materials to an architect." Yet this is followed by the humility of his own failure: "[W]e hear those primal warblings and attempt to write them down, but we lose ever and anon a word or a verse and substitute something of our own, and thus miswrite the poem." In the first role, he speaks as "emperor in his own right"; in the second, as "any permissive potentate" (*W*.III.8, 7). These oscillations correspond to his changing relationships with his reader; when he is needy, his "we" includes us; when he is strong, his "I" excludes us. There is no question, I think, that the latter condition gives him greater pleasure. He strikes out rhetorically at an opponent, be it idea, feeling, or person. The recoil from this encounter moves him from the desire for power toward the exercise of it. The essay gets underway with an attack on "umpires of taste" that carries Emerson to his true subject, the "man of Beauty." Barely restrained scorn for the "recent writer of lyrics" and other "men of talents" catapults him into an entirely different mood in which he imagines a thought so "passionate and alive" that it constitutes a "metre-making argument." He does not yet think this thought; his is still the passion of deprivation, not of possession. Nevertheless, the energetic rebound from the encounter with critics carries him onward and upward to "the aurora of a sunrise which was to put out all the stars" (*W*.III.4, 9–10). Sublimity is the effect of aggression, and also, as we shall see, of reading.

The memory of the auroras is one of the essay's high points, "high" both stylistically and by virtue of the sublime emotions it describes. Emerson mentions the appearance of the aurora borealis in September 1839, in his journal (*JMN*.VII.238–39). It was a fairly recent memory when he wrote the entry that forms the kernel of this passage. The journal editors speculate that William Ellery Channing the younger, who was visiting Emerson at the time, is the subject of this entry (*JMN*.VII.463n.). In that case, the "youth who sat near me at table" of the essay would really have been a youth who was a guest at his table. Instead of involving two young men of about the same age, as the essay passage implies, the anecdote concerns Emerson at thirty-nine and Channing at twenty-four. Furthermore, Emerson had serious reservations about Channing's ability. The essay, then, by setting the memory in the distant past of his own youth, invents a naïve Emerson. The quasi-paternal relationship that in fact prevailed between Emerson and Channing is reversed; Channing becomes the primary author, Emerson the reader of vast authorial ambitions. In the essay version, Emerson's heightened rhetoric is caused by his distance from the light. He has received the "good news" second hand: "I remember when I was young how much I was moved one morning by tidings that genius had appeared in a youth who sat near me at table." He seems not even to have actually read the "hundreds of lines" then composed. Even the poet "could not tell whether that which was in him was therein told." Emerson hears an account of the writing of a poem: a much-mediated vision. Yet his metaphors claim that for him, as well as for the youth, "all was changed." Space and time are reordered: "Boston seemed to be at twice the distance it had the night before ... Rome,—what was Rome?" Loci of past and present authority fall away. As verbs shift into the present tense ("These stony moments are still sparkling and animated!") he experiences directly the new heaven and new earth that a few sentences before were known only by report (*W*.III.10–11).

The justly famous auroras are the central metaphor for imagination in this passage. "Tidings" of good news, the silencing of the oracles, the advent of a world-changing youth draw on Gospel accounts of the Nativity. The nocturnal occasion—"all night ... these fine auroras have been streaming"— recalls the shepherds' vigil rewarded by an angelic visitation, the "sunrise which ... put out all the stars." Complicating the Nativity imagery with mythological associations, the auroras become sacred fires burning before oracles or, perhaps, the oracle itself as the voice or "fires" of nature. The metaphoric sequence ends magnificently in an image of the human face reminiscent of Blake's engraving "Glad Day": "all night, from every pore, these fine auroras have been streaming" (*W*.III.10–11).

The vision of nativity granted to Emerson is apparently as radical as that experienced by his "poet." His response depends on a suppressed syllogism: if genius can strike another here and now, it can strike me, too. The poet is ecstatic over his poem; Emerson, the reader, ecstatic with ambition. In the auroras passage, the reader senses his potential superiority to the poet. "Plutarch and Shakespeare ... and Homer" had been his teachers; the sources of his culture had been as remote as Greece, Rome, and England. The change to the present tense accentuates precisely that aspect of the occasion that so overjoys Emerson: "poetry has been written *this very day*.... [T]hat wonderful spirit *has not expired!*" (*W*.III.10–11, emphasis added). He forgets the other youth and puts himself in his place. The signs of power— light, fire, oracular voices—attest to the strength of his aspiration. The mere thought that "the spirit" has not died out, that he might be part of an unbroken apostolic succession reaching back to Homer, stimulates a fantasy of Orphic and prophetic powers. Exposure to poetic achievement so inflames Emerson's desire for literary greatness that he imaginatively elides his own development. Without having written anything, he attains the "condition of true naming" (*W*.III.16). The actual poem then composed matters only insofar as it proves that power is accessible.

But the rhetoric that bears witness to influx quickly recoils in the opposite direction. The rising sun gives way to collapse, the optative mood to self-mockery. The next paragraph breaks in half with the "but" in "Such is the hope, but the fruition is postponed." Suddenly the future, not the past, is remote. Emerson is betrayed, allegedly by the man who soars only as high as "a fowl or a flying fish," but also, Icaruslike, by his own desire for "the all-piercing, all-feeding and ocular air of heaven" (*W*.III.12). The absurd poet, flapping his stubby wings, is as much a victim of this desire as his follower.

Emerson's shifts in tone and stance are usually brought about by antithetical or negative reactions. The triple epithet—"all-piercing, all-feeding ... ocular"—offers a clue as to the antagonist that makes possible the shift from sublimity to humor here. Personified as a transparent eyeball looking downward, the aggressor seems to be the air itself. "Piercing" describes the power of vision and "all-feeding" the nourishing quality of a manna-bestowing heaven. Yet "piercing" can also mean "wounding" and "all-feeding" suggests "devouring." Like Blake's sky god Urizen, this is an image of the sublime conceived as an external objective rather than discovered within by that key Emersonian motion, surprise. Desire that is too self-conscious ends up reflecting on itself from a distance. Under the scrutiny of the "objective" mind, the yearning for transcendence appears ridiculous. The speaker parodies his own aspiration: "I shall mount above these clouds and opaque airs in which I live" becomes "this winged man ... whirls me into mists, then leaps and frisks about with me as it were from cloud to cloud." Emerson hears the winged man "still affirming that he is bound heavenward," a deft ironic touch. Colloquialisms—"I tumble down ...

into my old nooks"—effect a stylistic descent and convey his comic disillusion before he asserts it outright: "I ... have lost my faith in the possibility of any guide who can lead me thither where I would be" (*W*.III.12–13). All this reads like an echo and a parody of Hugh Blair, who, with serious misgivings, popularized the Romantic sublime:

> The Poet is out of sight, in a moment. He gets up into the clouds; becomes *so abrupt in his transitions*; *so eccentric and irregular* in his motions, and of course *so obscure*, that we essay in vaine to follow him, or to partake of his raptures.[3]

The "of course" is priceless.

Every transcendental flight in "The Poet" is similarly denied or negated, usually at once, by "descents of the spirit ... as fraught with ecstasy as any ascent Emerson could make," and often fraught with humor, as well.[4] The pattern strongly suggests that descent is caused by ascent. The reflex is skeptical rather than nihilistic; inventive and witty, not despairing. As readings of two or three subsequent passages will show, Emerson's reversals or inversions of sublimity are characterized by playful images (fowl and flying fish), a comic stance ("tumbling down"), and an ironic tone ("being myself a novice"). Here, the fantasy of poethood cannot stand the return of reflection. One way of conceiving of Emerson's task in the essays is as an effort to find a sublime that does not dissolve under the scrutiny of the critical, self-conscious mind.

Directly following his "tumble" into disappointment, Emerson entertains "new hope," and we wonder if the cycle of ascent and descent is about to repeat itself. However, this part of the essay (paragraphs 10–24) exhibits tendencies somewhat different from those of the opening section. A new element appears: nature, the world of "things." This permits Emerson to avoid an excessive imaginative investment in mortal writers. He turns away from poets who mislead their "victims" to seek a guarantee for the poetic office in the earth itself: Nature "has insured the poet's fidelity to his office of announcement and affirming ... by the beauty of things." For the moment, Emerson theorizes that art originates in nature instead of in the poetic imagination. But power, although attributed to nature, still takes linguistic forms. Everything signifies. Men who take advantage of nature's offer of a "picture-language" are rewarded with "a second, wonderful value," the "new and higher beauty" conferred by expression (*W*.III.13). Meaning is intensified as symbolic parts join to form wholes symbolic to the second power. Images express ideas; body reveals spirit; form conveys character. The reader and would-be poet beholds a redundancy of signifiers: images, symbols, beauty, language. Significance need not be created, for it surrounds us. In shifting from poet to nature, Emerson has substituted text for author—a strategy that temporarily relieves him from considerable anxiety.

"Everything signifies" has as its corollary "every man is so far a poet as to be susceptible of these enchantments of nature." Insofar as one is a "susceptible" reader of nature, one is a poet. Where "all men have the thoughts whereof the universe is the celebration," democracy prevails among men and objects alike. "Nature" is a leveling agent who demotes winged pretenders while elevating mean subjects and low language. If poetry is defined as responsiveness to things, not just "men of leisure and cultivation" but also "hunters, farmers, grooms and butchers" are potential artists. A characteristic "not more ... than" construction suggests the presence of shadowy authorial opponents: "The schools of poets and philosophers are not more intoxicated with their symbols than the populace with theirs" (*W*.III.15–16). The extended fable of collaboration between egalitarian society and nature is Emerson's revenge on the anti-democratic, over-educated poet.

After the first celebration of nature, we seem to encounter a detour, but the accidental discovery of the immanent "secret of the world" reveals one of the advantages of setting nature up as artist. A favorite passage from Spenser's "Hymn to Beauty" precipitates a new cognition or, since Emerson knows at once where he is, a recognition:

> Here we find ourselves suddenly not in a critical speculation but in a holy place, and should go very warily and reverently. We stand before the secret of the world, there where Being passes into Appearance and Unity into Variety. (*W*.III.14)[5]

The change in "place" is actually a change in *topos*, for it describes the shift from "critical speculation" to "holy," that is, Miltonic and Biblical, tones; from analysis to sublimity. We can only discover the holy place inadvertently; we "find ourselves suddenly" arrested. This is how we escape critical speculation. Surprise evades the dangers of self-consciousness, particularly the excess of hope which led to the too-strenuous and disillusioning pursuit of the "winged man." Emerson surrenders the initiative to what he calls "nature" in order for the world to take him by surprise; truth seems holier for being found, not earned.

As long as nature possesses the language-making power, the structures of sentences and paragraphs tend toward parallel repetitions and away from distinctions or oppositions. Emerson's demonstration of democratic symbolism takes the form of a series of equations in which the forceful voice of individual ambition yields to the language of the common man and of nature itself: "the north wind ... rain ... stone and wood and iron.... Lowell goes in a loom, and Lynn in a shoe, and Salem in a ship.... [T]he cider-barrel, the log-cabin, the hickory-stick, the palmetto" (*W*.III.16). But the lull in Emerson's rhetoric of aggression is only temporary. Among the *sententiae* that compose the interchangeable parts of the paragraph beginning "Beyond this universality of the symbolic language," one stands out: "We can come to use [symbols] yet with a terrible simplicity." Such heightenings signal, or effect, the reentrance of the poet. Catalogues have filled the world with words, facts, and men, but these begin to vanish. Simplicity is realized as he "disposes very easily of the most disagreeable facts." The sense of accelerating motion (nature adopts them "very fast") and hyperbole ("the fact of mechanics has not gained a grain's weight"; "[l]ife ... can dwarf any and every circumstance") create a rhetorical updraft (*W*.III.17–19). The winged man is once more among us.

With him come the combative distinctions of the opening paragraphs. The poet who purportedly heals "dislocation and detachment" also brings them into being. In this part of the essay, the motif of the circle represents the poet's relationship to others. The beehive and the "geometrical web" are images of the symmetrical whole that forms around him wherever he unifies by his "insight" a landscape that appears "broken up." Nature's "vital circles" repeat the poet's appropriating gesture. It persists through the "centred mind," the "curve of the sphere," and the situation of the country boy who centers himself in the city as the poet has in the landscape. The circle can be a figure of either inclusion or exclusion, depending upon one's point of view. Initially it incorporates "millions" of "particulars," as the poet draws nature into his gravitational field. When he begins to dominate, however, its circumference excludes the speaker of the essay and us, its readers. We are "intelligent" but not original; we "inhabit symbols," but do not recognize them. The poet is the active agent who "turns the world to glass", we are the spectators to whom he "shows ... all things" in their correct order. He is "nearer" to the center than we are, and shares the fluidity of the world's molten core while the objects we perceive stand "dumb and inanimate" at the petrified surface (*W*.III.18–21).

The distinction between "us" and "Him" signals a resurgence of the poet's authority at the cost of nature's—and at the cost of Emerson, the reader. This is one of the intriguing moments when Emerson seems to elect inferiority or to prefer vicarious to direct gratification. An act of aggression establishes the poet's dominance; the world is "put under the mind for verb and noun." Things fall "under" his mind, both as subjects live "under" their ruler and as we view a cell "under" a magnifying glass. Perception becomes a metaphor for power, as it always does in Emerson's writings. In a synaesthetic celebration of several kinds of power, he asserts that perception makes possible control, expression, and kinesis. "[T]hat better perception" discovers perpetual motion, first in thought, then in things. Emerson blurs the distinction between the "stability of the thought" and the "fugacity of the symbol" with the notion of "multiform" thought. Energy is contagious, a force "within ... every creature ... impelling it to ascend into a higher form." Instinct and rhetoric combine in speech that "flows with the flowing of nature." This influx brings about the predicted condition of "terrible simplicity," but the achievement of transparency definitively casts "us"—including Emerson—in a subordinate role: "As the eyes of Lyncaeus were said to see through the earth, so the poet turns the world to glass, and shows us all things in their right series and procession." This is the holy place where the poet "alone" witnesses "metamorphosis," the "secret of the world." He is "one step nearer to things" than his readers (*W*.III.20–21). Once again, Emerson experiences a moment of sublime vision at the cost of dependency. The trappings of the Romantic sublime here do not result in the elevation of the reader over the author who has overimpressed him. The linearity of the catalogue—"sex, nutriment, gestation, birth, growth"—gives way to vertical motion as particulars pass "into the soul of man, to suffer there a change and reappear a new and higher fact." "[A]stronomy, chemistry, vegetation and animation" are realigned on the sublime axis of height and depth: "[the poet] knows why the plain or meadow of space was strown with these flowers we call suns and moons and stars; why the great deep is adorned with animals, with men, and gods." The last sentence of the paragraph grows out of the first. The mind that put the world under it becomes the poet who rides "the horses of thought" (*W*.III.21). In the space between the two metaphors, thought has subsumed things and taken flight.

Just as the conquest of nature by the poet is at hand, Emerson reverts to the theory of poetry as natural process. He apparently feels no need to reconcile what seem to us competing claims. Language making is first willed, then as automatic as the growth of "a leaf out of a tree." The poet's authority as "Namer" is taken over by a mother who "baptizes herself." Emerson delights at one moment in the "detachment or boundary" established by names; at another, in attachment or continuity when naming is redefined as "a second nature, grown out of the first as a leaf out of a tree" (*W*.III.21–22). This was a familiar paradox even in Shakespeare's time—*vide* Polixenes and

Perdita on nature's art.[6] The peculiarity of Emerson's version is that he will neither recognize the paradox nor resolve it. Man and nature, as creators, do have substantive differences in "The Poet," however. As I suggested earlier, the poet is self-conscious and nature, as sheer process, is not. There seems to be a trade-off. The attributes of power—vision, motion, voice—accrue mostly to the poet. Nature bears no burden of consciousness, but her powers of transformation are less radical. The strain of poethood seems to make Emerson want an unreflective, nonhuman, and wholly natural art. When nature is dominant, on the other hand, he grows restless with her benign organic forces and yearns for his antithetical hero. "Nature" frequently appears to stand for an intermittent, saving forgetfulness. Here it no doubt saves the speaker from the bathetic collapse that resulted from his first episode of enthusiastic soaring.

Emerson's attitude toward nature here is somewhat different from the "nostalgia" attributed by de Man to Romantic poets, despite the fact that de Man describes their similarly "alternating feelings of attraction and repulsion ... towards nature."[7] Emerson's rhetoric reveals more clearly than theirs his awareness that nature's authorship is a fiction. We hardly need ask ourselves whether he means that names literally grow out of nature "as a leaf out of a tree"; we know to take this as hyperbole. Throughout "The Poet," the rhapsodic status of his assertions is obvious:

> What we call nature is a certain self-regulated motion or change; and nature does all things by her own hands, and does not leave another to baptize her but baptizes herself; and this through the metamorphosis again. (*W*.III.22)

The repetitive "and-and-and" construction of this sentence expresses enthusiasm without demanding our rational assent, and Emerson's acknowledgment of the figurative meaning of "what we call nature" conveys his sophisticated awareness of its metaphoric quality.

After substituting nature for the poet, Emerson suddenly—but not, by now, surprisingly—reintroduces the human author. He falls upon the Orphic poet, whom his argument has just rendered unnecessary, a repeated gesture that indicates how little sentiment he really has for nature. He would have us believe that the words of the Orphic poet which follow are especially persuasive, uttered by one possessing particular authority. In *Nature*, the voice of the Orphic poet is a serious, heightened one. In "The Poet," however, as in other essays, Emerson is more skeptical about Orphic powers. This bard sounds too much like the disillusioned speaker earlier in the essay to be convincingly sublime. As before, our expectations of sublimity are aroused, then deflated by parodic images, a comic fall, and a humorous tone. Quantitative extremes ("billions of spores," "two rods off") and hyperbolic adjectives ("a fearless, sleepless, deathless progeny") sound comical, not weighty. "[V]ivacious offspring" of the poet take to the air, beating their emblematic wings; the "new self" has become outrageously plural. Emerson keeps his brood alive with *ad hoc* allegorizing. Suddenly we have not one flock but two. The songs "flying immortal from their mortal parent" are pursued by "clamorous flights of censures, which swarm in far greater numbers and threaten to devour them." This time, instead of Emerson tumbling down into his old nooks, critics "fall plump down and rot." "Censures," not desirous emulators, pursue the poet. Their motive is not aspiration but attack, and their ensuing collapse is thus thoroughly deserved. With villains substituted for victims, the airborne songs "ascend and leap and pierce into the deeps of infinite time" unscathed (*W*.III.23–24).

The Orphic poet is fair game; Emerson has little patience with expert testimony, even of his own invention. The Poet waxes hyperbolical until Emerson's skeptical reflex reacts and his own overstatements strike him as funny. The longer he dwells on a thought—particularly a "sublime" thought—the more susceptible he becomes to laughter. Hence Emerson's climaxes are often comical. In this instance, I think it is the mechanical aspect of nature's activity that begins to amuse him. He parodies his own complicated metaphoric apparatus of fungus, gills, spores, and sowing in the anatomical details of the flying melodies and their "plump" pursuers. He uses the devices of allegory to ridicule the excesses of allegory itself. The object of his humor is the Orphic speaker of the parable. Nature and poems mockingly collaborate to escape poet and critics. The device of the Orphic poet is a witty turn against the wrong kind of sublimity.

As we continue to read through "The Poet," we find that the essay repeats itself. Certain tones and attitudes generate each other in predictable ways: the desire for and the exercise of power, the celebration of and skepticism about the hero-poet, sublime transcendence and ironic descent. Alternation between these, not a developing argument of "dialectical" synthesis, accounts for the progress of the essay. Each repetition is also a variation, however, so the cumulative effect is expansive, not reductive. We learn the full implications of each stance and motion. More importantly, we learn that there is, finally, no resolution; such motions are unending. In the paragraph following the bard's speech, another one of these cycles begins. Emerson first returns to the theme of "organic" expression. Objects automatically generate the poems of which they are the subjects. But almost immediately, authorial inspiration revives and nature yields to the supernatural. Language appears that we will associate with the poet at the height of his powers as liberating god. Metaphors of transparency ("making things translucid to others") and excess ("intellect doubled on itself") are part of this mood, as is the occasional touch of Old Testament grandeur ("his speech is thunder, his thought is law"). Motion accelerates. Metamorphosis "does not stop"; following and suffering, flowing and circulating speed up until the poet's "centrifugal tendency" is great enough to fling him "out into free space" (*W*.III.25–28). Organic process gradually gives way to instantaneous and unnatural change described as magic, madness, and drunkenness. The speaker once more participates vicariously in inspiration. As eyewitness, Emerson again interprets the work of art as a prophecy of his own poem. This time, he is not defended by irony His youthful memory of the unnamed sculptor repeats the previous account of the auroras. "I knew in my younger days" echoes "I remember when I was young," and the dawn that imbues Phosphorus recalls the auroral light. Like the youth who "could tell nothing but that all was changed," the sculptor is "unable to tell directly what made him happy or unhappy, but by wonderful indirections he could tell" (*W*.III.24).

Through a complex sequence of similes, the poet's power begins to grow. Passive Lockean perception ("in the sun, objects paint their images on the retina of the eye") is likened to the way things "paint a ... copy of their essence in his mind." Then "the metamorphosis of things into higher organic forms" illustrates "their change into melodies." Finally, the eye's reflection of form is analogous to the musical image of "its daemon or soul." Emerson uses the word "daemon" to mean an attendant spirit or genius. But the daemon's stance "over everything" betrays a power that belongs to other connotations of the daemonic, a "field of force" occupied by the "more than rational energy of imagination."[8] Daemonization—taking the daemon that stands over nature into his own "melody"—is the poet's reward for his boldness in entering that field: "his speech is thunder, his thought is law, and his words are universally intelligible as the plants and animals." The quest traditionally routed through the underworld is implicit in the movement "into" and "through": "new passages are opened for us into nature; the mind flows into and through things hardest and highest, and the metamorphosis is possible." The "passage out into free space" follows the journey down into the earth (*W*.III.25, 27–28).

We encounter the following dynamic, then. The "possessed and conscious intellect" of the aspiring poet wants to augment "his privacy of power as an individual man." His goal is to know the world directly, which means, for Emerson, to control matter ("he disposes of disagreeable facts"), other men (as liberator, teacher, language maker), and, ultimately, time. Perceiving "a great public power" out there in "things," he sees the world as the object of his desire. He defines the "Not Me" (*CW*.1.8) as what the self would be: ethereal, auroral, divine. Although the poet flows out into and mingles with things, his identity does not dissolve. On the contrary, he absorbs nature into himself. Speaking for and as the Not Me, he mediates between it and all other men. What looks like loss is aggrandizement. Emerson's hero acknowledges power other than his own only to "take advantage of it" (*W*.III.26, 28). He risks losing his soul in order to gain the whole world. The inebriation caused by a heady draught of "instinct" calls for restrictions, as though Emerson seeks to discipline his dream of power. No "spurious mode of attaining freedom" is permitted; these lead into "baser places" where poets are "punished for that advantage they won, by a dissipation and deterioration" (a phrase that condemns both aggression and substance abuse). The habit of living "on a key so low that the common influences ... delight him" protects the poet from an excess or the wrong kind of imaginative stimulation. Midway between the bare common of *Nature* and the bleak rocks of "Experience," "the lonely waste of the pinewoods" is an appropriate setting for the "radiance of wisdom" in "The Poet" (*W*.III.28–29).[9]

Throughout these paragraphs, the speaker of the essay has been vicariously benefiting from the poet-hero's progress. After all, it has been a characteristic of the sublime since Longinus that the mind of the reader "swells in transport and inward pride, as if what was only heard had been the product of its own invention."[10] Having himself escaped from "the custody of that body in which he is pent up, and of that jail-yard of individual relations in which he is enclosed," the poet leads his readers "out of a cave or cellar into the open air." As the poet resigned himself to the Not Me, we yield to him and are similarly compensated. The mind of the "beholder" is liberated: "Men have really got a new sense and found within their world another world, or nest of worlds; for the metamorphosis once seen, we divine that it does not stop" (*W*.III.28, 30). A list of representative metaphors follows (*W*.III.30–31). Having described the consequences of reading poetry, Emerson now offers us a practical demonstration.

The experience of reading, however, reminds him how much he dislikes this secondary role (which he nevertheless has consistently elected). If "tropes" are liberating, books are oppressive. In the next paragraph, he argues that freedom is given to us in books in order that we may be free *from* them.

> An imaginative book renders us much more service at first, by
> stimulating us through its tropes, than afterward when we arrive
> at the precise sense of the author. I think nothing is of any value
> in books excepting the transcendental and extraordinary. If a man
> is inflamed and carried away by his thought, to that degree that
> he forgets the authors and the public and heeds only this one
> dream which holds him like an insanity, let me read his paper, and
> you may have all the arguments and histories and criticism.
> (*W*.III.32)

That "I think" arrogantly dismisses everything except "the transcendental
and extraordinary" in a tone encountered here for the first time in the essay,
the unmistakable hubris of the reader's sublime. The initial distinction
between "tropes" and "the precise sense of the author" quickly stiffens into
the opposition between "this one dream which holds him like an insanity"
and "all the arguments and histories and criticism," though even here
Emerson tends to forget his own strength as reader in his contemplation of
the writer. Strengthened by vicarious liberation, the first person voice tries
itself against an opponent in the familiar "us versus them" tactic. The
sharpening antithesis and growing outrageousness of tone go together.
Emerson's self-enjoyment derives from the exhilarating clarification of his
stance that the antagonist permits. Put another way, friction between the
speaker and books that presume to instruct him generates the energy that
inflames and carries away this pronouncement. "We" disappears in favor of
the unabashed "I." The apotheosis of the reader-critic displaces the poet just
recently deified. Emerson excepts from his general denunciation only the
author who "forgets the authors and the public." That is, he reads in order
to have his own rebellious readings confirmed. While he avows that his
admiration for a pantheon of writers is exempt from the general curse, the
breezy tone in which he declares that "all the value" of this group is "the
certificate we have of the departure from routine" still thrills to its own
audaciousness. The closing *fortissimo* suggests that the "emotion" with which
a reader responds to a trope is an empathetic fantasy of origination. Feeling
like a creator, he usurps the poet's Orphic powers:

> the magic of liberty ... puts the world like a ball in our hands.
> How cheap even the liberty then seems; how mean to study, when
> an emotion communicates to the intellect the power to sap and
> upheave nature; how great the perspective! nations, times,
> systems, enter and disappear like threads in tapestry of large

figure and many colors; dream delivers us to dream, and while the drunkenness lasts we will sell our bed, our philosophy, our religion, in our opulence. (*W*.III.32–33)

Emerson never feels so free as when he is rejecting "nations, times, systems," "arguments, and histories, and criticism." His poetics are polemical; freedom is always freedom *from* and power, always power *over*.

But once again, Emerson voluntarily renounces his goal just as it is achieved. This habit of abandoning authority once he has it saves his will to power from brutality. Before the superman can oppress anyone, he resigns and joins the revolution that would have resisted him. After an apparent victory, the Orphic reader surrenders. Again "fruition is postponed" (*W*.III.12). Suddenly "the poor shepherd, who ... perishes in a drift within a few feet of his cottage door" is an "emblem of the state of man." Drunken opulence has left the speaker washed up on "the brink of the waters of life." Spatial metaphors situate us once more on the periphery of a circle of which the circumference is everywhere, the center nowhere: "The inaccessibleness of every thought but that we are in, is wonderful.... [Y]ou are as remote when you are nearest as when you are farthest." Deprivation revives desire and the tone of affectionate longing: "we [readers] love the poet, the inventor, who in any form whether in an ode or in an action or in looks and behavior has yielded us a new thought" (*W*.III.33).

Desire reinstates the hierarchical distance between reader and poet which, as we could have predicted, leads Emerson to discover a new opponent. He attacks the literal-minded reader or writer. The crucifying "mystic" "nails a symbol to one sense" and so makes it "too stark and solid." The poet, with his unfailing powers of invention, is unperturbed by the temporary nature of his productions. His faith in himself is so immense that any one symbol is "held lightly" (*W*.III.34–35). The mystic, on the other hand, is capable of only one good idea which he anxiously and possessively insists on. To dramatize the distinction and reprove the mystic's heavy-handed symbolism, Swedenborg materializes. Readers of "Swedenborg, or The Mystic" cannot help but find it strange that he should be deployed as a corrective to mysticism, for in *Representative Men*, Emerson attributes to him precisely the tedious fixity here ascribed to mystics (*W*.IV.132). Emerson habitually mocks the literal-mindedness of Swedenborg while conceding the "literary value" of his "epical parables" (*CW*.I.68).[11] "I commended him as a great poet," he reports in a journal entry of July 1842. This was hardly good enough for Sampson Reed, who "wished, that if I admired the poetry I should feel it as a fact." But Emerson dismissed Swedenborg's beliefs as

"Absurd." "'Otherworld?' I reply, 'there is no other world; here or nowhere is the whole fact.'" In the end, though, Emerson resolves, "I can readily enough translate his rhetoric into mine" (*JMN*.VIII.183).

We have an example of such translation in "The Poet." Pieces of visions from Swedenborg's writings are joined into Emersonian "rhetoric." His adaptation results in some stylistic peculiarities. The nonparallelism between figs and grapes, between affirming a truth and a blossoming twig, between gnashing and thumping and disputing voices is bewildering; so is the imagery of dragons in heavenly light and men in a cabin. The visions become progressively more alarming as we shift disconcertingly between distance and nearness, inside and outside. Whose point of view do we share? Swedenborg? The protagonists of his visions (who "to each other ... appeared as men")? The reader? Or Emerson, who wonders how others perceive him? When the poet inspires "awe and terror" because of the quality of "perception in him," every point of view finally postulates a perspective beyond itself (*W*.III.36). Emerson seems to have committed the intellectual sin he would later attribute to Swedenborg, that is, "a confounding of planes ... which is dislocation and chaos" (*W*.IV.140).

The result is closer to farce than poetry. Emerson betrays not the slightest hint of a smile; indeed, he apparently assumes that he has shown us sublimity itself when he calls Swedenborg "an object of awe and terror." Awful and terrible, it should be noted, by virtue of a potentially comic doubleness: "men may wear one aspect to themselves and their companions and a different aspect to higher intelligences." At such moments, "[t]he question Emerson raises," writes Barbara Packer, "is not primarily what he means by these bizarre associations, but whether or not he was aware of how funny they sound."[12] After the annunciation of Swedenborg's awful aspect, the writing gets even funnier. To see men as dragons is one thing, but priests as "dead horses"? In a moment of slight detachment, irony enters and "instantly" Emerson comically reimagines the material to which he has just alluded. "Epical parable" is repeated as joke:

> instantly the mind inquires whether these fishes under the bridge, yonder oxen in the pasture, those dogs in the yard, are immutably fishes, oxen, and dogs, or only so appear to me, and perchance to themselves appear upright men; and whether I appear as a man to all eyes. (*W*.III.36)

Yet Emerson does not admit his own humor even now. He presents, still in the key of high seriousness, Brahmins and Pythagoras, wheat and caterpillars, until he arrives at a restatement of the first sentence of the paragraph, which invested Swedenborg with the full regalia of the poet. We are left, in Packer's words, with "the Tyger of Wrath as Cheshire Cat."[13]

This adaptation of Swedenborg's cosmic fantasies is the third ironic episode in "The Poet," along with the fables of the "winged man" and of the "clamorous flights of censures." Taken together, these passages give us an insight into the relationship of irony and the sublime in Emerson's prose. Such episodes, and the many others like them scattered throughout the essays, resemble the closing paragraph of "Intellect" as it originally appeared in the journals. Its development illuminates the motivation of Emerson's ironic fables.

> Of these unquiet daemons that fly or gleam across the brain what trait can I hope to draw in my sketch book? Wonderful seemed to me as I read in Plotinus the calm & grand air of these few cherubim—great spiritual lords who have walked in the world— they of the old religion—dwelling in a worship that makes the sanctities of Christianity parvenues & merely popular; for "necessity is in intellect, but persuasion in soul." This band of grandees Hermes, Heraclitus, Empedocles, Plato, Plotinus, Olympiodorus, Proclus, Synesius, & the rest, have somewhat so vast in their logic, so primary in their thinking, that it seems antecedent to all the ordinary distinctions of rhetoric & literature, & to be at once poetry & music & dancing & astronomy & mathematics. I am present at the sowing of the seed of the world. With a geometry of sunbeams the Soul lays the foundations of nature. The truth & grandeur of their thought is proved by its scope & applicability; for it commands more even than our dear old bibles of Moses & Swedenborg the entire Schedule & inventory of things for its illustration. But what marks its elevation & has a comic look to us if we are not very good when we read, is the innocent serenity with which these babe-like Jupiters sit in their clouds & from age to age prattle to each other and to no contemporary; perfectly assured that their speech is intelligible & the most natural thing in the world, they emit volume after volume without one moment's heed of the universal astonishment of the poor human race below, who do not comprehend a sentence.... The angels are so enamoured of the language that is spoken in heaven that they will not distort their lips with the hissing & unmusical dialects of men but speak

their own whether there be any near, who can understand it or not. (*JMN*.VII.413–14)

The journal entry opens with a Miltonic flourish in rather hushed tones of desire, wonder, and praise appropriate to a subject both "vast" and "primary." Once again we hear the "holy place" motif in a vision of Being "antecedent" to Appearances—"I am present at the sowing of the seed of the world." With the reference to "our dear old bibles of Moses and Swedenborg," though, gravity gives way. The very next sentence begins with a pivotal "But" which confesses the "comic look" of what Emerson has just imagined. Comic, that is, "if we are not very good when we read." Irony is a delicious sin, then, a temptation the "good" reader and, surely, the "good" writer must try to resist.

This temptation perhaps besets Emerson more often than usual when Swedenborg is his subject. (In the published version of "Intellect," interestingly enough, the reference to the "bibles of Moses and Swedenborg" drops out and Emerson's laughter is more decorous [*CW*.II.204–5].) Emerson regards Swedenborg's visions as exercises in point of view that can be enjoyed as intellectual play, whatever the author's intentions. Add his mixed feelings about Swedenborg, and it is not surprising that the impulse to irony frequently prevails. It prevails far too often to be accounted for by his response to a single writer, however. The fact that the representative mind of "Intellect" undergoes a metamorphosis from high seriousness to high good humor suggests that the ironic moment is central to Emerson's literary philosophy and method. The Transcendentalist is, by his own definition, an ironist. His analysis of "The Comic," the best possible gloss on his ironic passages, bears this out:

> [T]he best of all jokes is the sympathetic contemplation of things by the understanding from the philosopher's point of view.
>
> This is the radical joke of life and then of literature. The presence of the ideal of right and of truth ... makes the yawning delinquencies of practice remorseful to the conscience, tragic to the interest, but droll to the intellect.
>
> [T]he occasion of laughter is some keeping of the word to the ear and eye, while it is broken to the soul. (*W*.VIII.153, 154, 157)

This definition of humor shows why Emerson laughs at Swedenborg's "confounding of planes." "The comic" is profoundly ironic, generated by several points of view belonging to different faculties that come into play together: conscience, interest, and intellect; Understanding and Reason ("the philosopher's point of view"); ear, eye, and soul. "Yawning" discrepancies in the responses of the various faculties provoke laughter. In each case, the superior faculty laughs. The philosophical sense and the soul are amused by what the understanding, eye, and ear take seriously. (The superiority of intellect to conscience is questionable, however.) Humor requires an "ideal of right and truth." The more high-minded we are, the more likely we are to find life comical, since our soul is that much more remote from our senses.[14] If the higher faculties mock the lower, however, the lower also expose the higher. In comic moments, the soul acknowledges the understanding, whereas in sublime moments, the soul defeats the understanding. It is the "truth and grandeur" of Emerson's "band of grandees" in "Intellect" which trigger the ensuing parody, suggesting that the lower faculties can function as the antagonists. As the syntax reveals, "what marks ... elevation" is what "has a comic look." Clearly, irony is essential to Emerson's oscillation between the mood of awed desire and that of irreverent self-aggrandizement. It shatters monolithic perceptions and frees the observer into laughter.

The apparent inadvertence of Emerson's irony is thus deceptive. Irony is one of the intentions of an art of multiple points of view and tones of voice. The argument that Emerson is a consciously ironic writer accommodates the accidental genesis of any given passage. In its full range of meanings, irony pervades Emerson's works. Its essential "halfness" or "break" recurs in his theory of transition and in stylistic discontinuities. Repetition, the chance for second thoughts, also precipitates irony. Finally, as the reference to the comic sense as a reader's affliction implies, irony strikes when Emerson contemplates the works of other writers. Since the "transcendental and extraordinary" never fill a whole book, the reader inevitably perceives the author's "yawning delinquencies of practice" that miss the soul and impress only the lower faculties. The very structure of the act of reading involves assent on one "plane" and mockery on another. Emerson thus grounds his theory of literary influence in this bifurcated response to past masters.

The essay's final movement represents this double, or ironic, reading in dramatic terms as it repeats the central action of the work: deprivation provokes critical distinctions that bring about an influx of power. Emerson as reader displaces his poet-hero, only to close by invoking him once more. He begins the closing section by recapitulating his call for assistance. The poet of America, "the timely man," is late in arriving. ("The principal event in chronology," as Emerson told us once before, "is postponed.") "We" delay the emergence of the poet within us: "We do not with sufficient plainness or sufficient profoundness address ourselves to life, nor dare we chaunt our own times and social circumstances. If we filled the day with bravery, we should not shrink from celebrating it." The speaker as representative reader turns against himself, and this gesture begins his metamorphosis. The call for a "genius" to recognize "the value of our incomparable materials" initiates this recognition (*W*.III.37). An "astonishingly prideful figure presents itself unabashedly as the very figure of the ideal poet for which it calls," Porter observes. "*It summons itself.*"[15] I would revise this. What really materializes out of Emerson's evasive arrogance is not the poet, but the critic. He finds his own version of the American poem inadequate, but denies that anyone has yet produced a better one. Outraged and outrageous, he dismisses all of European literature:

> If I have not found that ... which I seek, neither could I aid myself to fix the idea of the poet by reading now and then in Chalmer's collection of five centuries of English poets. These are more wits than poets, though there have been poets among them. But when we adhere to the ideal of the poet, we have our difficulties even with Milton and Homer. Milton is too literary, and Homer too literal and historical.

The American provincial regards five centuries of English poetry as an anthology into which he dips "now and then"; his revenge is an "ideal" that no poet who has ever lived can match. In a demonstration of the aggressive uses of criticism, Emerson's British and classical competitors are dispatched by a theoretical double bind which rules them either too literary or not literary enough. The mask of the humble critic ("I am not wise enough for a national criticism") cannot hide the speaker's egotism. Acting as archangel to the poet's Adam, he assumes the privileged role of mediator who discharges an "errand from the muse to the poet concerning his art" (*W*.III.38).

Emerson chooses not to end at the height of his critical powers. The poet once more becomes the central figure. He is in the throes of a painful adolescence. If Emerson yields to the poet, then it is to a youthful one whose anxieties are very close to those of Emerson-as-reader. Emerson lyrically reimagines the poet's development as quest romance, then as pastoral. These somewhat fanciful treatments effect a rhetorical diminuendo; more importantly, they recapitulate the frustrations Emerson experienced as a maturing writer. The older speaker who looks to the poet for revelation and the struggling youth represent two phases of Emerson's development. Even as the hero of the essay is displayed in the soft colors of pastoral and romance, he strives to find a voice that will shatter the nostalgic style which praises him.

In the first fable, the quest romance, poets "found or put themselves" (an interesting equivocation) "in certain conditions ... exciting to [their] intellect." Encountering these "conditions" suggests tales in which the hero lies down to sleep under an enchanted tree, drinks from magical waters (tasting "this immortal ichor"), or trespasses half-deliberately on haunted ground (the journal passage reads "I see the beckoning of this Ghost" [*JMN*.IX.71]). A vision initiates the quest: "He hears a voice, he sees a beckoning ... he pursues a beauty, half seen, which flies before him." The "charm" of his own "original and beautiful" utterances lures him further on his way until the strangeness he desires is his, at least, in "our way of talking." The quest fable is clearly an allegory of the creative, agonistic release of what is "in me, and shall out." Pursuit of an external object changes to the ejaculation of "thought ... as Logos." Like the young Emerson, the poet is rendered speechless by external and internal constraints; he is both "balked" and "dumb." He perceives the audience by whom he is "hissed and hooted" as the antagonist with whom he is to "strive." Convinced nightly in solitude of his capacity to conduct a "whole river of electricity," he finds himself blocked during the day in public. Afraid of the force of his own imagination and unwilling to appear shamelessly egotistical (they go together), he hides the ambition that rages within him. Belief in his own potency and aggression toward a perceived oppressor once again generate each other. When the poet accepts his own power, antagonism evaporates momentarily. He reconciles himself to the world by imaginatively absorbing it: "All the creatures by pairs and by tribes pour into his mind as into a Noah's ark, to come forth again to people a new world" (*W*.III.39–40).[16]

The Biblical story of nature saved from the Flood becomes a fable of nature pouring into the mind as flood and undergoing there an imaginative transvaluation. In the closing paragraphs of the essay, the Biblical landscape of rain, flood, covenantal rainbow, and greening trees repeats and naturalizes the drama of desire, agon, and power. Instead of dreaming electric dreams, the poet lies "close hid with nature," smitten with "an old shame before the holy ideal." A hint of harshness remains in his sentence; he "must pass for a fool and a churl for a long season" in the eyes of Capitol and Exchange. In the end, though, the poet dwells harmoniously with his fellow creatures in an "actual world." The landlord metaphor seems to describe stewardship and at-homeness rather than dominance. "Impressions" do not flood the poet's mind, but "fall like summer rain, copious, but not troublesome." The rain recurs in the gentle parody of the Eucharist that closes the essay: "[T]here is Beauty, plenteous as rain, shed for thee." This benign image of plenitude without excess signals the transformation of the "liberating god" into the "well-beloved flower" of Pan (*W*.III.41–42).

The peculiar repetition that ends "The Poet" tells us a good deal about Emerson's conception of closure in his prose works. Our feeling that the essay is winding down is achieved entirely by rhetorical and imagistic means. The closing episodes recall earlier passages: dumbness attributed to "some obstruction or ... excess of phlegm in our constitution"; the poet "isolated among his contemporaries by truth and by his art, but with this consolation ... that they will draw all men sooner or later"; the solitary who rejects Boston and New York for "the lonely waste of the pine woods." These elements recur in the closing allegories of trial, but there is no reason why these repetitions should be more meaningful than the many earlier ones. The idiom of supernatural romance acts as a foil for the quieter, naturalistic fable that follows. The shift into a more soothing tone and setting confirms our sensation of closure. This sensation depends in part on the illusion that the generative oppositions which have sustained the essay have been healed. We have had this sensation before in "The Poet" and should know by now that it is only a temporary resting place. Even as we are seduced by the trappings of sublimity—the long apostrophes ("Doubt not, O poet, but persist"), the prophetic mood ("the ideal shall be real to thee"), archaisms, and Biblical resonances ("thou shalt")—we recognize them for the conventional flourishes they are (*W*.III.6, 5, 29, 40–42). The gratuitousness of the ending reminds one of the conclusion to "Fate." In three paragraphs all beginning "Let us build altars to the Blessed Unity" or "to the Beautiful Necessity," Emerson pulls out the same peroratorical stops (*W*.VIII.48–49). Burke's phrase, "the machinery of transcendence," expresses our sense that at such moments Emerson lowers on us the stylistic equivalent of *deus ex machina*.[17] The ostentatiousness of the coda betrays its arbitrary character. It has been imposed on a text that could continue its oscillations indefinitely.

The concluding pages of "The Poet" verify what the rest of the essay has already taught us. Emerson composes by depicting the stages of his own development. But his prose is by no means autobiographical, for the essayistic representation of his progress is significantly different from his personal reminiscences. Emerson became a writer by identifying criticism with power and by making reading necessary to writing. En route to these discoveries, he made himself miserable. In essays like "The Poet," he chooses to relive the particular exasperations of his twenties. The repetition apparently is motivated by his desire to repeat the movement from deprived ambition to aggressive criticism. The fact that he repeatedly chooses positions disagreeable in themselves strongly suggests that his greatest pleasure is in the willing reenactment, freely and playfully dramatized, of slow and painful change.

NOTES

1. Bishop, *Emerson on the Soul*, p. 131.

2. Ibid., p. 184.

3. Hugh Blair, *Lectures on Rhetoric and Belles-Lettres*, edited by Harold F. Harding (Carbondale: Southern Illinois University Press, 1956), II, 354–56.

4. James M. Cox, "R. W. Emerson: The Circles of the Eye," in *Emerson: Prophecy, Metamorphosis, and Influence*, edited by David Levin, English Institute Essays (New York: Columbia University Press, 1975), p. 70.

5. The source of this passage must be Spenser's Garden of Adonis, that other secret place which guards the mystery of metamorphosis. Emerson's reference to the moment as "here" also recalls Wordsworth's "here the Power so called" (*The Prelude* VI.ll.592–616). Wordsworth, too, stops before the secret of the imagination and represents its mystery as a creative, unitary power: "like the mighty flood of Nile / Poured from his fount of Abyssinian clouds / To fertilize the whole Egyptian plain." "The Poet" and *The Prelude* describe encounters between the self and regenerative power in versions of the Renaissance allegory of a place where life originates.

6. *The Winter's Tale*, IV.iv.ll.88–90. Joel Porte adduces the same scene in a discussion of Emerson's changing conceptions of nature and fate, *Representative Man*, pp. 226–28.

7. Paul de Man, "Intentional Structure of the Romantic Image," in *Romanticism and Consciousness: Essays in Criticism*, edited by Harold Bloom (New York: W. W. Norton, 1970), p. 71.

8. *Shorter Oxford English Dictionary*, 2nd ed. s.v. "demon." Geoffrey Hartman, *Beyond Formalism* (New Haven: Yale University Press, 1970), p. 319.

9. Entered in Emerson's journal a few months after his son's death, the first version of this passage is preceded and followed by meditations on that event: "This beloved and now departed Boy, this Image in every part beautiful, how he expands in his dimensions in this fond Memory to the dimensions of Nature" (*JMN*.VIII.205). Waldo seems to have vanished into the landscape that both reminds Emerson of his loss and veils a consoling "Spirit." Only the poor, hungry, and simple—those who have purged themselves of "fashion and covetousness"—earn a glimpse of the *genius loci*. (As usual in Emerson's value judgments, socioeconomic, moral, and aesthetic capacities are conflated. Wisdom discriminates against the residents of Boston and New York, who have grown jaded by consuming imported culture—"wine and French coffee" [*W*.III.29]). He is among the needy by virtue of the grief that has left him unsophisticated. However, the pain of Waldo's death is ameliorated by his ghostly return as the light of Wisdom. Cox's hypothesis that Emerson habitually

converts the deaths of family members into imaginative energy seems borne out by this passage, both in its original form and as it appears in "The Poet" (Cox, "The Circles of the Eye," pp. 71–73).

10. *Longinus on the Sublime*, translated by William Smith, p. 55. "For the mind is naturally elevated by the true *Sublime*, and so sensibly affected with its lively strokes, that it swells in transport and inward pride, as if what was only heard had been the product of its own invention."

11. See also *JMN*.VI.312; VII.30, 127; VIII.221.

12. Barbara Packer, "Uriel's Cloud: Emerson's Rhetoric," *Georgia Review* (Summer 1978), p. 326.

13. Barbara Packer, *Emerson's Fall: A New Interpretation of the Major Essays* (New York: Continuum, 1982), p. 15.

14. Vivian Hopkins, *Spires of Form: A Study of Emerson's Aesthetic Theory* (Cambridge: Harvard University Press, 1951), pp. 196–97.

15. Porter, *Emerson and Literary Change*, p. 194.

16. The conflated images of salvation, matrimony, and nature recur in Harold Bloom's description of the outcome of "The Internalization of Quest-Romance," a plot that this passage illustrates very neatly. In *Romanticism and Consciousness*, p. 71.

17. Kenneth Burke, "I, Eye, Ay—Concerning Emerson's Early Essay on 'Nature' and the Machinery of Transcendence," in *Language as Symbolic Action* (Berkeley and Los Angeles: University of California Press, 1968), p. 200.

RICHARD BRODHEAD

Hawthorne, Melville, and the Fiction of Prophecy

As an, instance of tradition formation, Melville's relation to Hawthorne is peculiar on at least two grounds. Figures of tradition stand as the great past for their successors. But Hawthorne was emphatically not past when Melville encountered him. Hawthorne was 46, or still in mid-life, when Melville (then 31) met him in August 1850; and Hawthorne was still very much in mid-career. In the summer of 1850 Hawthorne was the writer of the two collections, *Twice-Told Tales* and *Mosses from an Old Manse*, and only just of *The Scarlet Letter*: three of the four long romances we think of as Hawthorne's major work were still unwritten when Melville discovered him. Hawthorne's most productive period came, in fact, just at this moment. *The Snow-Image and Other Tales* was assembled and *The House of the Seven Gables*, *A Wonder Book*, and *The Blithedale Romance* were all written between September 1850 and April 1852, or during the time of these writers' close involvement.

The Hawthorne–Melville connection presents the unusual spectacle of literary tradition being formed while the parent work is itself still in the forming. And Hawthorne's non-*pastness* also accounts for this relation's second oddity: that in this instance literary influence takes place without the usual removal from living, personal ground. When authors pass up into that sort of potent past that inspires tradition, they get objectified—or, as we say, immortalized—in the process. They become the authors of their work: their

From *The School of Hawthorne*. © 1986 by Oxford University Press, Inc.

literary self, the self achieved and expressed through their writing, supplants the more transient self of living personality, as the one meant by their name. (Who is Shakespeare after 1623? The author of Shakespeare's plays.) Hawthorne was eventually to undergo this sort of abstraction in a virulent form, but since Melville came to him before this process set in, he still knew Hawthorne in his person. Every surviving source makes clear that it was the living, embodied Hawthorne—not just the Hawthorne of the page—that Melville found attractive. In the month after they met Hawthorne and Melville both read each other avidly, but they also exchanged visit after visit, as if seeking a pleasure only full personal presence could supply. (During this time Melville told Mrs. Hawthorne that "Mr Hawthorne was the first person whose physical being appeared to him wholly in harmony with the intellectual & spiritual.") Melville claimed to be fixed and fascinated by Hawthorne's tales in 1850, but even twenty years after their friendship was over he was still attributing Hawthorne's power to his personal aura. Vine, the Hawthorne portrait in Melville's *Clarel* (1876), is introduced as "A funeral man, yet richly fair— / Fair as the sabled violets be," whose "charm of subtle virtue shed / A personal influence coveted."[1]

In Hawthorne and Melville's case, a complex literary relation is superposed on and in part mediated by a complex relation between whole, not just literary, personalities. For this reason it does a central violence to this relation to read it as an interaction in the written realm merely. But the difficulty here is that while the Hawthorne–Melville relation does not function wholly in literary terms, it never functions wholly outside such terms either. Hawthorne deeply charmed Melville in their personal meetings. To bring this charming other into his own orbit Melville resorted to unparalleled feats of hospitality. ("I keep the word 'Welcome' all the time in my mouth,"[2] he says in his first surviving letter to Hawthorne.) His successes in winning Hawthorne's full communion touched off similarly unparalleled satisfactions—Melville's reply to Hawthorne's praise of *Moby-Dick* is outdone perhaps only by Whitman's Calamus poems, among nineteenth-century expressions of masculine social fulfillment. But the fact remains that it was the *author* Hawthorne whom Melville found personally magnetic. In 1850 and 1851 Melville (in his words) "regard[ed] Hawthorne (in his books) as evincing a quality of genius, immensely loftier, & more profound, too, than any other American has shown hitherto in the printed form."[3] And surely it was what he embodied in literary and cultural terms that made Hawthorne such a riveting person. No doubt Melville brought all kinds of personal needs to bear on Hawthorne. I have no trouble believing that he regarded Hawthorne, as Edwin Haviland Miller has suggested, in light of his needs for fatherly approval and male comradeship. But it is no less true that Melville connected Hawthorne, with special and overriding intensity, to his specifically authorial needs: put Hawthorne in the service of helping him conceive an urgently desired new *literary* identity.

What makes the Hawthorne–Melville relation a genuine case of tradition formation—rather than a chapter in the history of literary friendships only—is the fact that Melville seized Hawthorne as a figure of literary possibility. Melville used Hawthorne to reveal what literature in its most fully realized form could do, and so too to know what he, as a writer, could aspire to achieve. His construction of a new plan of authorship on the basis of Hawthorne's example is itself a literary event of the first importance. It is important because it led to the great phase of his own career: that burst of creativity and sustained exploration that reaches forward from *Moby-Dick* through *Pierre* to *The Piazza Tales* and beyond. But it is important in a more historical sense as well.

We are beginning to have a much more adequate understanding of the cultural organization of literature in America between 1840 and the Civil War. The older researches of William Charvat—still the cornerstone for the study of this subject—established this as a time when an expansion in the market for fiction began to make it more practicable for an American to take up a career solely as a writer, but also when cultural separations among different kinds of audiences and interests a writer might appeal to had not yet been well-established. Recent workers returning to Charvat's study of the history of literature's cultural ground have established the new social position American fiction moved into in the 1840s much more concretely. We can now see that the literary market expanded so rapidly after 1840 not out of an innate tendency to grow, but because of its conjunction, at this time, with a social development that provided new encouragement for reading: the new organization of work, family life, gender-roles, and moral structures of insurgent middle-class domesticity. As it removed women from the sphere of productive labor and made them custodians of nonmaterial values, the cult of domesticity created both a new domestic leisure reading could help fill and a new ethic to support that pastime. (As both a cultivating and a nonproductive labor reading became woman's work in a double sense, under nineteenth-century domesticity.) In consequence, after 1840 and critically so around 1850, fiction writing took on the power to reach very large audiences in America, on the condition that it align itself with the values the new domesticity was constituted around.[4]

These changes in fiction's cultural place entailed immediate consequences for writers and the roles they could claim. One form of these consequences is seen in the literary ladies' men Ann Douglas has described: the writers like N. P. Willis, George William Curtis, and Donald G. Mitchell ("Ik Marvel"), who found new power and prosperity open to them as managers of domestic culture's literary organs on the condition that they serve domestic interests and become, in literary terms, unassuming. Another consequence is seen in the (painfully named!) literary domestics Mary Kelley has recently studied: the writers like Susan Warner, Maria Cummins, Mrs. E. D. E. N. Southworth, and Sara Parton ("Fanny Fern") who inaugurated the bestseller as a cultural phenomenon in the 1850s. As Kelley shows, such writers took advantage of fiction's new conjunction with middle-class domesticity to pioneer a role for women in the public or extradomestic sphere. But the hidden cost of this linkage was that they remained constrained, even as public figures, within traditionally domestic definitions of their identities. They won access to literary expression, but only on terms that made literature a willing servant of domestic ideology. They realized the will to write, but without thereby becoming able to assert their right to such a will: they continued to claim that family needs, the sphere of woman's most traditionally approved concern, prompted their labors instead.[5]

Such study has greatly enriched our sense both of the kinds of writers who were active in pre–Civil War America and of the relation of all writing of that time to its social ground. But what is this study to do with a Melville—a writer who is the exact contemporary of Willis and Curtis and Warner and Parton; who worked in the same, *not* a different, literary and social milieu, but who stands not just in a different but in virtually the opposite relation to literature and its cultural accommodations? Myra Jehlen has hazarded that the difference between Melville and the domestic authors he emerged alongside of is a difference not only in their cultural politics but in "their relationship to writing as such." Melville (in Jehlen's phrases) "took himself seriously," he "*assumed* himself": he engaged in writing as the act an independent identity could be composed through. If he is not (like Kelley's domestics) "conceptually totally dependent," it is because writing, so seized, gave him a vantage point outside the affirmations of his culture: "his novel in the sentimental mode [*Pierre*] could take on sentimentalism because he had an alternative world on which to stand: himself."[6] These are important claims, but, if we accept them, they raise an anterior, historical question. Unless we are willing to grant that some writers simply transcend their historical occasion, they require us to ask: where, in his situation, did Melville find the means for his extremely different way of occupying that situation? How did Melville find, and how did Melville construct, the organizing *idea* of authorship that let him engage literature on such radically altered terms?

It is exactly here that Melville's relation to Hawthorne is so instructive. Hawthorne figured in the drama of self-conception that produced the fiercely self-*assuming* Melville of Melville's mid-career. In Melville's eyes, Hawthorne was what enabled him to conceive and assert himself as an author on altered terms. Hawthorne's influence on Melville takes the form first of a personal interaction, then of a literary relation. But both of these form part of a larger story too: the story of how (in Melville's term) an "other way" of authorship got established as an artistic possibility, in America in the 1850s.

We recognize Hawthorne's effect on Melville by the fact that, immediately upon encountering Hawthorne, Melville broke into new levels of expressive energy. Within days of reading Hawthorne, Melville, the author heretofore of a few short reviews, produced his critical masterpiece, the sustained rhapsody "Hawthorne and His Mosses." In Hawthorne's presence the man who told Sophia Hawthorne that he "was naturally so silent a man, that he was complained of a great deal on this account" became so voluble that she likened his talk to "tumultuous waves."[7] Melville's letters, never unexpressive, abruptly double, then triple their length, when he begins writing to this corespondent. Within this flow of talk, and as if animating it, Melville is aware that he is seizing on powers that are fundamentally new to him. Melville becomes truly confessional, for the one time in his correspondence, in his letters to Hawthorne, but it is not simply that he is sharing confidences. Instead (as in the famous meditation beginning "From my twenty-fifth year I date my life")[8] it is as if he is bringing himself *to* self-knowledge in the letters, grasping, in Hawthorne's imagined presence, the logic of his mental life. Similarly, Melville becomes boldly philosophical in his letters to Hawthorne, but it is not as if he is outlining positions already held. He seems to be coming *to* understanding as he writes, and gaining, through such writing, confidence that the great life mysteries are his to address.

The reason Hawthorne touched off this excited self-extension has something to do with Hawthorne, but it has much more to do with the point Melville had reached in his career when he met Hawthorne—a point I want to reconstruct with some care. Melville, we might begin by remembering, had become an author only five years before he met Hawthorne. In his debut Melville came to writing with considerable natural aptitude, but certainly with no special dedication to writing as a calling. Having had some experiences in exotic lands in his early manhood, Melville found that by writing them up in a form "a little touched up ... but *true*" he could win an enthusiastic popular response for his work. After this venture he took on, as the organizing and sustaining idea of his work, the one he found in this reception. Having pleased a large, general public, Melville now adopted the aim so *to* please as the end of his writing: "calculated for popular reading, or for none at all," is his working motto in 1846. Having found a ready market for his adventures, Melville similarly accepted the idea of resupplying that demand as his authorial identity: "South Sea Adventure" is, still in late 1847, "the feild where I garner."[9]

But this plan of authorship, newly constructed after the success of *Typee*, did not hold for long. This idea of literary self and purpose was sufficiently strong to govern the production of a second Polynesian novel and to start him on a third. But Melville then staged the first of those reorientations in midcourse that become a kind of signature of his career. As he told his publisher, while writing *Mardi* he had a "change in my determinations."[10] Having started another "narrative of *facts*," without removing its initial traces he altered the book's plan to permit greater latitude, changing it first into an allegorical quest-romance, then into a travelling symposium, a free-floating feast of thought and talk. What Melville is searching for, in these revisions, is a format that will open his work more directly to the workings of his mind. Wrenching free from obligations either to rehearse real experience or to spin a continuous story, his effort in *Mardi* is to make each chapter an independent mental occasion: a chance for him to address whatever occurs to him as vigorously as he can, for the sake of finding out what he might have to say on that topic, without becoming bound to continue it or any other line.

Whitman once spoke of "a secret proclivity, American maybe, to dare and violate and make escapades."[11] This proclivity comes over Melvillean authorship with the writing of *Mardi*, and it takes the special form there of adventuresomeness *toward* the literary. What governs *Mardi*, after its early chapters, is the will, without knowing in advance where it will lead, to find out what else a writer can be than a garnerer in a fixed "feild." I might note in passing that, as he undertakes this exploratory self-extension, Melville already grasps how the reworking of literary tradition can help effect a reconstitution of authorial project and role. The first signs of *Mardi*'s eventual deviance from Melville's earlier way of writing are his early allusions to Burton's *Anatomy of Melancholy* and imitations of Sir Thomas Browne. These allusions—the first of many in this much more literature-conscious work—have behind them Melville's recently begun reading in Evert Duyckinck's "choice conservatory"[12] of older literatures. But they also display Melville's hereafter typical act of annexing the contents of libraries directly onto his own work in progress. In these instances, as later, Melville draws the most far-flung readings in around the project he is working on. Seizing their procedures, he at once converts them into voices *he* can try on. And it is through this quick apprehension, then assimilation of other writing into his own that Melville grasps new ideas of what writing can be and do.

This adventure of thinking through writing and of exploring writing's resources through imitation absorbed Melville for more than a year. The immediate yield of this project was the book *Mardi*. But in a more crucial and enduring sense its yield was the revolutionized idea of authorship that Melville became drawn to after this book. Several new strains enter Melville's thinking in *Mardi*, then move, in the year that follows (1849–50), to the center of his self-conception. For the first time in *Mardi*, then very strongly thereafter, Melville comes to identify writing with a wholly inward impulsion. "You may think me unwise to have written this sort of book," Melville writes his new English publisher in June 1849, "but some of us scribblers ... have a certain something unmanageable in us, that bids us do this or that, and be done it must—hit or miss."[13] Melville does not know this something's name, but he knows its forms and procedures. As he images it here and in other writings of this time, this "something" is a strong drive or will. It is imperious, simply not to be resisted: it bids us do things, and be done they must; in *Mardi*'s nautical image, it is a "blast resistless." And its action, when it cuts on, is to seize the work of writing and put that work in its own service: the "blast resistless" drives *Mardi*'s writer from his intended course; or in an even more violent image of the coercion of writing: "an iron-mailed hand clenches mine in a vice, and prints down every letter in my spite." The accession of this will produces a much more intense engagement of the writer in his work—composition as *Mardi* images it is a "seething" and "riveted" activity. But above all this will works to shift the ground of authorship within. Where before Melville thought of writing as produced for an audience's pleasure, now he speaks of it as produced by an inward urge: "My *instinct* is to out with the romance."[14] Where previously writing's proper form was dictated by market demand, now it answers its own demands: be done it must, hit or miss.

As it becomes associated with this other form of will, Melvillean authorship also becomes allied with a different mode of literary ambition. The literary ambition of *Typee*—if it can properly be said to have one—is to get published and, if possible, to get liked. The literary ambition of *Omoo* and at first of *Mardi* is to make *Typee*'s success a regular thing. But in *Mardi* and its wake Melville is reborn as a literary overreacher: a writer with grand notions of literary greatness, and with a strong will to realize himself on that scale through his work. "Permanent reputation" and "things immortal"[15] now become his obsession: the Melville of 1849–50 is more rawly hungry for literary immortality than any other nineteenth-century novelist I know of. Also at this time his reading—still voracious, heterogeneous, and actively appropriative—turns literature, much more than before, into a kingdom of greatness. Emerson, first heard in early 1849, is immediately greeted as an "uncommon man," "elevated above mediocrity." Shakespeare, first attentively read in this same season, becomes an incarnation of both literary genius and messianic spiritual power:

> Dolt & ass that I am I have lived more than 29 years, & until a few days ago, never made close acquaintance with the divine William. Ah, he's full of sermons-on-the-mount, and gentle, aye, almost as Jesus. I take such men to be inspired.... And if another Messiah ever comes twill be in Shakesper's person.[16]

Melville's generosity in passages like these is extraordinary, but it also shows the workings of his own giant will. For what he invests in great writers at this time is that enlarged personal power he hopes might be his in prospect.

As it links up with ambitions of this scope, writing also revises its sense of its cultural placement. The 1847 motto "calculated for popular reading, or for none at all" gives way, so soon as the "something unmanageable" letter of 1849, to the disdainful phrase "calculated merely to please the general reader."[17] What lies behind this change is not just the growth of Melvillean snobbery, but the fact that Melville has begun to rethink the cultural basis of literary value. The undifferentiated audience of general readers he had earlier aimed to please begins to be split, by his act of mind, into elite and popular audience zones, each supporting radically different levels of artistic activity. His writings of 1849–50 insist that there is one kind of writing for the many, another for the few, "those for whom it is intended"; that one aspires "simply for amusement," the other to be a "literary achievement"; that one audience's approval helps establish popularity, but the other's "permanent reputation." Wrapping himself in the conceit of "higher purposes,"[18] Melville mentally removes his work from the situation where general acceptance determines its value. In his new thinking writing becomes nonpopular, possibly even anti-popular, in aim: the proof that *Mardi* has "higher purposes," he tells his publisher Bentley, is the fact that it has not been generally accepted.

The last of these new developments—the hardest to name but the most important to grasp—is that after *Mardi* Melville comes to identify writing as the means to profundity of thought. Anyone who knows Melville between 1848 and 1851 knows that he is American literature's great victim of raptures of the deep; and the self-delighting activity he calls diving is intimately connected, for him, with his new, more driven kind of writing. In its seething *Mardi* already displays the movement we know best from his 1851 letters: a move in which Melville feels beckoned to address ultimate life mysteries; then, as he engages them, finds himself thrown churning forward from surmise to surmise, so that understandings entirely new to him seem to be being produced through the activity of articulation. The Melville of *Mardi*, as he becomes aware of a separate will to writing, also moves toward the concept that such writing is what *produces* the great writer's expanding "world of mind."[19] As he splits it into high and low, Melville now also divides writing into the kind that refuses and the kind that allows writing's potentially thought-creating powers.

Melville's state in the year after *Mardi* is that of a writer for whom writing has become, quite suddenly and unexpectedly, the focus of powerful new drives and ambitions. But to know his state in full we need to recognize that these ambitions, electrifying in the power they seemed to promise him, were also sources of intense new uncertainties and confusions. When he published *Mardi*, Melville discovered that readers and critics did not have much liking for work produced on that plan. He now learned in hard practice what he had airily accepted in theory: that if he was going to write in that self-delighting "other way," he would jeopardize the income his growing family depended on, and forfeit too the sort of public approval that had emboldened him to experiment in the first place. Quite as daunting as this lesson in the impracticality of his ambitions was the fact that these ambitions, so compelling to their bearer, were in crucial ways unable to validate the giant presumptions they touched off. Melville's idea of a literary culture of the happy few and higher purposes is plainly a validation device: an attempt to specify a ground other than that of popular approval on which the special merits of his project could be confirmed. But we need to remember, when we see this device in action, that this separate high literary culture was an imaginative invention of Melville's, not a historical reality. Prose fiction, Melville's genre, had never been given as a high cultural form in the England or America of Melville's time: its status at his moment was exactly as the form that merged high and low into a "universal" popular audience. (Witness the cases of two other authors Melville's English publisher also published: Cooper and Dickens.) In any case, there certainly was not, in Melville's America, such a thing as a formalized alternative audience a writer could appeal to against a popular one; this was not fully established until well after

1850, and was at best almost wholly incipient at *Mardi*'s time.[20] Since such an alternative audience did not exist in reality, Melville had to try to improvise it from the available materials (hence the appointment—not Melville's last—of Evert and George Duyckinck as *Mardi*'s "real" audience). More, since it did not exist in reality, the "assurance"[21] it could offer Melville's presumptions was at best a matter of anxious hope. So too with another ground of potential validation: the writing itself. It would be one thing to be seized with a sense of personal profundity and prospective immortality if one had just written, say, *The Divine Comedy*. But the author of *Mardi* quickly recognized that his work was grotesquely more impressive in its ambitions than in its displayed achievement. When he recognized its callowness, the work that should have established his right to such identifications threw them instead into deep doubt. The chapter of *Mardi* that bares Melville's presumption to immortality also shows him racked with anxiety that this presumption may be an insane delusion. He ends his reflections desperate for but at a perfect loss for evidence of his election:

> Ah, Oro! how may we know or not, we are what we would be?
> Hath genius any stamp and imprint, obvious to possessors? Hath
> it eyes to see itself; or is it blind? Or do we delude ourselves with
> being gods, and end in grubs?[22]

The Melville of 1849–50 then is inspired, we might even say afflicted, with a sense of literary calling in the highest degree elating. But he is almost completely uncertain, either that his ambitions can be made practicable or that he has any real warrant to hold such ambitions. His condition, accordingly, is one of anxiety-fraught suspension of purpose. He is sufficiently committed to his hoped-for future work to have disdain for work produced on his old plan of authorship. (He associates his two new "unmetaphysical" novels of this year with the degradation of mere manual labor: "they are two *jobs*, which I have done for money," he keeps telling everyone, "being forced to it, as other men are to sawing wood.") But he is not yet sure enough of the warrant for his hopes to convert them into a working authorial identity. It is still only his "earnest desire" "to write those sort of books which are said to 'fail.'"[23]

This highly charged state of vocational hope and confusion is the state Melville was in when he encountered Hawthorne in the summer of 1850. And if that encounter was a "shock" to him, it was because, in Hawthorne, he seemed to see his own most wildly imagined ambitions realized, and so purged of their attendant uncertainty. His encounter with Hawthorne is the supreme instance of the process by which, since the time of *Mardi*, Melville has gone out to other writers, magnified their praise, and thereby used them to help him grasp the idea of his own prospective career. Melville met Hawthorne on August 5, 1850; he read Hawthorne's *Mosses from an Old Manse* in the following days; and no more than a week later, he wrote his electrified recognition-piece "Hawthorne and His Mosses." In this essay we can watch him bringing forth, as if from Hawthorne's writing, an idea of incandescent importance to his writing life.

Melville begins this essay knowing only that Hawthorne is obscurely fascinating as a writer. To account for this fascination, he puts together as best he can a portrait of the author characterized by the *Mosses* pieces (in fact, this is also the Hawthorne of Hawthorne's early critical reputation): a genial author, too fine for broad popularity, associated with the rhythms of nature and the white melancholy of a "contemplative humor" (1156).[24] But Melville has what Henry James calls a *grasping* imagination, and so no sooner does he sketch this picture than he moves to get back behind it. His way of attempting this is to surmise that Hawthorne's manifest geniality must be the index to another, antithetical form of power. Hawthorne's visible soarings in the sun prove, Melville argues, that he must have a corresponding gift for penetrating depths, must have "a great, deep intellect, which drops down into the universe like a plummet" (1158). Melville now looks back to the tales for evidence of this so far purely surmised other Hawthorne, educing possible examples until, with a burst, he is able to say what that Hawthorne's power consists of. Having cited "Earth's Holocaust," Melville begins as if to take up two more relevant tales, but suddenly what he has been driving at is ready to be said:

> "The Christmas Banquet" and "The Bosom Serpent" would be fine subjects for a curious and elaborate analysis, touching the conjectural parts of the mind that produced them. For spite of all the Indian-summer sunlight on the hither side of Hawthorne's soul, the other side—like the dark half of the physical sphere—is shrouded in blackness, ten times black. (1158)

On the basis of this recognition, Melville can now completely revise his initial account. Hawthorne is *not* a nature author but the diviner, behind appearances, of the hidden guilt Calvinism called "Innate Depravity." Hawthorne is *not* a gentle author but the terrifying wielder of that "terrific thought." His light or bright side, so far from being even a complementary aspect, is there only in conjunction with that dark knowledge, to make that darkness visible: "You may bewitched by his sunlight,—transported by the bright gildings in the skies he builds over you;—but there is the blackness of darkness beyond; and even his bright gildings but fringe, and play upon the edges of thunder-clouds" (1159).

This reading of Hawthorne is so famous that we need to remember to wonder at the authority and sheer mental speed with which Melville moves to this conception. (When he wrote this passage he had read one book by Hawthorne, and not even all of that.) In any case, having reached this point, Melville clearly exults in the sense that he has now *known* Hawthorne, and for the first time: "In one word, the world is mistaken in this Nathaniel Hawthorne," he crows; "he himself must often have smiled at its absurd misconception of him" (1159). But this very exultation fuels a further extension of Melville's inquiry, instead of bringing it to an end. What the knowledge of human depravity gives Hawthorne's fiction, Melville explains, is "the infinite obscure of his back-ground." Then, since this is itself obscure: "that back-ground, against which Shakespeare plays his grandest conceits." Then, since this requires amplification in turn (articulation now comes in wave on wave):

> it is those deep far-away things in him; those occasional flashings-forth of the intuitive Truth in him; those short, quick probings at the very axis of reality; these are the things that make Shakespeare, Shakespeare. Through the mouths of the dark characters of Hamlet, Timon, Lear, and Iago, he craftily says, or sometimes insinuates the things, which we feel to be so terrifically true, that it were all but madness for any good man, in his own proper character, to utter, or even hint of them. Tormented into desperation, Lear the frantic King tears off the mask, and speaks the sane madness of vital truth.... And if I magnify Shakespeare, it is not so much for what he did do, as for what he did not do, or refrained from doing. For in this world of lies, Truth is forced to fly like a scared white doe in the woodlands; and only by cunning glimpses will she reveal herself, as in Shakespeare and other masters of the great Art of Telling the Truth,—even though it be covertly, and in snatches. (1159–60)

This passage is one of the great displays of Melville's powerfully synthetic habits of mind, and more particularly of his use of reading as a means to mental realization. His former reading stays livingly present to Melville, such that when he wants to grasp a new mental stimulus he instinctively moves to fuse it with other ones: Hawthorne is known, here, in conjunction with Shakespeare, but also with an array of uncited sources. (Carlyle's "The Hero as Prophet" is a palpable presence in this passage. So is Evert Duyckinck's 1845 essay on Hawthorne, where Melville would have found this passage: "No conventionalist art thou, or respecter of show and outside, but as keensighted a moralist as tempest-stricken Lear whose sagacity flashes forth from his exceedingly vexed soul like the lightning from the storm-driven clouds.")[25] At the same time that he amalgamates work with work, Melville also draws this amassing whole of his reading directly into the sphere of his own deepest preoccupations, such that the texts of his reading become at once saturated with those concerns and made an imagery in which those concerns can be thought through.

What Melville synthesizes through this process is a highly articulated notion of literature as a prophetical activity. In this passage's glowing conception great artists have the gift to pierce through what passes for reality and to know a more essential order people's ordinary sense of things excludes. Their power and their office, then, is to deliver knowledge of this alienated reality back to the world that would forget it. And the way they know, as the way they deliver knowledge, is through their special use of the word. Literature's special form of language, when its power is fully realized, becomes a flashing-forth or *speaking* of vital truth. The art created through such a language neither imitates the familiar world nor fabricates an aesthetic replacement for it but bears witness to what is-a great Art of Telling the Truth.

Literature seriously considered as a prophetical activity is a new idea to Melville—more properly, is an idea we watch Melville in the act of conceiving—in "Hawthorne and His Mosses." And if this essay is almost uncontrollably euphoric, it is because the idea Melville forges here has such immediate and profound bearings on his own urgent obsessions. This notion of literary prophecy has the peculiar power to take the confused strains of Melville's post-*Mardi* idea of authorship up into itself and there fuse them into a coherent literary program. More, it has the power, in so doing, to supply those urges with the validation they had anxiously lacked. Within a conception like this, it becomes seriously *thinkable* that the will to writing Melville called "something unmanageable" might be no stray compulsion but a privileged inner prompting, the pressure of the Word one has been specially chosen to speak. In that case unleashing that urge to expression would represent no mere self-indulgence, as *Mardi* feared itself to be, but a high obedience to a specially appointed vocation. *What* that expression brings forth—the speculation *Mardi* loves but fears may be only pompous pseudoprofundity—could be seriously identified as new or neglected Truth: that grasp of ultimate things it is such speakers' privilege to deliver. And the problem of audience could be rethought too. In "Hawthorne and His Mosses" Melville is still obsessed with the difference between "circumscribed renown" (1159) and "mere mob renown" (1160). But as he works out this prophetical conception Melville transforms his old and quite vulnerable ideas of high and low into ones that require no actual, historical audience to confirm the writer's high purposes. The mere mob is unreceptive in Melville's new thinking not because it is lowbrow or culturally unenlightened but because, like ordinary humanity to the prophet's eyes, it *refuses the Truth*. Conversely, great art is great not because it is an artistic achievement but because it is possessed of the Truth. That it is not received, that it thrusts itself against the acceptances of its hearers, is the chief proof of its truth—the mark that it possesses that higher spiritual authority that sets the prophet apart.

In the idea of prophetical authorship, Melville's disruptive artistic impulses get *justified*. They get made into the central elements of another *kind* of writing, a kind carrying the most extreme form of privilege Melville can imagine. This is why, once Melville has fully seized this idea, his essay turns from a work of criticism into a virtual hymn of self-annunciation. The ostensible subject of "Hawthorne and His Mosses'" second half is America's coming cultural independence, but in reality Melville borrows the millennial rhetoric of 1840s American nationalism to announce the actual practicability, in the contemporary American world, of that spiritually potent authorship he has just dreamed. Baptist-like, Melville here proclaims that the "coming of the literary Shiloh of America" (1169) has already taken place, that our "American Shiloh, or 'master Genius'" (1169) is even now with us—in Hawthorne, as unrecognized in our midst as Christ was by the Jews he lived among (1154, 1162). And he manages his annunciation of Hawthorne in such a way as to make Hawthorne imply the advent of other writers of comparable power. "I commend to you, in the first place, Nathaniel Hawthorne" (1165), Melville proclaims—Hawthorne, that is, as he implies others coming behind him. He ends the essay prophesying, on the basis of Hawthorne, a plural incarnation of genius, a general infusion of literary-spiritual power that could live in him as well:

> May it not be, that this commanding mind has not been, is not, and never will be, individually developed in any one man? And would it, indeed, appear so unreasonable to suppose, that this great fullness and overflowing may be, or may be destined to be, shared by a plurality of men of genius? (1169)

The action of "Hawthorne and His Mosses" is of Melville first thinking a new idea of authorship, then, on the basis of that thought, emboldening himself to assert his own literary-prophetical vocation. And when we know this, we know Hawthorne's power for Melville. When they met in 1850, Hawthorne moved into the highly charged field of Melville's authorial anxieties and ambitions. Projecting these concerns out onto Hawthorne, Melville seemed to see in Hawthorne the kind of writer he aspired to be. And recognizing the "real" Hawthorne the world had mistaken enabled Melville to recognize his own potential literary identity: to attain to a new conception of literature's possible power, a conception that could legitimate the most extreme of his presumptions. To Melville Hawthorne hereafter stood as he who incarnated, and so showed the living, present possibility of, literary power prophetically imagined, and as he who licensed Melville's belief that such power might be his to claim.

The most telling evidence that the prophetical conception of authorship is what bound these two writers together, at least on Melville's side, is found in their so-called personal relationship. Melville, I have said, opened himself to Hawthorne in unprecedented ways. But it might be more helpful to say that he specialized a certain version of himself for presentation to Hawthorne. Among the other selves he can also be, the one Melville displays to Hawthorne always has certain sharply particularizing features: it is hyperenergized; it readily shifts into what might be called the gear of transcendence, an overdrive that thrusts beyond immediate occasions to cosmic or ontological topics; and it gets caught up in an endless forward movement of conception as it engages those topics. ("I can't stop yet" is the regular refrain of his letters.) This is the Melville we see in "Hawthorne and His Mosses." This is the Melville we find in every one of his letters to Hawthorne. And this is, by abundant testimony, the Melville Hawthorne always met in conversation. Already in February 1851 Melville is saying that the "pleasure" of a visit from Hawthorne is "getting him up in my snug room here, & discussing the Universe with a bottle of brandy & cigars." In May 1851 Sophia Hawthorne writes that "to Mr Hawthorne [Melville] speaks his innermost about GOD, the Devil & Life if so be he can get at the Truth," then adds: "Nothing pleases me better than to sit & hear this growing man dash his tumultuous waves of thought up against Mr Hawthorne's great, genial, comprehending silences." In August 1851, after Melville came over to spend his birthday with Hawthorne, Hawthorne records:

> After supper, I put Julian to bed; and Melville and I had a talk about time and eternity, things of this world and of the next, and

publishers, and all possible and impossible matters, that lasted pretty deep into the night....

Even five years later, when their close friendship had already been over for four years, the person who called on Hawthorne in Liverpool is still the same old Melville:

> We soon found ourselves on pretty much our former terms of sociability and confidence.... Melville, as he always does, began to reason of Providence and futurity, and of everything that lies beyond human ken, and informed me that he had "pretty much made up his mind to be annihilated"; but still he does not seem to rest in that anticipation; and, I think, will never rest until he gets hold of a definite belief.[26]

Melville obviously thought of Hawthorne as inviting or sponsoring a particular form of communication. And, very strikingly, the self Melville expressed toward Hawthorne is what we must call his prophetic self: the driven or compelled speaker, wildly unpopular in his conceptions, to whom God and Devil, "visable truth" and cosmic Powers are immediately present. The surviving letters, our chief record of the "ontological heroics"[27] Melville directed toward Hawthorne, are charged with this vein of speech, and return obsessively to the idea of the prophet's power and situation. The letter of 16 April 1851—written in response to Hawthorne's gift of *The House of the Seven Gables*—is a perfect piece of that overheated, heaven-aspiring, and forwardly driving style that is the Hawthorne style for Melville. ("What's the reason, Mr. Hawthorne, that in the last stages of metaphysics a fellow always falls to *swearing* so? I could rip an hour," it concludes.) It also puts forward (again identifying it as Hawthorne) a yet bolder version of the "Mosses" essay's heroic figure—a man who takes his stand on his own deep sense of things, over against both the mystifications of the cosmos and the deceived affirmations of ordinary thought: "There is the grand truth about Nathaniel Hawthorne. He says NO! in thunder; but the Devil himself cannot make him say *yes*. For all men who say *yes*, lie."[28] A letter eight weeks later links the writer even more directly to the prophet as persecuted bearer of alienated truth:

> Try to get a living by the Truth—and go to the Soup Societies. Heavens! Let any clergyman try to preach the Truth from its very stronghold, the pulpit, and they would ride him out of his church

on his own pulpit bannister. It can hardly be doubted that all Reformers are bottomed upon the truth, more or less; and to the world at large are not reformers almost universally laughingstocks? Why so? Truth is ridiculous to men.... Though I wrote the Gospels in this century, I should die in the gutter.[29]

(By now Melville has worked his idea of the prophetic back to its radical Protestant sources. The accents here are those of Frank Lloyd Wright's militantly religious grandfather, whose motto was "TRUTH AGAINST THE WORLD"; or even of Milton, who calls Enoch in *Paradise Lost*:

The only righteous in a World perverse,
And therefore hated, therefore so beset
With Foes for daring single to be just,
And utter odious Truth.)[30]

Melville's relation to Hawthorne, I would be the last to deny, was played out on many levels, and in many moods. But the whole of that relation was framed within a dominant structure, on Melville's side at least. What structured this relation—and what Melville therefore had at stake on its success—was the concept of the real possibility of the prophetical artistic career. Hawthorne impressed Melville because he seemed to embody the writer gifted to know and speak hidden truths, if only covertly and by snatches. He drew Melville to him because he seemed seriously to allow what Melville was most ambitious to do. He seemed to license Melville to speak and write as he felt compelled to, in confident hope that such speaking might be of transcendent spiritual weight.

The reason we pay attention to Melville and Hawthorne's encounter is that just after this encounter, and in some crucial way in the wake of it, Melville undertook to write the book that became *Moby-Dick*. The facts of this matter are well known. In May 1850 Melville claimed to be half-done with a book that appears to have treated his whaling years on the same terms that *White-Jacket* had treated his naval experience. By late June Melville wrote to his English publisher that he would have a romance of the sperm whale fishery done by autumn. On August 7 (two days after the Hawthorne–Melville meeting) Evert Duyckinck, Melville's houseguest, reported that Melville had "a romantic, fanciful & literal & most enjoyable presentment of the Whale Fishery" "mostly done."[31] But then, for the second time in his career,

Melville changed his determinations. He so massively reconceived the book he was writing that it took him another full year of driving labor to complete it (this, from the author who wrote *Redburn* in eight weeks); and, in its new form, the book that had been "most enjoyable" to Duyckinck the summer before had become annoying and disturbing to him instead.[32]

The reconceived *Moby-Dick* was written in Hawthorne's near neighborhood, during the time of Melville's close involvement with Hawthorne. And it is clear that Melville regarded it too as part of that special kind of communication Hawthorne seemed to sponsor. He entrusted Hawthorne with *Moby-Dick*'s "motto (the secret one)—Ego non baptiso to in nomine—but make out the rest yourself"; when the book was finished, he dedicated it to Hawthorne; and when Hawthorne read it understandingly, Melville announced that in its proper form it would have been written just to Hawthorne as its audience fit, though few:

> I should have a paper-mill established at one end of the house, and so have an endless riband of foolscap rolling in upon my desk; and upon that endless riband I should write a thousand—a million—billion thoughts, all under the form of a letter to you.[33]

Rarely has one writer's great book been so variously bound to another, contemporaneous author as *Moby-Dick* is to Hawthorne. But it is a further measure of the nature of this relation that, in each of these instances, Melville specifically ties *Moby-Dick* to Hawthorne by way of the concept of authorship born in "Hawthorne and His Mosses." The motto Melville shares is thus a "secret" one: part of that covert, deeply *un*public, ordinary-belief-inverting communication Melville there says great truth tellers exchange. His dedication is to Hawthorne "In Token of my admiration for his genius": that quasi-autonomous faculty, in his essay's thinking, whereby "spiritual truth" lodges "in" (1160) such authors. Most crucially, when Melville is gratified by Hawthorne's response to *Moby-Dick*, his pleasure takes the quite specific form of literary-prophetical confirmation. His letter of thanks casts Hawthorne as the audience specially empowered to confirm that his wildest authorial ambitions are warranted by his work. What Hawthorne saw to praise, as Melville imagines it, was less the book than the spirit that impelled it—a spirit he then links to classical figures of inspiration and divine possession:

> You did not care a penny for the book. But, now and then as you read, you understood the pervading thought that impelled the

book—and that you praised. Was it not so? You were archangel enough to despise the imperfect body, and embrace the soul. Once you hugged the ugly Socrates because you saw the flame in his mouth, and heard the rushing of the demon,—the familiar,— and recognized the sound; for you have heard it in your own solitudes.

Since, in aspiring to such a privileged identity, Melville had run the risk of accepting a seriously insane self-identification, Hawthorne's recognition of the authenticity of his genius brings not gratified vanity but something much more intense: "unspeakable security." And since Hawthorne's own incarnation of genius has recognized a parallel incarnation in Melville, these two have become not fellow-artists merely but joint manifestations of the spirit:

Whence come you, Hawthorne? By what right do you drink from my flagon of life? And when I put it to my lips—lo, they are yours and not mine. I feel that the Godhead is broken up like the bread at the Supper, and that we are the pieces. Hence this infinite fraternaty of feeling.[34]

I may seem to be waxing mystical when I say that, at the time of *Moby-Dick*, Melville made Hawthorne the guarantor of his literary-prophetical identity. But that is what Melville claims in this climactic letter to Hawthorne (the only non-family letter he ever signed "Herman"). And if we take this notion seriously, we get a much more adequate notion of how exactly Hawthorne affected the writing of *Moby-Dick*. The question what Hawthorne did for *Moby-Dick* has produced such answers as that he "fortified" Melville, that he made Melville "feel full of possibility," that he inspired Melville with "psychic energy and poise," "euphoria" and "confidence," and these things are all well said.[35] But what we can add here is that Hawthorne chiefly gave Melville these powers by enabling him to believe in the practicability, as an organizing idea for his work, of the prophetical model of literary authorship. There would have been no *Moby-Dick* without the accession, in Melville, of new levels of intellectual, imaginative, and rhetorical energy. And it was Melville's ability seriously to identify himself with this exhilarating concept, I would argue, that unleashed *Moby-Dick*'s new energies of thought and speech. Writing *Moby-Dick* did indeed take fortitude: it was an act of serious risk for Melville to divert a year's labor into a project of this sort, this time in full knowledge of the support he would thereby forgo. (We do not commonly remember that Melville contracted a $2050 loan at 9% interest while writing this book.)[36] And it was his ability to believe that his self-willed, publicly unsupported writing efforts had the exalted value this concept promised, I would claim, that gave him the courage to write "the other way." Hawthorne's gift to Melville was not so much that he outlined the book *Moby-Dick* as that he helped Melville think the terms on which he could become the writer of *Moby-Dick*. He helped Melville realize himself as a writer on an altered basis: if Melville (in Jehlen's words) assumed himself in his, writing, took himself seriously, made himself a point to stand on outside and against his culture's affirmations, it was by embracing the prophetical conception of his art that he became able to do so.

The way Hawthorne acts on Melville's plan of authorship determines such influence as Hawthorne has inside this text. In approaching *Moby-Dick* it is important not to overstate Hawthorne's directing presence. The author of *Moby-Dick* is an author of very various gifts, few of which can find their likenesses in Hawthorne: Melville would look in vain, in Hawthorne's work, for models for *Moby-Dick*'s sort of inventive pedantry, or violent physical action, or racy cross-cultural comedy, or self-delighted rhetorical display. But one strand of this book does show Hawthorne's direct and decisive influence: Melville's figuring of his hero, and of the action he projects. All evidence suggests that Ahab and his quest were conceived into *Moby-Dick* after Melville rethought this work in late 1850. When Ahab is first invoked, he is imaged in the idiom of the heroic tradition at large. But when Melville reaches the point where he needs to specify the motives for Ahab's quest and the status it is to have as a statement about the world, he turns very directly to Hawthorne as an aid to conception.

As he looks to Hawthorne's fiction from the vantage of his new project, Melville's interests become much more tightly focussed than they were in "Hawthorne and His Mosses." He now identifies Hawthorne with a handful of tales, and within them, with a single figure. The mark of this figure, as Melville reconstructs him, is that he has passed through a radical reorganization of selfhood, a process at once of extreme intensification and extreme reduction. In the chapters "Moby Dick" and "The Chart" Melville twice rehearses, in explicating Ahab's motive, a transformation repeatedly replayed in Hawthorne ("Ethan Brand" and the analysis of Chillingworth in Chapter 10 of *The Scarlet Letter* provide its classic versions)—a self-fracturing or self-fractioning whereby a faculty that has existed alongside others in an integrated personality suddenly separates itself off and assumes what Melville calls an "independent being of its own" (1007).[37] This now-independent faculty next extends its domination over the rest of the self, absorbing its collective powers into its one form of agency—as Ethan Brand's "intellect" absorbs the energies of "heart"; or as, in the "furious trope" of *Moby-Dick*, Ahab's "special lunacy stormed his general sanity, and carried it, and turned all its concentred cannon upon its own mad mark" (991). What results is a prodigious concentration of being, in which the desires available for the ordinary self's various projects get fixed and focussed on one object, and the energies available for the self's various moves get redirected into movement toward one end. What was once a person is now a project. Living becomes, for the hero thus transformed, a drive along the straight line toward a goal (so Ahab can say: "the path to my fixed purpose is laid with iron rails, whereon my soul is grooved to run" [972]). So consolidated are his being and his object that we name him fully in naming his goal: Ahab *is* he who hunts the White Whale, as Ethan Brand *is* he who searches for the Unpardonable Sin.

The figure (in a phrase Melville repeats from Hawthorne) mastered by one Idea, and compelled, by his Idea, to the unswerving execution of an inflexible program, is not, of course, Hawthorne's exclusive invention. The structure of selfhood I describe Melville as imitating from Hawthorne Angus Fletcher finds in all of allegory: Fletcher likens allegory's simplified agents to figures possessed by a daimon (Melville, who knows this concept both from Goethe and from its classical roots, spells it "demon," as in his reference to "the rushing of [Socrates's] demon,—his familiar"; but I will continue to use spellings based on the alternate form "daimon," to make clear that the devil and the diabolical are not being referred to.) that form of intermediate deity whose effect as it descends on the human self is to narrow it to one function and direct it to one end.[38] The consolidation of the self that Hawthorne's fiction displays is also a standard feature of the gothic—I think of Godwin's Caleb Williams, who slips as easily from having ideas to being had by Ideas as Ethan Brand ("it was but a passing thought. And yet ... the idea once having occurred to my mind, it was fixed there forever"); or I think of Frankenstein, like Ahab and Chillingworth both agent and victim of an idea that converts wholeness of being into a will for one thing ("one by one the various keys were touched that formed the mechanism of my being; chord after chord was sounded, and soon my mind filled with one thought, one conception, one purpose.")[39] But what Melville marks in Hawthorne is the fusion of monomania as a personality type with a peculiar mode of figuration. In Hawthorne the self recentered within a single faculty sees the world recentered in a parallel way. Its attention fixes on a single object, which it lifts out of the continuum of objects and makes into the sign of its obsession.

Aylmer, the perfectionist bridegroom of "The Birthmark," isolates and resignifies Georgiana's facial blemish in this way, projecting his inward preoccupations upon it in such manifold and insistent ways (Hawthorne says that he connects it "with innumerable trains of thought, and modes of feeling")[40] as to convert it into a figure for the sum of his dreads, "the symbol of his wife's liability to sin, sorrow, decay, and death." He is in this the prototype for Hawthorne's idea-possessed men, who in the moment that they succumb to obsession also find an object—Reverend Hooper's black veil, Roderick Elliston's bosom serpent, Arthur Dimmesdale's scarlet letter—in which obsession lodges as an overdetermined meaning. Melville has clearly noticed the conjunction of monomania and figure-making in Hawthorne, because when he recreates Hawthorne's account of the daimonic consolidation of the self in *Moby-Dick*, he insists that its products are a pathology and a metaphor. According to Melville, Ahab's loss of his leg to Moby Dick generates a rage that activates and absorbs every other possible form of human rage until rage is so intense that it achieves a fusion of previously separate things, makes Ahab "*identify* with [the whale], not only all his bodily woes, but all his intellectual and spiritual exasperations" (989). As if still struggling to grasp this notion Melville runs through every way he can think of to say that Ahab's madness is a madness of metaphor: "the White Whale swam before him as the *monomaniac incarnation* of all those malicious agencies which some deep men feel eating in them"; or again: "*deleriously transferring* its idea to the abhorred white whale"; or again: "all evil, to *crazy* Ahab, was visibly *personified*, and made practically assailable in Moby Dick" (989; my italics).

The curious thing about emblem-makers in Hawthorne is that although it is clear, both to themselves and others, that the meanings they read into their chosen objects originate in an act of obsessive projection, once that projection is completed it takes on an oddly objective and authoritative status. Aylmer selects the birthmark as the symbol for a human condition that he cannot accept, but once he has done so neither Georgiana nor Hawthorne can work free of the notion that this is indeed the birthmark's meaning. Reverend Hooper converts a black veil into the symbol of that secret sin the knowledge of which torments him, but when he presents his neurotic emblem before others it takes on an "awful power"— the power to disclose them to themselves as the secret sinners Hooper claims them to be. Roderick Elliston, the chief case in Hawthorne of what might be called the symbolist as aggressor, thrusts his bosom serpent upon others as their meaning-he "makers] his own actual serpent ... the type of each man's fatal error, or hoarded sin, or unquiet conscience." But the effect of this energetic self-projection is to bring forward the serpent that is them—"by obtruding his own bosom-serpent to the public gaze" he "drag[s] those of decent people from their lurking-places."[41]

Obsession in Hawthorne, this is to say, is associated not just with figuration but with figuration as a means to knowledge. The Hawthornesque obsessive deforms reality, subjects it to a perverse pressure that distorts and violates its familiar contours; but through this deformation he discovers another state of things that is instantly known to be more deeply real, and that is not to be known otherwise than through his obsessive deformations. Similarly, the Hawthornesque symbolist is a pure projectionist, writing out onto the world a condition that starts within himself; but through his projections he brings a real and general condition to expression, one that is not available except through his expressive projections.

The descent from here to Ahab is clear: for Ahab is above all a knower, and a knower on the same terms that Hawthorne's heroes are. Like Elliston or Hooper, he is a testifier: he embodies a statement of how things are in the world. Like them, his statement has no referent in the visible world. *He knows by his obsession*: he knows what he knows by his rage, as Hooper knows what he knows by his guilt. But the lack of objective external sanction for his frantic projection does not make it less authoritative. He is mad and therefore sees another world than the one we see—in Ahab's case, sees malign gods where we see only natural processes. But although it is known to be the product of insanity, this antithetical vision carries the power to make others recognize that they too know its truth. So it is that Ahab's insane symbolization can make the faithful Starbuck acknowledge life's "latent horror"; so it is that his insane quest can present itself to Ishmael as "mine" (973, 983).

Here it begins to come clear, I think, what Melville is finding in Hawthorne as he writes *Moby-Dick*. When Melville looks back to Hawthorne at this time, it is with a clarified will to practice a Hawthornesque mode of prophetical authorship—but also with a new curiosity, we might surmise, about how such authorship expresses itself inside a text. If the daimonized hero fixes and fascinates him now, it is because he seems to incarnate, in an imitable textual structure, such authorship's essential action: the process by which an ordinary self gets seized by an imperious will, becoming the witness, through this mastery, to a reality ordinary reality denies. Melville identifies the daimonic hero both with his prophetical ambitions and as the fictional structure that might express such ambitions. And this idea governs the way he transforms this figure as well.

With the Hawthornesque sources of Ahab as in "Hawthorne and His

Mosses," Melville's way is to seize the operative idea of work that impresses him as quickly as he can, then to amalgamate it with many other sources, struggling, through the vigor or even violence of such conjunctions, to release the whole form of the concept each source partially expresses. At the same time that he recomposes this figure from Hawthorne, then, Melville freely assimilates it with every other form of strong selfhood he can call to mind: with Milton's Satan, Shakespeare's Lear and Macbeth, Tamburlaine, Prometheus, Goethe and Carlyle's myths of the hero, and so on.[42] (What other character in literature is *alluded* into being so much as Ahab is?) Through this process, Melville drives Hawthorne's hero-as-obsessive back into a full-scale heroic mode. Hawthorne's heroes are flattened by the daimons that seize them. But as Melville redraws this figure he makes it not two-dimensional but larger than life in the dimensions of its being. Reimagined on Melville's plan the obsessive hero becomes a character of authentic magnanimity, of greatly expanded powers of self-hood: great in its power of will, great in its power of reflection, great above all in its power of suffering. (Ahab never seems more outsized than when he lets out a "loud, animal sob, like that of a heart-stricken moose," or when, crushed by Moby Dick in his final pursuit, "far inland, nameless wails came from him, as desolate sounds from out ravines" [966, 1383]).

As he magnifies Hawthorne's hero, Melville also drives back toward a deeper motive for this hero's unnatural selfhood. In Hawthorne daimonization is commonly a kind of fate, an irresistible process whose sources remain obscure. Aylmer's quest for mastery of nature is obviously rooted in some sort of elemental revulsion from our natural, mortal, embodied condition, but we learn nothing further about that revulsion: his inflection of character is simply *given*. But when Melville seizes on this sort of figure, he wants to know where its form of identity comes from; and in thinking this out he makes this character's extremely peculiar state be a response to our general condition, unmitigatedly faced. As Melville imagines him Ahab is against nature because he feels the full affront of the fact that nature is inhuman, is not structured as human things are, is not the world humans want and needfully feels the fact (in Wallace Stevens's words) "that we live in a place / That is not our own and much more, not ourselves / And hard it is in spite of blazoned days." Ahab would assert his unconditional mastery over nature because he knows so unrelievedly that nature is our master: that it creates and uncreates (and mutilates) us without our will, that we are at best deposed heirs of the kingdom we feel we ought to rule.

Conjoining the obsessive hero with other heroic types, Melville restores him, we might say, to the great ground of his obsession. He restores him too to the tradition of great speech. Hawthorne's heroes express themselves largely symbolically. But by crossing this figure with the Miltonic and Shakespearean heroes of the great oration, Melville makes Ahab talk, as well, with real magniloquence. In particular he makes him, like Satan addressing the sun, or Lear on the heath, a great apostrophist: one who addresses the inanimate as if it were there to listen; and who makes that object be present as he speaks it, through the sheer power of his speech.

And it is through the raw lyricism of his addresses that Ahab speaks the world he knows. "Oh, thou dark Hindoo half of nature, who of drowned bones hast builded thy separate throne somewhere in the heart of these unverdured seas," Ahab prays in "The Dying Whale," "All thy unnamable imminglings float beneath me here; I am buoyed by breaths of once living things, exhaled as air, but water now" (1323). And as he speaks, the apparent world is supplanted by, then reseen as the work of, a cosmic power Ahab alone knows: a power that is life-creating but not life-sustaining; seen as whose product inanimate nature is not matter merely, but the corpse of the life nature lets depart; so that we read, in every sight of inanimate nature, the promise of our own future extinction. In "The Candles," where the crew sees only the natural sublimity of St. Elmo's fire, Ahab sees another order: a god of pure force, nature ruled by a power perfectly omnipotent and perfectly impersonal. That god is present to Ahab—in the Carlylean phrase Melville superbly literalizes it glares or flares in upon Ahab[43]—but not to other men. But it gets *made* present to us, palpably and powerfully, through the power of Ahab's speech: the magnificent aria beginning "Oh! thou clear spirit of clear fire, ... I own thy speechless, placeless power; but to the last gasp of my earthquake life will dispute it unconditional, unintegral mastery in me" (1333).

To a student of Hawthorne and Melville's relation, Ahab's profession of faith in unregenerating nature sounds like a more poetical version of Melville announcing that he had made up his mind to be annihilated. Ahab's address to Power in "The Candles" even more directly recalls Melville's "NO! in thunder" letter, with its vision of humanity as an assertion against the cosmic powers that would make it dependent. These resemblances are more than casual. For it is through Ahab, and more particularly through the heroic speech-function Melville devises for Ahab, that Melville's own prophetic strain finds expression in *Moby-Dick*. In building his monomaniac hero Melville traces a figure he finds outlined in Hawthorne. Vigorously expanding on it, he gives this figure powers it never had in Hawthorne's original. But it is exactly through this construction that he gives vent to what he thinks of as Hawthorne's sort of artistic assertion. This is how his own work unfolds a "background," makes an obscure further order seem directly present in the apparent world. This is how he speaks a world alien to common understanding, realized to us through his utterance. This is how he makes himself what Hawthorne let him dream: the writer who grasps and reveals an unseen world, through the special action of his speech.

Melville of course distances himself from his prophetic impulse by putting it in the character of Ahab. And if that impulse gets expressed in *Moby-Dick*, it is also powerfully contained. A Hawthornesque or prophetic reading of *Moby-Dick* always tends to understate the dominance, over the great mass of the book, of Ishmael: of a voice that knows that its dives cannot escape from the domain of thought and language into ultimate reality; and that therefore can exploit the impulses of prophecy not to reach at Truth but to fuel exploratory, self-delighting mental play. But in terms of Melville's career, his prophetic yearnings, not the containment mechanisms he devises for them in *Moby-Dick*, have the greater staying power. In his next book those yearnings show themselves much more nakedly, seize a more imperious control of the work at hand, and so bring Melville to a literary crisis *Moby-Dick* managed not to reach.

Pierre follows a Hawthornesque original even less strictly than *Moby-Dick* does, but it too organizes itself around the kind of action Melville links with Hawthorne above all. The plot Melville constructs here turns on a young man's discovery of his illegitimate sister and, through that, of the illicit sexual life of his idealized father. Melville tries hard to make this plot carry the burden of the sort of initiation he regards as Hawthornesque. (Isabel, Pierre's beckoner into new knowledge, lives, as Hawthorne did in 1851, in a red rural cottage, prominently adorned with two other Hawthorne emblems: mosses and gables.) Pierre's discovery of illicit parental sexuality, as Melville describes it, opens his eyes to a heretofore-hidden blackness of life in general, a "darker, though truer aspect of things" (84).[44] The revelation of this buried order immediately also shows Pierre that reality as he has known it has been a matter only of "hereditary forms and world-usages" (108), a cultural convention-system organized to keep this "truer aspect" out of sight. ("Men are jailers all; jailers of themselves" [110], Pierre cries, in profound echo of Hawthorne's vision of the social contract as a league of mutual repression.) And as it produces this revision of social reality Pierre's discovery also brings a transformation of self. As Pierre comes to know "the hidden things" (80) an "incipient off-spring" begins "foetally forming in him" (128). This new self wrests Pierre from the world of ordinary social engagements and remakes him as that trans-social or transcendent self who "know[s] what *is*" (80). As it does so it makes him too a man with a mission: against "the diving and ducking moralities of this earth" to "square myself by the inflexible rule of holy right" (129), and so to enact the true law of brotherhood in a world that refuses to know that law.

Melville works many new sources and conceptions into his retelling of the story of daimonization in *Pierre*.[45] But the most interesting difference in this book's treatment of this now-familiar process is that in *Pierre* daimonization is so much more undisguisedly linked with Melville's own artistic ambitions. Pierre like Ahab is a "profound willfulness" (393), but this time that willfulness is very intimately linked to the strain of personal messianism so marked in Melville's literary thinking after *Mardi*. Pierre's self-within-a-self is a "heaven-begotten Christ" (128) born within him, another version, that is, of the new Messiah Melville looked for in "Shakespers person" and the "literary Shiloh" whose coming haunts "Hawthorne and His Mosses." As it links up with Melville's strong christological urges (Melville was in his thirty-third year when he wrote *Pierre*), Pierre's special incarnation ties itself too to Melville's aspirations to literary genius. The "accession of the personal divine" in Pierre drives him in one way to lead a life of Christlike sacrifice, but in another to undertake a "deep book" (355). And the literary ambitions that propel this book are, transparently, those of Melville's own prophetical yearnings. Pierre's "burning desire" as a writer is "to deliver what he thought to be new, or at least miserably neglected Truth to the world" (329), or as he even more exaltedly declares, "I will gospelize the world anew, and show them deeper secrets than the Apocalypse!" (319). (Compare Melville to Hawthorne: "Though I wrote the Gospels in this century, I should die in the gutter.")

That web of highly charged aspirations that entered Melvillean authorship with Mardi, then reached their crisis of self-acceptance when Melville met Hawthorne, are directly implicated in the plot of Pierre's career. And as if because they surface here in such undisguised form, Melville finds these ambitions considerably harder to control. *Pierre*, a book full of ideas about how it might organize itself, has some quite brilliant notions of how it might contain the will to prophecy this time around. It has obviously occurred to Melville to try to read Pierre's prophetical impulses sociohistorically, as by-products of the new form of family life gaining ground in his time. It has also occurred to him to study these impulses psychologically, in terms of the mind's self-disguise of its illicit desires. (In this phase of his project Melville has *The Scarlet Letter* quite directly before him.) But such plans get abrogated in *Pierre*—and abrogated, quite visibly, by the resurgence of the prophetical will itself. Pierre, once treated in part as a victim of domestic culture or of sexual self-deception, increasingly becomes a "noble soul" persecuted by the "dastardly world" (315) as the book goes on. As this happens the book falls increasingly into Pierre's own prophetical frame of vision—into a vision antagonistic, self-pitying, and addicted to stark, transcendently abstract moral polarizations, as in: "The wide world is banded against him; for to you! he holds up the standard of Right, and swears by the Eternal and True!" (315).

What Pierre charts—and harrowingly, because in full knowledge that its own governing ambitions are its real subject—is the story of where the prophetical impulse leads, when embraced so unrestrainedly. In this respect it is the story, for one thing, of the spiritual and even physical destructiveness of ambitions so defined. The accession of the personal divine produces no new gospel in *Pierre*, but rather the drainage, from the bearer, of the energies of ordinary life. "Gifted with loftiness" (393)—the phrase can remind us of Ahab, "gifted with the high perception," but also of Melville's own assurance of "higher purposes"—Pierre suffers the diseases of excessive elevation: the "superhuman" (361) is associated, in late *Pierre*, with the bad transcendence of living women turned to "marble girl[s]" (415) or of the amaranth flower, sterile and immortal. Pierre himself shows the final yield of his election and elevation when, in a really frightening passage, he becomes simply affectless, dead to stimuli of any sort—"utterly without sympathy from any thing divine, human, brute, or vegetable" (392); then, in an intensification even of this, devitalized in the radical sense: "he did not have any ordinary life-feeling at all" (395).

As it wrecks its bearer's common life, the ambition *Pierre* studies and is sick with wreaks a corresponding violence on its own transcendent goals. The mark of Pierre's prophetical incarnation is that he organizes his life in harsher and ever-more-abstracted polarities. But it is the nature of these polarities that, when insisted on in such absolute form, they collapse in on themselves. "Henceforth I will know nothing but Truth" (80), Pierre declares at his prophetical awakening. Nothing is so inspiring to him as "to think of the Truth and the Lie!" (353). (Compare Melville: "For in this world of lies, Truth is forced to fly....") But when he so relentlessly stakes himself on the existence of a Truth he never attains, the very notion of a deep or essential reality explodes itself—"Truth" shows its "everlasting elusiveness" (393)— and the antithesis True/False annihilates itself as a form of significant opposition. "To follow Virtue to her uttermost vista, where common souls never go" (318), in a parallel discovery, is to reach not the place of the Right but the place where Virtue and Vice collapse into indistinguishable "trash," then into empty "nothing" (319). In literary terms, to insist strongly enough on the opposition between the "deep book" and "some shallow nothing of a novel" (355) produces not a realized Art of Truth but a collapse of the deeps into the shallows and of all writing into "coiner's book[s]" (414). Promising to lead to a perfect authenticity of life, knowing, and speaking, prophecy's animating conceit leads instead to an explosion of its own organizing concepts, abolishing, in the process, the mental equipment whereby any kind of significant direction or opposition could be thought. Its end is the "neuter" (418) condition, a white world of perfect undifferentiability:

> it is not for man to follow the trail of truth too far, since by so doing he entirely loses the directing compass of his mind; for arrived at the Pole, to whose barrenness only it points, there, the needle indifferently respects all points of the horizon alike. (196)

What *Pierre* demonstrates—in full knowledge that it does not thereby escape from this predicament—is the inherent tendency of a prophetical conception of authorship to collapse its own ground. And this lesson has a larger application than to Melville's case alone. After all, Melville is not the only author of his time to organize his work around a prophetical literary conception. This conception is equally central to such exact contemporaries of Melville's as Whitman, or Thoreau, or Jones Very (who intermittently believed he was the Second Coming.)[46] Historically, this is *the* other literary self-conception, besides the domestic one, operative in American writing of the 1850s. It is the other idea writers there could find ready access to, to motivate their work. And it is the idea that released what, along with the new popular literature of domesticity, is the other authentic literary product of the American 1850s: that massively individuated, morally as well as formally innovative writing, unpurchased by the public but undaunted by its lack of public support, of which *Moby-Dick*, *Leaves of Grass*, and *Walden* are the three great examples. (Harriet Beecher Stowe, who spent some time in later life trying to plot out a tradition of female prophecy, authorizes the assertion of *Uncle Tom's Cabin* through this conception too, and so shows that the prophetic and domestic strains of 1850s authorship could be combined.) Melville's case demonstrates what it is about this authorial conception that lets it activate a literature of these features. His case shows how this conception excites and energizes the writer, defends him against the public's wishes, and warrants him to believe that his most eccentric impulses are the ones he is most bound to pursue. But his case also dramatizes the fact that the same features that equip this conception to unleash such unconventional imaginative energies also make it unsustaining, as a program of authorship. *Pierre* shows that the conception of prophecy, promising to release him from the world of lies or fictions, tempts its bearer to embrace it as an actual identity, not a temporarily assumed role, but that it is a psychic and artistic disaster when so embraced. (Jones Very and Hawthorne's demented devotee Delia Bacon—witness to the truth that the *real* Shakespeare was not Shakespeare—show the real-life consequences of taking prophetical appointment too literally.) *Pierre* also suggests that it is the nature of the prophetical conception, when persisted in, to demand of the author more than he can create—and so to stymie the labor it first inspired. We might read, in this, the reason why the American careers founded on this conception take the form of short bursts of dazzling creativity followed by increasingly impaired efforts to renew that level of achievement—Whitman's and Thoreau's pattern as it is Melville's. (This pattern persists for the more modern writers who have been drawn to the prophetical literary conception—James Agee, James Baldwin, and Flannery O'Connor are three very various examples.)

Since Melville entered into the idea of prophetical vocation by way of Hawthorne, it might occur to us to ask, at this point, how Hawthorne avoided the extremities Melville reaches in *Pierre*. And might not the answer just be that Hawthorne stayed clear of the whole prophetic syndrome? As a personality structure and as a way of mobilizing personal belief and its expressions, prophetical selfhood is a powerful form in America in the 1850s. We need only read evangelical sermons or reformist speeches of this time, or remember Henry Adams's claim that antislavery threw Massachusetts back onto Puritan holy warfare,[47] to learn that what we see in Melville, or Whitman, or Thoreau is only the more purely literary expression of a much more widespread cultural phenomenon. But Hawthorne displays the prophetical personality about as little as anyone one could name from his time. The evidence is that this is the one human type he could least abide: I remember here Coverdale's ennui at Hollingsworth's "prolonged fiddling upon one string," or Hawthorne's remark on John Brown, the great political avatar of the prophetic type in the 1850s, that "nobody was ever more justly hanged."[48] Writing inspired by the idea of prophecy is known at once by its air of intense conviction, and America produced as much self-convicted writing in this decade as anyone would ever care to read. But Hawthorne's writing is known by its feints and indirections, not its professions of its beliefs; in fact Hawthorne may be the literary writer of his time whose writing is freest from such strains.

As the orientation point for his own prophetical program, this would imply, Melville lighted on the one major author of his time who was seriously immune to such authorship's attractions. And this would lead to a further conclusion that students of the Melville–Hawthorne relation must, at some point, face: namely, that Melville was just totally wrong about Hawthorne as an authorial model—so wrong, we might say, that it would take a genius to *be* so wrong. But another reading is possible as well. It would be easy to produce, from inside Hawthorne's writings, a massive censure and repudiation of prophetical ambitions. (What could Melville have thought when he read this, in *The House of the Seven Gables*? "Persons who have wandered, or been expelled, out of the common track of things, even were it for a better system, desire nothing so much as to be led back.")[49] But, as Melville noticed, Hawthorne shows a recurring fascination with art's possibly reality-disclosing power (as when Holgrave, in that same book, literally uncovers the "secret character" beneath the "merest surface" of his sitters' presented selves through his act of portraiture). And at times something very close to what Melville understands as prophecy seems to be taking place in Hawthorne's books. In the forest scene of *The Scarlet Letter*, for example, Hester (and the book she now seizes control of) is mastered by a powerful will; that will makes her strong in speech; and what that speaking does is first to disclaim the truth of merely social designations of obligation or value, then (on the authority of its own convictions) to *speak* a drastically revised moral covenant: "what we did had a consecration of its own."[50]

It is easy to see how Melville might read such a scene as literature, however covertly, gospelizing the world anew. But if we concede that energies like those of prophecy are at work in Hawthorne's writing, the crucial question then becomes on what terms those energies are entertained. Obviously, in *The Scarlet Letter* these energies are fiercely contained— contained first by Dimmesdale, who uses the vigor Hester inspires in him to redeliver their love to the authority of the old law; then by Hester, who chooses to resubject herself to the badge of censure she had removed in this scene; and throughout by the book itself, which, on every rereading, always releases Hester's assertion as a living possibility, then always forbids it to become an achieved reality. Readers of Melvillean persuasions usually dislike this movement of limitation, taking it as sign of a failure of courage. But the logic of lost nerve is not really the logic of *The Scarlet Letter*'s return. After all, what generated Hester's powers of moral reimagination is the action of the law that condemned her. Before her punishment, Hester's illicit desires are strong enough to have led her into adultery. But it is her experience of legal condemnation, her constant, painful coercion into the category of the transgressive, that turns her vitalities "from passion and feeling, to thought,"[51] and so generates in her the much more powerfully transgressive free-*thinking* she achieves in the forest scene. But since her passionate counter-perception is itself the product of the orthodoxy it inverts, it cannot, as it tells itself in the forest scene, stand wholly apart from that scheme. Hester's imaginativeness is not a power by itself but one half of a larger structure the other part of which is the law that constrains her: the two forces, conceptually opposite, are grasped as interdependent and even mutually generative in the powerful thinking of *The Scarlet Letter*. When Hester resumes her letter, it is in no simple surrender to the authority of worldly law. It is in recognition of the inextricableness (imaged in her letter) of subversion from the authority that calls forth subversion, of freedom from the law whose breaking creates freedom's possibility, of imaginative creation from the restricting conventions that allow such creation to be.

Hawthorne's difference from his more overtly prophetical contemporaries, such an account would let us say, is not that his work is closed to prophetical energies, but that it eludes the conceptual commitments such energies bring along. Prophecy is the mode of fierce either/ors—of the Truth against the Lie, the Right against the Wrong—but Hawthorne exploits the energies of prophecy without accepting its schemes of mutually exclusive opposition. His work realizes the prophetical impulse neither as the Truth nor as a violation of the natural order but as part of a system whose elements imply and affirm their opposites: in which conventionality breeds anticonventional aggressions, imaginative assertion helps validate the shared conventional world, and so on.

Read in this way, Melville did not just get Hawthorne wrong: he got him right and wrong at the same time. By approaching Hawthorne in a prophetical mood, Melville was able to discover the authentically prophetic strains of Hawthorne's imagination. (Who else had even seen these before Melville?) But his own prophetical interests made Melville read this as the only true Hawthorne, so that in the act of grasping this aspect Melville also failed to grasp its allegiance to its apparent opposites. Melville got the full benefit of this mistaking. By reading Hawthorne as he did, Melville won crucial backing for his own, altogether more adventurous imaginative ambitions-backing to which we owe the realization of *Moby-Dick*. But this mistaking was not without its cost. In *Pierre* Melville reaches the point where prophecy's cherished idea of Truth manages first to delegitimate any kind of existing conventional structure as a Lie, then to explode the idea of Truth as a basis for work or thought. Melville's work might have averted this self-abolition if it had learned a different lesson in Hawthorne's school: that prophecy is most productive as an artistic program when it does not quite believe it knows the whole, grand truth.

I said before that Melville experienced Hawthorne as confirming his prophetical aspirations when he read and praised *Moby-Dick*. There is evidence that he experienced the later abortion of his prophetical career through Hawthorne's eyes as well.

One of the most powerful fantasies to emerge toward the end of *Pierre* is the cool, philosophical face of Plotinus Plinlimmon, leering at Pierre as he attempts to write. Virtually every detail of this portrait ties Plinlimmon to Melville's Hawthorne. Pierre has found Plinlimmon's work unmemorable, as Melville had found Hawthorne's, before he meets him in person. In his person, Plinlimmon has Hawthorne's blue eyes and famous detachment of manner. He has a "face of repose" (339), a standard word for Hawthorne's manner around 1850; his face is systematically voided of affect or expression, as Melville later remembered Hawthorne's to be (he writes in *Clarel*: "not responsive was Vine's cheer, / Discharged of every meaning sign"); his clothes, like his face, "seemed to disguise this man" (338) (compare Hawthorne on his publicly visible self in the newly written preface to *The Snow Image*: "these things hide the man, instead of displaying him.")[52] Plinlimmon's disengagement from his own feelings is haunting because it speaks a disengagement too from the life issues that might inspire strong feeling. Plinlimmon is honored as a profound thinker, but he himself prefers not to engage in philosophical speculation (as Hawthorne returned silence to Melville's energetic divings; Plinlimmon, possibly like Hawthorne, prefers his followers' champagne to their ontological heroics.) His only known philosophical position, expressed in his pamphlet "EI" or "Chronometricals and Horologicals," is that the ethical norms that prevail in the world are just communal conventions, radically disjoined from "Heaven's own Truth." But he affirms that both of these systems are valid in their own way, and that "by their very contradictions they are made to correspond" (249).

The power not to get vexed by the mysteries of life—the power not even to want to go into them—is what the ardently speculative Melville must have found incomprehensible in Hawthorne as their relation went on. And Plinlimmon's thought has just the feature Melville's must have found exasperating in Hawthorne's: the ability to affirm the simultaneous validity of apparently exclusive opposites, and specifically to affirm the value of the conventional in full knowledge that it is merely conventional. Plinlimmon, we might say, is Hawthorne reseen as something very different from a prophet; and this is what gives him his new, eerie power. Plinlimmon appears just after Pierre undertakes to write his truth-delivering deep book, and he appears as a nightmare-projection of such authorship's deep self-doubts: Pierre comes to believe that "by some magical means or other the face had got hold of his secret" (342), and sees Plinlimmon as silently mocking him for his presumptions. This, we can suppose, is how Hawthorne must have looked to Melville as he pressed on through *Pierre*: as a figure after all not engaged in his same project; but as the man who was in on the secret of his project; and so as one who knew him for an egotistical fool.

If my reading is right, it reminds us of how the personal side of Hawthorne and Melville's relation fed into and amplified its literary aspect. Hawthorne's reserve commonly made others feel that he was looking for them to initiate a relation. But then, when he failed to join in the exchange he seemed to invite, he made others feel embarrassed at their own sociability. (When Hawthorne died, Emerson lamented his lifelong failure to "conquer a friendship" with him: "It was easy to talk with him,—there were no barriers,—only, he said so little, that I talked too much, and stopped only because, as he gave no indications, I feared to exceed.")[53] Melville obviously went through this same cycle of feeling specially "drawn out" by Hawthorne's "sociable silences," then feeling reproached, by those same silences, for talking as he did.[54] But since he invested his authorial ambitions in his personal relation with Hawthorne, he set the end-points of this cycle at much greater extremes. Having projected his risky ambitions onto Hawthorne, Melville gave him the power, whenever he seemed responsive, to seem to be confirming his right to such aspirations: when Hawthorne liked *Moby-Dick*, Melville felt "unspeakable security." By the same token, whenever Hawthorne's silence seemed less than fully sociable, Melville felt his reserve as reservation about his artistic project—reservation truly devastating since it came from the figure chosen to underwrite that project's validity.

When Melville's authorship reaches the crisis it reaches in *Pierre*, and when Hawthorne becomes mixed up with such punishing self-criticisms in Melville's mind, we might assume that their relation is at its end. But Melville continued to look to Hawthorne in 1852 and 1853, as he struggled to find a way for his authorship to go on. The first writing project Melville undertook after *Pierre* was a work he outlined at length in a letter to Hawthorne and tried to get Hawthorne to write: the story of the patient fidelity of a Nantucket woman whose sailor-husband deserted her, then came back long after he was thought dead. The "Agatha" letters of 1852 show Melville again trying to plant an idea of authorship on Hawthorne, then to receive it back *from* Hawthorne as a project Hawthorne had invited him to. The letters show too how Melville felt after his great attempt at such a supporting exchange had failed: abandonment is the content of the Hawthorne relationship as the "Agatha" letters image it.

But in a sense the most interesting thing about the "Agatha" letters is that they show Melville paying attention to a new part of Hawthorne's work: to what Melville calls "your *London husband*,"[55] or the early tale "Wakefield." "Wakefield" is an intriguing tale for Melville to be thinking about because it renders the same Hawthornesque figure who had always fascinated Melville in a somewhat different way. Like Hooper, or Brand, or Ahab, or Pierre, Wakefield is a man found out by a fate, by an idea that descends on him, wrests him from the world of ordinary habits and relations, and compels him to unwavering adherence to a peculiar personal program. This is the familiar process of daimonization; but in "Wakefield" daimonization is a process almost perfectly opaque. Wakefield's personal program—to live one block away from home for twenty years while never going home—has no motivation even suggested for it. His program leads to no symbolic counter-expression: Wakefield is the hero as literally uncommunicative man. If his special fate makes Wakefield seem like a "figure" for some unknown truth of our condition, that truth remains almost perfectly elusive. Hawthorne hazards the moral that, by stepping out of our social places even for a moment, "a man exposes himself to a fearful risk of losing his place forever."[56] But Wakefield remains a fascinating freak, impressive because so little susceptible to explication.

"Wakefield" presents Hawthorne's daimonic agent acting in a reversed role—as a figure not of assertive will but of withdrawal and passivity, and as the bearer not of revelation but of mystery itself. The lesson is not lost on Melville. In "Bartleby the Scrivener," the first work he published after *Pierre*, Melville creates his own version of this passive, unimpassioned, unexplained, and inexpressive character. And in "Bartleby" Melville also catches—from "Wakefield," we can surmise—a new idea for his work. In "Bartleby" Melville's fiction becomes, for the first time, *short*: curtailed in its expression, no longer aiming at what Melville had called "full articulations." His fiction now emulates the detachment it had found so distressing in *Pierre*: it sets itself apart from its author, no longer offering to speak or develop his personal mind. Above all, his fiction does not try to penetrate the depths of a more essential reality. Like "Wakefield" it builds power through the secrets it keeps, not those it tries to tell.

In the more secretive stories of *The Piazza Tales*, then in *The Confidence-Man*, which finds fiction's analogy not in the gospels but in the apocrypha or scripture without a warrant, Melville goes on to explore the new ways fiction can be conceived that open up when a prophetical conception gets pressed to its limits. Hawthorne does not preside over this new work quite as much as he once did,[57] but I think it instructive that Melville should find his way to this work in part by rethinking Hawthorne's example. It is a mark of Hawthorne's persisting power to help other writers see their work, as it is of Melville's persisting creativity as a reader of Hawthorne's aims, that Melville can still take guidance from Hawthorne even in learning how to move away from him—can use him to help frame a post-prophetical plan of authorship, as he used him to frame a prophetical one before.

NOTES

1. *Melville Log*, p. 924; *Clarel*, ed. Walter E. Bezanson (New York: Hendricks House, 1960), pp. 91 and 94–95. Consideration of Melville's encounter with Hawthorne has the status almost of a *topos* in American literary criticism. For a useful survey of earlier discussions, see James C. Wilson, "The Hawthorne–Melville Relationship: An Annotated Bibliography," *American Transcendental Quarterly*, 45–46 (1980), 5–79. Among the discussions Wilson reviews, two deserve special mention for their success, despite the overstatement both indulge in, at bringing forth features of the dynamics of this exchange. They are Edwin Haviland Miller's *Melville* (New York: George Braziller, 1975), a biography that makes Melville's relation with Hawthorne virtually the sole determinant of his mental life, and Sidney Moss's "Hawthorne and Melville: An Inquiry into Their Art and the Mystery of their Friendship," *Literary Monographs*, 7 (1975), 45–84, the fullest consideration of this relation's meaning from the Hawthorne side. Perhaps the best short treatment of this relation is Walter Bezanson's discussion of Vine in his Introduction to the Hendricks House edition of *Clarel*, pp. xc–xcix.

2. *Letters of Herman Melville*, p. 119. For the remainder of this chapter this volume will be abbreviated *LHM* in the notes.

3. *LHM*, p. 121.

4. On the advent of the cult of domesticity and its stimulus to reading, see Nancy F. Cott, *The Bonds of Womanhood: "Woman's Sphere" in New England, 1780–1835* (New Haven: Yale University Press, 1977) and Ann Douglas, *The Feminization of American Culture* (New York: Knopf, 1977), especially pp. 3–13 and 44–79. Charvat's historical researches were collected by Matthew J. Bruccoli in the volume *The Profession of Authorship in America*.

5. See Douglas, *Feminization*, pp. 227–40, and the whole of Kelley's *Private Woman, Public Stage*.

6. Myra Jehlen's important essay "Archimedes and the Paradox of Feminist Criticism," *Signs* 6 (Summer 1981), 575–601, takes the Melville/literary domestics dichotomy as a test case in its call for a comparatist and historical study of men's and women's authorship. The phrases cited come from p. 593.

7. *Melville Log*, pp. 925 and 926.

8. See *LHM*, p. 130.

9. *LHM*, pp. 46, 39, and 66.

10. *LHM*, p. 70.

11. From an 1863 note by Whitman on Emerson, printed in Edmund Wilson, ed., *The Shock of Recognition* (New York: Farrar, Straus, and Cudahy, 1955, 2nd ed.), p. 272.

12. *LHM*, p. 102. Duyckinck's importance for Melville is that he urged literary nonderivativeness as a patriotic duty, while also giving Melville access to his library (and deep personal knowledge) of older writing. On Duyckinck's literary nationalism, see Perry Miller, *The Raven and the Whale* (New York: Harcourt Brace, 1956). For a specimen of the depth and seriousness of his learning, see Donald and Kathleen Malone Yannella's edition of his 1847 diary in *Studies in the American Renaissance*, ed. Joel Myerson (Boston: Twayne, 1978), pp. 207–58, where we see Duyckinck (for instance) reading Machiavelli, indexing Walton's *Compleat Angler*, and planning a study of Sidney's *Arcadia*.

13. *LHM*, p. 86.

14. *Mardi*, pp. 1213, 1023, 1254, 1256; *LHM*, p. 71. (Since it embodies the only complete edition of the authoritative text of Melville's prose, the three-volume Library of America edition [New York, 1982–84] is the source of my quotations from Melville's novels. *Mardi* is printed with *Typee* and *Omoo* in the first of these volumes, to which these page numbers refer.)

15. *LHM*, p. 85; *Mardi*, p. 1262.

16. *LHM*, pp, 78–79 and 77.

17. *LHM*, p. 86.

18. *LHM*, pp. 86, 71, 85, 86.

19. *Mardi*, p. 1214. On Melville's theory of writing as thought-generating or mind-producing activity, see my "*Mardi*: Creating the Creative," in *New Perspectives on Herman Melville*, ed. Faith Pullin (Edinburgh: Edinburgh University Press, 1978), pp. 29–53.

20. Charvat makes this point about American literary culture in *Profession of Authorship*, p. 211. (His chapter "Melville," pp. 204–61, is an important discussion of Melville's interaction with a culturally unstratified audience.) On the nonsegregation, in the 1840s, of cultural levels that became segregated later on, see especially Lawrence W. Levine's "William Shakespeare and the American People: A Study in Cultural Transformation," *American Historical Review* 80 (1984) 34–66. As I argue in the next chapter, Evert Duyckinck, Melville's mentor at the *Mardi* phase of his career, was an important agent in early (and still quite unsuccessful) movements to institutionalize a high artistic culture in America. Melville's Duyckinck connection thus provides the real social basis for his imaginative assertion of a "high" counter-public—when Melville spoke of *Mardi* reaching "those for whom it is intended," the Duyckincks are the actual readers he had in mind.

21. *LHM*, p. 86.

22. *Mardi*, p. 1262.

23. *LHM*, pp. 91–92.

24. Page numbers refer to the text of "Hawthorne and His Mosses" printed in the third volume of the Library of America edition of Melville's complete prose.

25. Duyckinck's 1845 essay on Hawthorne for the *Democratic Review*—an essay that prefigures a number of other turns and phrases from "Hawthorne and His Mosses" as well—is reprinted in J. Donald Crowley's valuable *Hawthorne: The Critical Heritage* (London: Routledge and Kegan Paul, 1970), pp. 96–100. (Duyckinck, one of Hawthorne's two or three most influential critics before 1850, was Melville's houseguest when Melville met Hawthorne and wrote this essay.) For the source of the Carlyle echoes—first noted by Luther S. Mansfield and Howard P. Vincent in their notes to the Hendricks House edition of *Moby-Dick* (1952)—see *On Heroes, Hero-Worship, and the Heroic in History* (Lincoln: University of Nebraska Press, 1966), pp. 42–68. Two recent essays helpful for describing Melville's use of reading as a means to thought are Robert Milder's "Nemo Contra Deum ...: Melville and Goethe's 'Demonic,'" in *Ruined Eden of the Present*, ed. G. R. Thompson and Virgil L. Lokke (West Lafayette, Ind.: Purdue University Press, 1981), pp. 205–44, and James McIntosh's "Melville's Use and Abuse of Goethe: The Weaver-Gods in *Faust* and *Moby-Dick*," *Amerikastudien* 25 (1980), 158–73.

26. *LHM*, p. 121; *Melville Log*, pp. 926, 419, and 528–29.

27. *LHM*, p. 133.

28. *LHM*, pp. 124–25.

29. *LHM*, pp. 127–29.

30. Frank Lloyd Wright, *An Autobiography* (New York: Horizon Press, 1977, rev. ed.), p. 27; *Paradise Lost*, XI:701–704.

31. *LHM*, pp. 198–109; *Melville Log*, p. 385. Robert Milder usefully surveys the evidence about *Moby-Dick*'s composition and the theories of composition this evidence has invited in "The Composition of *Moby-Dick*: A Review and a Prospect," *Emerson Society Quarterly* 23 (1977) 203–16.

32. I say this in view of the very mixed review Duyckinck wrote for the *Literary World* in November 1851. This review is reprinted in the Norton Critical Edition of *Moby-Dick*, ed. Harrison Hayford and Hershel Parker (New York, 1967), pp. 613–16.

33. *LHM*, pp. 133 and 143–44.

34. *LHM*, p, 142.

35. Newton Arvin, *Herman Melville* (New York: William Sloane Associates, 1950), p. 138; Sidney Moss, "Hawthorne and Melville," p. 62; Hyatt H. Waggoner, *The Presence of Hawthorne* (Baton Rouge: Louisiana State University Press, 1979), p. 137. For another important assessment, see Leon Howard, *Herman Melville: A Biography* (Berkeley and Los Angeles: University of California Press, 1967), pp. 168–69.

36. *Melville Log*, p. 410.

37. References to *Moby-Dick*, taken from the Library of America volume that also includes *Redburn* and *White-Jacket*, are followed by page numbers in parentheses.

38. Angus Fletcher, *Allegory: The Theory of a Symbolic Mode* (Ithaca: Cornell University Press, 1964), pp. 25–69 and 279–303.

39. William Godwin, *Caleb Williams* (New York: Holt, Rinehart, and Winston, 1960), p. 124; Mary Shelley, *Frankenstein* (New York: New American Library, 1965) p. 47.

40. *Mosses From an Old Manse*, p. 39. "The Birthmark" is one of the most heavily marked tales in Melville's copy of *Mosses*. For the record of Melville's marks and annotations see Walker Cowan, "Melville's Marginalia: Hawthorne," *Studies in the American Renaissance* (1978), 279–302.

41. *Twice-Told Tales*, Centenary Edition volume 9, p. 49; *Mosses*, pp. 277–78.

42. The place to begin the study of the heroic sources of Ahab is in Mansfield and Vincent's notes to the Hendricks House edition of *Moby-Dick*, especially pp. 637–52; see also Howard, *Herman Melville*, pp. 169–73. Charles Olson describes the Shakespearean origins of Ahab in *Call Me Ishmael* (San Francisco: City Lights, 1947) pp. 35–73; on Ahab and Goethe, see Milder, "Nemo Contra Deum"; on Ahab and Carlyle, see Jonathan Arac, *Commissioned Spirits: The Shaping of Social Motion in Dickens, Carlyle, Melville, and Hawthorne* (New Brunswick: Rutgers University Press, 1979), pp. 139–63.

43. See Carlyle, *Heroes and Hero-Worship*, pp. 45–46.

44. Page numbers refer to *Pierre* as printed in the third Library of America volume of Melville's complete prose.

45. Other sources, much more incoherently amalgamated than the sources for Ahab are in *Moby-Dick*, include Romeo and Hamlet; the Romantic tradition of inspiration through a female muse or damsel with a dulcimer; and especially, I think, Emerson, who states the principle of being Pierre acts out in "Self-Reliance": "O father, O mother, O wife, O brother, O friend, I have lived with you after appearances hitherto. Henceforward I am the Truth's;" "when good is near you, when you have life in yourself, it is not by any known or accustomed way; ... the way, the thought, the good, shall be wholly strange and new."

46. On prophetical authorship in the American Renaissance, see Roy Harvey Pearce's Introduction to the 1860 edition of *Leaves of Grass* (Ithaca: Cornell University Press, 1961), pp. xv–xviii; Stanley Cavell, *The Senses of Walden* (New York: Viking Press, 1974), pp. 14–20; Lawrence Buell, *Literary Transcendentalism* (Ithaca: Cornell University Press, 1973), pp. 30–45; and Buell, "Literature and Scripture in New England Between the Revolution and the Civil War," *Notre Dame English Journal* 15 (Spring 1983), 1–28. Buell's essay, pp. 17–18, anticipates my sense of the instability of prophecy as a literary program. Of course the prophetical program of authorship, so seriously enacted by American authors, is also a strong element in the English Protestant poetic tradition. For considerations of this program's pre-American life see, among many other sources, William Kerrigan, *The Prophetic Milton* (Charlottesville: University Press of Virginia, 1974); Geoffrey Hartman, "The Poetics of Prophecy," in *High Romantic Argument*, ed. Lawrence Lipking (Ithaca: Cornell University Press, 1981), pp. 15–40; and John Guillory, *Poetic Authority: Spenser, Milton, and Literary History* (New York: Columbia University Press, 1983).

47. *The Education of Henry Adams* (New York: Modern Library, 1931), pp. 25–26. I do not know of a comprehensive treatment of the antislavery movement's crucial dependence on the prophetic as a personality type and rhetorical stance.

48. *The Blithedale Romance*, Centenary Edition volume 3, p. 56; "Chiefly About War Matters," *Miscellanies: Biographical and Other Sketches and Letters by Nathaniel Hawthorne* (Boston: Houghton Mifflin, 1903), pp. 397–98.

49. *The House of the Seven Gables*, p. 140.

50. *The Scarlet Letter*, Centenary Edition volume 1, p. 195.

51. *The Scarlet Letter*, p. 164.

52. For an important connection of Hawthorne with "repose," see Poe's 1847 review of Hawthorne, *Edgar Allen Poe: Essays and Reviews* (New York: Library of America, 1984), p. 579. Melville had used this word for Hawthorne in "Hawthorne and His Mosses," p. 1156. *Clarel*, p. 256; Preface to *The Snow Image*, Centenary Edition volume 11, p. 4.

53. Stephen E. Whicher, ed., *Selections from Ralph Waldo Emerson* (Boston: Houghton Mifflin Riverside Edition, 1957), p. 403.

54. For evidence of such embarrassment, see Melville's letters to Hawthorne of 1? June and 29 June 1851, *LHM* pp. 126–32, where Melville's venting of his prophetical voice keeps pivoting him into an abased consciousness of himself as "conceited and garrulous" and of his talk as "my old foible-preaching." The anxiety and self-criticism Hawthorne's reserve inspired in Melville were no doubt reasons why their close friendship dissolved after 1851; but the larger truth is that their relation, literary as well as personal, was worn out by the energies it had unleashed.

55. *LHM*, p. 155. The "Agatha" letters appear on pp. 153–63 of this volume.

56. *Twice-Told Tales*, p. 140.

57. Not that his presence disappears. In *The Presence of Hawthorne*, pp. 131–43, Hyatt Waggoner has convincingly argued that Hawthorne is pervasive in *The Piazza Tales* ("The Bell Tower" is certainly the most straightforwardly Hawthornesque tale Melville ever wrote); he is present again in the Vine sections of *Clarel*, and it would be possible to argue that *Billy Budd* is an amplified version of the sort of allegorical parable Melville found in Hawthorne's tales.

LAWRENCE BUELL

The Literary Significance
of the Unitarian Movement

That there is an intimate connection between the American Unitarian movement and the so-called American literary renaissance has been long known and loudly proclaimed. One of the first full-dress national literary histories, Barrett Wendell's turn-of-the-century *Literary History of America* went so far as to insist that "almost everybody who attained literary distinction in New England during the nineteenth century was either a Unitarian or closely associated with Unitarian influences."[1] George Willis Cooke's contemporaneous *Unitarianism in America* cites chapter and verse:

> Ralph Waldo Emerson was the son of William Emerson, the minister of the First Church in Boston.... George Bancroft was the son of Aaron Bancroft, the first Unitarian minister in Worcester, and the first president of the American Unitarian Association. To Charles Lowell, of the West Church in Boston, were born James Russell Lowell and Robert T. S. Lowell.[2]

Triumph by genealogy—a familiar Brahmin tactic. Cooke goes on to claim Unitarian prominence in virtually every genre, fictive and nonfictional—except, significantly, drama, which in proper traditional New England fashion he silently omits. As reinforcement, he quotes my opening quotation from Wendell. But "more even than that may be said," adds Cooke, "for it is

From *American Unitarianism*, 1805–65. © 1989 by Northeastern University Press.

the Unitarian writers who have most truly interpreted American institutions and American ideals" (p. 435).

The extravagance of these claims must immediately be discounted in view of their status as artifacts of late-century Brahmin ethnocentrism and collegiality. Still, Wendell, if not Cooke, was more right than wrong. In New England, if not in America at large, Unitarianism clearly did exert a literary influence far out of proportion to its denominational size. My recent research on the careers of New England authors during the Renaissance or Middle period (from the War of 1812 to the Civil War) indicates that something like one-quarter of all creative writers of any significance were at some time in their lives Unitarians, including fully half of the region's writers who might arguably be called "major."[3] The region's first substantial intellectual quarterly, the *North American Review*; its first important denominational periodical of literary cast, the *Christian Disciple* (which evolved into the still more ambitious *Christian Examiner*); its most prestigious literary magazine, the *Atlantic Monthly*; and its most prestigious publishing house, Ticknor & Fields, were overwhelmingly (although not exclusively) sponsored and dominated by groups of Unitarians who together formed a kind of interlocking directorship whose fraternal networking became publicly concretized for the region's literati most conspicuously by the institution of Boston's Saturday Club at mid-century.[4]

So far I have merely been reciting the ABC's of the Unitarian preeminence in the region's antebellum literary culture. Almost equally familiar are the explanations of the rise of that hegemony. As numerous scholars have shown, the Unitarians were well positioned to play a leading role within the region as writers and tastemakers because of their status as the liberal wing of its best educated and most socially prestigious denomination, a denomination which at the beginning of the nineteenth century still enjoyed a sizeable majority in number of churches throughout the region. In New England's intellectual capital, Boston, the liberal presence was especially strong and conspicuous. The Unitarians and their Arminian precursors were far less inclined than were Orthodox Congregationalists to draw a sharp distinction between sanctified and unsanctified pursuits, between sacred and profane letters, between piety and conduct. For the Unitarians, the path to salvation was the growth and maintenance of Christian character, rather than a special conversion experience that marked the individual off from the rest of the world as the recipient of grace. To this end of character formation, the Unitarians welcomed art and literature as potential aids, all the more readily so given that the transmission of doctrine as such mattered less to their theologically liberal perspective than the raising of ethical consciousness.[5] Even in the pulpit, Unitarian ministers did not hesitate to make sweeping claims like the following about the spiritual value of "secular" art:

> books, to be of religious tendency, to be ministers to the general piety and virtue, need not be books of sermons.... *whatever* inculcates pure sentiment, whatever touches the heart with the beauty of virtue and the blessedness of piety, is in accordance with religion; and this is the Gospel of literature and art.[6]

Thus Unitarian reviewers turned to the serious examination of Walter Scott's fiction while the Orthodox continued to debate the propriety of novel reading; and in the hands of the Unitarian preachers, as Cooke put it, the sermon became "a literary product," as ministers "ceased to quote texts, abandoned theological exposition, refrained from the exhortatory method, and addressed men and women in literary language about the actual interests of daily life" (*Unitarianism*, p. 416).

This quick review shows the scholarly consensus as to the link between the development of Unitarianism and of literary culture in America (specifically New England) and the reason for the intimacy of that link. But it is tedious and unnecessary to continue on this level of well-established truths. Rather than give the kind of familiar panoramic survey of the epic of the Unitarian contribution to nineteenth-century arts and letters, I wish to isolate two special problematic features thereof to analyze in detail. Both points, I confess, have a sort of in-group character to them as being in the nature of admonitions directed especially to my own tribe of literary scholars; but I think they bear stating in mixed company as well.

I

The first point arises from my sense that literary scholars like myself typically experience as we approach the study of Unitarianism an irresistible temptation to depict it in the image of our own disciplinary interests, to overstate its aesthetic cast as we discuss its place in nineteenth-century culture. Unitarian–Orthodox debates about hermeneutics and doctrine (not to mention church government) do not in themselves concern the average literary specialist at all; from our point of view, American Unitarianism signifies primarily "the transition from religion to aesthetics" or, as Perry Miller put it in his seminal essay "From Edwards to Emerson," the rolling away of "the heavy stone of dogma that had sealed up the mystical springs in the New England character."[7] Although Miller is careful not to claim that the Unitarian–Transcendental continuum is in itself primarily an aesthetic one (indeed Miller stresses here and elsewhere that Transcendentalism was first and essentially a religious movement), it is clear that Unitarianism especially interests Miller, and his successors in American English departments to an even greater degree, for the service it performed as a kind of antidoctrinal solvent to release the New England imagination from its parochial confines and into confluence with the larger currents of European romanticism.

What I particularly want to stress about this reductionist view of Unitarianism's character, however, is not its element of disciplinary narcissism but its resemblance to the pronouncements of Unitarianism's own early historians such as Cooke, who seems positively to require us to read his chapter on "Unitarianism and Literature" as the key to his whole book. "The early Unitarian movement in New England," states Cooke, "was literary and religious rather than theological." Its early leaders—among whom Cooke incidentally reckons Emerson the most important—"made no effort to produce a Unitarian system of theology; and it would have been quite in opposition to the genius of the movement, had they entered upon such a task." Likewise, Joseph Henry Allen, another pioneer historian of the movement, identifies English Unitarianism with the romantic poets and the classic phase of American Unitarianism with William Ellery Channing, specifically with the power of Channing's voice: "its melody and pathos in the reading of a hymn were alone a charm that might bring men to the listening, like the attraction of sweet music." Likewise, memoirist O. B. Frothingham, summing up the creed of his father—whom he presents as a representative example of the early Unitarian establishment—calls it "rather rhetorical than dialectical" ("It would not have contented Abelard, though it might have pleased Emerson"), commends the elder Frothingham's genteel cultivation while apologizing for his rudimentary and unphilosophic reasoning, and quotes from among the funereal tributes Frederic Henry Hedge's assessment that although weak as a doctrinalist and theologian, Frothingham senior was gifted in hymn-writing and exquisitely polished in speech. "Nothing awkward," insists Hedge, "ever fell from his lips. His words expressed with unerring fitness the thing most fit to be expressed."[8]

At such moments, it begins to seem that late nineteenth-century Unitarian historiography was engaged in some kind of tacit conspiracy to set up the history of Unitarianism to be read in an aestheticist way. First, there is the tendency to represent William Ellery Channing as the star of the movement's pioneer era and to depict Norton, the Wares, Gannett, Tuckerman, and others as minor satellites by comparison, operating at the edges of Channing's penumbra in a not too interesting backroom or wheelhorse capacity. Second, and following from the first point, is the tendency to proclaim (usually with pride) the softness of Unitarianism as a theology and as a sect, and to locate its main source of intellectual energy in its powers of eloquence and cultivation. Third, and again related, is the tendency to cast the Unitarian net as wide as possible and base the prestige of the denomination broadly on the cultural accomplishments of non-mainstream figures like Emerson, and in particular to redefine the Transcendentalist schismatics as the most exciting and central of the second-generation figures.

Up to a point, this approach is very much in the tradition that characterized Unitarianism from the first. Unitarianism took shape in reaction against Orthodox formalism, always resisted movements to form binding creeds, often went to great lengths to preserve the spirit of free inquiry. At the same time, the late-century passages quoted earlier also often represent a skewed rewriting of Unitarian's classic phase for reasons the totality of which are obscure to me but which certainly include the sense of historical distance that two generations had created on the controversies of the formative period. From the standpoint of 1882, Unitarianism, as Allen put it, "so far as it is destined to survive at all, must understand that it has outgrown its old theological limits; and, as it was once the liberal side of the old Congregational body, so now it must know itself as the Christian side of the broader scientific movement of our time."[9]

It is in light of that retrospective standpoint, I surmise, that we must interpret Allen's earlier, seemingly dithering statement that he finds it hard to say "just what the Unitarian opinion is on any given matter, or what it is that Unitarians believe in general"; that indeed "I am a little impatient that they should ever be judged by their theology, which was so small a fraction of either their religion or their life!" (p. 30). While there is *some* truth to this, it greatly understates the importance that not only the old "moderate" Unitarians but even liberals like Channing and radicals like Theodore Parker attached to the issues of theology and ecclesiastical polity that concerned them. It is a too-conveniently literal reading of early pronouncements like Parker's "Now Arius, and now Athanasius is lord of the ascendant."[10] In this remark from *The Transient and Permanent in Christianity*, Parker is making a serious theological point, even though his aim is to dismantle theological structures, just as classical Unitarianism had been doing in its arguments against Calvinism. The late-nineteenth-century tendency to reduce early

Unitarian discourse to aesthetic impressionism reflects at least in part the
period's disinterest in the issues that earlier discourse addressed. The
readiness to expose theological argument as mere rhetoric. was indeed a
legacy of classical Unitarianism, but only after the fact did it come to seem
the legacy.[11]

In short, when literary scholars think about the aesthetic cast of the
Unitarian sensibility, we need to compensate not only for our own
disciplinary ethnocentrism, but also for the effect of insider testimonials like
the ones I have cited. Nor would I direct this caveat at literary researchers
only, although we are the ones most predisposed to reduce Unitarianism to
an aesthetic movement. Scholarship on early Unitarianism as a whole has
often shown the same sort of bias in, for example, its intense concentration
on Channing relative to Andrews Norton, on whom to this day there is no
full-length biography or monograph. Part of this skewing—although
certainly not all of it—clearly reflects a lingering anti-institutional
aestheticist bias in favor of the inspired eloquence of the individual
performer as against the laborious ratiocination of the organization man. I
suspect that this prince-of-the-pulpit-centered perspective would have been
offset to a greater degree than it has so far been had not the anti-
institutionalism of Frothingham, Allen, Cooke, and others become
paradigmatic.

II

The second major point I have to snake, however, is opposite my first:
namely, that even though literary scholarship has probably overstated early
Unitarianism's status as an aesthetic movement, in another sense it has not
taken that aspect of the Unitarian legacy seriously enough. Even though a
great deal of attention—arguably a disproportionate amount of attention—
has, during the past decade, been paid to Arminian aesthetics from
Buckminster on, even though Daniel Howe has driven home the point that
"Harvard Unitarianism probably had its greatest impact on American society
through its influence on American letters," and David Robinson has
reinforced it in his recent history of the Unitarians and Universalists,[12] the
average student of American literature still tends (taking a cue from
Emerson's pronouncements in his quotably waspish moments) to look at
Unitarianism as a benighted state of cultural privation from which the really
important New England writers had to break away in order to accomplish
anything interesting. This indeed has remained standard doctrine ever since

American literary scholarship began to become a major growth industry in the 1930's. F. O. Matthiessen, in his monumental study *American Renaissance*, declared that "the most immediate force behind American transcendentalism was Coleridge."[13] Perry Miller, embroidering on this line of thought, stated a decade later that the function of Unitarianism for the Transcendentalists was to teach them that theology was a dead end:

> Therefore this revival of religion had to find new forms of expression instead of new formulations of doctrine, and it found them in literature. It found them in patterns supplied by Cousin, Wordsworth, Coleridge, and Carlyle. (*Transcendentalists*, p. 9)

Here, as in Matthiessen, we have the emphasis on major European literary and intellectual talents as the catalytic agents, with Unitarianism figuring as nothing more than a launching pad.

In taking this position, Matthiessen and Miller were not being solipsistically perverse but were taking their cue from the pronouncements of the Transcendentalists themselves, particularly Emerson, who had called Unitarianism "corpse cold," declared in exasperation that he could never find his "heavenly bread" in Longfellow or Lowell, and said of his contemporaries in general that "Goethe was the cow from which all their milk was drawn."[14] The rhetoric of the Transcendentalist literati easily yields a myth of revolution against, as opposed to evolution from, its Unitarian background.

The tendency to relegate Unitarian literary and intellectual culture to the status of mere background has been reinforced by other factors as well. One is the rise of so-called Puritan legacy scholarship, in response to and in reaction against Perry Miller's research: that is, scholarship seeking to define American literary and cultural distinctiveness in terms of America's Puritan antecedence. The effect of this approach is by and large to reaffirm the Milleresque contrast between Unitarianism as representing a negative phase of secularization vs. Transcendentalism as representing a reenergized expression of Puritan spirit. As today's justly most influential spokesperson for Puritan legacy studies, Sacvan Bercovitch, puts it in *The American Jeremiad*, "When Unitarianism proved a dead religion, [Emerson] remembered that America was bound to shape the religion of the future," and he expressed this vision by "building upon the old jeremiadic ambiguities."[15]

The ultimately more important reinforcer, though, of the tendency to sideline Unitarian literary culture as a trivial if not positively baleful epiphenomenon in the history of American letters is what might be called "high canonicalism." By "high canonicalism" I mean the practice of defining American literary history quintessentially in terms of a small number of great heroes and mountainpeak literary achievements that count. The history and limiting effects of this mode of literary historicizing, first institutionalized by nineteenth-century romanticism and revived in America in the 1920's and 1930's, have only recently begun to be documented and analyzed, most particularly by students of minority and women's writing.[16] By now it is a matter of record that until quite recently, American literary anthologies increasingly tended to represent fewer authors in greater depth, and American literary scholarship to focus intensely on a limited number of "classic" texts in proportion to the totality of the field. The full historical explanation for this rise of high canonicalism is complex, but two key factors, clearly, were these. First, was the prestige of the so-called New Criticism, which valorized the individual complex text, stigmatized contextual research as merely "extrinsic," and tended (following in the footsteps of T. S. Eliot) to represent literary history as a series or symposium of the most eminent figures. Second, was the anxiety of American literary studies to establish its status as an autonomous field, to locate a body of work that would rival without imitating the achievement of European literatures, and with that goal of excellence-with-a-difference in mind to define the great American tradition specifically in terms of its anticonventionalism, both literary and ideological: for example, in terms of Melville's resistance to nineteenth-century novelistic standards, Whitman's resistance to traditional prosody and Victorian sexual taboos, and so forth.

This anticonventionalist reading has tangled ideological roots. It can be diagnosed, up to a point, as a form of academic rarefaction (the valorization of the complex for its own sake over the straightforward), but also, again up to a point, as a form of democratic populism (to the extent that "conventionalism" is equated with genteel Anglophile culture); but, on the other hand, it is also an anti-populist elitism (to the extent that it rejects popular culture and ways of thinking for the sake of the few truly original thinkers and doers that rise above the herd); but, yet again, this valuation of cantankerous titans could itself conceivably be seen as a mainstream American value. Be that as it may, the bottom line with respect to Unitarian literary culture is that high canonicalism relegates it to the sidelines if not the dustbin and reinforces the myth of the New England Renaissance as beginning in earnest with Emerson's dramatic refusal to administer the Lord's Supper rather than with Buckminster and the Anthologists, the North American Reviewers, and all the rest. Notwithstanding the dozens of names smugly listed by Cooke in his chapter on "Unitarianism and Literature," in today's normative myth of nineteenth-century American literature there not only is no Unitarian playwright but no bona fide nineteenth-century Unitarian novelist (unless we count Hawthorne, whose Unitarian side most readers refuse to see) and indeed not even any noteworthy Unitarian poet apart from Emerson, because from the high canonical standpoint the rest of Transcendentalist poetry boils down into a few decent lyrics and the more conventionally Unitarian schoolroom poets like Bryant, Longfellow, Holmes, and Lowell hardly exist at all.[17]

Precisely at this juncture, however, researches into Unitarianism as a literary and aesthetic movement have a valuable contribution to make, although it has not yet been pressed as vigorously as it might be. So far, such work has mostly been in the nature of foundational studies chronicling various pleases of Unitarian literary culture, such as those of Daniel Howe, Joel Myerson, David Robinson, and Lewis Simpson. This work has been indispensible in providing better bibliographical tools, quality editions of inaccessible texts, and biographical and historical studies of themes, figures, and episodes within the Unitarian movement—most particularly of course its Transcendental offshoots. But of special note for present purposes, it has also been valuable analytically in demonstrating beyond all possible refutation that the relationship between Unitarian literary culture and the literary texts produced by the major Transcendentalists of "canonical" stature (Emerson, Thoreau, and in recent years Fuller) must be conceived much more in terms of a continuum than in terms of an opposition.

In stating this, I do not mean to erase all difference: to preempt William Ellery Channing as a Transcendentalist aesthete; or, on the other hand, to deny any distinction between Emerson's Divinity School Address and Unitarian sermonizing.[18] Transcendentalist discourse surely discomfited middle-of-the-road Unitarians not just because its style seemed self-indulgently fanciful, elliptically discontinuous, and neologistic compared with their more pellucid prose, but because the fancifulness and neologism arose from a post-Kantian intellectual framework that privileged the individual's creative and intuitive powers to an extent that the Unitarians' epistemology, based on old-fashioned faculty psychology, did not permit. Still, without the Unitarians' own prior adjustment of the relative priority of reason and revelation, argumentation and intuition, empirical evidence and eloquence, Emerson might not have recognized the significance of the Coleridgean distinction between Reason and Understanding, or if he had, he might not have felt empowered to do anything more creative with it than, say, James Marsh, the moderate Calvinist who introduced. the distinction to America.

Literary scholarship of the past several decades has, again, sketched in this picture quite fully, though it is not yet complete. A great deal more work needs to be done on just about every non-canonical literary figure on Cooke's list of Unitarian writers, and the relationships among them. We might start, perhaps, with Longfellow, whose enormous nineteenth-century popularity is today much more often laughed at than understood, and who I am increasingly convinced seems as much more interesting figure than has been realized if looked at as an exemplar of the Unitarian imagination. For example, Longfellow's most popular poem, "A Psalm of Life," which posterity (with some justice) has tended to see as the quintessence of facile banality, seems culturally if not aesthetically more resonant when we read it as a direct response to a "Calvinistic" ethos of determinism in the name of an "Arminian" ethos of effort. A more pervasive sign of Longfellow's Unitarian sensibility is his characteristic fondness for drawing loaded contrasts between religious ideologues and people of intuitive sensitivity (as in his portrayal of Puritanism in *The New England Tragedies*), or between obtuse utilitarians like Miles Standish and artist- or scholar-figures like John Alden. Also symptomatic is the amazing catholicity of Longfellow's grasp of diverse literary and mythological bodies of knowledge, in which we find a counterpart to the syncretism that made the Unitarian-Transcendentalist movement the cradle for the study of comparative religion in America, from the "ethnical scriptures" Thoreau edited for the *Dial* to James Freeman Clarke's *Ten Great Religions*. There is a more than fortuitous relationship between the globe-circling plot of Longfellow's "Keramos," which finds the biblical image of the artist/God as potter in every culture, and Whitman's globe-circling "Saint au Monde," where the persona declares solidarity with the world's population at large. The Transcendentalist assumption of the identity of human nature that Whitman extracted from Emerson is the child of the liberal ecumenicism expressed in Longfellow.

In recent years, feminist revisionary scholarship has demonstrated how a literary culture long believed shallow can be seen to have great resonance; and its rediscoveries include, among others, important literary Unitarians like novelist Catherine Maria Sedgwick.[19] But as the example of feminist revisionism also indicates, an even more fundamental priority than fleshing out further the record of literary careers and relationships, or rediscovering the virtues of this or that forgotten author, is to show that a mountainpeaks approach to charting literary history is an impoverished approach, that we need a more capacious theory to explain whatever literary achievement we consider significant, whether it be a *Walden* or an *Evangeline*. We need, to be specific, a theory that will not merely or even mainly seek to explain literary history as a dialogue between strong poets, or an intertextual web in which the only nodal points are marked by names like Dante, Shakespeare, and Wordsworth. A truer and more useful theory of literary achievement will try to explain that achievement not simply in terms of other supposedly great masterpieces and not simply as a maverick deviation from the supposed conventionalism of its day, but will in addition show the masterpiece's affinities with and dependence upon the normal literary culture of its milieu, and the extent to which the individual artist was nurtured as well as nettled by a cohort of mostly forgotten contemporaries who at the time, however, cross-fertilized each other through their more or less mutual interests.

In the historical phenomenon of literary Transcendentalism arising from the seedbed of Unitarian literary culture, we have an already well-researched exemplary case of the symbiosis of conventional achievement and more radically innovative genius. We see from this case that the works of the latter—the masterpieces of Emerson and Thoreau—took shape both in differentiation *from* the norms of the former and in dependence upon them. One sharp limitation of classical Unitarian aesthetics, for example, is its commitment to ethical idealism, which limited both the reading matter it could comfortably endorse and the range of its literary practice, steering it toward nonfictional prose and toward a certain kind of poetry, placing its practice of fiction within rather prim boundaries, and steering it away from drama. Emerson and Thoreau take their energy to a considerable extent from quarreling with these constraints, but they also stay within them; their strengths and weaknesses as writers are distributed over the different genres in *precisely* the same way as the Unitarian literati as a whole.

The symbiosis of genius and convention is a two-way street: on the one hand, it links the classic with the residuum of conventional achievement, while on the other hand it resists conceiving of the latter as merely formulaic. In the average literary history, the lesser figures assume the status of flat comic characters in a Dickens novel. In the model I am proposing, one would be careful to differentiate, say, the sermon styles of Nathaniel Frothingham and Orville Dewey and F. W. P. Greenwood—all of whom were noted as pulpit stylists in the early years of the Unitarian movement, but for very different effects—and also to recognize the inherent complexity of the Unitarian's "formulaic" literary gestures as such.

Once more to cite the analogue of feminist criticism, it has shown very clearly that the so-called storybook ending device to the Cinderella plot of the typical nineteenth-century domestic novel was a complex ideological artifact, involving a problematic balance between the heroine's aspirations to self-realization versus submission to constraints of patriarchy. A good example of this kind of thing in Unitarian writing is what might be called the discourse of miracles.[20] On the surface this topic might seem out of place in a discussion of the literary aspects of Unitarianism, yet I do not think so, because the doctrinal controversy over miracles in the early days of Unitarianism and its struggles with the heresy of Transcendentalism almost immediately bled over into the realm of the literary.

Most Unitarian theologues assumed uneasily and self-consciously the role of apologists for gospel miracles as seals of the divine authority of Jesus' mission. They realized that miracles were a sticking point for the majority of their flocks, and often they themselves were disposed either to doubt or to evade the position that the authenticity of the gospel miracles is the empirical test that validates Christianity's claims to special authority. Consequently, defenses of miracles by Unitarian spokespersons tend to take one of two forms, both of which have the effect of trying to lessen the alterity of the miraculous: either the argument that suspension of the normal laws of the universe is reasonable given God's all-powerfulness, or the argument that miraculous events are (if we look at them closely) conceptualizable as part of the natural order itself, or at least might be if our knowledge were perfect.[21] This second argument is the more interesting one for our purposes because it tends to lean so heavily on metaphor. As one preacher explained the meaning of the miracle at Cana (turning water into wine), "We do not know anything about the conflict or concord between the chemical laws and the spiritual laws.... But we do know that there are presences, there are influences in the world, possessing a mysterious, and, if you will, a miraculous power, to transform things common and homely into things rare and beautiful." And he goes on to give a string of analogies.[22]

Analogy here compensates for and disguises the evaporation of the distinction between the natural and the supernatural which is the original reason for making an issue of miracles to start with, and constitutes a direct link between this moderate Unitarian discourse and the Transcendental menace of Emerson, who notoriously proclaimed in his Divinity School Address that miracle was "Monster." Or did he? In reality, if we look at that Emerson passage very closely, we see that it too is part of this same subtype B of miracle discourse, for never does Emerson flatly deny that the gospel miracles happened (he only says that in the way our churches talk about them they give "a false impression," meaning that they sound unnatural: they are "not one with the blowing clover and the falling rain"). In fact Emerson uses much the same ploy used in the sermon just quoted and used also, indeed, in some of the very sturdiest Unitarian defenses, such as Orville Dewey's 1836 Dudleian lecture, which Emerson may partially have been writing against.

Dewey begins with a hard-nosed argument that, like it or not, miracles are the foundation of faith, but he sweetens the pill as he goes on by the device of naturalization through analogy and metaphor, calling the character of Jesus a moral miracle, asserting that "the act of creation is but the grandest of miracles." Emerson makes much the same move in opposition to miracles that Dewey makes for the sake of pill-coating rhetoric in favor of miracles. "He spoke of miracles," says Emerson of Jesus, "for he felt that man's life was a miracle, and all that man doth, and he knew that this daily miracle shines as the man is diviner."[23] Emerson, like the Unitarian apologists for miracles (and specifically apologists of type B), redeems miracle from the realm of monstrosity via metaphor, which renaturalizes its unnaturalness. Emerson differs from them, of course, in his pugnacity toward the churches and in his implication that miracle can *only* be interpreted figuratively. But it is also significant that Emerson never makes a frontal attack on the historicity of miracles; his strategy is to redefine the concept in ways that to the practiced eye look familiar enough to keep him as much within as without the boundaries of normative Unitarian discourse on miracles.

If we scrutinize the delicate rhetorical ballet of consensus and dissent in which the Divinity School Address participates, we arrive at a better appreciation both of the dependence—even at Emerson's most "radical" moment—of high-canonical achievement on the terms of "conventional" discourse and of the richness and multilayeredness of that conventional discourse in itself. Just as the conventional discourse on miracles greatly illuminates our understanding of Emerson at this point, so, conversely, the Emersonian deviation brings out the complexity of implication, rhetorical subtlety, and tonal nuance that results from the "mainstream" Unitarian impulse to naturalize miracles while at the same time maintaining their status as a special sort of phenomenon. The elegance and diversity of the intellectual and literary powers called forth in the furtherance of that project is grossly flattened if we simply see it in terms of a model of obtuse dogmatic consensus disturbed by the iconoclastic Emerson.

III

My conclusion from this chain of remarks is that, although the literary approach to the study of Unitarianism is in some respects excessively seductive and ought not to be undertaken before one purges oneself insofar as possible of historical innocence, nevertheless when warily negotiated it promises to yield not only results of significance for the understanding of

Unitarianism and American literary history as discrete bodies of knowledge but also an important—and in our time positively crucial—lesson for literary theory about how canonical and conventional achievements relate to each other and must be read in light of each other. In a way admittedly different from what Cooke and Allen would have understood, we need to claim Emerson and even Thoreau (for example) as legatees of Unitarianism and place them in the company of the more moderate and timid denominational poetasters whom Transcendentalist radicalism rendered distinctively uncomfortable. In the long run, however embarrassing it might have been for both parties, the memory of both is greatly enriched by the juxtaposition.

We will probably not thereby be led to anything like a consensus opinion as to the precise extent to which mainstream Unitarianism anticipated Transcendentalism or the precise extent to which Emerson and Thoreau retrained tied to their Unitarian roots. My own experience, at any rate, is that the more one contemplates, say, the Emerson–Unitarianism relation, the more one sees the possibility of competing arguments over the question of how far Unitarianism anticipated and encompassed Emersonian discourse. But that type of unresolvability should not concern us. On the contrary, our aim should be precisely to expose the untenability of clear-cut distinctions between genius and convention: to recognize, for example, that "conventional" frames of reference can in fact positively stimulate as well as negatively inhibit the most "individualistic" gestures, as James Duban has recently shown in Thoreau's case by pointing to the basis in Unitarian moral thought of his theory of civil disobedience.[24]

That sort of discovery is not altogether pleasant. It may, indeed, be more likely to distress than to gratify many literary scholars, pointing as it does toward the necessity of mastering dozens of "minor" writers (many of them "nonliterary") at a moment in history when the minimum bibliographical requirements for respectable literary scholarship seem to be expanding with unprecedented rapidity in another direction owing to the advancement of literary theory. Here I have no consolation to offer; if historical understanding is to be achieved, the work must be done. Literary scholars must be prepared, as social historians during the last two decades have learned to be, to commit themselves to a more truly "vertical" mode of research that takes into account the plateaus as well as the peaks, if only to the extent of learning the flimsiness of all such metaphors of stratification.

Notes

An earlier version of this paper was prepared for a May 1987 conference on American Unitarianism, 1805–1865, sponsored by the Massachusetts Historical Society, the proceedings of which (including the present essay) will be published in 1989 by Northeastern University Press under the above title, edited by Conrad E. Wright. Permission to publish this essay in *ESQ* is gratefully acknowledged.

1. Barrett Wendell, *A Literary History of America* (New York: Scribners, 1901), p. 289.

2. George Willis Cooke, *Unitarianism in America* (Boston, 1902; rpt. New York: AMS Press, 1971), p. 413; also see p. 435.

3. Lawrence Buell, *New England Literary Culture: From Revolution Through Renaissance* (Cambridge and New York: Cambridge Univ. Press, 1986), esp. p. 388 and n.

4. For a brief narrative survey of this network, see Buell, *Literary Culture*, pp. 37–49.

5. Recent scholarship that develops this argument in detail includes Daniel Howe, The *Unitarian Conscience: Harvard Moral Philosophy* (Cambridge: Harvard Univ. Press, 1970); Lawrence Buell, *Literary Transcendentalism: Style and Vision in the American Renaissance* (Ithaca and London: Cornell Univ. Press, 1973); Philip Gura, *The Wisdom of Words* (Middletown, Conn.: Wesleyan Univ. Press, 1981); and David Robinson, *Apostle of Culture: Emerson as Preacher and Lecturer* (Philadelphia: Univ. of Pennsylvania, 1982).

6. Orville Dewey, "The Religion of Life," *Works*, new ed. (Boston: American Unitarian Association, 1883), p. 125.

7. Perry Miller, "From Edwards to Emerson" (1940), rpt. in *Errand into the Wilderness* (Cambridge: Belknap of Harvard Univ. Press, 1956), p. 197.

8. Cooke, *Unitarianism*, p. 415; Joseph Henry Allen, *Our Liberal Movement in Theology* (Boston, 1882; rpt. New York: Arno Press, 1972), pp. 13, 49; Octavius Brooks Frothingham, *Boston Unitarianism, 1820–1850: A Study of the Life and Work of Nathaniel Langdon Frothingham* (New York: Putnam, 1890), pp. 41, 235–236.

9. Allen, *Liberal Movement*, p. 116.

10. Parker, *A Discourse of the Transient and Permanent in Christianity* (1841), rpt. in Perry Miller, ed., *The Transcendentalists: An Anthology* (Cambridge: Harvard Univ. Press, 1950), p. 266.

11. The most ambitious history of Unitarian thinking produced within the classic period itself shows this difference very clearly: George E. Ellis, *A Half-Century of the Unitarian Controversy* (Boston: Crosby, Nichols, 1857).

12. Howe, *The Unitarian Conscience*, p. 174: David Robinson, *The Unitarians and Universalists* (Westport, Conn.: Greenwood Press, 1985), p. 25.

13. F. O. Matthiessen, *American Renaissance* (London and New York: Oxford Univ. Press, 1941), p. 6.

14. *The Journals and Miscellaneous Notebooks of Ralph Waldo Emerson*, ed. William H. Gilman et al. (Cambridge: Belknap of Harvard Univ. Press, 1960-82), IX, 376; XI, 382.

15. Bercovitch, *The American Jeremiad* (Madison: Univ. of Wisconsin Press, 1978), pp. 182–183.

16. See for example Nina Baym, "Melodramas of Beset Manhood: How Theories of American Fiction Exclude Women Authors," *American Quarterly*, 33 (1981), 123–139; and Paul Lauter, "Race and Gender in the Shaping of the American Literary Canon," *Feminist Studies*, 9 (1983), 435–463.

17. In this regard, see Buell, *Literary Culture*, pp. 105–107, which comments on previous scholarship on the American poetic tradition, among which Harold Bloom's essays in a series of books from *The Ringers in the Tower: Studies in Romantic Tradition* (Chicago and London: Univ. of Chicago Press, 1971) through *Agon* (London and New York: Oxford Univ. Press, 1982) have been particularly influential.

18. Conrad Wright comments on the fallacy of conflating Channing with Transcendentalism in "The Rediscovery of Channing," *The Liberal Christians* (Boston: Beacon Press, 1970), pp. 34–40. For the argument that the difference between the Divinity School Address and liberal Unitarianism was rhetorical rather than substantive, see Mary W. Edrich, "The Rhetoric of Apostasy," *Texas Studies in Language and Literature*, 8 (1967), 547–560; for my own partial demur and modification, see *Literary Transcendentalism*, pp. 29–41.

19. See especially Nina Baym, *Woman's Fiction* (Ithaca and London: Cornell Univ. Press, 1978); Sandra Gilbert and Susan Gubar, *The Madwoman in the Attic* (New Haven and London: Yale Univ. Press, 1979); Mary Kelley, *Private Woman, Public Stage: Literary Domesticity in Nineteenth-Century America* (New York: Oxford Univ. Press, 1984); Jane Tompkins, *Sensational Designs: The Cultural Work of American Fiction, 1790–1860* (New York: Oxford Univ. Press, 1985); and Judith Fetterley's editorial "Introduction" to *Provisions* (Bloomington: Indiana Univ. Press, 1985).

20. William R. Hutchison provides an authoritative historical account of the miracles *Controversy in The Transcendentalist Ministers* (New Haven: Yale Univ. Press, 1959), pp. 52–97. For selections from many of the key documents, see Miller, *Transcendentalists*, pp. 157–246.

21. The difference between the two types of Unitarian insider explication of miracles, as well as the frequent porousness of the boundary is pretty well indicated comparing W. H. Furness, *Remarks on the Four Gospels* (Philadelphia: Carey, Lee, & Blanchard, 1836), esp. pp. 146–158, which undertakes a "naturalistic" response to W. E. Channing's more supernaturalist position in "The Evidences of Revealed Religion" (Channing, *Works*, 11th ed. [Boston: Channing, 1849], vol. 3), with Channing's own argument in full. Channing hurries through his direct defense, referring his audience to Paley (3: 131) and lingers on arguments that would minimize the non-naturalness of what he fundamentally feels constrained to admit are departures from the natural order.

22. George Putnam, *Sermons* (Boston: Houghton, Osgood, 1879), p. 323.

23. Dewey, "The Argument from Miracles," *Works*, p. 449; Emerson, *The Collected Works of Ralph Waldo Emerson*, vol. 1, *Nature, Addresses, and Lectures*, ed. Robert E. Spiller and Alfred R. Ferguson (Cambridge: Belknap of Harvard Univ. Press, 1971), p. 81.

24. James Duban, "Conscience and Consciousness: The Liberal Christian Context of Thoreau's Political Ethics," *New England Quarterly*, 60 (1987), 208–222.

JOHN HOLLANDER

Introduction to
Leaves of Grass

We have yet had no genius in America, with tyrannous eye, which knew the value of our incomparable materials, and saw, in the barbarism and materialism of the times, another carnival of the same gods whose picture he so much admires in Homer; then in the Middle Age; then in Calvinism. Banks and tariffs, the newspaper and caucus, methodism and unitarianism, are flat and dull to dull people, but rest on the same foundations of wonder as the Town of Troy and the temple of Delphi, and are as swiftly passing away. Our logrolling, our stumps and their politics, our fisheries, our Negroes, and Indians, our boasts, and our repudiations, the wrath of rogues, and the pusillanimity of honest men, the northern trade, the southern planting, the western clearing, Oregon, and Texas, are yet unsung. Yet America is a poem in our eyes; its ample geography dazzles the imagination, and it will not wait long for metres.

It did not. Twelve years after Emerson concluded his essay "The Poet," there appeared a remarkable volume, prefaced with an echoing declaration that "the United States themselves are essentially the greatest poem," and likening itself and its "forms" to "the stalwart and wellshaped heir" of him whose corpse has just been carried from the house. *Leaves of Grass* was published by the author himself during the week of Independence Day 1855, and a few days later the corpse of his own father, Walter Whitman, Sr., left its house at last. Self-published, self-reviewed (more than once), self-proclaiming, self-projecting, self-inventing, the corpus, the opera, the body

From *Leaves of Grass*. © 1992 by John Hollander.

of work and life of Walt Whitman, Jr., gave birth to itself in an astonishing volume; augmentations, revisions, and rearrangements would occupy the poet's creative life.

The 1855 *Leaves of Grass* comprised twelve long stretches of a new sort of free verse, untitled, unglossed, and generically unframed, including the great poems now known as "Song of Myself," "The Sleepers," "Faces," "I Sing the Body Electric," "A Song for Occupations," and "There Was a Child Went Forth." Its title was—and remains—as deeply problematic as its appearance: are the leaves literally the pages of books—not "those barren leaves" which Wordsworth's speaker wanted shut up to free the reader for the texts of nature but pages which were paradisiacally both green and fruitful? Or are they rather metaphors for the poems, here not the "flowers" of old anthologies but green with newness? Are they the leaves which, broadcast by the wind, served the Cumaean Sibyl for her prophetic pages? Are they revisions of the oldest poetical leaves of all, those figurations of individual lives in Homer, Virgil, Dante, Milton, and Shelley; and is the grass likewise also that of all flesh mown down by death in Isaiah and the Psalmist? Are they *leavings*—residues of the act of "singing," departures for worlds elsewhere that are always regions of here? And in what way are the leaves pages *of* grass: made of, about, for, authored by? "Leaves of Grass"—hard words, putting body, life, text, presence, personality, self, and the constant fiction of some Other all together.

The poetry, like its title, looks easy and proves hard. Who was this and to whom was he talking? Was this "you" he invoked variously a version of himself, a companion, a muse, a reader? Why should a reader care about "Walt Whitman," "one of the roughs," even if he did regard himself as being "so luscious"? What appeared difficult and problematic immediately included the centrality of body, the placing of *homo urbanus* at a visionary frontier, the homoerotic realm as a token of both independence and connectedness, the confused addressing of reader, body and soul, by a nonetheless unfractured voice, the innovative formats for the framing of metaphor. Now, just a hundred years after the poet's preparation of the "deathbed" edition of his works, these issues seem virtually classical. Nevertheless, Whitman's growing and ongoing book, insisting on its role and nature as the poem of Democracy and the poem of the great poem of "these United States," defies easy characterization the more one reads it. The poet here insists that he stands for all of America—that he is America, and, lest you not believe him, he will play out that theme in energetically crowded detail. It is difficult because of its celebration of self-possession in scattered multitudes of tropes of self-dispersion, or in confusing images of the incorporation of wonderful arrays of particulars; it is difficult in its propounding the song of body, in compounding a body of song. And, as always, it presents us with the perpetual problem of the Old and the New, the Early and the Late. When Milton at the beginning of *Paradise Lost* proposes that his ad-venturous song will accomplish "Things unattempted yet in prose or rhyme," his very words are those of a successful precursor (Ariosto) flamboyantly making the same promise. Whitman implicitly allows that celebrations and singings had indeed one on in the past ("the talkers were talking .... the talk of the beginning and the end," by which he means that the Bible was Bibling); still, he declares,

> There was never any more inception than there is now,
> Nor any more youth or age than there is now;
> And will never be any more perfection than there is now,
> Nor any more heaven or hell than there is now.

He demands to be taken literally and requires to be taken figuratively. ("I and mine do not convince by arguments, similes, rhymes, / We convince by our presence," he chants, which has to be either a lie or a metaphor.) What the poet of "Song of Myself" invokes as "O perpetual transfers and promotions" are his tropes and his hyperboles, his profoundly nonliteral tallyings and ecstatic reportage, his episodic pictures fading in and out of parable. Robert Frost—that most un-Whitmanian of major twentieth-century American poets—characterized the essentially poetic as "saying one thing and meaning another, saying one thing in terms of another, the pleasures of ulteriority." Whitman's metropolis of ulteriorities hums and buzzes with lives and busynesses, but below its streets are pulsing countercurrents. His proclamations of openness ("Unscrew the locks from the doors! / Unscrew the doors themselves from their jambs!") only concern outer layers of closure, for the most important matter inside the house remains ever safe: as he proclaims and concedes in "As I Ebb'd with the Ocean of Life,"

> before all my arrogant poems the real *Me* stands yet
> untouch'd, untold, altogether unreach'd,
> Withdrawn far, mocking me with mock-congratulatory signs and
> bows,
> With peals of distant ironical laughter at every word I have
> written,
> Pointing in silence to these songs, and then to the sand beneath.

This "real Me" or "Me myself" is an elusive being. For all the openings and accessions and outreachings propounded in the poems, it can never really bear to be touched, save by the mothering presences of night or the sea, perhaps, and thereby by death. Whitman's difficult ulteriorities are often reversals of this sort. When he announces his expansions, containments, and incorporations, he is frequently enacting a contraction and a withdrawal. Likewise with Whitman's varying figures of the filling and emptying of the Self and the Everything Else, the "I contain the X,Y,Z" and the "I leak out into the XYZ." They are as easy to mistake as are his purported identifications of Self and Other, which D. H. Lawrence shrewdly observed have nothing to do with feeling and sympathy ("Agonies are one of my changes of garments, / I do not ask the wounded person how he feels, I myself become the wounded person").

In "Song of Myself" the singer is very shifty about his mode of *standing for*, whether in the relation of the poet's "I" to the massive particulars he so ecstatically catalogs and inventories or in his relation to the other components of his being-his soul and his "the real Me," not at all of one substance with the authorial father. The Personal, the Individual, instead of the Collective—but so overwhelmingly adduced that it is easy for the dulled reading spirit to glue all the vibrant particulars into a slab of generality. For enough people to be able to be in a crowd, each without losing self-identity, self-respect, and dignified particularity, would be to transform the meaning of "crowd" utterly. Whitman is a remarkable celebrant of dignity and confounder of shame: the only shame he feels is, manifestly, the moment at the end of "Song of Myself" 37—"Askers embody themselves in me and I am embodied in them, / I project my hat, sit shame-faced, and beg"—where his riot of inclusions entraps him in the begging that would have been so sinful in his Quaker upbringing. (But it is this moment which leads to the remarkable self-recognition and recovery in section 38.) More generally, his implicitly pronounced shame is at shamefulness itself.

"Do I contradict myself? / Very well then I contradict my-self" he slantingly avers toward the end of "Song of Myself," but there is no paradox of self-reference here, and that is one of the things that makes this poem such a hard one. Starting out with the work of "loafing," which is more than the trivially paradoxical industry of idleness, the speaker poses quirkily, a *flâneur*, or dandyish observer of the life of the city street, whose sympathies are always effortlessly outgoing:

> Apart from the pulling and hauling stands what I am,
> Stands amused, complacent, compassionating, idle, unitary,

Looks down, is erect, or bends an arm on an impalpable certain
   rest,
Looking with side-curved head curious what will come next,
Both in and out of the game and watching and wondering at it.

Along with Whitman's celebration of bodily projection comes an ambivalence about old stories. "As if the beauty and sacredness of the demonstrable must fall behind that of the mythical!" he exclaims in the 1855 Preface; but it is just the complex mythopoetic elevation and concentration of the "demonstrable" that his poetry effects. Wordsworth had, at a crucial moment in his Preface to *The Excursion*, proclaimed the betrothal of ancient myth and the quotidian:

           Paradise, and groves
Elysian, Fortunate Fields—like those of old
Sought in the Atlantic Main—why should they be
A history only of departed things,
Or a mere fiction of what never was?
For the discerning intellect of Man,
When wedded to this goodly universe
On love and holy passion, shall find these
A simple produce of the common day.
—I, long before the blissful hour arrives,
Would chant, in lonely peace, the spousal verse
Of this great consummation.

Whitman, subsequently, but more audaciously, comes "magnifying and applying" in section 4.1 of "Song of Myself" as a collector of old images of "the supremes," the obsolete gods, buying them up at auction, reproducing them, "Taking them all for what they are worth and not a cent more, / Admitting they were alive and did the work of their days." He even uses them for a poetic coloring book: "Accepting the rough deific sketches to fill out better in myself [*by* myself, *with* myself], bestowing them freely on each man and woman I see, ... / Not objecting to special revelations, considering a curl of smoke or a hair on the back of my hand just as curious as any revelation." By the end of the section's ode to the Olympus of Everything ("The supernatural of no account"), the poet himself, "waiting my time to be one of the supremes," half-astonished, acknowledges his own role as the sole originator. In a powerful vision that colors in the rough sketches which both the first chapter of Genesis and the opening invocation of *Paradise Lost* have become for him, he feels his near rape of the primordial darkness and chaos into which prior myths of the universe have now sunk: "By my life-lumps! becoming already a creator, / Putting myself here and now to the ambush'd womb of the shadows." He can also move from the acutely "demonstrable"— the detailed vignettes of sections 10 and 12 of "Song of Myself"—to the puzzlingly "mythical," as in the beautiful parable of section 11, with its twenty-eight young men who are also days of the month and the lunar lady who comes to join them in the spray.

Oddly enough, a chief difficulty of Whitman's poetry for every reader comes not from his ecstatic vocabulary, his self-descriptive "barbaric yawp," but from his hard, ordinary words. These include basic verbs of motion, like "drift" and "pass," located somewhere between "sing" and "sally forth." There are also complex terms like "vista," which can mean (1) what is seen, (2) the point or place from which one sees it, (3) the structure of mediating or intervening opacity past or through which one does the seeing. There are rarer but stunning verbs like "project," which has both physical senses (to throw or cast out or away, to jut out from, to make something jut out from, to cast images or patterns onto a surface, et cetera) and mental ones (transitively, to plan, contrive, devise; to put before oneself in thought, to imagine). The interplay of these senses helps energize that remarkable moment in "Out of the Cradle Endlessly Rocking" when he calls out to the bereft, widowed mockingbird, "O you singer solitary, singing by yourself, projecting me" (to which, darkling, he listens and reciprocates with "O solitary me listening, never more shall I cease perpetuating you").

Most famously problematic has been the matter of Whitman's free verse and his formal innovations generally. A map of the "greatest poem," the United States themselves, shows us shapes formed by both natural contours—seacoasts and lakeshores, demarcating rivers, and so forth—and surveyed boundary lines—geometric, unyielding, and ignorant of what the eye of the airborne might perceive. Whitman's poem of America purported to have dispensed with all surveyors, with arbitrary strokes of a mental knife which score out legal fictions like state boundaries or city limits. It declared that all of its component lines, stanzas, and structures would be shaped only by the natural forms they organically exuded. Which meant, as in every great poet's high ulterior mode, that the art which shaped them would teach older formal paradigms and patterns to dance, rather than negate them utterly. As a poet, you can only, in Wordsworth's phrase, "Let nature be your teacher" after yourself having taught nature how to speak. Very complex are the linear and strophic patterns in which Whitman would claim to "weave the song of myself" ("Song of Myself," section 15, where he fuses melodic lines and horizontal warp threads of a growing fabric), and their formal modes as well as their complex articulations of those modes are all in themselves subtle and powerful formal metaphoric versions of more traditional ones.

The revisionary character can be more easily observed at the. level of trope or fiction than in the realm of scheme or formal pattern. Some of his greatest imaginative figures—leaf, grass, bird, star, sea, flowering branch, city, river, road, ship, the Wanderer, the Original—have all the freshness and imaginative power that come only from the revision of traditional figurations. And often the rhetorical deed of a poem or movement in a poem will be ceremoniously to enact such a revision, as when, for example, the poet substitutes his domestic, American, erotic, spring-blooming lilac for the more traditionally emblematic flowers on the funeral hearse of the Lost Leader in "When Lilacs Last in the Dooryard Bloom'd": "O death, I cover you over with roses and early lilies, / But mostly and now the lilac that blooms the first." He is hereby also substituting his own kind of poetry (text and bouquet, poesy and posy having been associated since antiquity), and the original gesture earns its memory of "Lycidas" and "Adonais" by also mourning a complex mythological personage on the occasion of the death of an actual person. Or there is the substitution of the native American mockingbird for the romantic nightingale and skylark. These are simple and manifest instances of a phenomenon occurring throughout Whitman's poetry.

In its formal aspect, Whitman's poetry adopts almost unvaryingly an end-stopped line, characteristically connected to its near companions by anaphora (formulaically repeated opening word or phrase) or parallel syntactic form in a ramified growth of subordinate clauses (the familiar formats of his fascinating array of modes of cataloging). In context, his form is as identifiable as a quantitative or accentual syllabic line would be, marked not by a tally of its parts but by the way it is shaped to be part of an epigram, a strophe, an aria or sonata form—like "movement," or a block of stipulations. There are his strophic forms: sometimes, in his later work (as in "Eidolons" or "Dirge for Two Veterans" or "Darest Thou Now O Soul"), suggesting in their format classical stanzas; more often some form of ad hoc rhythm developed by linear groupings, as in the opening of "Song of Myself," 6. (There a pattern of two and then one, three and then one, four and then one develops in the responsive suppositions rising in answer to the child's—and the reader's—"*What is the grass?*")

And always, there is the marvelous deployment, throughout lines and strophes, of the rhythms of speech as well as the totally unspeakable rhythms generated only by writing: the cadences of the inventoried, parallel modifying phrases and dependent clauses (who *talks* like that?); the mannered: Frenchified noun–adjective inversions; the rhythmic jolts provided by intrusions of weird diction. The rhythmic patternings of long and short fines—aligned, variously interjected, refrained, extended, receding-were not exactly, as Whitman put it to his friend Horace Traubel, analogous to

> *the Ocean*. Its verses are the liquid, billowy waves, ever rising and falling, perhaps wild with storm, always moving, always alike in their nature as rolling waves, but hardly any two exactly alike in size or measure, never having the sense of something finished and fixed, always suggesting something beyond.

But the fixer and finisher, the poet himself, is far more crafty a puller of waves than the coldly regular moon. He might just as well have likened his long anaphoric catalogs to urban crowds through which the reader himself will pass, jostling, pushing, sometimes striding, sometimes pausing.

A word or two about Whitman's basic form of cataloging: it exhibits a variety of structural modes. In the third strophe of "Song of Myself," 31, for example, the little list begins with the generality "In vain the speeding or shyness," then reiterates the qualifier "In vain" to introduce each item in the list of ascending entities (in archaeological time and humanly scaled space—from "plutonic rocks" to the auk). The conclusion is the burden of this song: "I follow quickly; I ascend to the nest in the fissure of the cliff," which itself follows quickly on the last line, as well as on the whole series of ineffectually evasive beings, all of which the poet "follows quickly." But it is as if the particular following—the climb up to the high point, to the nest of the great bird—becomes a momentary archetype of all the others. And one great function of the list may have been to explore fully the meaning of "the speeding or shyness." Without the array of instances, it could not be grasped; fully informed by the items of the catalog and the musical patterning in which they are unrolled, it becomes a unique phrase, Whitman's—and the reader's—own. The central matter is not the extent of Whitman's lists but rather their internal structure, the narrative of their development, the ways in which they are—as in this case—variously framed by enveloping initial predications or shape their own closures by the framing gesture of the last entry.

Consider the great catalog of specifications preceding the "I tread ... such roads" in "Song of Myself," 33. Starting after the declaration that "I am afoot with my vision," there are nearly eighty lines of "Where"s ("Where the quail is whistling ... / Where the bat flies ... where the great goldbug drops ... / Where the brook puts out ...," et cetera), "Upon"s, "Through"s, "Pleas'd with"s that make up subsections of their own. Through these and beyond, the whole passage itself treads roads of country, city, farm, factory, wild and domestic animal, marine nature, and industry, and moves toward a hyperbolic envelopment. Its electrifying last entry functions like the dancing figures on Achilles' shield in *The Iliad*, which seem to sum up the whole story of the making and describing of the vision of human life represented on it:

> Speeding amid the seven satellites and the broad ring, and the
>   diameter of eighty thousand miles,
> Speeding with tail'd meteors, throwing fire-balls like the rest,
> Carrying the crescent child that carries its own full mother in its
>   belly.

The concluding line is packed with complex figuration: the "new moon with the old moon in its arms" (from "Sir Patrick Spens" and Coleridge) invokes the barely discernible full sphere shadowed within the bright crescent, being connected—through the literal Latin sense of "crescent"—to the curved form of the enwombed fetus. It concludes, sums up, and reaches beyond the preceding elements in the list with a marvelous image of containment.

From the Homeric list of ships and the Biblical genealogies through the rhetorically rough inventories of goods; the blazons of erotic details of a desired body, the stacks of clauses and conditions and contingencies on a contract or lease; the inventories of rescued necessities by a Robinson Crusoe or Swiss Family Robinson or of what Tom Sawyer received in barter for the whitewashing; the wondrously detailed names of those who came to Jay Gatsby's parties—the rhetoric of cataloging in our literature has encompassed everything from the high heroic to the low quotidian. Whitman's catalogs often consist of lists of ramified predications. Sometimes their litanies of specimen instances are his sort of chanting of the laws—as only in Biblical times and rituals—of the Great Poem of America as a self-acknowledged legislator of the world. Generally they are transcendental: they include and metaphorically revise these and other nonliterary modes of inventorying. With Whitman, lists become basic topoi, places in, by, and through which his poems develop themselves. Through their internal structures and rhythms of syntactic and semantic grouping, they articulate their own boundaries and purposes.

Whitman the poet is "afoot with his vision" not only in the poem but throughout his life, in his constant textual revisions, as well. The nine editions of *Leaves of Grass* after 1855 not only rearrange material in, the preceding ones but add many new poems, subtract a good many, sometimes reinsert a previous subtraction. The leaves of the book remain green and growing throughout his life. There is an academic industry of interpreting the continual changes Whitman made in his work from 1855 to 1891, with a number of interpretive agendas; each running roughshod over the partial applicability of the others. There is the school whose central agenda is the matter of varying explicitness about homosexuality; another of developing explicitness about poetic intention; those who see greater obliqueness, increased second-guessing of a growing audience, and so forth. Such impulses can indeed all seem to be at work differently, at different times and places in the text. Whitman's evolving thoughts on formal structures are reflected in his renumbering—and thereby reconstituting—of strophes and sections ("Song of Myself," unnumbered and unnamed in 1855, falls into 372 numbered strophes-ranging from couplets to full odes—in 1860 but does not acquire its calendrical division into 52 sections until 1867). Likewise interesting in this regard are the opening and form of "Out of the Cradle"; the sheer play of retitling generally, sometimes reframing, sometimes clarifying an intention, sometimes obscuring or transforming one; the addition of clusters in later editions; the segmentation, in 1856, into genres of poems, and so forth.

The history of Whitman's reputation seems to me to be less interesting than the history of any reader's reaction to the poetry. But generally one may say that The Poem gets reinterpreted into The Works of the Bard. "Song of Myself," with, again, the ambiguous resonances of the grammatical construction (composed of, by, to, about, for myself? "of myself" as it might be "of itself"? et cetera) starts out untitled in 1855, becomes "Poem of Walt Whitman, an American" (which introduces the ambiguous "of"), and "Walt Whitman" thereafter until 1881, when it assumes its familiar title. New leaf forms—asides, communiqués from Parnassus, blurbs for the universe, position papers, self-commissioned laureate verses, ghosts of leaves that are really only *Albumblätter*, et cetera start filling up the pages. They work their way into thematized sections—he calls them "clusters" from 1860 on-as part of a program to extend his formal metaphor of organic structure from line to strophe to poem to poem group to the ever-growing oeuvre itself. "Chants Democratic"; "Leaves of Grass" (a synecdochical subtitle); "Enfans d'Adam"; "Calamus" (again, like "leaves," a complex figure, blending the stiff phallic rush or cane, the musically tuned pipe cut from a reed, the writing reed, the green, growing, and emphatically fragrant plant, into an object of erotic, musicopoetic instrumentality); "Messenger Leaves"—these appear in the

1860 text: some fall off and die in later editions, others continue to flourish and are joined by newer ones, often when entire books, like the volume of Civil War poems, *Drum-Taps* and *Sequel* of 1865, are subsequently "annexed" to later editions.

Sometimes putting a previously published poem into a new cluster in a later version of the book amounts to a gloss on that poem. So with, for example, the gnomic "Chanting the Square Deific," with its four strophes erecting a weird pantheon composed of (1) Jehovah-Brahma-Saturn-Kronos, (2) Christ-Hermes-Hercules, (3) Satan, and (4) a subsuming Santa Spirita identified with the bard himself, who ultimately squares the circle of "the great round world" itself. It first appeared along with the beautiful little "I Heard You Solemn-Sweet Pipes of the Organ" in the *Sequel* to *Drum-Taps* (1865–66), but by 1871 It had been gathered into the cluster entitled; from the second poem in it, "Whispers of Heavenly Death," as if implicitly perhaps to avow its cold agenda. "An Adam Early in the Morning" originally appeared in 1860 as the last a poem (15) in the "Calamus" cluster, but without the first two words; the added simile may only make manifest what was latent in the original use of the word "bower," but it certainly brings to the little poem an additional assertion of Originality—it is as if Whitman were now off to name all the animals for the first time. Sometimes it is only a privileged glance at a manuscript which reveals some of the heart of Whitman's revisionary process. That traditionally formed emblematic poem "A Noiseless Patient Spider" emerged from a passing simile in a meditation on unexpressed love on an occasion of unseized erotic opportunity: in the published poem, the matter of a street pickup is put through what Hart Crane called "the silken skilled transmemberment of song" and becomes a greater matter of the soul's far-flung "gossamer thread" catching somewhere, of the song being heard.

There is also the effect, noted earlier, of the many retitlings. In some of his notebooks, Whitman projects poems with titles like "Poem of Kisses" or "Poem of the Black Person," where, as in his overall title, the "of" is fruitfully ambiguous. Most original with him is the simple compound form, for instance, "Sundown Poem" (the original title of "Crossing Brooklyn Ferry": canceling it dims the prominence of the westwardness of the crossing from Brooklyn to Manhattan underlined by the occasion and allows the alternative directions of so many trips and crossings to emerge) or "Banjo Poem" (one of these projected—what would it have been like?). The two great shore poems, odes of the figurative littoral—"Out of the Cradle Endlessly Rocking" and "As I Ebb'd with the Ocean of Life"—that dominate the "Sea-Drift" cluster were differently titled. The first was originally published as "A Child's Reminiscence," then "A Word out of the Sea" (with the subtitle "Reminiscence" at the start of the second strophe, and with an additional line before the present third one: "Out of the boy's mother's womb, and from the nipples of her breasts," thus giving Whitman's familiar Quaker designation of September, "the Ninth-month midnight" an additional significance). The second was initially "Bardic Symbols," then number 1 of the cluster entitled "Leaves of Grass" in 1860 (again, with the added opening "Elemental drifts! / O I wish I could impress others as you and the waves have been impressing me"), then "Elemental Drifts," and, finally, when those two lines were canceled, the present incipit title it now bears.

But we also sort through Whitman's leaves and form our own readers' clusters, generic groupings that seem to emerge among the finished poems as if from unstated or unavowed intentions. Walk Poems; Panoramic Poems; Talk Poems; Optative Exhortations (including the brilliant and sardonic "Repondez!" an ironic inversion of that mode dropped after the 18–76 edition); Poems of Pictures—following the fragmentation of that never-printed early manuscript poem "Pictures" (it survives both as the tiny "My Picture-Gallery" and, more importantly, throughout all the poems, starting with the well-known vignettes of sections 9 and 10 of "Song of Myself").

Then there are the musical odes, such as the midpoint chant of "Song of Myself" (section 26); "Italian Music in Dakota"; the splendid "Proud Music of the Storm"; "That Music Always Round Me"; "I Heard You Solemn-Sweet Pipes of the Organ"; section 5 of "A Song for Occupations"; section 3 of "Salut au Monde!" and, of course, "I Hear America Singing." These tend to use Whitman's catalog format in a unique way: their prototype is a pattern of layered lines of verse, each embodying a polyphonic voice, instrumental, vocal, or "natural" (the wind in the trees, birdsong, sounds of moving water, et cetera, to which Whitman adds the noises of human work and enterprise, constructive, destructive, or whatever). This is a device that persists from Spenser through the romantic poets. Whitman employs it in a poetic revision of musical polyphony, even extending the symphonic format beyond phonetic materials to include specimens of all human activity. Section 15 of "Song of Myself," for example, opens with a Whitmanian duet: "The pure contralto sings in the organ loft, / The carpenter dresses his plank, the tongue of his foreplane whistles its wild ascending lisp" (and how Homeric this last half line!) but then continues with about sixty varied glimpses of What Is and of What Is Done, musical relations between parts having been only an introductory paradigm for a more general organic assemblage of "the beauty and sacredness of the demonstrable."

Here and there throughout the poetry lurks a notion that the Poem of America—whether in the notion of the United States as "greatest poem" or in *Leaves of Grass* itself—had already been written by Walt Whitman in some earlier phase of consciousness and self-projection. It is not only among the animals in whose selectively described moral condition ("Not one kneels to another, nor to his kind that lived thousands of years ago, / Not one is respectable or unhappy over the whole earth") the poet finds "tokens of myself." (It might nevertheless be added that Walt Whitman does not eat his young, or remain incapable of knowledge of death or acknowledgment of anything.) It is rather about all his inventoried and chanted phenomena that he surmises "I wonder where they get those tokens, / Did I pass that way huge times ago and negligently drop them?" Still, his continuous "transfers and promotions" remain his greatest generosities and sympathies, his widest- and farthest-reaching hands or filaments: "And there is no object so soft but it makes a hub for the wheel'd universe" means, of course, that the imaginative faculty which can construe as a hub a caterpillar or a drop of sweat or a hair on the back of a hand—and can construct the right concentric circles radiating from it—is the breath of Democratic life itself.

Democracy, for Whitman's poetry, begins with questions of "representation"—that is, of metaphor. His literal is elusively figurative, and his favorite figure-synecdoche, the part for the whole, the whole for the part, the container and the things contained variously figuring one another—is itself metaphoric, and even more ulterior. American democracy entails a representative government and a deference to a body of opinion with a propensity to slacken toward self-identifications of the synecdochical sort. We clamor for public officials who are members of whatever group of which we constitute ourselves; we want to be represented by a lump of our region, district, race, sect, caste, or ethnic strain (but seldom of our intelligence, our moral nature, our imagination, our prudence, our regard for others). A system of metaphoric representation (and British Parliament, or perhaps our Senate—rather than our House of Representatives—has been more like this) would have us wish the best and most skilled advocate to argue and negotiate for us (which is a different a business from singing), even if he or she were nothing like a neighbor, a workmate, a cousin, or a fellow congregant who would know our song by heart. Such a representative would *stand for us* in another way.

Whitman's affirmations thus always engage our Democratic paradoxes: that if there is to be no selfishness there must be true self-containment. Responsibility starts with the mutual obligations among the components of one's own identity; acknowledging the dignity of things and beings requires a zoom lens to home in on the minute and otherwise help get by the false worth of mere magnitude. Self-respect, as Whitman liked to say, mocks and dissolves aristocracies. Wallace Stevens observed that "Pareto's epigram that history is a cemetery of aristocracies becomes another: that poetry is a cemetery of nobilities" (for Whitman, these two assertions are the same). American Democracy is both uniquely equipped for, and uniquely in need of, interpreting itself. Its own bodily and empirical constitution is framed anew in all the languages of many sorts of lives—from "The blab of the pave" to the complex poem of celebration that takes back with one hand what it gives with another, perpetually claiming that reading it poses no problems and thereby generating a multitude of them, yet always extending the ultimate perpetuating connection of poet and reader, interpreter and reinterpreter, citizen and citizen. Like his own great poem of poems, "Democracy," said Whitman in *Democratic Vistas*, is "a word the real gist of which still sleeps, quite unawakn'd."

KATHY KURTZMAN LAWRENCE

Margaret Fuller's *Aesthetic* Transcendentalism and Its Legacy

"It is right that forms of religion should not be bestowed directly by God himself, but as the work of eminent men."
Eckermann's Conversations With Goethe,
Feb. 28, 1830

Perhaps the one constant throughout Margaret Fuller's brief and angst-ridden existence was her devotion to artistic genius. She strove to establish criteria for aesthetic excellence and then sacrificed health and friendship to champion her standards. Even amidst the cannon volleys of the siege of Rome in 1848, after she had transformed herself from Boston transcendentalist to international cosmopolite and war correspondent, Fuller interspersed dispatches on the revolution with commentary on the Classical, Renaissance, and contemporary art that surrounded her, as evidenced for example in one dispatch entitled "Art, Politics, and the Hope of Rome" and another late dispatch called "Kings, Republicans, and American Artists" (Reynolds and Smith 131 and 260). In fact, Fuller's radicalism was at first an *aesthetic* radicalism, which she never abandoned. Political sophistication followed and was fused with aesthetic sophistication as she pursued her dream of an America, and later of a world, of equals, but of equals who would read Goethe, appreciate Beethoven, and admire Canova. Fuller shared this passion for art—literary, musical, pictorial, and sculptural—with her close friend Emerson, and indeed with the circle of young Boston intellectuals who surrounded them in the 1830's and 1840's, inspiring many to write poetry, study music, paint, and even sculpt. These various artistic pursuits of the young transcendentalists were motivated not by dilettantism but rather by German Romantic idealism that sought expression of the soul in every medium.

Fuller also shared with Emerson a profound love for America. While both Fuller and Emerson sought to safeguard the moral and intellectual life of their country, Fuller in particular worried about America's artistic future. On the eve of her departure for Europe, she wrote, "I go to behold the wonders of art, and the temples of old religion. But I shall see no forms of beauty and majesty beyond what my country is capable of producing in myriad variety, if she has but the soul to will it; no temple to compare with what she might erect in the ages, if the catchword of the time, a sense of *divine order*, should become no more a mere word of form, but a deeply-rooted and pregnant idea in her life" (*LWLW* 355). Although she supposedly carried her manuscript on the history of the Italian *Risorgimento* in the frigate *Elizabeth* in which she and her young family drowned when it foundered off the coast of Fire Island in 1850, she no doubt also brought newly-honed opinions about literature and art that would have insured both her livelihood and a significant voice in American culture once she resumed writing criticism for Horace Greeley's *New York Tribune*.

Fuller's love of art, and effort to analyze it, did not exist in a vacuum. Lacking schools, teachers, and traditions, antebellum Americans nevertheless struggled to amass old master paintings and nurture native talent in their young country.[1] Antebellum Boston, Fuller's milieu, vied with New York and Philadelphia in collecting, displaying, and discussing art. While Boston's august *North American Review* reigned as literary arbiter, the Boston Athenaeum initiated America's first exhibitions of painting and sculpture.[2] Although Fuller benefited from her exposure to the Athenaeum's connoisseurship, her stance towards art, literary and plastic, differed from *North American Review* critics and Brahmin collectors. Not herself a Boston Brahmin but rather descended from humble Puritan farmers on her mother's side and Orthodox Calvinist ministers on her father's side, Fuller made a bid for prominence through aesthetic rigor. As she observed, "Our nation is not silly in striving for an aristocracy. Humanity longs for its upper classes. But the silliness consists in making them out of clothes, equipage, and a servile imitation of foreign manners, instead of the genuine elegance and distinction that can only be produced by genuine culture" (*LWLW*).

While contemporary Boston critics such as the now largely forgotten Henry Theodore Tuckerman weighed the moral tone of art and literature, basing his evaluations on the Christian rectitude of author, painter, or sculptor rather than the quality of the art, Fuller judged by aesthetic values that surpassed outworn piety.[3] Fuller's inspiration, shared with Emerson, came from the German Romantic philosophers and Coleridge, derived fundamentally from neo-Platonic and Kantian aesthetics.[4] But ultimately Fuller's aesthetic ideas were distinctly American. Although she cared about form and execution, she demanded revelation of the divine through human genius. She sought essentially the American Sublime.

As in her appreciation of art, in German language and literature Fuller benefited from Boston's early cultivation of this Weimar phenomenon. Beginning in 1815 with George Ticknor and Edward Everett, Harvard sent an advance guard of its precocious sons to Gottingen to import this profound and enigmatic culture to their Cambridge outpost, and Fuller participated in this rich collegiate atmosphere.[5] But Fuller differed in the intensity of her adoption of German ideas, particularly those of Goethe. She reveled in Goethe's individualism and self-culture, in his belief in the artist as prophet. Just as Boston art patrons had recoiled at the display of Horatio Greenough's naked cherubs at the Athenaeum, requiring their tiny pudenda to be draped, so Boston intellectuals railed at Goethe's lack of allegiance to normative Christianity. The *North American Review* and *Christian Examiner* decried the increasing popularity of *The Sorrows of Werther* and *Wilhelm Meister*. Even Emerson vacillated in his estimation of the great German, writing to Carlyle that "the Puritan in me accepts no apology for bad morals in such as *he*," and protesting Goethe's "velvet life" (*CEC* 20 Nov. 1834, p. 106).

Fuller's decision to translate Eckermann's *Conversations With Goethe* in 1839 for fellow transcendentalist George Ripley's series *Specimens of Standard Foreign Literature* had particular significance for her later prominence as a critic. These conversations, recorded by Goethe's personal secretary Eckermann, revealed the ripened musings of the great man near the end of his life and corroborated Fuller's critical stance that art must be sublime and need not be moral. Still wary of public reaction to Goethe, Fuller wrote in the "Translator's Preface" that "whatever may be thought of his views (and they are often still less suited to our public than to that of Germany,) his courteous grace, his calm wisdom and reliance on the harmony of his faith with his nature, must be felt, by the unprejudiced reader, to be beautiful and rare."[6] For the frontispiece to her translation, Fuller chose the following quotation from Milton's *History of Britain, Book III*:

> As wine and oil are imported to us from abroad, so must ripe understanding, and many civil virtues, be imported into our minds from foreign writings;—we shall else miscarry still, and come short in the attempts of any great enterprise.

This passage was echoed by Fuller in her first article for the *Dial*, "A Short Essay on Critics," where she again pleaded for openness to European high art, that while Americans were "delighting in the genial melodies of Pan, can perceive, should Apollo bring his lyre into audience, that there may be strains more divine than those of his native groves." (*Dial* I.1, July 1840: 5–11) She advocated not "a servile imitation of foreign manners," but a recognition of genius. Fuller reiterated this idea in the "Preface" to her first collection of miscellanies:

> It has been one great object of my life to introduce here [in America] the works of those great geniuses [foreign authors], the flower and fruit of a higher state of development, which might give the young who are soon to constitute the state, a higher standard in thought and action than would be demanded of them by their own time. I have hoped that, by being thus raised above their native sphere, they would become its instructors and the faithful stewards of its best riches, not its tools or slaves. I feel with satisfaction that I have done a good deal to extend the influence of the great minds of Germany and Italy among my compatriots (*PLA*, vii).

Although Fuller recognized the popularity of Lydia Maria Child, Nathaniel Parker Willis, Cooper, Irving, and others, she regarded antebellum sentimentalism as inferior to the High Romantic Sublime (*PLA* 129–131). Genre mattered over nationality or gender.

The fact that transcendentalism valued intuition and encouraged artistic experimentation did not mean that its main proponents lacked artistic standards. In fact, Fuller and Emerson together shared a deep aversion to bad poetry and bad art, generating between them during the early 1840's a heretofore untallied corpus of editorial rejection slips. Emerson, at first cultivating a circle of young poets who experimented with amorphous poetic form—Jones Very, Henry David Thoreau, William Ellery Channing II, Christopher Pearse Cranch, and Charles King Newcomb—quickly became disillusioned with them. Originally impressed with Very's "truth and illumination," Emerson ultimately concluded that Very's poems had "no composition, no elaboration, no artifice in the structure of the rhyme, no variety in the imagery; in short no pretension to literary merit [...]."[7] In February, 1839 Emerson announced to Fuller that "My Henry Thoreau has broke out into good poetry and better prose" (*Letters*, II, 182). By July 1840, however, Emerson warned Fuller that "we must mend him if we can" (*Letters*, VI, 320). And by 1842 Emerson lamented "These [verses] of H. T. at least have rude strength, and we do not come to the bottom of the mine. Their fault is, that the gold does not yet flow pure, but is drossy and crude" (*Journals*, VIII, 257). Emerson repeated this pattern of initial interest and later disillusion with Channing, Cranch, and Newcomb. Emerson was frustrated by their lack of form, bad grammar, and bad spelling. As he wrote to Elizabeth Hoar, "Is the poetic inspiration amber to embalm and enhance flies and spiders? As it fell in the case of Jones Very, cannot the spirit parse and spell?" (*Letters*, II, 331).

Fuller was equally strict. Rejecting a critical piece for the *Dial* by the young William Wetmore Story, Fuller admonished him that "the latter part has many bad faults in style and imagery. I mention this because if Mr. Story is inclined to take the pains to sift and write it over I would insert it in the April number.... I wish too he would compress his article. It is too long for us, and would also be improved thereby—and take heed of such expressions as, 'hang for hours on the head' of Augustus, etc. etc." Far from insulted by this criticism, Story apparently took it to heart, later publishing his improved review in another transcendental periodical, *The Harbinger*.[8] He kept this early rejection slip among his papers in Rome for half a century.

Fuller's defenses of Goethe that followed during her editorship of the *Dial* from 1840 to 1842 were a corroboration of her own aesthetic standards. The first was a response to scathing criticism by Goethe's countryman Menzel in his book on German literature that had been translated as another of Ripley's volumes of *Standard Foreign Literature*. Contradicting Menzel's moral condemnation of Goethe's work, Fuller predicted that criticism of Goethe will "end in making more men and women read these works ... till they forget whether the author be a patriot or a moralist, in the deep humanity of thought, the breathing nature of the scene" (*Dial* I.3, Jan. 1841:340–347). Thinking perhaps of the sentimental literature that surrounded her, Fuller continued, "While words they have accepted with immediate approval fade from memory, these oft-denied works of keen, cold truth return with every new force and significance." Fuller wanted her readers to experience the moral and intellectual vertigo of the Sublime brought on by reading Goethe, "that the highest flight should be associated with a steady sweep and undazzled eye of the eagle."

It was not her defense of Goethe but rather her concern for the future of American literature that threatened Fuller's social position in her narrow Boston world. Her essay "American Literature," written from the geographical and intellectual distance of New York and included among reprinted miscellanies in *Papers on Art and Literature* (1846), questioned the promise of two of Boston's local heroes, Henry Wadsworth Longfellow and James Russell Lowell, one married to Brahmin daughter Fanny Appleton and the other a scion of Boston's most powerful Brahmin clan. Of Longfellow, Fuller wrote the following: "Longfellow is artificial and imitative. He borrows incessantly, and mixes what he borrows, so that it does not appear to the best advantage. He is very faulty in using broken or mixed metaphors. The ethical part of his writing has a hollow, secondhand sound" (132). Fuller tempered her biting critique by adding that "He has, however, elegance, a love of the beautiful, and a fancy for what is large and manly, if not a full sympathy with it. His verse breathes at times with much sweetness; and, if not allowed to supersede what is better may promote a taste for good poetry. Though imitative, he is not mechanical."

Lowell was not as fortunate. Fuller evaluated him with utter contempt and dismissal: "We cannot say as much for Lowell, who, we must declare it, though to the grief of some friends, and the disgust of more, is absolutely wanting in the true spirit and tone of poesy. His interest in the moral questions of the day has supplied the want of vitality in himself; his great facility at versification has enabled him to fill the ear with a copious stream of pleasant sound. But his verse is stereotyped; his thought sounds no depth, and posterity will not remember him." Although Fuller lacked Goethe's genius as prophet-poet, still she could be a prophet-critic. While she was beyond the intellectual gravitational pull of genteel Boston, Emerson was not. He asked Horace Greeley that, in assembling a posthumous edition of Fuller's works, "let the notices of Longfellow and of Lowell be omitted. These two critiques of two writers of such respectable ability were exceptional in their severity from Margaret's pen, and there is no need to repeat the wounds" (*LRWE*, Aug. 5, 1850, pp. 225–226). Emerson's qualification, "respectable ability," revealed his social caution rather than his belief in the artistic distinction of these poets.

Fuller's courage in questioning the aesthetic quality and future of these two poets can not be underestimated. Not a Boston Brahmin herself, fatherless, unmarried, and continually on the verge of poverty, Fuller lacked social protection in spite of her wide network of friends. Still she ventured to deliver her prophecy. Although in New York, she was not beyond the reach of spiteful Boston provincialism and paid dearly for this act of aesthetic discernment. Lowell retaliated with an excoriating *ad hominem* strike on Fuller in *A Fable for Critics* (1848). His thinly-veiled satirical portrait of the sibylline "Miranda," Fuller's name for herself in the autobiographical sketch in "The Great Lawsuit" (*Dial* IV.1, July 1843:1–47), ended "when acting as censor, she privately blows / A censer of vanity 'neath her own nose." Later criticized by his friend William Wetmore Story for this mean-spirited attack, petulant Lowell denied knowing Fuller's weak condition, both financial and physical. Professing regret, nevertheless Lowell retained the offending verses in subsequent editions of the work, even after Fuller's tragic death by drowning.

Equally concerned that painting possess "that transparent depth which I most admire in literature" and demanding that if "the great writer would go beyond my hope and abash my fancy, should not the great painter do the same," Fuller turned to the work of Washington Allston, another of Boston's sacred cows. Because Allston professed to aim "at the Ideal" and not paint "direct from nature," he was in Fuller's territory. Her review in the *Dial* of Allston's exhibition of 1839 thus focused primarily on his paintings of biblical subjects that "present no impediment to the manifestation of genius." Fuller was not impressed by Allston's *Restoring the Dead Man by the Touch of the Prophet's Bones* or his *Massacre of the Innocents*, both of which contained figures "offensive to the sensual eye." *Jeremiah in prison dictating to Baruch* had "great merit, but not the highest." But it was Allston's *Miriam* that most disappointed Fuller because "There is hardly a subject which, for the combination of the sublime and the beautiful, could present greater advantages than this," and Allston failed "to satisfy our highest requisitions." Fuller lamented, "What a figure this might be! The character of Jewish beauty is so noble and profound!" One wonders if Fuller envisioned herself as a modern-day Miriam when she asked her readers to "Imagine her at the moment when her soul would burst at last the shackles in which it had learned to move freely and proudly, when her lips were unsealed, and she was permitted before her brother, deputy of the Most High, and chief of their assembled nation, to sing the song of deliverance. Realize this situation, and oh, how far will this beautiful picture fall short of your demands!" If attempting the Ideal, then artist-prophet would have to do justice to biblical prophet. Clearly, Allston did not attain this status in Fuller's opinion. She concluded, "The Prophets and Sibyls are for the Michael Angelos. The Beautiful is Mr. Allston's dominion. There he rules as a Genius, but in attempts such as I have been considering, can only show his appreciation of the stern and sublime thoughts he wants force to reproduce" (*PLA* 115). Although Emerson wrote to Fuller that "I stoutly admire the entire criticism" (*LRWE*, II, 275), other Bostonians were incensed and transcendental painter Sarah Freeman Clarke wrote Emerson a letter of protest in defense of her former teacher Allston.

The primal truth that Fuller sought in art was that expressed by the ancients, both Hebrews and Greeks, and prized by the Romantics. As she wrote to her friend Caroline Sturgis in 1839, "I shall never be happy unless I could live like Pericles and Aspasia. I want the long arcade, the storied street, the lyre and the garland. I want the Attic honey on the lip, the Greek fire in the eye" (*LMF*, II, 41). She wanted no superficial culture to take root in America's virgin soil, threatened but still largely free of philistine amusements. Whenever she could, not only in her well-attended "Conversations" for women of 1839–1844 but even earlier as a teacher of elementary school children in Providence, Fuller asked her students to look for models to David, Apollo, and Psyche. Diligently copying her pronouncements on the beauty of Greek culture in their journals, Fuller's Providence schoolchildren engaged in heresy probably never guessed by their parents. The dutiful Mary Ware Allen, aged eleven, copied the following verbatim from Fuller: "The heathen had many gods, while we have but One—but they separated the qualities which we believe to exist in One, and gave them to different beings ... Some indeed in ancient times had correct views of a God—very few now surpass the idea Socrates had."[9]

While the young innocently endorsed Fuller's views, the Boston women of the "Conversations" bristled at her suggestion that they should emulate the ideas of pagans. Discussing the Greek gods in her 1839–40 series of "Conversations," Fuller expressed "a fervent enthusiasm in recalling the joyous life of the Greeks [...] and said we sometimes could not but envy them submerged as we are in analysis and sentiment." No less a personage than Mrs. Josiah Quincy "immediately caught this up, and expressed wonder and some horror at the thought of *Christians* enjoying *Heathen Greeks.*" But Fuller averred that "These fables and forms of gods were the reverence for and idealization of the universal sentiments of religion—aspiration— intellectual action of a people whose political and aesthetic life had become immortal. We should approach it then with respect—and distrust our own contempt of it."[10] Fuller's fused her childhood knowledge of classical civilization with Romantic thought to create her own brand of American Hellenism.

Fuller's search for truth sometimes carried her to dizzying heights, especially as she tried to find the divine spirit not only in painting, sculpture, and literature, but also in friendship, in lived life. As she once wrote to a friend, "The best that we receive from anything can never be written. For it is not the positive amount of thought that we have received, but the virtue that has flowed in to us, *and is now us*, that is precious. If we can tell no one thought yet are higher, larger, wiser, the work is done. The best part of life is too spiritual to bear recording" (Higginson 118). With bemused wonderment as well as caution, Emerson entered the emotional realm of Fuller and her circle as they included him in their exchange of journals, letters, and private poems (Strauch). As he wrote to Samuel Gray Ward after Fuller's death on the subject of a "Life of Margaret," "I think it could really be done, if one would heroically devote himself, and a most vivacious book written, but it must be done *tête exaltée*, and in the tone of *Spiridion*, or even of Bettine, with the coolest ignoring of Mr. Willis, Mr. Carlyle, and Boston and London" (*LRWE*, Aug. 2, 1850, 222). By associating Fuller with *Spiridion*, George Sand's mystical work, as well as Goethe's effusive admirer Bettine, and in advocating "the coolest ignoring" of the urbane Willis and skeptical Carlyle, Emerson was essentially mythologizing Fuller, acknowledging the sublime quality even of her mundane existence, a quality that would lead eventually to Henry James's fictionalization of her. As James understood, "She has left the same sort of reputation as a great actress" (James, *Hawthorne* 62). Fuller's various epithets, the "American Corinne," the "Sibyl," and the "American Bettina," all attested to this enraptured side of her writing and her behavior. In lieu of any real contact with Europe, enduring frontier privations, Fuller needed to take on these personae, to mythologize herself. Once in London, Paris, and Rome, actually meeting and befriending women of this High Romantic stripe—George Sand, Elizabeth Barrett Browning, Princess Belgiojoso, and Madame Arconati—she became their confidant, friend, and fellow revolutionary, and no longer needed any augmentation of her persona. Although at the end of her life she finally acquired an imposing title, the Marchese Ossoli, this title never succeeded in describing her. Although Emerson used the surname "Ossoli" in the memoir he published with James Freeman Clarke and William Henry Channing, in private letters to Carlyle and others his friend was still "Margaret Fuller." Henry James also balked at using this foreign cognomen, sensing its ironic alienation from the sufferings and dislocations of Fuller's American Romantic life that had moved him to fictionalize her in stories and novels. Her aristocratic title was an encumbrance.

Perhaps the most difficult part of reconstructing the culture of antebellum New England is to understand the tenor of this ardor. Bettina von Arnim's fervent outbursts derived from German Romantic "enthusiasm," that is High Romantic emotionalism, not its less authentic but often substituted half-sister, Victorian sentimentalism. The line separating these related modes, though hard to draw, relied on the High Romantic emphasis on aesthetic rather than moral considerations. In the medium of painting, this Sublime mode allowed for the conflicting emotions of beauty and terror, while in writing it countenanced agony. This Goethean rapture explained Bettina's introductory proviso that her book, *Goethe's Correspondence With a Child*, "is for the good and not for the bad"—that is only for those who would not take its ecstatic expressions of passion for her mentor Goethe as inappropriate sexual advances from an admirer who was actually a young woman in her twenties, not a child.

This High Romantic emotionalism found its way into not only the journals and letters of the transcendentalists but also into their poetry where it was often in danger of declining from noble sentiment to saccharine sentimentality. If the goal was to pierce through the veil of matter to inner spirit, then sometimes the poet was propelled on extremes of emotion. The charm of these poems now is their ability to help us enter that lost world of fervency, what Henry James, with a tone of irony, has Olive Chancellor call "the heroic age of New England life—the age of plain living and high thinking, of pure ideals and earnest effort, of moral passion and noble experiment" (*The Bostonians* 173). Fuller's effusions of the soul found their way into verse, although she was not gifted as a writer of either poetry or fiction. In spite of the fact that she wished to be an author, she knew that her own verse was perhaps guilty of the excessive sentimentality for which she criticized others.

Two of her poems are of particular interest as statements of her project for high art in American culture, one published in her first book *Summer on the Lakes, in 1843* (1844) and the other by Emerson in her *Memoirs* (1852). Both poems are meditations on sculptures she had seen at the Boston Athenaeum in late 1830's, Bertel Thorwaldsen's *Ganymede* (1820) and Thomas Crawford's *Orpheus and Cerberus* (1843). Although never anthologized, these poems are of particular interest because of their extended use of the literary device of *ekphrasis* (the poetic description of a pictorial or sculptural work of art), connecting them to Keats' "Ode on a Grecian Urn," to Ephraim Lessing's aesthetic treatise *Laokoön* (1763), and ultimately back to Homer's description of the shield of Achilles in *The Iliad*. Fuller's poems reveal her love of sculpture as the art most capable of embodying the Ideal and her desire to introduce her country to this medium, still rare in antebellum America. More importantly, they reveal Fuller's bid to connect American culture and indeed American soil to Europe and to a continuous strand of Western high culture. While *ekphrasis* was employed by Renaissance poets to engage in the *paragone* or contest among the arts, Fuller initiated her own American *paragone* which was a contest not among media but between *genres*, between the high and middlebrow, a vertical rather than a horizontal *paragone*.

The first of the two ekphrastic poems, "Ganymede to His Eagle," subtitled "Suggested by a Work of Thorwaldsen's; Composed on the Height called the Eagle's Nest, Oregon, Rock River," occurred to Fuller as she contemplated the rough landscape of Illinois on her trip West in 1843 (*SL* 54–56). Fuller thought "The whole scene suggested to me a Greek splendor, a Greek sweetness, and I can believe that an Indian brave, accustomed to ramble in such paths, and be bathed by such sunbeams, might be mistaken for Apollo, as Apollo was for him by West." In a moment of Sublime inspiration, Fuller envisioned the American landscape as ancient Greece and the American Indian as Apollo. She referred to the famous anecdote of American painter Benjamin West arriving in Rome in 1760 as the first American Grand Tourist and exclaiming upon seeing the *Apollo Belvedere* "How like a Mohawk warrior!" But Fuller reversed the experience of neophyte among the sophisticated to self-made woman and city-dweller among the savages, arriving in the virgin wilderness and proclaiming of the American Indian, "How like the Greek god Apollo!" (Although Fuller added, "I do believe Rome and Florence are suburbs compared to this capital of nature's art," she no doubt inwardly amended that Emersonian irony four years later when confronted by the actual sight of these capitols of art.)

Significantly, Fuller dated the poem "July 4th, 1843," suggesting that the birth of her nation was also the rebirth of the Greek ideal. Fuller's poem was a double-ekphrasis, transuming the very rocks into Nature's sculpture, into America's own version of Thorwaldsen's exquisite neoclassical work and giving life both to Thorwaldsen's masterpiece and to its geological analogue. While Jefferson had envisioned America as the new Greek democracy, here Fuller connected that political dream to an aesthetic one where the Greek ideal of purity and grace as embodied in Thorwaldsen's statue was literally fused with the land. Fuller's choice of this statue connected her poem as well to Goethe's poem on Ganymede and to her own earlier association of Goethe's Sublime with the eagle.

Whereas Fuller had described Ganymede asking to be borne upward "to the serene heights" and his "earthlier form into the realms of air," her "Orpheus," following the leaning lineaments of Crawford's actual sculpture, imagined the ardent lover descending to the abyss. Recalling Goethe's dictum that "the Seeker is nobler than the Meister" (*Dial*, II.1: July 1841), Fuller's Faustian Orpheus "Must melt all rocks free from their primal pain; / Must search all nature with his one soul's fire." Crawford's sculpture had arrived in Boston with great fanfare, its size and weight necessitating its own purpose-built gallery on the grounds of the original Athenaeum on Pearl Street. Crawford traveled from Rome to oversee the final details of his first great work's installation, including the choice of purple paint on the walls to offset the sparkling marble. Fuller was thus confident that many of her readers would be familiar with this work and thus be able to visualize her ekphrastic descriptions, including her final rhymed couplet, "If he already sees what he must do, / Well may he shade his eyes from the far-shining view." Describing the statue's uplifted arm that presumably shades his eyes as he peers into Hades, Fuller suggested that her Goethean Orpheus, like Wilhelm, must undertake a *Wanderjahre*, exposing himself to the depths of despair before he can ascend to noble heights. As in her description of the ideal Miriam, Fuller no doubt saw herself in Ganymede and Orpheus, presaging her eventual exposure to life's horrors as overseer of the Hospital of the *Fate-Bene Fratelli* for the wounded revolutionaries and her loss of virginity to the young and handsome Marquis Giovanni Angelo Ossoli.

Fuller's poetry, like her criticism, was not an abstract exercise but an influence on of her life.[11] She changed herself by listening to her own poetry and criticism. Fuller's "Orpheus" thus used the device of *ekphrasis* to transmogrify not a rock on the prairie into an Aegean god but rather a cold lifeless work of antebellum American neoclassicism into a passionate seeker of lost love, embodying Fuller's own quest for love, spirit, and aesthetic understanding she sought unsuccessfully in her unrequited love for Samuel Gray Ward, William Clarke, and perhaps even Emerson himself. But in addition to personal healing, Fuller's poem advanced her project for American culture. Somewhat awkward in proportion and lacking naturalism in its expression of motion, Crawford's "Orpheus" was a somewhat crude attempt at Romantic-Neoclassicism. Fuller overlooked the statue's flaws to see instead the possible meaning the statue could impart as well as the potential for American high art that it portended. Fuller implicitly engaged in and won the *paragone* between literature and sculpture as she was able to attribute feelings and ideas to Crawford's *Orpheus* that were impossible to carve into stone. Fuller's rigorous requirements for the emotional pliability of marble contributed to William Wetmore Story's later attempts to embody emotion in stone, essentially the invention of the hybrid style "Romantic-Neoclassicism."

Henry James, like Emerson, could withstand and even appreciate Fuller's strong personality and critical judgment. Far from reacting to her character with the defensiveness of Lowell and Hawthorne as some critics have suggested, James inherited Fuller's critical acumen and drew upon her singular and unconventional persona for characters in numerous short stories and novels. Fuller's critical standards and personality survived her in the work of Henry James, a curious extension of her brief life that amounted to a double legacy. James's infamous laundry list of American deficiencies in his early biography *Hawthorne* (1879) parallels a similar list by Fuller in the *Dial* of 1839. Both James and Fuller had the temerity to judge American art by European standards. While James wrote that America had "No sovereign, no court, no personal loyalty, no aristocracy, no church, no clergy...," Fuller wrote that America had "no established faith, no hereditary romance no such stuff as Catholicism, Chivalry afforded. What is most dignified in the Puritanic modes of thought is not favorable to beauty" (*Dial* I.1:75).

Interestingly, James's first sustained employment was as a critic for the *Tribune*, although under a different editor from Fuller's, and, like Fuller, James became a critic not just of literature but of painting. In keeping with their respective eras and aesthetic commitments, while Fuller had looked for the Sublime in art, James looked for psychological depth. He found that brand of realism in the portraits of the young John Singer Sargent. Difficult to fathom now in this era of adulation for Sargent, James, like Fuller before him, had to persuade the American Puritan conscience that the sensual and glittering portraits of Sargent were not decadent and profane, especially after the debacle over Virginie Gautraux's infamous pose as Madame X. James's 1887 review in *Harper's* was instrumental in bringing Sargent's work to national attention and succeeded in claiming Sargent as an American painter in spite of the fact he had never set foot on his parental and familial soil.

Coincidentally, James also substantiated Fuller's positive critical appraisal of Robert Browning, Fuller and James bracketing Browning's career at beginning and end with praise. Fuller's love of Browning was another of the connections between her and Henry James. Fuller also shared with James a lukewarm regard for the poetry of his wife, Elizabeth Barrett Browning, each of them publishing unenthusiastic evaluations of this poet. As in her work on Goethe, Fuller did not apply her critical acumen only to tear down but also to admire genius, although in the case of Browning, Fuller's role was not to defend but to explain. Fuller's review of Browning for the *Tribune*, reprinted in *Papers on Literature and Art*, was an example of prescient critical insight about a difficult poet that many would struggle to comprehend. In her understanding and appreciation of Browning, as in her political and social views on women and Native Americans, Fuller was ahead of her time. Fuller's frontier situation was perhaps never more powerfully expressed as when she apologized to her readers that her "first acquaintance with this subtle and radiant mind was through his 'Paracelsus,' of which we cannot now obtain a copy, and must write from distant memory," or "'Sordello' we have never seen, and have been much disappointed at not being able to obtain the loan of a copy now existent in New England" (*PLA* 31–32). Alone in Rome two years later, weary, pregnant, and poor, Fuller would write to Emelyn Story in Florence to please bring her a copy of *Bells and Pomegranates*, the only thing that Fuller could think of to soothe her mind.[12]

Henry James had no trouble fording books by Browning in Newport, Rhode Island a decade or so later, thanks perhaps to Fuller's partisanship. Browning, the hero of James's youth, became the mystery of his adulthood and no doubt provided the prototype for the authors in his short stories "The Lesson of the Master" (1891) and "The Private Life" (1892). While Fuller had made it a priority to meet Browning and his wife in Florence soon after her arrival in 1847, James made the same effort in London three decades later. Browning, like Fuller herself, fascinated James both as aesthetic exemplar and persona, and possibly, like William Story, another close friend of Fuller from her Italian days, could provide James with anecdotes of Fuller during the many candlelit dinners James shared with Browning in Victorian London society (Edel *The Conquest of London* 330). While James tied Fuller to Goethe in *Hawthorne*, he connected her to Browning in *William Wetmore Story and His Friends*, where James recognized Fuller and Browning as the two central consciousnesses of the Anglo-American expatriate community. Reading Story's private letters, James also must have noticed that Fuller had introduced the two lifelong friends, Story and Browning, and had written to congratulate Story on the connection. While Fuller was a critical precursor for James, Browning's dramatic monologues of internal consciousness possibly furnished James with an aesthetic precursor, as Ross Posnock has shown. But Browning's influence, as fictional persona and technical instructor, appeared earlier than Posnock has suggested. James's early tale of Italy, "At Isella" (1871), which has been accused not only of being "apprentice work" but of being merely a pastiche of entries from James's travel diaries, is actually a parody in miniature of romances set in Italy, among them *The Ring and the Book*. This little tale announced James's intention of further projects haunted by Italy's gothic atmosphere, namely *Roderick Hudson* (1875) and *The Portrait of a Lady* (1881), but also revealed his early exploration of and fascination with the antebellum Anglo-American expatriate community.

James not only echoed Fuller's critical bias, he also deeply resonated with her situation as a cultural sophisticate in a frontier society. Hints of James's interest in Fuller abound in his work, both criticism and fiction.

James's two biographies, the early *Hawthorne* (1879) and the late *William Wetmore Story and his Friends* (1903) both single out Fuller for discussion almost as often as the ostensible subject. James was, indirectly but not unconsciously, Fuller's most devoted nineteenth-century biographer. In both works, Fuller figures as the most important of "friends." James introduces Fuller into his narrative on Hawthorne early on as an example of cultural deprivation, and one wonders whether James is not describing a version of his own young self.

> There flourished at that time in Boston a very remarkable and interesting woman, of whom we shall have more to say, Miss Margaret Fuller by name. This lady was the apostle of culture, of intellectual curiosity; and in the peculiarly interesting account of her life, published in 1852 by Emerson and two other of her friends, there are pages of her letters and diaries which narrate her visits to the Boston Athenaeum, and the emotions aroused in her mind by turning over portfolios of engravings. These emotions were ardent and passionate—could hardly have been more so had she been prostrate with contemplation in the Sistine Chapel or in one of the chambers of the Pitti Palace. The only analogy I can recall to this earnestness of interest in great works of art at a distance from them, is furnished by the great Goethe's elaborate study of plaster-casts and pencil-drawings at Weimar. I mention Margaret Fuller here because a glimpse of her state of mind—her vivacity of desire and poverty of knowledge—helps to define the situation. (pp. 55–56)

This narration of Fuller's experience in antebellum Boston mirrors James's description of his own childhood in antebellum New York in *A Small Boy and Others* (1913) as he turns over the pages of books with frontispieces in his father's library in Washington Square or a bit later gazes intently at paintings in Boston galleries. Like Fuller, James also frequented the Boston Athenaeum, to which he returns with reverent nostalgia in *The American Scene* (1907). One generation did not change materially the circumstances of an American culture-seeker hungry for art. Significantly, James compares Fuller to Goethe in this paragraph, thus recalling her defense of him in the *Dial* and implicitly connecting all three—Goethe, Fuller, and James—as a triad of critics who transcend narrow piety, frustrated visionaries who outgrew their homeland. In spite of his role as main proponent of American realism, James cast himself here as possessing fundamentally a Romantic spirit, the core of his connection not only to Fuller but to Isabel Archer and Milly Theale, in other words to his ardent American girls.

James also shared with Goethe and Fuller a yearning to see Italy, and all three did eventually journey to the Sistine Chapel and the Pitti Palace. Another curious passage in *Hawthorne* implicitly concerned Fuller in this regard. James remarked that "we are unable to rid ourselves of the impression that Hawthorne was a good deal bored by the importunity of Italian art, for which his taste, naturally not keen, had never been cultivated" (127). James added:

> The plastic sense was not strong in Hawthorne; there can be no better proof of it than his curious aversion to the representation of the nude in sculpture. This aversion was deep-seated; he constantly returns to it, exclaiming upon the incongruity of modern artists making naked figures. He apparently quite failed to see that nudity is not an incident, or accident, of sculpture, but its very essence and principle; and his jealousy of undressed images strikes the reader as a strange, vague, long-dormant heritage of his straight-laced Puritan ancestry.

This passage presciently connected James's *Hawthorne* with his late biography of William Wetmore Story, the Boston expatriate sculptor with whom Hawthorne was most friendly in Rome and whose *Cleopatra* figured prominently in *The Marble Faun* as Kenyon's own statue. James subtly recalled Fuller once again as she implicitly joined James and Story in winking at Hawthorne's provinciality and artistic philistinism. James had just told us of her passion for the statues at the Athenaeum and engravings of Renaissance works, which were, of course, nudes. And James, frequent visitor to Story's Thursday *conversazione* for expatriates in his apartments in the Palazzo Barberini, undoubtedly knew not only of Fuller's close friendship with the Story's and reliance on them for understanding once her son had been born, but also of Fuller's aesthetic influence on the young Story in his decision to abandon the law for art, and specifically for sculpture.

But, more importantly, Fuller appears implicitly when this passage is read in tandem with James's later description of Fuller in Rome in *William Wetmore Story and His Friends* where Fuller is James's surrogate as culture-starved American Romantic abroad. While Hawthorne maintained a "constant mistrust and suspicion of the society that surrounded him" (121) in Italy, Fuller "had bitten deeply into Rome, or, rather, *been*, like so many others, by the wolf of the Capitol, incurably bitten" (*WWS*, I, 129). And while Hawthorne is "irritated" by the "influences of the Eternal City," Fuller "met the whole case with New England arts that show even yet, at our distance, as honest and touching; there might be ways for her of being vivid that were not as the ways of Boston." Hawthorne's provinciality, his "duskiness" as James called it, excluded him aesthetically from Fuller's "little circle of interlocutors."

While Fuller appeared prominently in James's *Hawthorne*, she figured even more centrally in *William Wetmore Story and his Friends*. Within the strictures of the insular and usually self-congratulatory genre of Brahmin memoir, for example Edward Everett Hale's *James Russell Lowell and His Friends* and James T. Fields' *Nathaniel Hawthorne and His Friends*, James has secreted the story of the fate of the American romantic abroad as well as that of his own initiation into the mysteries and sensuality of Italy. James's choice of this title alludes obliquely to Fuller, for what became Fuller's *Memoirs* was originally intended to be *Margaret Fuller and Her Friends*. Story's key "friends" are Fuller, Browning, and James. If *William Wetmore Story and His Friends* is seen as the beginning of James's cycle of autobiographies that continues with *A Small Boy and Others* (1913), *Notes of a Son and Brother* (1914), and his unfinished *The Middle Years*, then his Story biography is transformed from a commissioned puff-piece and financial necessity to the cornerstone of a tetralogy. James dubs Story and his generation as the "precursors," meaning that they cleared the path to Europe for others to follow. But this is an overloaded term to use for those who merely initiated travel. Its real meaning suggests James's artistic and critical belatedness to this generation.[13] They, and in particular Fuller, are James's *aesthetic* precursors. Fuller is James's precursor as American cosmopolite expatriate and serious critic.

James's other epithet for Fuller is the "Margaret-ghost," an appellation recently excoriated by critics as denigrating, patronizing, and misogynist. Nothing could be further from the truth. This title is proof of James's belatedness to Fuller as critic and covert indebtedness to her persona as fictional inspiration. As James relates, "The unquestionably haunting Margaret-ghost, looking out from her quiet little upper chamber at her lamentable doom, would perhaps be never so much to be caught by us as on some such occasion as this. What comes up is the wonderment of *why* she may, to any such degree, be felt as haunting" (*WWS*, I, 127). For the author of "Owen Wingrave," "The Way It Came," *The Turn of the Screw*, and numerous others tales of brushes with the supernatural, the word "ghost" is significant, not casual or flippant, a microcosm of Jamesian consciousness of the mystical relation of souls, of the interdependence of higher natures.

"Ghost" here is revelatory of the structure of James's aesthetic and moral universe. James keeps repeating in *William Wetmore Story and His Friends* that he is writing a "history," but he cares mainly for the "history" of Fuller's American Romantic consciousness that evolved into both the characters and the morality of his postbellum psychological realism.

Critics who discuss James's preoccupation with the young American girl of moral spontaneity usually refer to his beloved cousin Minny Temple who died at twenty-four of consumption in 1870 as James's model, and she is no doubt the main inspiration for Isabel Archer and Milly Theale, as James divulged in letters home and in *Notes of a Son and Brother*.[14] But we must add Fuller to Minny Temple as possible prototype for "the struggle of the spontaneous spirit with institutionalized manners" (Anderson 24). The Fuller–James connection offers another perspective on the "American Henry James." While Minny provided the image for James's American girls abroad, Fuller helped provide the spiritual and intellectual ballast to complete these complex characters. In fact, what James saw in Minny was Fuller, and he continued to search for Fuller's moral and cultural descendants for the rest of his life. He sought out her friend Caroline Sturgis Tappan, whom he says in *Notes of a Son and Brother* "became fairly historic, with the drawing-out of the years, as almost the only survivor of that young band of the ardent and uplifted who had rallied in the other time to the 'transcendental' standard, the movement for organized candour of conversation on almost all conceivable or inconceivable things which appeared, with whatever looseness, to find its prime inspirer in Emerson and became more familiarly, if a shade less authentically, vocal in Margaret Fuller" (*NSB* 364). James saw Fuller as well in Clover Hooper Adams, Tappan's niece, who was mystified when she "had a farewell letter from Henry James, Jr., written Tuesday at midnight on the eve of sailing. He wished, he said, his last farewell to be said to me as I seemed to him 'the incarnation of my native land'—a most equivocal complement coming from him."[15] Hooper Adams and others used to thinking of James as a "young emigrant" (*LMHA* 320) who preferred "a quiet corner with a pen where he can create men and women who say neat things and have refined tastes and are not nasal or eccentric" did not understand James's deep connection to the vestiges of ardent American idealism that he sought in Clover Hooper herself.

James's Fulleresque characters are painted either with nostalgia and devotion, like Isabel Archer and Milly Theale, or with irony and satire, like Henrietta Stackpole and Olive Chancellor. The Emersonian Ideal is always in danger of decline and self-parody. While Isabel Archer and Milly Theale represent the fulfillment of Fuller's romantic sacrifice, Henrietta Stackpole and Olive Chancellor stand for its caricature and perversion. Strangely, James has recently been lambasted for his depiction of Olive Chancellor and Miss Birdseye as vehemently as he was originally by Boston readers when *The Bostonians* was published in 1885. But Olive is not the only representative of Fuller in *The Bostonians*. So is Verena Tarrant, and Verena possesses "a strange spontaneity in her manner, and an air of artless enthusiasm, of personal purity" (*The Bostonians* 48). James calls Verena, not Olive, by Fuller's own nickname, the "American Corinne," as he does Gilbert Osmond's ubiquitous but absent mother, despised and ridiculed by Madame Merle and by Osmond as strongly as Fuller's spiritual daughter Isabel.

With Verena, as with Isabel, James achieves what one might refer to as "the Great Zenobia Shift," in essence reversing the negative image of Fuller painted by Hawthorne as the willful Zenobia in *The Blithedale Romance*. Concealing his own influences and sources, James protests too loudly in *William Wetmore Story and His Friends* that the legend of Hawthorne "having had her in his eye for the figure of Zenobia, while writing 'The Blithedale Romance,' surely never held water" (*WWS*, I, 129). James here contradicts his own earlier opinion in *Hawthorne* that "As Margaret Fuller passes for having suggested to Hawthorne the figure of Zenobia in *The Blithedale Romance*, and as she is probably, with one exception, the person connected with the affair who, after Hawthorne, offered most of what is called a personality to the world, I may venture to quote a few more passages from her memoirs—a curious, in some points of view almost a grotesque, and yet, in the whole, as I have said, an extremely interesting book" (*Hawthorne* 62). James goes on for two more pages on *Fuller*, not his ostensible subject, Hawthorne. The "one exception" to Fuller for possible model for Zenobia was Fuller's close friend, Brook-farmer, and renowned New England beauty, Almira Penniman Barlow, whose Brahmin name James borrows for Aunt Penniman in *Washington Square*. James would have learned the petty gossip and legends of this circle years later from Caroline Sturgis Tappan, Caroline Healey Dall, Clover Hooper Adams, and others of Fuller's circle of bluestockings whom James courted. James, more than anyone, experienced the belatedness he described in *Hawthorne*: "Her tragical death combined with many of the elements of her life to convert her memory into a sort of legend, so that the people who had known her well grew at last to be envied by later comers." James's envy for information on vanished transcendentalists was that of the tenacious novelist.

One opinion that James does not conceal or change in the years between writing *Hawthorne* and *William Wetmore Story and His Friends* is his estimation of Fuller's writing. James's stance towards Fuller's writing is even

more conflicted than that towards Hawthorne's and reveals an anxiety of
influence to Fuller stronger than that to Hawthorne. On this subject, James
does not wait three decades to contradict himself but contradicts himself in
the very same paragraph. First he writes in *Hawthorne* that Fuller "left
nothing behind her nothing but the memory of a memory. Her function, her
reputation, were singular, and not altogether reassuring: she was a talker."
But James follows this verdict in the same paragraph with "Some of her
writing has extreme beauty, almost all of it has a real interest [...]" (*Hawthorne*
62). After an entire career of portraying Fuller, and of having continued her
critical precedent, James writes in *William Wetmore Story and His Friends* that
Fuller's history "matters only for the amusement of evocation—since she left
nothing behind her, her written utterance being naught" (*WWS* 1: 128).
James does not suffer here from a bad memory but from a powerful need to
conceal an important source and strong influence.

Perhaps James's uneasiness vis-à-vis Fuller concerned not just her
influence but her fate. Fuller's "strange history" and "strange destiny" were
that of someone who, like James, had "a magnificent, though by no means
unmitigated, egotism" and who exchanged familiarity and comfort for the
uncertain existence of the expatriate. Fuller's condition as "brilliant, restless,
and unhappy" also applied to James himself. For James imbibed not only
Fuller's critical posture, not only her persona, but also her aesthetic
transcendentalism, that is her liberalism. James imbibed this liberalism, as he
imbibed Emersonianism, like a tonic, and absorbed it into his deeply
introspective nature. Along with Emerson's faith, Fuller's faith was
transmogrified into James's sense of the sacred in art. Fuller's love of truth in
art became James's search for form and for a genre far elevated above
American sentimentalism. James traded Fuller's religion of art and action
into a life solely of art. Like Fuller, James loved word and image, book,
painting, and sculpture, and imported into his fiction a plethora of ekphrastic
descriptions of great works in defiance of aesthetic mediocrity. Fuller's
suffering and loss might have frightened James into a withdrawal from overt
action but not from moral work. He did not desist in this other "Great
Succession," that of continuing Fuller's aesthetic transcendentalism. His
fiction is doing that work still.[16]

NOTES

1. For American antebellum culture see Neil Harris, *The Artist in American
Society: The Formative Years, 1790–1860* (Chicago and London: Chicago University
Press) 1966. I do not agree with Lawrence W. Levine, *Highbrow–Lowbrow: The*

Emergence of Cultural Hierarchy in America (Cambridge, MA.: Harvard University Press, 1988) that distinctions between high and middlebrow culture did not form in America until the Gilded Age and argue here that Fuller played a significant role in distinguishing and promoting a canon.

2. For the cultural role of the Boston Athenaeum, see Robert F. Dalzell, Jr., *Enterprising Elite: The Boston Associates and the World They Made* (Cambridge, MA.: Harvard University Press) 1987; Paul DiMaggio, "Cultural Entrepreneurship in nineteenth-century Boston: the creation of an organizational base for high culture in America," in Richard Collins, James Curran, et al., eds. *Media, Culture, and Society: A Critical Reader* (London and Beverly Hills: Sage Publications, 1986); Ronald Story, "Class and Culture in Boston: The Athenaeum, 1807–1860," *American Quarterly* 25.2 (May 1975): 178–199; and Mabel Munson Swan, *The Athenaeum Gallery, 1827–1873: The Boston Athenaeum as an Early Patron of Art* (Boston: The Boston Athenaeum) 1940; *A Climate for Art: The History of the Boston Athenaeum Gallery, 1827–1873*. Boston: The Boston Athenaeum, 1980.

3. Henry Theodore Tuckerman, *American Artist Life comprising biographical and critical sketches of American artists, preceded by an historical account of the rise and progress of art in America*, 2nd ed. (New York, 1867).

4. Stanley M. Vogel, *German Literary Influences on the American Transcendentalists* (New Haven: Yale University Press), 1970.

5. For the influence of German culture on antebellum America, see Henry A. Pochmann, *German Culture in America* (Madison: University of Wisconsin Press, 1957).

6. *Eckermann's Conversations With Goethe*, trans. S. M. Fuller (Boston: Hilliard, Gray, and Company) 1839, x.

7. See William M. Moss, "'So Many Promising Youths': Emerson's Disappointing Discoveries of New England Poet-Seers," *The New England Quarterly* 49.1 (March 1976): 46–64.

8. William Wetmore Story Papers, courtesy of the Harry Ransom Humanities Research Center, University of Texas at Austin.

9. Mary Ware Allen, Journal, Greene Street School, Providence, Dec. 19, 1837, p. 29. Quoted courtesy of the American Antiquarian Society.

10. Nancy Craig Simmons, ed., "Margaret Fuller's Boston Conversations: The 1839–1840 Series," in *Studies in the American Renaissance 1994*, ed. by Joel Myerson (Charlottesville: The University Press of Virginia), p. 204.

11. For the concept of this phenomenon in literary characters, see Harold Bloom, *Shakespeare and the Invention of the Human*.

12. William Wetmore Story Papers, Margaret Fuller to Mrs. Emelyn Story, January 7, 1849. Courtesy of the Harry Ransom Humanities Research Center, University of Texas at Austin.

13. For his theories of the anxiety of influence and literary belatedness, see Harold Bloom, *The Anxiety of Influence, A Theory of Poetry* (New York and Oxford: Oxford University Press), 1997.

14. See Lyndall Gordon, *A Private Life of Henry James: Two Women and His Art* (London: Chatto and Windus), 1998.

15. Ward Theron, ed. *The Letters of Mrs. Henry Adams, 1865–1883* (Boston: Little, Brown, and Company) 1936, p. 384, May 14, 1882.

16. Fuller's influence on James equal to that of Hawthorne will be discussed in my forthcoming book entitled *The Margaret-Ghost: Henry James and the Legacy of Aesthetic Transcendentalism.*

PRIMARY SOURCES FOR MARGARET FULLER

Ossoli, Margaret Fuller. *At Home and Abroad, or, Things and Thoughts in America and Europe.* Ed. Arthur B. Fuller. Boston: Crosby, Nichols, 1856.

————, *Art, Literature, and the Drama.* Ed. Arthur B. Fuller. Boston: Brown, Taggard and Chase, 1860.

————, *Life Without and Life Within; or, Reviews, Narratives, Essays, and Poems.* Ed. Arthur B. Fuller. Boston: Brown, Taggard and Chase, 1860.

Fuller, Sarah Margaret. *Papers on Literature and Art.* New York: Wiley and Putnam, 1846.

————, *Conversations With Goethe From the German of Eckermann,* Vol. IV in George Ripley, ed. *Specimens of Foreign Standard Literature.* Boston: Hilliard, Gray & Co., 1839.

————, *Summer on the Lakes, in 1843.* Boston: Charles C. Little and James Brown, 1844.

————, *Woman in the Nineteenth Century, and Kindred Papers Relating to the Sphere, Condition and Duties, of Woman.* Ed. Arthur B. Fuller. Boston: John P. Jewett, 1855.

————, *The Letters of Margaret Fuller.* 5 vols. Ed. Robert N. Hudspeth. Ithaca and London: Cornell University Press, 1983.

————, ed., the *Dial* 1–4, 1840–44.

————, *The New-York Tribune,* 1844–46.

————, *'These Sad But Glorious Days.'* Eds. Larry J. Reynolds and Susan Belasco Smith. New Haven: Yale University Press, 1991.

————, *Love-Letters of Margaret Fuller, 1845–1846.* ed. Julia Ward Howe. New York: D. Appleton & Co., 1903.

Emerson, Ralph Waldo. *Letters of Ralph Waldo Emerson.* 9 vols. Ed. Ralph L. Rusk. New York: Columbia University Press, 1939.

Emerson, Ralph Waldo, and Thomas Carlyle. *The Correspondence of Emerson and Carlyle.* New York: Columbia UP, 1964.

Higginson, Thomas Wentworth. *Margaret Fuller Ossoli.* Boston: Houghton, Mifflin, 1884.

SECONDARY SOURCES

Strauch, Carl F. "Hatred's Swift Repulsions: Emerson, Margaret Fuller, and Others." *Studies in Romanticism*, 7: 2 (Winter 1968), 65–103.

PRIMARY SOURCES FOR HENRY JAMES

Autobiography. Ed. Frederick Dupee.

Complete Stories 1, 1864–1874, New York: The Library of America, 1999.

Complete Stories 2, 1874–1884, New York: The Library of America, 1999.

The Notebooks of Henry James. Ed. F. O. Matthiessen and Kenneth B. Murdock. New York: Oxford University Press, 1947.

Henry James Letters, 1843–1875, ed. Leon Edel, Cambridge, MA: Harvard University Press, 1974.

The Portrait of a Lady, Oxford and New York, Oxford University Press, 1995.

Roderick Hudson. New York: The Library of America, 1994.

Daisy Miller. London: Penguin Books, 1986.

William Wetmore Story and His Friends, 2 vols., Boston: Houghton, Mifflin, 1903.

Notes of a Son and Brother, New York: Charles Scribner's Sons, 1914.

Literary Criticism, vols. 1 and 2, New York: The Library of America, 1984.

The Letters of Mrs. Henry Adams, ed. Ward Thoron, Boston: Little, Brown and Co. 1936.

Selected Letters of Henry Adams, ed. Newton Arvin, New York: 1951.

SECONDARY SOURCES

Anderson, Quentin. *The American Henry James*. New Brunswick, N.J.: Rutgers University Press, 1957.

Bloom, Harold. *The Anxiety of Influence*. Oxford and New York: Oxford University Press, 1997.

Edel, Leon. *The Conquest of London*. New York: J.B. Lippincott, 1962.

Long, Robert Emmet. *The Great Succession: Henry James and the Legacy of Hawthorne*. Pittsburgh: University of Pittsburgh Press, 1979.

Posnock, Ross. *Henry James and the Problem of Robert Browning*. Athens: University of Georgia Press, 1985.

ELIZABETH SCHMIDT

A Mourner Among the Children:
Emily Dickinson's Early Religious Crisis

I have perfect confidence in God and his promises & yet I know not why, I feel the world holds a predominant place in my affections. I do not feel that I could give up all for Christ, were I called to die. Pray for me Dear A. that I may yet enter into the kingdom, that there may be room left for me in the shining courts above.
—Emily Dickinson, Letter to Abiah Root, 8 September 1846[1]

Christ is calling everyone here, all my companions have answered, even my darling Vinnie believes she loves and trusts him, and I am standing alone in rebellion, and growing very careless. Abby, Mary, Jane, and farthest of all, my Vinnie have been seeking and they all believe they have found; I can't tell you *what* they have found, but *they* think it is something precious. I wonder if it *is*?
—Emily Dickinson, Letter to Jane Humphrey, 3 April 1850[2]

I

Until the age of sixteen, when Emily Dickinson wrote the first of the letters above, her life was the model of all that a girl's life in New England in the 1840s could be. She was the popular, brilliant, witty, attractive and beloved daughter of one of Western Massachusetts's most esteemed and financially secure families, whose ancestors were among the earliest settlers of the Massachusetts Bay Colony.[3] Her father's family was instrumental in founding Amherst College and they cared deeply about religion and education, encouraging their sons and daughters to excel in matters of the spirit and the mind. The primary school that Dickinson and her sister attended in Amherst, which her grandfather helped start, was among the best and most serious of schools in the country for girls. In the fall of 1846, a particularly intense wave of religious revivals swept through Western Massachusetts. Dickinson refused to stand up in public and "give up all for Christ,"[4] as she wrote to her best friend Abiah Root, and this choice set her apart, for the first time, from her family and closest circle of childhood friends. The crisis of faith and consciousness that followed this decision painfully distinguished her from the people she loved, while also setting her on a course of independent thinking that would determine her future development as a poet.

Generations of Dickinson scholars and biographers, from Richard B. Sewall to Alfred Habegger, have explored this early religious crisis. But their discussions have viewed the event as an important one among others in the poet's childhood and life. This essay will reexamine this early religious crisis as *the* crucial event in the formation of Dickinson's poetic voice. As a young woman, she was forced to measure her own belief in God against the stringent and fervent religious demands of her community. Richard Sewall believed that Dickinson "wrote her poems in much the same way that her devout contemporaries prayed. It was a daily ritual with her ... a very organic part of her religiously oriented life ... a communion with her soul and her maker in the very best Puritan tradition."[5] What set her apart from her Puritan forebears, however, was her pointed criticism of the popular religious practices of her time. She was deeply committed to recording and probing her own private religious beliefs—one could say it is the only abiding theme in her nearly 2,000 poems—but it was not a process that she felt had any connection to the group dynamic that characterized the evangelical fervor in Western Massachusetts in the 1840s and 1850s. Dickinson may well have written her poems as a kind of prayer, but I would add that they are prayers of a most defiant bent. Read alongside her letters they are the scrupulous record, the latter-day spiritual autobiography, of a miraculously gifted individual, who could not partake of the religious conventions of her day, and who had to forge her own at once painful and exhilarating understanding of what is lost and gained when one comes to believe, as Dickinson wrote during the early 1860s, that "The Brain is just the weight of God"[6] (#632).

As a young woman, Dickinson was caught between two counter forces: the Calvinist tradition of examining one's inner life in preparation for religious conversion, and the public pressure at conversion meetings to stand up in front of a crowd of witnesses and join "the saved." For Dickinson this was an impossible collision of the public and the private. As her early letters show, she thought long and hard about religious matters—and she agonized about how, when, and if she should convert. The counter forces at work during what has come to be called "The Second Great Awakening in New England" were much more at odds with the secularization of American culture in the mid-1800s than they were during earlier periods of widespread conversion and religious evangelicalism.

In poem after poem, habits of prayer and of song, in the form of the Issac Watts hymns, have the paradoxical effect of separating the speaker further from God. When one has been schooled to pray and to sing in God's name, what happens when God has slipped out of sight? Prayer and song turn inward, and, in Dickinson's case, the subject of her poetry becomes the reevaluation of spiritual life, though she's not always certain God can hear. I am especially interested in the strength of the speaking voice in relation to God's presence or absence. Very often, when God is a definite presence, the speaker is diffuse and passive; when God is reduced to a "furthest Spirit" (in poem #789) the strong sense of the "Columnar Self" is ample recompense.

The letters that Dickinson wrote during the 1840s and 1850s, especially the twenty-two written to her close friend Abiah Root, are the best record of her emotional and intellectual development during this time. They can be read as a spiritual autobiography in the sense that they are relentless, often anguished evaluations of her readiness for conversion. She can't accept the demands of public conversion, but she is still anxious about being lost to God. At the same time, these letters also record the process by which she was forced to acknowledge the power of her worldly interests and ambitions. These letters prefigure many of the concerns she would develop throughout her poetry, and several poems are illuminated by passages in the Root correspondence, illustrating how well Dickinson knew her mind even at such an early age. The letters reveal her anxiety about conversion pressure and her criticism of a public process that had more to do with the power of collective emotion than with a careful and rigorous theology.

Root was a classmate of Dickinson's at Amherst Academy, and one of the group she called "the special five" of her closest circle of friends. Root was the only one who preserved Dickinson's letters for herself and posterity,[7] and they remain the best record of the changes in her written expression during the Second Great Awakening in Amherst and South Hadley, where she went away to school when she was seventeen. The friendship deepened during their ten-year correspondence—it's significant to note that Dickinson and Root went to school together for less than a year and saw each other only once very briefly after Root left Amherst.

In the early letters to Root, Dickinson presents herself as someone who happily takes part in the social and intellectual life of her peers. In the first known letter to Root, Dickinson mentions going "to singing school Sabbath evenings to improve my voice ... Don't you envy me?"[8] The first mention of anything remotely religious in her letters is an unpious account of spending the Sabbath improving her voice. This description corresponds to one of the few passages that recount how Dickinson behaved at her family's church, The First Church of Christ in Amherst.[9] A memoir written by her pastor's son, David Jenkins, recalls the primarily social role church played for Dickinson as a girl. He recalls that during a period of church reconstruction, the congregation met in a small, temporary building:

> It was during this period that Miss Emily Dickinson was attending church and mixing in the social activities of the town and college. It was in this somber little building that she first began to place, on occasion, bouquets of flowers in the pews of her more intimate friends. Their color and fragrance did much, I am sure, to dispel the depressing effect of the somewhat austere surroundings, and added a touch of private intimacy and interest to the ritual of public worship that certainly did no harm. This practice she continued for some time, and when she no longer attended the services, the devoted Lavinia would bear her offerings and place them as directed.[10]

Jenkins remembers Dickinson putting her own mark in the form of flowers on the Church, and thereby transforming the building from a place of worship into a place where she could perform her own social and aesthetic rituals.

The fourth letter to Root, written in late September, 1845, is the first letter in which Dickinson alludes to the Bible. The tone of the letter is breezy and conversational, especially when one considers that it was written, as indicated in the postscript, after a period of illness. It is chatty, full of details about mutual friends and descriptions of her life at home because she wasn't going to school that term. Its confident, upbeat tone is a good touchstone for seeing how differently she would write about religion once she was exposed to the revivals. Her life was full of potential and she prided

herself on being a bright and desirable part of her family, friends, and
Amherst community. In a passage in which she describes learning how to
bake bread and keep house in general she writes:

> I think I could keep house very comfortably if I knew how to
> cook. But as long as I don't, my knowledge of housekeeping is
> about of as much use as faith without works, which you know we
> are told is dead. Excuse my quoting from the Scripture, dear
> Abiah, for it was so handy in this case I couldn't get along very
> well without it.[11]

The quote from James 2.17, "... Faith, if it hath not works, is dead," is folded
neatly into her description of keeping house. Her "excuse" acknowledges
that she's aware of being somewhat flippant in using the Bible and indicates
that Root is more religiously conservative than she is. Later in the letter she
alludes to Shakespeare with similar ease, indicating that scripture and
literature were on a par in her mind: both were available means of accenting
her written style with flashes of learnedness. Judging from these two early
references, the Bible and Church function chiefly as opportunities for
embellishing two early outlets for creativity and self-expression: leaving
bouquets and letter writing. This attitude by no means set her off from other
Amherst young women her age, most of whom learned to read from primers
that combined passages from scripture with popular ditties, songs, and
poems.

In her next letter to Root, written three and a half weeks later,
Dickinson jokes that she could be Eve:

> I have had a severe cold for a few days, and can sympathize with
> you, though I have been delivered from a stiff neck. I think you
> must belong to the tribe of Israel, for you know in the Bible the
> prophet calls them a stiff-necked generation. I have lately come
> to the conclusion that I am Eve, alias Mrs. Adam. You know there
> is no account of her death in the Bible, and why not I Eve?
> (*Letters*, 24)

The letter doesn't go on to clarify the distinction she intends by calling
herself Eve and Abiah one of "the tribe of Israel," but it's clear she's assigning
Abiah a place in the tribe, part of Old Testament biblical history, while
Dickinson's Eve can be thought of as almost outside biblical history, in the
sense that her action sets the history of the Bible in motion. Casting herself

and her friends as types, she makes light of finding present-day versions of Old Testament figures. All in all, there is a sense of religion as an enhancement, a light, interesting angle used to tell certain fictions about her life. The quote also reveals how carefully and originally she read the Bible; she knows there's no mention of Eve's death in the Bible.

All of this would change in the next of Dickinson's letters to Root, written at the very end of January 1846, when a particularly intense wave of religious revivals swept through Western Massachusetts. But in order to appreciate the change, one must first know something about the religious history of the Dickinson family in Amherst and about the intensity of the revivals themselves.

The Dickinsons were among the first Puritans who came to the colonies. There is record of a Nathaniel Dickinson on the same boat as John Winthrop in 1630. A Dickinson, therefore, heard Winthrop deliver his famous address, "A Model of Christian Charity.[12] Cynthia Griffin Wolf writes, "The men of the Dickinson family constituted a microcosm of the American experience as it sprang from the Puritan roots of New England."[13] The Dickinsons were devoted to preserving Winthrop's notion of the Massachusetts Bay Colony as "a city upon a hill": "The eyes of all people are upon us," Winthrop wrote at the end of his sermon, "we shall be made a story and a by-word through the world. We shall open the mouth."[14] Amherst was a community determined to keep this original message alive, while they felt the rest of the region was falling prey to the lax seductions of Unitarianism.

The founding of Amherst College can be seen as a reenactment of the English Puritan's break with the Anglican church. Connecticut Valley Trinitarians were strongly opposed to the liberal character of the increasingly powerful Unitarian Church, whose center of power was at Harvard in the early 1800s. In 1812 Samuel Fowler Dickinson, Dickinson's paternal grandfather, began a campaign in Amherst to raise money for Amherst Academy, to prepare boys and girls for the great Trinitarian colleges, Yale, Dartmouth, and Williams. In 1818, Samuel Fowler Dickinson felt that Amherst needed to start a college in order, as Wolf writes, to "uphold the Puritan virtues in an age when old-fashioned religion was beginning to fail." Emily Dickinson's paternal grandfather was "the moving force behind this idealistic endeavor, deliberately and self-consciously attempting to revive and reassert the fervor of John Winthrop's generation."[15] And her father was, for most of her life, a stern and highly rational man, who had to take on much of his father's financial burdens, including managing the always precarious finances of Amherst College. Edward Dickinson was a vital force in the building up of his family's church, known at different times as The First Congregational Church and The First Church of Christ, which was established in 1736. The beliefs of the founders of the college resonated with those of the town:

> In what did the founders believe? Broadly speaking, they were conservative Congregationalists of the orthodox Calvinistic type. As a body, with one or two possible exceptions, they would have stood by the doctrines of Jonathan Edwards, who had been a clergyman at Northampton from 1727 to 1750. They would have subscribed to the principles of original sin, justification by faith alone, salvation by grace, and atonement.[16]

Until Dickinson withdrew from society, she attended this church regularly with her family. The children of church families eventually had to "join" the church as individuals, and Dickinson was the only member of her family who did not become an official church member on her own.

The tone of Dickinson's letters to Abiah Root changed dramatically during the waves of religious revivals that swept through the Connecticut Valley, beginning when she was sixteen. Two and half weeks after Dickinson wrote Abiah Root the blithe letter in which she calls herself Eve, Dickinson wrote a letter entirely different in tone, expressing, for the first time, her religious uncertainties. This letter is a response to one in which Root must have mentioned that she was thinking seriously about converting in the religious revival of 1846.[17] At some point during the two and a half weeks since Dickinson's last letter, Root had written to Dickinson about contemplating her own conversion. Root was the first of Dickinson's close friends to contemplate conversion and the news, judging from Dickinson's letter in response, was greatly disturbing. This letter can be read as the piece of early writing that best describes the particular pressure upon young people during this era of the Second Great Awakening in New England.

The locus for the Amherst revivals was Amherst College. Edward Hitchcock, president of the college from 1845 to 1858[18] was instrumental in stirring up religious enthusiasm during his tenure. In his memoir, *Reminiscences of Amherst College*, he summarizes the waves of religious revivals during Dickinson's lifetime:

> Up to the present time (July, 1863) the College has enjoyed marked seasons of special religious interest in the following years, viz: 1823, 1827, 1828, 1831, 1835, 1839, 1842, 1846, 1850, 1853,

1855, 1857, 1858, and 1862. Besides these fourteen prominent revivals, many other seasons of special religious interest have existed in the institution, which, though not dignified by the name of revivals, have yet been of unspeakable importance in raising the standard of practical piety, and in fitting the successive classes to go forth in to the world with a more glowing and fresher love to God and man than otherwise they would have felt; and, moreover, in all such cases, a few are hopefully converted ... We think it not extravagant to say that probably as many as three hundred and fifty have begun their religious life here.[19]

Elsewhere in the memoir he describes the forms the revivals took, and how he and others associated with the college worked to inspire them: "... though impossible without the sovereign grace of God, like everything else in this world not miraculous, [revivals] are always connected with means as their antecedents, and if no means are used, we have no reason to expect revivals" (Hitchcock, 165). Chief among means was "the grand, all-essential ... presentation of truth" (165) by men who have undergone a private period of self-examination:

> ... in all the cases which I have traced out, I have found a silent preparation in the hearts of Christians to have preceded the revival. They have been deeply humbled by a sense of their selfishness, wordiness and want of interest in the cause of religion, and often the struggle in their bosoms has been long and painful, before they were brought into a state in which they could labor effectively to bring about a revival. If only a very few in a church are thoroughly permeated by such feelings and feel so straitened in their souls that they cannot but make manifest their emotions, and must strive to rouse their brethren to duty and impenitent men to repentance, we may hope for a revival, even though a large majority take no interest in the work. (Hitchcock, 166)

He goes on to say that it is the role of church pastors to detect such self-scrutiny in his congregation and to respond by intensifying his preaching to inspire the potential converts to step forward.

Hitchcock also writes that "private conversation with Christians is another admirable means to quicken the religious sensibilities." "All my experience," he adds, "goes to convince me that such private conversation is one of the most powerful of all means of grace in a college" (Hitchcock, 166). Theodora Ward's book *Capsule of the Mind* illustrates the extraordinary pressure revivals put on young people, especially those like Dickinson who were recalcitrant and undecided. Ward quotes from an account by Dr. Herman Humphrey, Hitchcock's predecessor, about an exchange between a young man who had come to him in private for spiritual advice:

> Inquirer: I do not feel anything. I have no sense of my sins, and how can I have? I wish I could feel as others do, but it is impossible.

> Pastor: My dear young friend, do stop and think what you are saying. You do not Feel! You have no sense of sinfulness! Astonishing! A sinner against a holy God, and under condemnation, and liable every moment to drop into a burning hopeless eternity—and yet cannot feel, cannot be alarmed, cannot "fell from the wrath to came." O, how stupid you must be![20]

Dickinson would have experienced the spectacle of the early 1840s Amherst revivals from a comfortable distance. At this point no one in her immediate family or her closest circle of friends had converted. She may have witnessed some emotional outbursts in her church, and the general atmosphere of religious enthusiasm seems to have moved her to serious religious reflection for the first time in her letters to Root. But by January 31, 1846, when she wrote to Root, she had begun to think seriously about where she stood in relation to the conversions. This letter is the most direct and sustained expression of her ambivalence about the revivals. She sincerely wonders if she ought to "give up all for Christ" and convert. In later letters, she looks back to this moment as one of two missed opportunities—one of two times she felt religiously inspired to renounce her worldly life. But she resisted, and her resistance was her first act of committing to her life as a poet.[21]

The letter begins with an uncharacteristically somber and direct apology for not responding sooner to Root's previous letter in which, we infer, Root recounts her own inclination to convert.[22] "I fear you have thought me very long in answering your affectionate letter and especially considering the circumstances under which you wrote," Dickinson begins. "But I am sure if you could have looked in upon me Dear A. since I received your letter you would heartily forgive me for my long delay" (*Letters*, 1, 27).

Compare this opening to the one that begins the letter in which Dickinson first quotes scripture: "I just glanced at the clock and saw how smoothly the little hands glide over the surface, I could scarcely believe that those self-same little hands had eloped with so many precious moments since I received your affectionate letter" (*Letters*, 1, 19). In the second letter, her playful ease with language and image has been replaced by a flat, colorless, formal apology, which brings to mind her famous poem #314, "After great pain, a formal feeling comes." This poem conveys the psychological numbness that follows emotional distress:

> The Feet, mechanical, go round—
> Of Ground, or Air, or Ought—
> A Wooden way
> Regardless grown,
> A Quartz contentment, like a stone—

News of Abiah Root's imminent conversion marked the first intrusion of the Massachusetts religious fervor into her inner circle of family and friends. (Her mother converted the year after Dickinson was born, but there is no evidence in letters that Mrs. Dickinson pressured anyone else in her immediate family to convert.) There are signs in earlier letters that Dickinson enjoyed a mild competition with Root: she had always been keen to know exactly what Root was studying and how far along she was with her piano playing. Dickinson often followed such inquiries with catalogues of her own related accomplishments in school and music. They are in some respects, letters typical of a teenage girl: full of inquiries about whom Root is seeing, how she looks, what boys she's interested in. And there must also have been a simple desire to keep pace, and thereby remain closer in terms of interests and intellectual growth, with the friends she never saw. One imagines that Dickinson saw Root's preparations to convert as the first signs of their eventual separation. The tone of her letters is never as playful after she finds out about Root's religious life.

This letter is the most sustained and detailed expression of Dickinson's early ambivalence towards conversion. "Under any other circumstances," she continues after the apologetic introduction, "I should have answered your letter sooner. But I feared lest in an unsettled state of mind in regard to which choice you should make, I might say something which might turn your attention from so all-important a subject. I shed many tears over your letter—the last part of it. I hoped and still I feared for you" (*Letters*, 1, 27). Dickinson is clearly conscious of how her own undecided state could influence Root. Edward Hitchcock, president of Amherst College at this time and leader of the 1846 Amherst revival was very concerned, at the time Dickinson was writing Root, about the negative influence of friends and family upon those who were debating conversion:

> How often have I seen the College church apparently in a humble waiting and anxious state, yet pleading and waiting in vain for revival. Something out of sight may have been wrong in all these cases. But may there not have been something wrong also in the churches of the land whose duty it is to pray and labor for the colleges? Especially may not something be wrong in the hearts of Christian parents and friends who have unconverted sons in college? In the revival of 1846, so suspicious was I that some foreign influence was exerted even more powerful than that in College, that I tried to ascertain how much of it proceeded from the prayers and efforts of the parents.[23]

So Dickinson was not only being instructed to scrutinize her own soul, she was being charged with influencing those who were ready to convert with her own ambivalence. President Hitchcock decided to air his suspicions in the 1846 revival publicly by publishing an account of the revival in several newspapers, which Dickinson, a voracious reader of local news, would certainly have read. The account was a list of excerpts from letters of parents whose sons were contemplating conversion. It was published, no doubt, to show readers the influence that letter writing could have upon someone evaluating conversion.

Dickinson goes on in the letter to explain how her ambivalence about Root's choice stems from her own religious indecision:

> I have had the same feelings myself Dear A. I was almost persuaded to be a christian. I thought I never again could be thoughtless and worldly—and I can say that I never enjoyed such perfect peace and happiness as the short time in which I felt I had found my savior. But I soon forgot my morning prayer or else it was irksome to me. One by one my old habits returned and I cared less for religion than ever. (*Letters*, 1, 27)

She sets up a revealing dichotomy here between conversion and peace of mind that plays out later in her letters and throughout her mature poetry. And there's a sense, even in this brief and in some ways evasive description of

her thinking, that converting means giving up a sense of self—her
preferences, habits and freedom to be "thoughtless" and "worldly." The
letter here has the kind of searing honesty that early conversion narratives
had, where the former sinner has left a record of all the sins committed along
the path to salvation.

The letter goes on to describe the 1846 revival in Amherst. She gives a
strong sense of the appeal that conversion had to people who couldn't think
for themselves:

> Last winter there was a revival here. The meetings were thronged
> by people old and young. It seemed as if those who sneered
> loudest at serious things were soonest brought to see their power,
> and to make Christ their portion. It was really wonderful to see
> how near heaven came to sinful mortals. Many who felt there was
> nothing in religion determined to go at once & see if there was
> anything in it, and they were melted at once.

Although it is difficult to parse her tone here, there seems to be a trace of
irony in her saying it was "wonderful" to see a crowd of simple-minded
people make a big spectacle of giving in. She makes the interesting
observation that it is the most vocal doubters who give in first. For someone
like Dickinson, who thought constantly about "serious things," who
repeatedly referred to conversion as "the all-important subject," and who was
interested in and curious about religious revelation, the burden of proof was
greater. She wasn't about to be persuaded by a mere show of emotion and
enthusiasm. Indeed, her strict and quiet Calvinist upbringing made her
innately suspicious of such loud and emotional proclamations of faith. And
though she seems to have longed for some assurance and peace of mind, she
enjoyed the secular world of intellectual thought and sensory experience too
much to give it up for something that didn't absolutely convince.

Her short, early poem #105[24] can be read as a narrative of the religious
dilemma she described to Root at this time:

> To hang our head—ostensibly—
> And subsequent, to find
> That such was not the posture
> Of our immortal mind—
>
> Affords the sly presumption
> That in so dense a fuzz—

You—too—take Cobweb attitudes
Upon a plane of Guaze![25]

The poem is a short narrative, told in two one-stanza parts. It begins with a cowed and humbled act, most likely of religious submission: "to hang our head," as though bowing in prayer or acknowledgement of God. But she's carefully chosen "hang" and not "bow" here, hang conveying a secular sense of dejection and defeat, rather than the more formal and participatory verb "bow." The word "ostensibly"—emphasized by its place at the end of the first line, by the surrounding dashes and its four-syllable length—changes the meaning of the head hanging: it's an act, a kind of pious put-on, a gesture meant to be read as a sign of religious submission but not perhaps truly revealing of the head-hanger's emotions and thoughts. If we read "to hang our head" as an act that implies conversion and giving into religious pressure, then the rest of the stanza shows the unhappy outcome: that the speaker has been mistaken, has found out too late that "such" head hanging was in fact "not the posture / Of our immortal mind." The words "posture" and "mind" work against "hanging" and "head" in the first line. "Posture" and "mind" are words with more expansive, dignified connotations. The question she puts forth here is: what if "hanging," submitting, isn't our "immortal mind's" true "posture"? The implied is: what if our thinking minds, the site of "internal difference" (as opposed to our heads, which is just what people see of our mind) were meant for grander, less subservient designs? We also see an early instance of how Dickinson establishes her own, personal meaning for the word "immortal" in the poetry. Immortality is most often connected to the products of the mind, to human accomplishment and to poetry; this is different from the word Eternity, which describes a frightening plan separate and oblivious to human life and achievement.

The poem's second stanza answers the questions posed in the first. The possibility of error means it is better to maintain some critical distance, to afford "the sly presumption" of taking "Cobweb attitudes." If we look at the poem in relation to her religious quandary, she seems to be writing a kind of justification for playing it safe at this point, for not giving in to the sway of conversion until she's more sure of her mind's posture. Thinking back to her letter to Abiah, the poem recommends being sly and cautious rather than being like those masses who "were melted at once" at the revival meetings, whose chaos and high emotionality may have felt to Dickinson like "so dense a fuzz." "Plane of Gauze" is a phrase that in itself reveals Dickinson's uncertainty about what exactly she would get if she gave up the world of the senses. In poems that debate conversion she frequently counters images of her immediate, sensory reality with vague, unfocused overwhelming metaphors for heaven. In the penultimate line, she goes so far as to recommend to others ("You—too—) that they should "take Cobweb attitudes." It's a puzzling image, but one which may express her need for some kind of veil or net to keep her from disappearing in "the acres of perhaps," one of her most striking metaphors for heaven.

Later in the letter to Abiah Root, Dickinson equates an imagined kind of pure "happiness"[26] with conversion. She distrusted the state of undifferentiated, limitless bliss that the converted preached to her, a state that was no substitute for the particular pleasures of her world, even if those pleasures were very often realized only through some kind of pain. Throughout her poetry, pain is proof of a kind of sensitized humanity ("the wounded deer leaps highest"), connected to insight and vision—the "imperial affliction" that made her a poet. But as a deeply introspective, sixteen year old, Dickinson was confused. Later in the letter to Root, she writes

> I feel I shall never be happy without I love Christ. When I am most happy there is a sting in every enjoyment. I find no rose without a thorn. There is an aching void in my heart which I am convinced the world can never fill. I am far from being thoughtless upon the subject of religion. I continually hear Christ saying to me Daughter give up thine heart. (*Letters*, 1, 27)

Here she very clearly articulates her dilemma: give up my heart, my emotional and intellectual independence, for what? As she grew older, she would mature as a poet, she would become a connoisseur of the "sting in every enjoyment," and become interested in exploring "the void" in her heart. But in this letter she makes a show of telling her best friend that she understands and is tempted by what conversion promises.

She then goes on to confess to Abiah that she stayed away from the revival meetings because she didn't want to give in:

> Perhaps you won't believe it dear A. but I attended none of the meetings last winter. I felt that I was so easily excited that I might again be deceived and I dared not trust myself. Many conversed with me seriously and affectionately and I was almost inclined to yield to the claims of He who is greater than I.

What Dickinson hated and feared was the hype of the religious meeting, her sense of feeling was easily excited by the group dynamic and giving in, not out of stringent belief, but on impulse. Stirring up excitement was a huge element of the public conversion spectacles, which were part religious ritual and part public entertainment. A decade earlier, the Reverend Charles Grandison Finney, who had led a wave of revivals in New York and out west, went as far as to say "that to expect to promote religion without excitements is unphilosphical and absurd."[27] Finney, a successful lawyer turned evangelist, ardently believed that "Christendom" had to compete with "the great political, and other worldly excitements," that "these excitements can only be counteracted by religious excitements. And until there is religious principle in the world to put down irreligious excitements, it is vain to promote religion except by countering excitements" (Miller, 3). Finney, whom Harold Bloom calls "the paragon of modern Evangelical revivalism," created "a new American form, at once religious revival, popular spectacle, and serious social crusade."[28] It was a form that was strikingly unappealing to Dickinson, and which may have ultimately kept her from converting in a more private and restrained manner.

Though Dickinson was clearly turned off by the emotional pitch of public conversions, much of the diction of her letter to Abiah Root reveals that she had intellectual as well as emotional reasons for resisting the pressure to convert. It appears from this letter "and from later letters that discuss conversion, that Dickinson had trouble with the fundamental idea of giving up her pleasure in independent thinking and in sensual response to the world in exchange for inclusion in a larger, boundless, thoughtless divine entity. In all such references, she emphasized her smallness in relation to an encroaching immensity. Yielding, to her mind, would mean losing the boundaries of the self, which she became increasingly interested in delimiting. The second half of the letter is a meditation on the "dreadful" concept of "Eternity":

> Does not Eternity appear dreadful to you. I often get thinking of it and it seems so dark to me that I almost wish there was no Eternity. To think that we must live forever and never cease to be. It seems as if Death which all so dread because it launches us upon an unknown world would be a relief to so endless a state of existence. I don't know why but it is but I cannot imagine with farthest stretch of my imagination my own death scene—it does not seem to me that I shall ever close my eyes in death. (*Letters*, 28)

These are concepts that Dickinson would continue to explore throughout her poetry. (And, of course, in many of her most famous mature poems that explore a speakers death scene). It's almost as if having opted to face the dread of Eternity on her own—without the comforts of Christianity, without the assurance, as she puts it towards the end of this letter, of knowing that she would join her converted friends and family in "one unbroken company in heaven"—she decides to try to overcome her fear of the unknown by imagining it in a variety of usually domestic and familiar scenarios. This courage to face her worst fears, to confront Eternity, gave her, through her poems, the assurance of achieving immortality, a way of making certain that the products of her mind would not be forgotten in some eternal plane of gauze.

By the time Dickinson wrote her next letter, two months later, Abiah Root had converted. In this letter there's a new, subtly defiant undertone. The letter, for the first time in what remains of their correspondence, is full of images of Dickinson as a writer. In the letter's second sentence Dickinson situates herself as set-off, behind her desk: "I am alone before my little writing desk, & wishing I could write news to you as joyful as your letter to me contained. I am alone with God, & my mind is filled with many solemn thoughts which crowd themselves upon me with an irresistible force" (*Letters*, 30). The first image this letter presents is of her thinking, writing self as still separate from God and Eternity. The charge often hurled to resisters like Dickinson was that she was "worldly." She looks back to the time before her previous letter, when she felt close to converting:

> I had a melancholy pleasure in comparing your present feelings with what mine once were, but are no more. I think of the perfect happiness I experienced while I felt I was an heir of heaven as of a delightful dream, out of which the Evil one bid me wake & again return to the world & its pleasures. Would that I had not listened to his winning words! The few short moments in which I loved my Savior I would not now exchange for a thousand worlds like this. It was then my greatest pleasure to commune alone with the great God & to feel that he would listen to my prayers. I determined to devote my whole life to his service & desires that all might taste of the stream of living water from which I cooled my thirst. But the world allured me and in an unguarded moment I listened to her syren voice. From that moment I seemed to lose interest in Heavenly things by degrees ..." (*Letters*, 31).

She now sees conversion as a choice between her interest in this world and the "dream" world of God. And she presents herself as a literary figure, an

Odysseus who loses track, gets derailed by the Siren's seductive voices. This is the first letter in which she appears to be self-conscious of herself as a writer, and conversion becomes at odds with her potential as a poet.[29] We see her mind playing with the spelling of "world" and "word" when she writes of being seduced by the Evil one's "winning words" about this "world."

She's far more adamant in this letter about remaining in her uncommitted state. She wrote about the pressure from her peers: "Prayer in which I had taken such delight became a task & the small circle who met for prayer missed me from their number. Friends reasoned with me & told me of the danger I was in of grieving away the Holy spirit of God." And still she holds her ground:

> I felt my danger & was alarmed in view of it, but I had rambled too far to return & ever since my heart has been growing harder & more distant from the truth & now I have bitterly to lament my folly—& also my own indifferent state at the present time. (*Letters*, 31)

There's also a stronger sense of the inviolable boundaries of her body, mind and sensibility: "my heart," "my folly," "my own indifferent state at the present time." The figure she uses for her heart—which "has been growing harder & more distant"—conveys her sense of withdrawing and shoring up her self as an entity that is separate from "the truth," significantly not capitalized here. Later in the letter she wrote, "There is now a revival in College & many hearts have given way to the claims of God. What if it should extend to the village church & your friends A. & E." "Hearts" is used without any kind of possessive modifier—those who have "given way" lose possession of their hearts in a generalized, undifferentiated, depersonalized mass of the redeemed. The letter ends with another heart image. Dickinson writes about the death of her friend, Sophia Holland:

> There she lay mild & beautiful as in health & her pale features lit up with an unearthly smile. I looked as long as friends would permit & when they told me I must look no longer I let them lead me away. I shed no tear, for my heart was too full to weep, but after she was laid in her coffin & I felt I could not call her back again I gave way to a fixed melancholy.
>
> I told no one the cause of my grief, though it was gnawing at my very heart strings. I was not well & I went to Boston & stayed

a month & my health improved so that my spirits were better.
(*Letters*, 32)

The letter ends with a powerful description of personal feeling, which
Dickinson locates in the inner recess of her own heart. The range of her use
of the sentimentalized terms "heart" throughout this letter plots a kind of
chart of the private, feeling self's integrity in the face of the force that
promises to wipe out all pain ("yet I shall meet her in heaven" Dickinson
wrote about her friend, halfheartedly) but at the same time all individualized
and precise personal feeling. This section of the letter also contributes to the
almost cherished, protective sense Dickinson has of her private emotions.
She gives a picture of herself at the funeral as at odds with the decorum of
grief. She looks too long and her friends have to lead her away. She tells no
one the cause of her grief. She removes herself to Boston to nurse her spirits.
This letter is the first very vivid self-portrait, written when Dickinson was
only sixteen, that resembles the portrait posterity will know: the writer who
withdraws from everyone and everything to write and explore the forces
"gnawing at her very heart strings."

For the first time in her correspondence with Root, Dickinson uses an
image that will occur repeatedly throughout her poetry and later letters in
expressing feelings about religion and about powerful emotions, such as
creativity and love.

> I feel that I am sailing over the brink of an awful precipice, from
> which I cannot escape & over which I fear my tiny boat will soon
> glide if I do not receive help from above. (*Letters*, 31)

What will change in her later work is a keen sense of pleasure and unabashed
interest in being at sea. An early poem, #76, explicitly celebrates this feeling
of being out at sea:

> Exultation is the going
> Of an inland soul to sea,
> Past the houses—past the headlands—
> Into deep Eternity—
>
> Bred as we, among the mountains,
> Can the sailor understand
> The divine intoxication
> Of the first league out from land?[30]

This is one of Dickinson's most striking definition poems—a poem in which an emotion ("exultation") is defined, or equated by the use of "is" followed by an image or a small narrative. Cynthia Griffin Wolf makes this distinction between 'Eternity' and 'Immortality,' which are similar insofar as each deals with an expanse that stands outside of time's passage. However, 'Eternity' is a term that is coldly indifferent to the existence of both mankind and God; by contrast, 'Immortality' refers explicitly to the infinite life of an integral consciousness, either human or divine."[31] If we accept this distinction,[32] then this poem is somewhat blasphemous: giving into "Eternity," a Godless timelessness, produces a kind of "divine intoxication"—in other words, "divine" "exultation" comes from the human act of letting go, not from any kind of pious understanding of the path to salvation. Dickinson puts tremendous pressure on the word "understand" in the second stanza. The first gives us the figure of setting out past "houses" and past "headlands"—past human marks on the land—into a "deep eternity." The second stanza pivots around the word "understand": how can we, who dwell on earth, possibly understand this letting go. The question is rhetorical, posed only to emphasize that of course we can't understand "the divine intoxication" of setting out on a course that's utterly different from what we have known.

In Dickinson's next letter to Root, written on June 16, 1846, she announces that she's planning to go away to school for the following term. Her excitement about going to Mount Holyoke Seminary in South Hadley eclipses her religious quandary. There's no mention in this short letter of Root's conversion or of Dickinson's equivocation.

> I am fitting to go to South Hadley Seminary, and expect if my health is good to enter that institution a year from next fall. Are you not astonished to hear such news? You cannot imagine how much I am anticipating in entering there. It has been in my thought by day, and my dreams by night, ever since I heard of South Hadley Seminary. I fear I am anticipating too much, and that some freak of fortune may overturn all my airy schemes for future happiness. (*Letters*, 34)

The letter is full of her details about her "worldly" life—excitement about being reunited with a former teacher, questions about mutual friends, and, most significantly, descriptions about her current intellectual interests. She mentions attending a lecture by a "converted Jew" on "the present condition of the Jews," and "a beautiful piece of poetry which has been going around." In her next letter, Dickinson does touch upon "the all important question" of conversion, but she continues to be less apologetic now for her interest in "the world":

> I am not unconcerned Dear A. upon the all important subject, to which you have so frequently & so affectionately called my attention in your letters. But I feel that I have not yet made my peace with God. I am still a s[tran]ger—to the delightful emotions which fill your heart. I have perfect confidence in God & his promises & yet I know not why, I feel that the world holds a predominant place in my affections. I do not feel that I could give up all for Christ, were I called to die. (*Letters* 1, 38)

It would turn out to be a grim irony, given her heady expectations for the next stage of her education, that going to Mount Holyoke would only place Dickinson at the center of a religious fervor so pervasive that she couldn't go home to her unflappable family and the safety of her room and writing desk to escape it.

Mount Holyoke College for women was founded in 1837 by Mary Lyon, a devout follower of Edward Hitchcock, Amherst College's most religiously zealous president. The college was first known as Mount Holyoke Female Seminary, and its official mission was to give young women of moderate means an opportunity to do college work in a religiously conservative setting, though in the late 1840s the place became famous for "saving" unconverted young women. Lyon was especially focused on the school's religious role. Summarizing the school's religious practice over the first ten years she emphasized the importance of "public worship, the Bible lesson, and other appropriate duties of the Sabbath; a regular observance of secret devotion, suitable attention to religious instruction and social prayer meeting."[33] And under the heading "Religious Culture" she wrote

> This lies at the foundation of that female character which the founders of this seminary have contemplated. Without this, their efforts would entirely fail of their design. This institution has been built for the Lord, that it might be peculiarly his own. It has been solemnly and publicly dedicated to his service. It has been embalmed in prayer in many hearts, and consequently around many a family altar ... The friends of this seminary have thought that this might be a spot where souls shall be born of God, and where much shall be done for maturing and elevating Christian character.[34]

And her students' weekly schedules were full of mandatory religious activities:

> virtually every student enrolled at Mount Holyoke during Mary Lyon's lifetime attended two services at the village church every Sunday, studies and recited a long Bible lesson over the weekend, spent a half hour in the early morning and another in the evening alone in private devotion, and received from Miss Lyon scriptural instruction at morning devotions and practical advice on conduct and morality at the general exercises in the afternoon. In addition, most of the girls joined one or more "social prayer" circles and attended at least one of the separate weekly meetings arranged according to the religious state in which students had classified themselves when they entered: as church members, as having no hope of salvation, or as somewhere in between.[35]

Parents of students and trustees of the Seminary were especially interested in the number of "unbelievers" converted each year. Edward Hitchcock noted in his biography of Mary Lyons, *The Power of Christian Benevolence Illustrated in the Life and Labors of Mary Lyon*, that in every year of her administration except for the first, the Seminary had a revival of "a thoroughness and extent almost unheard of in the modern history of the church." Hitchcock attributed this achievement to "the true secret of the extraordinary fidelity of the instructors."[36] On the college's twenty-fifth anniversary, the president of the board of trustees would note that out of the 3,400 students who had come through the college, he guessed "that about 1,000 had entered without hope, Of these 1,000 at least three fourths must have been converted during their stay at the Seminary."[37]

Dickinson entered the Seminary in the "no hope" category in regard to religion, making her private religious uncertainties painfully public. Her first letters to Root and to her family are full of logistics. She was settling in, studying furiously to enter a year ahead of her age, and getting to know her teachers and classmates. She was extremely homesick and these earlier letters are full of somewhat unconvincing resolves to cure her homesickness. It was after her first Christmas vacation, after her first extended visit home, that she began to feel the school's religious pressure most acutely. Her January 17, 1848 letter to Root mentions in a postscript that "there is a great deal of religious interest here and many are flocking to the ark of safety. I have not yet given up to the claims of Christ, but trust I am not entirely thoughtless on so important & serious a subject" (*Letters* I, 60). She resisted this wave of conversion and in the spring in her next letter to Root, she looks back ruefully to this period at her second missed opportunity to convert:

> I tremble when I think how soon the weeks and days of this term will have been spent, and my fate will be sealed, perhaps. I have neglected the one thing needful when all were obtaining it, and I may never, never again pass through such a season as was granted us last winter. Abiah, you may be surprised to hear me speak as I do, knowing that I express no interest in the all-important subject, but I am not happy, and I regret that last term, when the golden opportunity was mine, that I did not give up all and become a Christian. It is now not too late, so my friends tell me, so my offended conscience whispers, but it is hard for me to give up the world. I had quite a long talk with Abby while at home and I doubt not that she will soon cast her burden on Christ. She is sober and keenly sensitive on the subject and she says she only desires to be good. How I wish I could say that with sincerity, but I fear I never can. (*Letters* 1, 68)

In this passage Dickinson isolates two aspects of her sensibility that made it impossible for her to give in to the pressure to covert: she can't give up the world and she doesn't only desire to be good. The pressure on her would have been especially intense because it came both from the institution and from her cousin and roommate Emily Norcross, who had converted at Mount Holyoke the preceding year. Norcross wrote home: "Emily Dickinson appears no different. I hoped I might have good news to write with regard to her. She says she has no particular objection to becoming a Christian and she says she feels bad when she hears of one and another of her friends who are expressing a hope but she still feels no more interest."[38] Two weeks after the above letter to Root, Dickinson wrote to her brother Austin, saying she is disappointed that she won't be able to come home for a weekend visit because "it was contrary to the rules of the Seminary to be absent on the Sabbath" (*Letters* I, 68). Shortly after this letter Dickinson became dangerously ill and was sent home, thereby ending the second debate about conversion and beginning her life as poet committed to understanding her self in relation to the world.

II The "Lost" Poems

Poems 160, 256, 49, 472, 953 & 959
The six poems in this group are a subset of the sixty-five Dickinson poems

that contain some form of the word "lost" or "loss." Each of these six poems touches upon the biblical paradox of Matthew 16 (KJV): "whosoever will save his life shall lose it: and whosoever will lose his life for my sake shall find it." Dickinson's plays with the terms "lost" "found" and "saved" in these poems. Sometimes her speaker is saved because she hasn't let herself be lost to heaven as it is represented in the poem. Sometimes she is lost because she couldn't find, or join heaven.

The first five poems describe a brush with being "found" in the biblical sense. In poem 160, the speaker is almost lost, almost absorbed by the "disappointed tide" when she is "saved" by breath. In 256, and in what I call the "double loss" poems, the speaker is lost because heaven shows itself to the speaker and then shuts her out. In 959 the speaker has adjusted to feeling "a loss of something" and accepts the fact that she looks "oppositely / for the Kingdom of Heaven."

I have read each poem as a chronicle of the speaker's sense of self as manifest in the strength of the poem's "I" as the first-person narration unfolds. In most cases, the speaker's presence in the poem diminishes as the poem describes heaven or heavenly agents. In each poem, heaven descends in some form to touch the hesitant speaker.

Read together, with Dickinson's own early religious crisis in mind, these six poem form a sequence. In poem 160, the speaker fears losing her self to "Eternity" just as in the course of the poem "I" is gradually lost. 256 is the most sustained description of the speaker's encounter with "the Angels," and of the speaker's inability to, as Dickinson puts it in an early letter, "give up all for Christ." In the "double loss" poems, the speaker writes of being rejected by heaven; these poems are written in the after math of the encounter, when the speaker is still infuriated and dejected by the rejection.

The last poem, 959, can be read a kind of manifesto on the poetics of loss. This is the only poem in which the speaker is not "lost," not defined by her feelings of "loss." By the end of the poem she accepts, without remorse, a perspective of "looking oppositely / For the site of the Kingdom of Heaven."

160
Just lost, when I was saved!
Just felt the world go by!
Just girt me for the onset with Eternity
When breath blew back.
And on the other side
I heard recede the disappointed tide!

Therefore, as One returned, I feel
Odd secrets of the line to tell!
Some Sailor, skirting foreign shores—
Some pale Reporter, from the awful doors
Before the Seal!

Next time, to stay!
Next time, the things to see
By ear unheard,
Unscrutinized by Eye—

Next time, to tarry,
While the Ages steal—
Slow tramp the Centuries,
And the Cycles wheel!

Dickinson uses the symbol of the shoreline of an endless sea to represent the speaker's encounter with "Eternity." Eight lines in the poem end with exclamation points. All but three lines end with some form of decisive punctuation. This gives the poem a fragmented, exclamatory feeling. It takes shape as a sequence of disjointed narrative bursts. The speaker makes big, obvious gestures at telling a story, but never gets to its content, which is put off and delayed. We're told insistently that "next time" the speaker will be able to tell her tale. The impression is of someone just returned from an extraordinary experience who can't yet put the experience into words. This narrative failure is oddly convincing; it helps us believe she has actually, as Walter Benjamin puts it, "come from afar,"[39] that she truly has "odd secrets of the line to tell."

The first line compresses the poem's essential drama: the speaker was "just lost," when she "was saved." However, we have to wait until the second line to learn that she has reversed the conventional religious meaning of "lost" and "saved." The parallel construction of the first three lines creates an equation. "Just lost" equals "Just felt the world go by," which in turn equals "Just girt me for the onset with Eternity." Therefore, "lost" means losing this world; saved means having been blown back from Eternity by breath.

The diction in the third line reveals much about the speaker's dread of her heavenly encounter. The primary meaning of *gird*, to encircle with a belt, in "girt me," creates the impression of the speaker gathering up her inner resources in preparation for an attack, an "onset." And the use of "with" in "with Eternity" (instead of by eternity or of eternity) conveys a struggle between two more equal forces.

In the face of this encounter, the "I" as the active subject of the poem is withheld until the last line of the first stanza, when the speaker is safely on her "side" and recalls that she "heard recede the disappointed tide." In the three lines beginning with "just," the "I" is the elliptical subject of "lost," "felt," and "girt." When the "I" is the stated subject, in "I was saved," the passive voice conveys that she did not save herself. She was saved by a larger, greater force, as in being saved by one's belief in God.

We learn in line four, however, that the speaker was saved by "breath." Dickinson seems to mean a life force in general (what is human, mortal, worldly) and not her own breath in particular (it's not "my breath"). In any case, she clearly is saved by what is the opposite of "Eternity." In the process, however, the sense of self is lost to the point that even the objective "me" has disappeared from "when breath blew back." So far in the course of the poem, the speaker's grammatical presence has dissipated from passive subject ("I was saved") to elliptical subject to object ("girt me") to elliptical object.

After being blown back, she regains her subjective status; the "I" actively "heard recede the disappointed tide." The adjective creates a dynamic at greater length in other poems in this group: the notion that she is a resistant, hesitant object pursued by a heavenly agent (the tide here, Angels, God, and Heaven, elsewhere.) The tide is "disappointed"; it wanted to envelop her. She casts herself in the role of a triumphant survivor of a narrow escape, and the three "just"s underscore the narrowness of the escape.

The second stanza begins with the promise of a more active speaker as subject. The strong transitional gesture of "Therefore" at the start of this stanza indicates that she plans to tell us a consequence of the journey. And the speaker actively feels "as One returned." But in fact we learn nothing of consequence about the speaker herself. The "I" feels not as an "I" but "as One returned," devolving from an unadorned "I" to someone assuming roles. As the stanza goes on the roles become more specifically allegorical, intensifying to "Some Sailor" and then to "Some pale Reporter." And in these two instances the "as" in "as One returned" is lost; the speaker's grammatical self is lost entirely to her role. And as the twice-repeated "some" indicates, she's not even subsumed by a particular role.

In the end, this stanza becomes a set-up for the telling of some incredible secret that never gets told. As the only unrhymed end word in this stanza, "tell!" stands out and hovers with importance. She has gone to the brink of the hereafter and returned, now feeling a responsibility to communicate what she has seen. But as the verb shifts from present indicative to infinitive, the "I" recedes. "The line" implies she's one in the line of allegorical figures in heroic epics who have traveled to the hereafter and returned to tell their tales. She's thereby aligned with her great epic precursors, from Aeneas to Dante. And "of the line" also implies stories written in lines, that her secrets are of the line, composed of written lines.

As the sailor, she never makes it back. The image ends with the sailor still "skirting foreign Shores." As the "pale Reporter," the "from" tells us she's made it back from the "awful doors," but that's as far as that image goes. As the "pale Reporter," however, we get something that could be more like a self-portrait. The journey is specified as a religious one fashioned on The Book of Revelation. ("Pale Reporter" refers to the narrator of the Revelation, who is "as dead" from the shock of witnessing God; the "awful doors" are like the doors opening to heaven; and seals both clasp the book of judgement and the Lamb's Book of Life and are marks on the foreheads of the elect.) Nevertheless, nothing is reported about the return. The "Odd secrets" of this poem's speaker remain secret. They are left untold.

The two quatrains that end the poem merrily project to a "Next time" when the speaker can "stay" and "tarry." The poem's music shifts completely here. Longer lines of up to twelve syllables are: to alternating lines of four and six syllables. The "things to see" are a slightly rephrased version of 1 Co 2:9: "eye hath not seen, nor ear heard, neither have entered into the heart of man, the things which God hath prepared for them that love him."[41] The speaker claims to believe she'll have a second chance to be redeemed. The optimistic lilt of the iambic march in these lines builds towards the end with the final rhyme of "steal" and "wheel."

For all the poem's declared optimism and jaunty prosody here, the speaker is nowhere to be found. In the course of the poem she's dissolved from a feeling "I" to an "as One" to "some Sailor" to "Some pale reporter" to the elided first-person subject of the last lines' infinitive verbs. The strong verbs of the last three lines "steal" "tramp" and "wheel" (made all the stronger for contrasting with "to tarry") all belong to the world she will leave behind, to the impersonal forces which will carry on measuring time regardless of her departure.

256
If I'm lost—now
That I was found—
Shall still my transport be—

That once—on me—those Jasper Gates
Blazed open—suddenly—

That in my awkward—gazing—face—
The Angels—softly peered—
And touched me with their fleeces,
Almost as if they cared—
I'm banished—now—you know it—
How foreign that can be—
You'll know—Sir—when the Savior's face
Turns so—away from you—

This poem is divided into three parts: lines one to three (setting up a question about transport); lines four to nine (encounter with the Angels); lines ten through thirteen (bitter address to "Sir"). The speaker is lost now (banished) after having been found (communicated with the Angels). She questions whether her brief divine encounter will be sufficient "transport" for her imagination after the encounter has ended. The poem begins by asking how long the divine vision can last and ends on a note of dejection. In the last lines, the Savior's face has turned away from the speaker just as it is certain to do to the randomly addressed "Sir" who comes in without warning at the end of the poem. The many allusions to The Book of Revelation correspond to the general question of "transport," of poetic vision that this poem explores. The speaker's "awkward—gazing—face—" is like St. John the Divine's at the spectacles preceding the apocalyptic vision. The poem asks if she, too, will have enduring vision, if her own moment of transport will sustain vision.

The present tense of the first line is set against the past tense of the second in a cause-and-effect relationship created by "that": she's lost now because, earlier, she was found. In lines four and five, the poem defines "found" as a moment of religious revelation, the "Jasper Gates" suddenly opening (Rev 21:11–13, 18–19 and elsewhere).

Looking to Dickinson's early letters, we find she uses "found" as a term for converting to Christianity. In a letter written on 3 April 1850 from Amherst, Dickinson interrogates the term "found" in writing about her close friends' and sister's religious conversions:

Christ is calling everyone here, all my companions have answered, even my darling Vinnie believes she loves and trusts him, and I am standing alone in rebellion and growing very careless. Abby, Mary, Jane, and farthest of all, my Vinnie have been seeking and they all believe that they have found; I can't tell you what they have found, but *they* think it is something precious. I wonder if it is? (*Letters* 1, 94)

The difference between her use of *found* in this letter and in poem 256, is in the subject of found. In this letter, her friends and sister are the subjects; they have found. In the poem, the speaker "was found" by the Angels; they come to her before she is ready to fully accept them, before she believes, as this letter puts it, that "she loves and trusts" Christ.

In a letter written to her best friend two years earlier, when she was living away from home for the first time as a student at Mount Holyoke Seminary, Dickinson was much less confident about her religious questions:

Abiah, you may be surprised to hear me speak as I do, knowing that I express no interest in the all-important subject, but I am not happy, and I regret that last term, when that golden opportunity was mine, that I did not give up and become a Christian. It is now not too late, so my friends tell me, so my offended conscience whispers, but it is hard for me to give up the world. (*Letters* 1, 67).

In line three, poem 256 asks a similar question: "shall still my transport be" that once the "golden opportunity was mine"? This is a question she poses repeatedly in her letters, wondering if the brief moments of religious enthusiasm she felt were enough to justify the enormous sacrifice and the leap of blind faith she felt converting demanded of her. Would her awareness of the "opportunity" be transporting enough, even if she wasn't able to embrace the opportunity in a conventional or expected way.

The image of the gates blazing open "on me" in line four and the position of "on me" in the middle of the line surrounded by dashes underscores the sense of her being the object of the opening. Visually and grammatically, the speaker is caught in the middle of the line, stunned by the sudden revelation of the blazing world beyond the gates. The first stanza graphically and musically conveys the surprise at how the gates open. Line four is the longest line in the stanza, which draws out for several extra beats the possibility of the gates remaining open.

The middle section of the poem describes the speaker's encounter with the Angels, the brief experience that is her "transport." These lines about her transport are more musical than the rest of the poem because of the end-rhymes that hold the section together; and they also cohere because of the story they tell of the Angels softly peering in the speaker's face.

The only break in the poem comes after "suddenly" and the opening in the poem here enacts the opening of the "Jasper Gates." The "That" beginning the second continues the story beginning with "That once ... That in my awkward—gazing—face / The Angels—softly peered." Dickinson uses "awkward" to mean both turned the wrong way and lacking ease or grace. The speaker isn't ready or searching for salvation. Nonetheless, the Angels find her. They peer; she gazes. Gazing implies a certain, passive receptivity defined in Webster's Ninth Edition as implying "fixed and prolonged attention, as in wonder, admiration, or abstractedness"; she has been stunned into opening herself to the angels by the blazing gates. The difference between gaze and peer contributes to the sense of this speaker (like the speaker in other poems in this group) as unable to meet or answer the Angels' advance; she is stunned into a receptive—but passive—pose. They "softly" peer into her gaze, and touch her "with their fleeces." Dickinson transposes "softly" from "touched," which one would expect it to modify, to "peered," thus intensifying the sense of being penetrated bodily by the angels' look.

The poem abruptly ends the mellifluous second section with the phrase "Almost as if they cared." Indeed, the entire poem turns on this line, which is the reason the speaker is now lost. She doesn't believe the Angels care and therefore can't answer their soft, beseeching gesture. Returning to the above quoted letter, she writes that "Vinnie believes she loves and trusts him." Dickinson in a sense extends the definition of religious faith from simply believing in Christ, to believing that one "loves and trusts" Christ. In this line she defines the reason for her questions about unequivocal faith: she doesn't believe that the Angels really care. The line is shocking given the gentleness of the description of the Angels in this poem. Compared to the more fierce angels in the Book of Revelation, Dickinson's Angels are tentative in the delicacy of their approach. They came close enough for the speaker to read their expression and in it she found something she couldn't believe.

From this point on the poem disintegrates. The shattering of narrative and of meter and rhyme mirror the shattering of the speaker's religious conviction. Line ten, "I'm banished—now—you know it—" returns to the "now" of the first line as a different way of saying that she is now lost. Only here she breaks from the flow of the poem and addresses a new and random "you." The "you" destabilizes the poem, which heretofore had been an intimate, closed-world story about religious revelation. The revelation failed to take and so the speaker now joins the ranks of the unsaved or the lost. Her banishment makes the sense of her question about her transport in line three more clear. The poem asks: Will the just-described transport last, now that I am banished? Will this fleeting contact with the Angels be my only source of transport?

The poem makes apparent by music and narrative coherence that the transport does not outlast the actual moment of revelation. The ungainly insertion of the unannounced "you" becomes a "Sir" to whom the last section (lines 10 to 13) of the poem is addressed. The "it" at the end of line 10 interrupts the alternating-end-rhyme scheme. The present tense of "you know it" returns abruptly to the present tense of the first line. And "you know it" goes clumsily with "I'm banished—now," as if to imply that some random bystander just happened to witness the speaker's personal catastrophe.

The end of the poem switches to the future tense, cruelly predicting the you's inevitable banishment. The tone becomes spiteful here. The speaker appears to enjoy foretelling the you's fate. The accented overly formal "—Sir—" gives the penultimate line a shocking note of sarcasm. The last two lines describe how the speaker is (and the you will be) banished: "How foreign that can be— / You'll know—Sir—when the Savior's face / Turns so—away from you—." Dickinson takes the cliché "Misery loves company" one step further by creating a situation where misery creates her own company. The you's detachment from the rest of the poem is italicized by the fact that it is the last, unrhymed word of the poem. The two other unrhymed end words in occur in the first two lines, connecting the "you" to the lost speaker who begins the poem. When the speaker is "lost," in the first and third sections of the poem, the lines don't rhyme, the poem has lost its transporting music.

Ending the poem with "You" leaves the poem hanging. It's the only poem in this group (and the rare poem among all of her poems) that does not end with a rhyming word. And this "you" enacts a final unraveling of the narrative by pointing the poem in an unknown direction. Dickinson tells us nothing about the "you" other than that he can also be addressed as "Sir." With the last line, then, the poem itself turns away from the rest of the poem, just as the Savior's face has turned away from the speaker and is sure to turn away from the "you." "Turns so" means "turns like this"—that is, "away from you" as well as away from the rest of the poem.

She uses "Savior" here, rather than Angels, to heighten the pain of not being saved. Calling Christ here "one who saves" offers the possibility of being saved just as it takes that possibility away. The poem's logic tells us that the Savior turns away because the speaker couldn't believe the Angels "cared." She's left at the end on a par with the random you instead of in the company of the interested Angels.

49
I never lost as much but twice,
And that was in the sod.
Twice have I stood a beggar
Before the door of God!

Angels—twice descending
Reimbursed my store—
Burglar! Banker-Father!
I am poor once more!

The form of the poem emphasizes the "twice"-ness of the experience. Two verse units. Two sentences in first stanza, each of two lines. Two complete sentences in the second stanza, interrupted by the outburst "Burglar! Banker-Father!" And, most significantly, two characters in the drama: "I" and "God." There's more anger in this poem than in other "double loss" poems (472, 953). The speaker is an active subject of "lost," "have ... stood" and "am." The poem reads as an outcry. Speaker has asked—begged—for something twice and been not only denied but robbed and violated.

The defiant tone begins in the first three words: "I never lost." The negation is then reversed by "as much." She has, then, lost, but never as much as she did on two occasions. The second line describes where the losing took place: "in the sod." The preposition "in" makes it sound as though the speaker was dead and buried when she lost. The word "sod" connects the speaker with ground, earth, and grass. But sod is also short for sodomite, one who is damned, and although this use does not fit grammatically, Dickinson has clearly chosen the most debased term she could find for earth, a word she uses often in other poems as a more neutral counterpoint to heaven.

Losing twice in this poem means losing twice in the same way. The tone in the last two lines of this stanza is pure frustration: not once, but twice, have I begged at God's door. The other double loss poems (953, 472) stress that the double loss is composed of two different losses—a general loss of faith and a more personal rejection. This poem, in all its evident frustration, stresses the redundancy of the two experiences. The redundancy is felt in the hammering rhythm of monosyllables throughout the first stanza, especially in "And that was in the sod." A kind of relentlessness (relative to other Dickinson poems) also comes through the more conventional use of punctuation in this half of the poem, one of her few stanzas with no dashes. The strong diction of "beggar" is italicized by its place as the first two-syllable word in the poem since "never" in line one. And the speaker's apparent anger at God stands out in the rhyme of "God" with "Sod" in a stanza that is otherwise conspicuously bereft of internal rhyme and sound repetitions.

By contrast with the first, the second stanza begins melodically. There is a play of alliterative S's in "Angel's—twice descending" and more variety in terms of longer and shorter words, with the poems only three-syllable words occurring in line five. Just as Dickinson smooths out the music in other poems when they turn towards heaven (256 and 953, in particular), this poem breaks here for a moment of hope. The angels come down and reimburse her store. "Reimbursed" implies that the angels are paying the speaker back for something they owe. And "store" implies that she will save the payment for future use, that the angels give her hope of joining them some day in the future. The possessive "my store" also conveys a sense of store as referring to the speaker's creative powers because of the etymological connection between "store" and story. The progressive form of "descending" expresses some hope in the continuing connection of the angels to the speaker beyond the past-tense confines of the poem's other verbs.

The biblical allusion to Jacob's dream of the angels ascending and descending the ladder is significantly abridged; in this poem the angels only descend. The ascending angels in Genesis 28 symbolize a reaching out from Jacob to God, who answers the gesture with his blessing in the form of the angels descending the ladder, coming down to meet and encourage Jacob. The King James Version of Genesis 28:12 reads: "And he dreamed and behold a ladder set up on the earth, and the top of it reached to heaven: and behold the angels of God ascending and descending." From the journey into the wilderness and the uncomfortable sleep upon stone pillows comes the vision that creates (or is created by) a gate to Heaven. The stages then are: exhaustion and despair; visionary dream; connection with God. In using "store" Dickinson connects her poem to these stages of Jacob; her creative "store" is the analogue to Jacob's dream. But she is unable to reach out from her store. In this poem there are no ascending angels. "The door of God" is shut to her. And it seems she has shut it herself.

The poem's jarring narrative and musical leap from line five to six communicates the violence of the loss. From the brief possibility of hope at the start of this stanza comes the devastation of hope. The outburst "Burglar! Banker-Father!" is an outcry against her robbed "store." In *The Western Canon*, Harold Bloom writes "The entity named 'God' has a very rough career in her poetry and is treated with considerably less respect and understanding than the rival entity she names 'Death'. Bloom goes on to say about this line in particular: "A poet who addresses God as father only after first calling him burglar and banker is up to something other than piety" (295). The idea of God as a burglar or thief is a common enough figure throughout the Bible ("the day of the lord so cometh as a thief in the night" (KJV 1 Th 5:2, for example), so the outcry is not exactly blasphemous or even disrespectful, as Bloom implies.

The poem turns upon the difference between the angels, who deign to come down to the speaker's level (just as they descended Jacob's ladder) and God, who stays in Heaven (just as in Jacob's dream he stands above the ladder and calls down to Jacob). The three-word sequence of this line descends from outrage at being robbed ("Burglar!") to a softer appeal to her "Banker-Father." (Edward Dickinson was lawyer, not a banker, but he did act as treasurer for Amherst college and gave the college considerable sums of money throughout his lifetime.) She replaces the exclamation point after "Banker" with a dash, which links "Banker" to "Father," and making of the two words a hybrid, or hyphenated "Banker-Father." "Banker" connects with "reimburse" earlier in the poem. She appeals to the father figure to reimburse her emptied store again. In an 1850 letter to a friend, Dickinson connects addressing God as "father" and psychological need: "How lonely this world is growing, something so desolate creeps over the spirit and we don't know it's name, and it won't go away, either Heaven in seeming greater, or Earth a great deal more small, or God is more 'Our Father,' and we feel our need increased" (*Letters*, 94).

The poem ends with God and the speaker on two separate lines. In the exclaimed last line, "once" contrasts starkly with the three earlier "twice"s. The poem shifts abruptly to the present tense here, indicating that this "poor" state will be the enduring state, made more painful because the twice-reimbursed speaker is now forever poor. The rhymes of "door," "store," "poor," and "more," draw a line from God's door to the speaker's poor inner store, renouncing the possibility of future reimbursement.

As in other poems in this group that touch upon the speaker's momentary connection with God, the speaker's active presence as an "I" disappears from the poem during the lines describing the connection. The "I" speaks actively throughout this poem's first stanza and in the last line, when the poem is safely on the "sod" side of "the door of God." But when the angels descend, in lines five and six, the "I" disappears from the poem. There is no intermingling of the "I" and the "Angels" or "God" in this poem.

472
Except the Heaven had come so near—
So seemed to choose My Door—
The distance would not haunt me so—
I had not hoped—before—

But just to hear the Grace depart—
I never thought to see—
Afflicts me with a Double loss—
'Tis lost—And lost to me—

Dickinson has arranged this poem to put the most pressure on its last word: "me." The poem is about rejection, a force over which the "I" has no control; it becomes a rejected "me." Losing doubly means both being hurt personally by the fact that "Heaven" shuts its doors and being lost in a more general religious sense, adding, so to speak, insult to injury. She is not only lost, she has been rejected. The entire poem, then, weighs heavily on its final "me," making the speaker the object of this monumental rejection. In other poems in this group, the encounter with heaven comes midway through the poem. This poem opens with heaven as the subject of most of the first stanza and ends with the speaker's reaction to the experience. The rejection (hearing "the Grace depart") is the subject of the last stanza. The extreme metrical regularity of the poem gives the poem a tonal flatness, in a sense the speaker sounds resigned to her status; though the experience continues to afflict her, there is little she can do about the rejection now. The tone is very different from the exclamatory #49, where the speaker appears still to be in the grips of outrage at being robbed of her religious faith.

Dickinson arranges the first stanza to stress the word "haunts" and to minimize the importance of the haunted "I" in the stanza's last line. The first two lines begin with conjunctions whose clauses reveal something about the way the distance haunts; it haunts because heaven had come so near, so near that it felt as though heaven had chosen the speaker's door to haunt. The repetition of the three "so"s holds the first three unrhymed lines together by the sound repetition. The effect of delaying and drawing out the action upon the "me" by beginning the poem with the clauses creates a drawing out, a kind of torture: the "me" being is out and chosen, only to be passed by. And of course the clauses tell the reader right from the start about Heaven's actions, not the speaker's, whose primary role in this poem is to be acted upon. We learn how the distance between the speaker and heaven haunts before we learn that the speaker is in fact haunted. The sense of heaven as a force, a being, even, that has come down and chosen the speaker's door prepares the reader for the poem's first active verb, "haunts," for thinking of heaven as a kind of ghost. "Haunts" is the only verb in the present tense in this stanza, setting the word off, italicizing it against the back drop of the past tense.

The last line of the first stanza stands alone as its own short sentence. We learn more about the nature of the haunting, that she is now haunted by hope. Heaven had come so near, the speaker got a taste of what she is missing. "Before" is emphasized both by its place at the end of the line, set off by dashes, and by its two syllables, coming after the four short beats of "I had not hoped." The tension created graphically (by the dashes) and musically (by the syllables) underscores the leap in time the poem makes from a before without hope to a present in which she is haunted and afflicted. The effect of withholding the "I" until the last line, helps convey the sense of the Heaven descending and invading the speaker's realm, just as the weight of the stanza sits on its last line. And the dashes surrounding "before" emphasize the once protected realm of the speaker that has been disturbed by Heaven's approach.

The speaker is a more active, if displaced, presence in the second stanza. The first two lines recap the earlier described abandonment, with the important distinction that in this stanza the speaker is the subject of the event, albeit the implied subject of "to hear." The use of two different senses ("to hear" and "to see") in these lines creates both a sense of confusion (the speaker's senses have been scrambled) and a sense of trauma affecting both senses at once. "See" here means both seeing in a religious sense (seeing the light, being illuminated, etc.) and in a specifically personal sense (she never thought that she herself would see the grace depart). The two meanings for see—the generally religious and the personal—prepare us for her definition for the "Double loss" in the last two lines.

"Afflicts" is in many ways the strongest word in this poem. It corresponds with "haunts," the only other word in the present tense. The action of the present tense verbs continue to work on the speaker after the Heaven's appearance and disappearance. But the position of "Afflicts" at the start of the line, as one of two multisyllable words that starts a line, gives the word graphic and musical emphasis.

The definition of the "Double loss"—" 'Tis lost—And lost to me"— reveals an imbalance in the doubleness of the loss. The first part of the definition ("'Tis lost"), concerning the general loss is short (two one beat words) and therefore seems less painful. The second part, concerning the personal loss, is set off and italicized by the surrounding dashes; it is drawn out, the loss is more painful because of its particular action on the speaker.

953   Variants
A Door just opened on a street—   ...street—] there opened—to a House
I—lost—was passing by—
An instant's Width of Warmth disclosed—
And Wealth—and Company.

The Door as instant shut—And I—   instant] sudden
I—lost—was passing by—
Lost doubly—but by contrast—most—
Informing—misery—   Informing] Enlightening—/Enabling—

This poem, unlike 472, doesn't relate the metaphor of the door to anything associated with heaven. The metaphor is in this sense a closed world. It is entirely about the misery of being shut out from the world viewed through the open door. The point of view of the speaker is stronger than in 472 because the poem is about the speaker's perception of the instant the door was open, of peering through into the world beyond the door, not about that world acting upon the speaker. The word "I" occurs three times. The objective "me" has no place in this poem. And the "I" is always set off by dashes and by its place at the start or the end of the line.

In a poem of only eight short lines, two are identical: "I—lost—was passing by." The repetition of this line and its place as the second line in both sections of the poem, best expresses the poem's devastating twiceness. The speaker was lost and passing by before the door opened; she was lost and passing by after the door closed. The view, the glimpse beyond, has left her unchanged, just as the lines themselves are unchanged.

In the first line, "just opened" conveys both the suddenness and the finality of the event. The only word revealing anything about the door opened is "just," meaning, in this context, barely, immediately, and simply. Dickinson uses "just" to convey the arbitrariness of the door, that it opened without regard to the disoriented speaker who had no time to prepare for what she was about to glimpse. The past tense of "opened" expresses finality; the poem's description of the event is a retelling; the word "opened" implies strongly that the door is now closed. "On a street" means that this door was just on a random, indefinite street. (And door, too, takes the indefinite pronoun compounding the sense that neither the door nor the street is particularly important to the speaker.) The first line ends as a complete sentence, which in this sense is significantly cut off from the single sentence of the second line. The door and the "I" of the poem are separated grammatically and spatially; the "I," is utterly separate from the world the door reveals. The basic past tense of "just opened" contrasts with the progressive past tense of "was passing." "Was passing" gives the sense of being in a process, being in motion, moving along in a way that will continue unaffected after the speaker has passed the open door. The word emphasized in line two is clearly "lost," italicized by its surrounding dashes.

Lines three and four describe the world beyond the door, and the poem here takes a distinctly mellifluous turn. Where the rest of the poem is broken into short, abrupt fragments, the lines here run together as a longer, flowing sentence linked by "and ... and." And the lines are further linked by the alliteration of "w"s in "Width" and "Warmth" and "Wealth" and the "s" sound in "instant's" and "disclosed." The diction here becomes surprising and engaging, the sudden opening of the door becomes "an instant's Width of Warmth." Dickinson capitalizes all words associated with the door and what it reveals, indicating the perceived superiority and formality of the door's realm. The capitals also contribute to the sense of this world's miraculous richness; that this rich sequence of adjectives can be packed into an "instant's Width" make them all the more remarkable. The "and ... and ... and" construction conveys a sense of the infinite space beyond the door as contrasted to the short and narrow view from the speaker's side. The brilliant word "disclosed" at the end of line three, means both unclosed (the door has suddenly opened) and revealed, made known or public. And each adjective used to describe the world beyond the door contrasts to the lonely world of the speaker, who is alone, "lost" and unadorned (in terms of what the poem discloses about her).

The period at the end of this stanza indicates a full and deliberate stop between the two stanzas. Looking at the manuscript of this poem, the deliberate dot of the period contrasts strongly with the dashes ending every other line of the poem. The period is a small dark circle; it has the look of having been colored in, or gone over several times with a pen because the mark is darker and fatter than any other mark in the poem. The dashes are light and convey a sense of speed, as though her pencil barely stopped between the words to make the dash; and most of the dashes have a slight downward slant that echoes the more elongated slanted line she uses to cross her "t"s. Visually the dashes appear to be a habitual, almost unconscious part of the pace at which she copied over the final version of her poems. The period in this poem looks like a somewhat awkward and deliberate mark that interrupts the sweep of her pen on paper. (A general note: periods seldom occur in Dickinson's poems. In the eight poems discussed in this packet, there is only one other period. She clearly preferred the more musical dash to indicate breaks in thought and lines. Her dashes also tend to give her poems a sense of speed as they move the poem along, linking, like small bridges, the words or lines connected on either side of the dash.) The period prepares us for the shutting of the door in the next line. The full stop in a sense shuts its own door on the warm world beyond the door, which will not in any way connect to the reflections of the speaker after the door has shut in the second part of the poem. The period anticipates the door shutting and communicates a sense of finality to the shut door. It also creates a barrier between the stanzas and therefore a barrier between what is on either side of the door.

The variant of "sudden" for "instant" in line five tells something more about how the door shut (suddenly, without warning). But Dickinson's final choice of "instant" creates a kind of cruel consistency to the mechanism of the door: it reveals in just the same way as it hides. This connects to her use of "disclosed" in line three, to the sense that the door is never really opened but rather "unclosed," is just a brief, sudden interruption of its usual closed state. By "Door as instant shut" Dickinson uses "instant" as an abbreviation of the adverb, "instantly." But it also works to think of the "as" a comparison, meaning that the door was like a shut instant, like a foregone conclusion in the sense that the instant was always meant to remain too fast, too narrow, and too fleeting an amount of time for the speaker to have ever entered through the opening.

Bringing "And I" up to the first line in the second stanza is the first sign that this second section of the poem will be more about the speaker's experience of the event and less about the event itself. The "I" is then repeated at the start of the sixth line where the "I—lost—" line is repeated. The two "I"s together give the sense of building up to a statement about the speaker, as though she must say her "I" twice before having the strength to continue. It is also a stutter. It is more difficult to get the words "I—lost" out at this stage in the poem, coming so close to the paradise behind the door.[42] The repetition also stresses the word "lost," as though the "I" can't stand on its own without being modified first by "lost" and then by "Lost doubly" at the start of the seventh line. "Lost" changes from adjective to verb at his point in the poem; the verb "lost" picks up on the "I" at the end of line five: "I ... lost doubly." "Doubly" meaning she was lost before the door opened and now has lost the vision of what was beyond the door, and the contrast of that view to her previous state of loss makes the new sensation of loss more acute.

The proliferation of dashes in the second stanza reveals a disturbed psychology; she can't stick to a train of thought at this point in the poem. The fragmented train of thought here becomes a manifestation of last line's "misery." Dickinson uses "Informing" to mean both giving form to/giving character or essence to misery, as well as imparting knowledge of misery. Misery is not the general state of being lost but rather that general state compounded by the more acute form of losing a world one has been allowed to see and therefore imagine joining. The use of the -ing form of "passing" and "informing" in this part of the poem extends the reach of each verb beyond the time frame of the poem's narrative. "Passing by" can be read as a metaphor for living, and the "informing" therefore lasting as long as the speaker lives. The manuscript of this poem indicates that Dickinson has two alternate words in place of "informing" in earlier version of the poem: "Enlightening" and "Enabling." Her ultimate choice of "Informing" indicates that she wanted to keep the first definition of inform, to show that the double loss not only tells us about misery by actually *is* the substance of misery.

959   Variants
A loss of something ever felt I—
The first that I could recollect
Bereft I was—of what I knew not
Too young that any should suspect

A Mourner walked among the children   walked] lurked
I notwithstanding went about   went] stole
As one bemoaning a Dominion
Itself the only Prince cast out—

Elder, Today, a session wiser
And fainter, too, as Wiseness is—
I find myself still softly searching
For my Delinquent Palaces—

And a Suspicion, like a Finger
Touches my Forehead now and then
That I am looking oppositely
For the site of the Kingdom of Heaven—

This is the only poem in this group that uses "loss" as a noun. The other poems use "lost" as a verb or as an adjective, a word that reflects directly on the speaker. "Loss" here is a general feeling the speaker has, an abiding part of her character, something she has accepted and learned to keep at a distance. The dominant religious metaphor is Eden; the speaker sees herself as one expelled from an ideal state in which she was not aware of the feeling of loss. The loss is never specified. At the start the speaker feels "a loss of something"; as a child, she recalls suffering "of what I knew not"; and when elder she finds herself "still softly searching." As the speaker ages through the course of the poem, she becomes more comfortable with the loss; the progression from "bereft" to "bemoaning" to "searching" to "looking."

"A," the indefinite article that begins this poem, casts a show of uncertainty on the entire poem. We never learn anything definite about "the something" from which the speaker suffers. But the suffering has caused the poem's speaker to live as its uncomprehending agent. The place of the "I" as the last word of the first stanza creates an image of the speaker being controlled by her suffering; she has been pushed by the feeling just as she has been pushed by the construction of this line to the outer limits of the poem. It's significant that the speaker is always an "I" in this poem. She wanders through the poem like a sleepwalker, like one who has been programmed by the loss to carry out its aims.

The first line is a setting for the vague, central word "something," which is surrounded by shorter words. "Ever," which modifies "something," is similarly vague, making this loss continue indefinitely. The use of the past tense "felt" gives the line a summarizing, introductory tone, raising expectations that what comes next in the poem will explicate the loss.

After the backward sweep of the first line, the remaining lines of the first two stanzas, the first half of the poem, look back to the speaker's childhood. She always felt a vague sense of loss, though the children around her weren't aware that "A Mourner walked among" them. The awkward phrasing of lines two and three: "The first that I could recollect / Bereft I was—of what I knew not" give a sense of disorientation. The placement of "Bereft" at the beginning of line three, emphasizes the word and dominates the "I" by coming before it. The poem shifts abruptly in the fourth line from discussing the speaker's emotions to illustrating how these emotions have isolated her from other children her age. Line four, "Too young that any should suspect," makes a shift in subject from "I" as to "any," meaning the other children. The word "suspect" hangs at the end of the stanza, compounding the speaker's sense of loss with guilt for feeling the loss.

Dickinson reverses the sense of a lost childhood as a kind of Eden; in her case the loss was most acute to her as a child because it separated her from other children, made her feel guiltily distinct.

The variorum shows that Dickinson had at some point written "lurked" for "walked" and "stole" for "went" in lines six and seven. The variants exaggerate her guilt, make her seem, in her bereft state, a predator to the other unaware children. To feel suspected because you mourn is a doubly sad situation. The next three lines use a kind of fairytale story to illustrate how she mourns. But the allegory of the cast-out Prince is a vague, generic explanation. And the "I" gets lost in the telling of the story, becoming a "one" then an "itself" then a "Prince." The capitalization of "Dominion," gives the word a heavenly meaning. "Dominion" is an interesting word to use here, as a major theme in this poem is the domination of the speaker by a loss of something; she's dominated by her search for a dominion.

The second half of the poem, the third and fourth stanzas, takes place in the present tense. The speaker characterizes herself as "Elder," "wiser" and "fainter." Instead of "bemoaning" her lost state, she finds herself "still softly searching / For my Delinquent Palaces—" She has grown from the position of a cast-out Prince mourning his dominion to an "I" "softly searching / for my Delinquent Palaces." The progression is towards ownership of her story; the "I" having been lost and distorted into an "itself" in the story of the Prince is here found; "I find myself," she writes, "searching for my Delinquent Palaces." Verb tenses shift from past tense ("felt I," "could recollect," "I knew not," "I was") to present tense, active verbs and participles ("I find myself ... searching," "a Suspicion ... touches," "I am looking"). Pulling the verbs into the -ing form gives the sense that the "searching" and the "looking" will continue into the future, beyond the scope of the poem. The shift from being cast out of "a Dominion" to being on the look out for "my Delinquent Palaces" implies a kind of control over the situation: the "a" becomes a "my"; the mourner, the rejected, becomes the searcher.

The "I" of the third stanza is a stronger presence than the "I" of the first two stanzas. The string of adjectives ("Elder," "wiser," and "Fainter") gives a more particular sense of the speaker; one could say she knows who she is in this stanza, for better or for worse. The idiomatic use of "I find myself" italicizes speaker's current status, by drawing out the reference to the self. In the previous stanza she was lost and cast out; in this, she is found searching for something she owns but can't find. In previous poems in this group, she was lost because she couldn't join heaven. In this case it is the speaker who finds herself. She finds herself searching, but perhaps she also finds herself by searching. The progression from "bemoaning" to "searching" certainly indicates a movement from active to passive. And the progression from "Dominion" to "Palaces" indicates a movement from a general region to a specific spot. The adjective "Delinquent," implies that these Palaces are particular to the speaker's life; that she is searching not for a collective ideal of Paradise, but for her own debased version of something lost.

This sense that this version of paradise is at odds with the more conventional lost "Dominion" of one's childhood becomes clearer in the last stanza, where she is "looking oppositely / For the site of the Kingdom of Heaven." Her guilt about choosing her own paradise becomes, here, a strange personification: "a Suspicion, like a Finger" periodically touches her forehead to remind her that she's looking in the wrong direction "for the site of the Kingdom of Heaven." The image is weirdly disembodied. The suspicion must be the speaker's own feeling. And yet the simile makes the feeling appear to be coming, "like a Finger," from outside the speaker. The image of the finger touching the forehead is gentle and comforting, and has something in common with the appeals from Angels in poems 49 (Angels—twice descending / Reimbursed my store—") and 256 ("... in my awkward—gazing—face— / The Angels—softly peered— / And touched me with their fleeces, / Almost as if they cared—").

To look down from Heaven implies that the speaker is looking to earth, looking at the world around for her own lost paradise. The tension Dickinson felt between the world and Heaven was one she described repeatedly in her letters to Abiah Root, one of her best friends, during the waves of religious revivals the swept though Amherst when Dickinson was sixteen. In a letter from late March, 1846, Dickinson wrote:

> ... the world allured me & in an unguarded moment I listened to her syren voice. From that moment on I seemed to lose interest in heavenly things by degrees. (*Letters* 1, 30)

Six months later she would again write to Abiah Root about the attraction of "the world": "I have perfect confidence in God & his promises & yet I know not why, I feel that the world holds a predominant place in my affections. I do not feel that I could give up all for Christ, were I called to die" (*Letters*, 38). A year and a half later, she was away from home for the first time, studying at The Mt. Holyoke Seminary. When she writes to Root, she is less confident about choosing the world over Christ: "... I am not happy, and I regret that last term, when that golden opportunity was mine, that I did not give up and become a Christian. It is not now too late, so my friends tell me, so my offended conscience whispers, but it is hard for me to give up the world" (*Letters*, 67).

But in this poem the speaker has learned to live with her attachment to the world. After a painful childhood of feeling like an outcast, she now accepts her focus on the world. The suspicion that gently intrudes "now and then" doesn't actually affect the "looking oppositely."

This notion of growing accustomed to the search, to "looking oppositely" as a way of life and perhaps also as a source of poetry is one that R. P. Blackmur touches upon in his essay "Emily Dickinson's Notation." He writes of Dickinson: "All her life she was looking for a subject, and the looking was her subject—in life as in poetry."[43] (182) If we think of "looking" as a metaphor for Dickinson's spiritual search, poem 959 shows the stage-by-stage process by which the search becomes a kind of affirmation of one's particular perspective on the world.

NOTES

1. *Letters* 1, 38.

2. *Letters* 1, 94.

3. Josephine Pollitt, *Emily Dickinson: The Human Background of her Poetry*, New York: Harper and Brothers Publishers, 1930, p. 8. Biographical material comes mostly from Richard Sewall, *Emily Dickinson: The Life of Emily Dickinson*, Ithaca: Cornell University Press, 1964, and Cynthia Griffin Wolf, *The Life of Emily Dickinson*, New York, Knopf, 1986.

4. *Letters*, 1, p. 38.

5. Millicent Todd Bingham, *Emily Dickinson's Home: Letters of Edward Dickinson and His Family*, New York: Harper & Row Publishers, 1955.

6. Johnson, *CP*, 312.

7. From Sewall, pp. 3720–399.

8. *Letters of Emily Dickinson*, Vol. 1, ed. by Thomas H. Johnson, p. 10.

9. TK: all the name changes of Dickinson family church.

10. MacGregor Jenkins, *Emily Dickinson Friend and Neighbor*, Boston, Little Brown, 1930. 71.

11. *Letters*, 1, p. 19.

12. Cynthia Griffin Wolf, *The Life of Emily Dickinson*, p. 13.

13. Wolf, p. 13.

14. John Winthrop, "A Model of Christian Charity," from *The Norton Anthology of American Literature*, Fourth Edition, Vol. 1, p. 180.

15. Wolf, p. 14.

16. Claude Moore Fuess, *Amherst: The Story of a New England College*, Boston: Little, Brown, and Co., 1935.

17. Root had by this time returned to Springfield MA, to live with her family, but this 1846 revivals was one which swept through Western MA and affected both young woman, who now living different places.

18. From *Amherst...* by Claude Moore Fuess. p. 127.

19. Edward Hitchcock, *Reminiscences of Amherst College*. Northhampton, MA: Bridgman & Childs, 1863, p. 162.

20. Reprinted in Richard Sewall's *The Life of Emily Dickinson*, Cambridge: Harvard University Press, 1974, p. 25.

21. Resistance to popular enthusiasm is a distinguishing characteristic of this period's writers. Hawthorne's fear of mesmeric spectacles and Dickinson's distrust of religious revivals are prominent examples.

22. Root's letters haven't survived; I'm inferring content by Dickinson's response.

23. Hitchcock, *Reminiscences of Amherst College*, p. 170.

24. Unless otherwise indicated, I will follow the chronology of poems that Thomas H. Johnson has established; it will be understood that his dating of the poems is approximate and I will base no reading on the presumed date of a poems, though it does seem safe to group poems in terms of early, middle and late poems based on what I have observed of and read about the changes in Dickinson's handwriting during her most prolific years.

25. *Complete Poems*, p. 51.

26. "Happiness" as a kind of mental illness, a delusional state that breaks down rational thought, etc. Unlike Emerson, Dickinson never really believed in or desired pure happiness. She liked and needed limits and boundaries in her emotional life. This made her an unlikely candidate for conversion.

27. Quoted in Perry Miller, *The Life of the Mind in America: From the Revolution to the Civil War*, San Diego: Harcourt Brace Jovanovich, 1965, p. 3.

28. Harold Bloom, *The American Religion: The Emergence of the Post-Christian Nation*, New York: Simon and Schuster, 1992.

29. Possible exploration of her use of "Eternity." Is it separate from Heaven or something synonymous?

30. Emily Dickinson, *The Complete Poems of Emily Dickinson* ed. by Thomas H. Johnson, Boston: Little, Brown, and Co., 1960, p. 40. Poems hereafter referred to in parentheses by their number according to and as they appear in this volume.

31. Cynthia Griffin Wolf, *Emily Dickinson*, New York Knopf, 1986, p. 293.

32. I'm not sure I agree with Wolf's distinction at this point, my sense is that she does uses these words interchangeably, which is Richard B. Sewall's reading.

33. Elizabeth Alden Green, *Mary Lyon and Mount Holyoke: Opening the Gates*, Hanover: University Press of New England, 1979, p. 197.

34. Edward Hitchcock, *The Power of Christian Benevolence Illustrated in the Life and Labors of Mary Lyon*, Northhampton: Hopkins, Bridgman, and Co., 1851, pp. 161–163.

35. Green, p. 299.

36. Green, 196.

37. Hitchcock, pp. 161–163.

38. Green, p. 251.

39. Sewall, 360.

40. Walter Benjamin, *Illuminations*, p. 84.

41. All biblical quotations come from the King James Version of the Bible.

42. This interruption in the form of stutter has a similar effect in the last line of Elizabeth Bishop's "One Art": "... though it may look like (Write it!) like disaster" (*CP*, 178). In both poems the poet shows herself breaking stride, just before writing the dreaded word "lost" (Dickinson) or "disaster" (Bishop).

43. R.P. Blackmur, "Emily Dickinson's Notation," from *Outsider at the Heart of Things* (Urbana: U of Illinois, 1989), p. 182.

Chronology

1800 Thomas Jefferson is elected President of the United States; John Chapman, "Johnny Appleseed," begins planting trees in the Ohio territory.

1803 Ralph Waldo Emerson is born in Boston, Massachusetts on May 25; Jefferson completes the Louisiana Purchase from France, doubling the size of the United States; Lewis and Clark begin a three-year exploration of the new territory.

1804 Nathaniel Hawthorne is born in Salem, Massachusetts on July 4; Napoleon is crowned Emperor of France; Immanuel Kant dies in Konigsberg, Germany.

1805 Admiral Nelson's British Fleet defeats the French Fleet at Trafalgar; Friedrich Schiller dies.

1806 Noah Webster publishes his dictionary in Hartford.

1807 Friedrich Hegel, *Phenomenology of Spirit*; England abolishes slavery.

1809 Abraham Lincoln is born in a log cabin in Kentucky.

1810 Sarah Margaret Fuller is born in Cambridgeport, Massachusetts.

1812 War of 1812 between the Americans and British begins (concludes in 1815).

1814 British Army destroys the White House.

1815 Wellington defeats Napoleon at Waterloo; Louis XVIII is restored to the throne.

1817	Henry David Thoreau is born in Concord, Massachusetts.
1818	Mary Shelley, *Frankenstein*.
1819	Walt Whitman is born on Long Island; Herman Melville is born in New York City.
1820	Missouri Compromise—Missouri admitted to the union as a slave state, Maine as a free state; War of Mexican Independence concludes; Mexico becomes independent from Spain.
1821	John Keats dies on February 23 in Rome; Napoleon dies on St. Helena on May 5.
1822	Percy Shelley drowns.
1823	President James Monroe declares Monroe Doctrine, enforcing United States sovereignty over the Western Hemisphere.
1824	Lord Byron dies of fever in Greece.
1825	Erie Canal opens; first railway service opens in England.
1827	Beethoven dies; William Blake dies.
1830	Emily Dickinson is born in Amherst, Massachusetts.
1831	Nat Turner leads a slave rebellion in Virginia killing 55 whites, and which brings about the eventual execution of most of the slave participants.
1832	Johann Wolfgang von Goethe, *Faust II*; Goethe dies.
1834	Samuel Taylor Coleridge dies.
1836	Samuel Morse invents the telegraph.
1840	Claude Monet is born.
1843	Henry James is born in New York City.
1846	United States goes to war against Mexico (war completed in 1848 with large annexations of south western territories and California); Second Great Awakening religious revival sweeps through the United States.
1848	Failed revolutions across Europe; Louis Napoleon becomes first President of France; Gold discovered in California; Karl Marx and Friedrich Engels, *Communist Manifesto*; Edgar Allen Poe dies.
1850	Nathaniel Hawthorne, *The Scarlet Letter*; Margaret Fuller dies in a shipwreck off Fire Island, New York on July 19; Compromise of 1850 signed by Millard Filmore; California admitted to Union as a free state.

1851	Herman Melville, *Moby Dick*.
1852	Herman Melville, *Pierre*; Harriet Beecher Stowe, *Uncle Tom's Cabin*; Louis Napoleon declares himself Napoleon III, Emperor of France.
1854	Henry David Thoreau, *Walden*.
1855	Walt Whitman, *Leaves of Grass*; Henry David Longfellow, *The Song of Hiawatha*.
1858	First trans-Atlantic telegraph cables lain; Czar Alexander II frees the Russian serfs.
1859	John Brown leads raid on the Federal Armory at Harper's Ferry, Virginia.
1861	American Civil War begins on April 12 in Charleston, South Carolina.
1862	Thoreau dies of tuberculosis on May 6 in Concord; Victor Hugo, *Les Miserables*.
1863	Emancipation Proclamation; Battle of Gettysburg fought in early July.
1864	Nathaniel Hawthorne dies in his sleep on May 18 while traveling in New Hampshire.
1865	Civil War ends, reconstruction of the South begins; Lincoln assassinated on April 14; Ku Klux Klan founded in Tennessee.
1869	Transcontinental Railroad completed.
1870	Fifteenth Amendment ratified, giving voting rights to all adult males, regardless of race; Ralph Waldo Emerson, *Society and Solitude*.
1871	Franco-Prussian War, foundation of German Empire; Great Chicago fire; Walt Whitman, *Democratic Vistas* and *A Passage to India*.
1876	Herman Melville, *Clarel*.
1877	End of Reconstruction.
1878	Henry James, *The Europeans*.
1879	Wallace Stevens is born.
1880	Henry James, *The Portrait of a Lady*.
1881	Booker T. Washington founds the Tuskegee Institute; Douglass, *Life and Times of Frederick Douglass*.
1882	Ralph Waldo Emerson dies on April 27 in Concord.

1883	Brooklyn Bridge opens.
1884	Mark Twain, *The Adventures of Huckleberry Finn*.
1886	Emily Dickinson dies on May 15 in Amherst.
1890	Emily Dickinson, *Poems*.
1891	Herman Melville dies on September 28 in New York.
1892	Walt Whitman dies on March 26 in Camden.

Contributors

HAROLD BLOOM is Sterling Professor of the Humanities at Yale University and Henry W. and Albert A. Berg Professor of English at the New York University Graduate School. He is the author of over 20 books, including *Shelley's Mythmaking* (1959), *The Visionary Company* (1961), *Blake's Apocalypse* (1963), *Yeats* (1970), *A Map of Misreading* (1975), *Kabbalah and Criticism* (1975), *Agon: Toward a Theory of Revisionism* (1982), *The American Religion* (1992), *The Western Canon* (1994), and *Omens of Millennium: The Gnosis of Angels, Dreams, and Resurrection* (1996). *The Anxiety of Influence* (1973) sets forth Professor Bloom's provocative theory of the literary relationships between the great writers and their predecessors. His most recent books include *Shakespeare: The Invention of the Human* (1998), a 1998 National Book Award finalist, *How to Read and Why* (2000), *Genius: A Mosaic of One Hundred Exemplary Creative Minds* (2002), and *Hamlet: Poem Unlimited* (2003). In 1999, Professor Bloom received the prestigious American Academy of Arts and Letters Gold Medal for Criticism, and in 2002 he received the Catalonia International Prize.

D.H. LAWRENCE, poet, novelist, and essayist, is the author of the novels *Sons and Lovers*, *The Rainbow*, and *Women in Love*, as well volumes of poetry, travel books, psychological treatises, and the book of critical essays, *Studies in Classic American Literature*. He is considered one of the most important literary figures of the twentieth century.

F.O. MATTHIESSEN was Professor of English at Harvard until his death. He is the author of the seminal volume *American Renaissance*, as well as books on the James family and T.S. Eliot.

CHARLES OLSON, a poet and critic, was visiting Professor and later rector at Black Mountain College, and was a visiting Professor of English at The University of New York at Buffalo and The University of Connecticut. His most famous work of criticism is *Call Me Ishmael*, and his many books of poems include *Collected Poems* and *The Maximus Poems*.

JORGE LUIS BORGES, distinguished poet, novelist, and critic, is the author of the collections of short stories, *Ficciones* and *Labyrinths*, as well as several volumes of poetry, and the collection of critical essays, *Other Inquisitions*. During his long lifetime Borges served as visiting Professor at the University of Texas, and was Charles Eliot Norton Professor at Harvard in 1967–8.

SHERMAN PAUL was Professor of English at the University of Iowa until his death. He is the author of many books on Transcendentalism and American Romanticism, including *Emerson's Angle of Vision: Man and Nature of Our Time*, *The Shores of America: Thoreau's Inward Explorations*, and *Hart's Bridge*.

RICHARD BRODHEAD is A. Bartlett Giamatti Professor of English and American Studies at Yale University. His books include *Hawthorne, Melville, and the Novel*, *Cultures of Letters: Scenes of Reading and Writing in 19th Century American Literature*, and *The School of Hawthorne*.

BARBARA PACKER is Professor of English at the University of California, Los Angeles. She is the author of many articles, including *The Transcendentalists* in *The Cambridge History of American Literature, Vol. II*, as well as a book, *Emerson's Fall*.

JULIE ELLISON is Professor of English at The University of Michigan. She is the author of several books, including *Emerson's Romantic Style*, *Delicate Subjects: Romanticism, Gender, and the Ethics of Understanding*, and *Cato's Tears*.

LAWRENCE BUELL is John P. Marquand Professor of English and American Literature, and Language at Harvard University. He has been editor of many volumes on nature writing, the environment, and

Transcendentalism, and is the author of several books, including *Emerson, Literary Transcendentalism: Style and Vision in the American Renaissance*, and *The Design of Literature*.

JOHN HOLLANDER is Sterling Professor of English Emeritus at Yale University. An accomplished poet and critic, his numerous books of poetry include *Reflections on Espionage, Selected Poems,* and *Picture Window,* while some of his critical works are *The Untuning of the Sky, Melodious Guile,* and *The Work of Poetry*.

KATHY KURTZMAN LAWRENCE teaches at Boston University. She is the author of articles on Margaret Fuller and Henry James, and is at work on a book about James and transcendentalism.

ELIZABETH SCHMIDT teaches at Barnard College and is poetry editor for *New York Times Sunday Book Review*.

Bibliography

Bercovitch, Sacvan. *The Cambridge History of American Literature*. New York: Cambridge University Press, 1991.

Bloom, Harold. *Poetics of Influence*. New Haven: Charles Schwab, 1988.

———. *Poetry and Repression*. New Haven: Yale University Press, 1976.

Borges, Jorge Luis. *Other Inquisitions*. Austin: University of Texas Press, 1964.

Brodhead, Richard. *The School of Hawthorne*. New York: Oxford University Press, 1986.

Buell, Lawrence. *Literary Transcendentalism*. Ithaca: Cornell University Press, 1973.

———. *The Environmental Imagination: Thoreau, Nature Writing, and the Formation of American Culture*. Cambridge: Belknap Press of Harvard University Press, 1995.

Chai, Leon. *The Romantic Foundations of the American Renaissance*. Ithaca: Cornell University Press, 1987.

Chase, Richard Volney. *Herman Melville, A Critical Study*. New York: Macmillan Co., 1949.

Ellison, Julie. *Emerson's Romantic Style*. Princeton: Princeton University Press, 1984.

Folsom, Ed. *Walt Whitman's Native Representations*. Cambridge: Cambridge University Press, 1994.

Howe, Susan. *The Birth-mark: Unsettling the Wilderness in American Literary History*. Hanover & London: Wesleyan University Press, 1993.

Lawrence, D.H. *Studies in Classic American Literature*. New York: Penguin USA, 1991.

Matthiessen, F. O. *American Renaissance*, New York: Oxford University Press, 1941.

Myerson, Joel. *Walt Whitman: A Descriptive Bibliography*. Pittsburgh: University of Pittsburgh Press, 1993.

Olson, Charles. *Call Me Ishmael*. San Francisco: City Light Books, 1947.

Packer, Barbara. *Emerson's Fall*. New York: Continuum, 1982.

Parker, Hershel. *Herman Melville: A Biography: 1819–1851 (Vol. I)*. Baltimore: Johns Hopkins University Press, 1996.

———. *Herman Melville: A Biography: 1851–1891 (Vol. II)*. Baltimore: Johns Hopkins University Press, 2002.

———. and Harrison Hayford. *Moby-Dick As Doubloon; Essays And Extracts, 1851–1970*. New York: Norton, 1970.

Paul, Sherman. *The Shores of America: Thoreau's Inward Exploration*. Urbana: University of Illinois Press, 1958.

Poirier, Richard. *A World Elsewhere: The Place of Style in American Literature*. New York: Oxford University Press, 1966.

Porter, David. *Dickinson: The Modern Idiom*. Cambridge: Harvard University Press, 1981.

Price, Kenneth M., ed. *Walt Whitman: The Contemporary Reviews*. Cambridge: Cambridge University Press, 1996.

Reynolds, David S. *Walt Whitman's America: A Cultural Biography*. New York: Knopf, 1995.

Richardson, Robert D. *Emerson: The Mind on Fire*. Berkeley and Los Angeles: University of California Press, 1995.

———. *Henry Thoreau: A Life of the Mind*. Berkeley: University of California Press, 1986.

Sewall, Richard. *The Life of Emily Dickinson*. New York: Farrar, Straus and Giroux, 1974.

Acknowledgments

"Emerson and Whitman: The American Sublime" by Harold Bloom. From *Poetry and Repression*: 235–266. ©1976 by Harold Bloom. Reprinted by permission.

"Herman Melville's *Moby Dick*" from *Studies in Classic American Literature* by D. H. Lawrence. ©1923 by Thomas Seltzer, Inc., renewed 1950 by Frieda Lawrence. ©1961 by the Estate of Mrs. Frieda Lawrence. Used by permission of Viking Penguin, a division of Penguin Group (USA) Inc.

"Method and Scope" by F.O. Matthiessen. From *American Renaissance*: vii–xvi. ©1941 by Oxford University Press, Inc. Reprinted with permission of Oxford University Press, Inc.

"Shakespeare" by Charles Olson. From *Call Me Ishmael*: 33–73. ©1947 by Charles Olson. Reprinted by permission.

"Nathaniel Hawthorne" by Jorge Luis Borges. From *Other Inquisitions*: 37–65. ©1964 by the University of Texas Press. Reprinted by permission.

"Introduction to *Walden* and *Civil Disobedience*" by Sherman Paul. From *Walden and Civil Disobedience*: vii–xxxix. ©1960 by Houghton Mifflin. Reprinted by permission.

"Whitman's Image of Voice: To the Tally of My Soul" by Harold Bloom. From *Agon*: 179–199. ©1982 by Oxford University Press, Inc. Reprinted by permission.

Index